LONDON CLAY

www.penguin.co.uk

LONDON CLAY

Journeys in the Deep City

TOM CHIVERS

doubleday

TRANSWORLD PUBLISHERS
Penguin Random House, One Embassy Gardens,
8 Viaduct Gardens, London SW11 7BW
www.penguin.co.uk

Transworld is part of the Penguin Random House group of companies
whose addresses can be found at global.penguinrandomhouse.com

First published in Great Britain in 2021 by Doubleday
an imprint of Transworld Publishers

A CIP catalogue record for this book
is available from the British Library.

ISBN 9780857526922

Typeset in 11/15.25pt Minion Pro by Jouve (UK), Milton Keynes
Printed and bound in Great Britain by Clays Ltd, Elcograf S.p.A.

The authorized representative in the EEA is Penguin Random House Ireland,
Morrison Chambers, 32 Nassau Street, Dublin D02 YH68.

Penguin Random House is committed to a sustainable
future for our business, our readers and our planet. This book
is made from Forest Stewardship Council® certified paper.

For Sarah

Contents

PROLOGUE   MAPPING   1

      I   SINKHOLE: UNLOCKING THE
          SECRETS OF ALDGATE   9
              A Hole in the City   11
              The Line of the Stage   21
              The Old Gate   27
              Whose Streets   36

     II   RETURN TO THE SOURCE:
          IN SEARCH OF THE AMBROOK   43
              Herne   45
              Effra   50
              Woods   54
              Grave   71

    III   LIQUIDITY: WALKING THE WALBROOK   81
              Panopticon   83
              Fulcrum   93
              Wall   99
              Bank   107
              Communion   113
              Mouth   121
              Going Dark   124

CONTENTS

IV   DESCENT: INTO THE RIVER OF WELLS   131

     Sewer   133

     Holy Water   141

     Drift   151

     Heath   163

V   FLOODLANDS: CROSSING THE WESTMINSTER DELTA   177

     Dawn   179

     Island of Thorns   182

     Holy Theatre   192

     Flood   197

     Eye   207

     Stone   224

VI   DEAD RIVER: TRACKING THE NECKINGER   233

     Tabula Rasa   235

     Skull   242

     Field   249

     Roundabout   257

     Anomaly   267

     First Contact   278

     Gallows   285

VII   BEATING THE BOUNDS: THE LOST ISLAND OF BERMONDSEY   293

     Fragments   295

     Lockdown   304

     Into the Lion's Den   316

     Sink Estate   327

CONTENTS

VIII   OLYMPIC CITY: EDGELANDS
OF THE LOWER LEA VALLEY   333
     Marsh Yoga   335
     Neverland   345
     Pandemonium   355
     Overflow   360
     Limmo   367
     Meridian   382

CODA   A ROSE BY ANY OTHER NAME   393

NOTES   411

THANKS   433

INDEX   435

Prologue:
MAPPING

'Geology is the study of pressure and time. That's all it takes really, pressure and time.'

Red, *The Shawshank Redemption*[1]

TAKE UP A HIGH position.
   Do it now.

You may need to climb to get there.

The Gherkin. The Royal Observatory, Greenwich. The highest point on Hampstead Heath.

Anywhere will do.

London shimmers beneath you. An orb of pale sunlight flares on the towers of Canary Wharf. The river is a tapeworm of poured silver. You can just make out the dome of Wren's cathedral of St Paul, or else it's hidden by the taller modern office blocks that catch the light and seem to sparkle but in equal parts obscure it, throwing down long shadows beneath them. Tower Bridge is there, its mock medieval turrets absurdly miniature; the Shard, bossing the skyline from its seat on the south bank of the Thames.

And now your eye is drawn beyond, to a landscape of tower blocks and municipal halls, spires and minarets, terraced streets, parks and heaths, of waterworks and rusting, derelict gas holders and, beyond even that, a band of dark woods where the land rises up to meet the horizon.

This is my city: you cannot see past the edges it doesn't have.

Now turn your gaze towards the east. Look for a messy fringe of streets and dimly lit alleys, a row of empty market stalls where the pavements are smeared with rain-softened cardboard boxes. A corner pub is chucking out. A kitchen porter empties a bucket and its swill forms a dozen rivulets that trickle across the street and pool beneath a four-storey building in London stock brick. Now look up, above the Nigerian textile shop that I guarantee will still be open this late. Can you see a flickering glow at the first-floor window? Peer in, if you can. Don't be shy. This is where you'll find me, working late and by candlelight, bent over a large, heavily creased map.

Collins Streetfinder (scale 1:17,500) presents London in all its familiar intricacy, but like all two-dimensional maps it bears only a faint resemblance to the real city as experienced by its inhabitants. I look down on a giant circuit board of white streets, yellow A roads and snaking, black railway lines, with Tube stations, parks and famous landmarks labelled in a clear, sans-serif font. From Hither Green in the south-east to Cricklewood on London's north-west frontier – the Streetfinder is a hymn to flatness. All the city's depth has been wiped away, the messy verticality of its hills and towers, tunnels and troughs reduced to one thin sheet. It is not enough; a partial truth. I want to go beneath, deep under London's streets, to find the essence of this place; to understand the city as a living, breathing landscape.

And so, here I am, in my one-bedroom flat above an East End market, obsessively modifying a street map with felt-tips and marker pens. I shade a block of orange over Trafalgar Square to represent the wind-blown clay and silt present deep beneath the bronze lions and the tourists lining up selfies. This is my task. To plot the geology of the city directly over the street plan; to create a hacked map of London, a palimpsest in which the present and the deep past are felt together, simultaneously, as two layers of the same place.

If you view the city from a height you are seeing London as it wishes to be seen: thrusting, monumental, its spires and skyscrapers reaching for the heavens. But what was here before the city? And what remains of it? What can still be felt, if not directly, then as an echo, a trace effect in the urban psyche?

The earliest maps of London, like Wyngaerde's sketches of 1543 or Hollar's *Long View* of 1647, were not really maps at all but panoramas.

They were drawn from real or imagined vantage points south of the river, and showed fields, forests and rolling hills surrounding the embryonic city, which was still mostly enclosed within the limits of its medieval walls. But even then much of what had defined the 'natural' landscape of London had already been erased: marshes drained for pasture; woodland stripped; streams paved over; the Thames itself embanked, contained, encroached upon by wharves and jetties. To appreciate the landscape on which the city was founded, we have to go much further back. But to go back we must first go down. So I have turned to the science of geology: the study of what lies beneath; the business of rock and sand, water and ice, laid down by forces unimaginably vast; the study of high pressure and deep time.

Using the British Geological Survey's website as a guide, my Street-finder has become a patchwork of different colours. Each shade represents a different geological stratum found beneath the streets – what geologists call 'superficial deposits'. The basic geology of London is that of the river valley: a broad basin dug out by thousands of years of water erosion. The Thames and its banks are underlain by alluvium, which I shade with a yellow felt-tip. From the Latin *alluere*, 'to wash against', alluvium describes the loose material deposited in the landscape by flowing water: a gloopy mixture of silt, sand, clay and gravel whose distribution indicates the full extent of the river's former floodplain. I turn whole neighbourhoods south of the Thames bright yellow. The great Victorian railway termini of Waterloo and London Bridge go under; Wapping marshes and the Rotherhithe peninsula are submerged.

I select four different pens for the next strata: variations of gravel deposited in terraces either side of the floodplain. Each represents a different stage in the river's shifting history, from the shallow platforms of Bermondsey and Stepney to the steep hills of Norwood and Hampstead that define the valley's limits. Cutting through these gravel terraces I add spidery fingers of alluvium: London's *other* rivers, from the Lea in the east to the hidden streams of Effra and Westbourne. Finally, I add strips of dark green to mark outcrops of the material that underlies all this. London Clay.

PROLOGUE

A stiff, bluish clay, rich in fossils, London Clay was formed in a shallow, tropical sea in the early Eocene Epoch (56 to 49 million years ago). Although it is a poor agricultural soil, London Clay makes good bricks and is an ideal material for tunnelling, and so it has always been a vital resource in the development of the city. In some places in London, the clay is 150 metres thick. It bursts through the surface in great clumps at Lavender Hill, Clapton, Norwood.

I step back from the map and survey the fruits of my labours. Half eccentric artwork, half primary-school science project. The city I have known for all my life recedes into a rainbow landscape of pinks and yellows, greens and browns. Geological time reduces the human story to a footnote in the history of the planet – and yet these ancient rocks determine our patterns of settlement and communication; they govern the sites of our temples, our institutions of power; they shape the very curvature of our streets. *This* London is rarely seen, but it is always there, pressing its immanence into our world.

London Clay is a book about the city beneath the city: a hidden landscape of lost rivers and secret woodlands, of marshes and islands long buried underneath the sprawling metropolis. Across eight documentary essays, I chart the unheard stories that emerge from my hacked and tattered Streetfinder. I detect the tears in the map where the past emerges as a disruptive force into the modern city, flashing across the synapses of historical and geological time.

The Streetfinder is my guide – and yours. Its mysteries will trigger journeys of discovery, journeys across, underneath and into the deep city.* We will encounter a landscape fundamentally configured by water, but which has been drained and tarmacked over. We will follow the

* I am borrowing this term from Nick Papadimitriou, author of *Scarp* (Sceptre, 2013) and purveyor of 'deep topography'.

5

course of London's lost rivers, buried and degraded streams that persistently threaten to break their shackles, undermining developers' ambitions and offering alternative ways of seeing the city. We will uncover islands in the Thames obscured by centuries of terraforming and erased from the records. And we will explore the edgelands of London, where wildflowers burst through concrete flyovers and ghosts of the deep past can be felt as a buzzing in the skull.

At the heart of my project is a desire to understand the place I was born by exploring it on foot. It is a fool's quest, of course; London is always changing around us. Its omnivorous appetite consumes everything we throw at it. I have chosen places with depth, places which leap from the map into the imagination. Some are locations where my personal memories connect with a greater story of change across millennia, and each reveals different aspects of the city's character that are still recognizable today. Consider these your doorways, or portals, into a place you thought you knew. Together, they tell an alternative story of London.

I make no apologies for the composition of this book, which is partial, subjective and incomplete; I am neither historian nor geographer, but write with the poet's compulsion for rumour and conjecture. London is the most written-about city on the planet. (Not to mention the most observed, with over half a million CCTV cameras.) It is those things *outside* the official narrative – and beyond the gaze of the camera – that interest me: the folk tales and urban myths buried within rabbit holes of unauthorized hyperlinks.

London Clay is not a traditional guidebook, then. We're going off map, drifting through familiar locations – the Houses of Parliament, the Square Mile and beyond – to uncover a hidden world of ruined Tube stations, flooded sewers, underground temples and abandoned industrial sites. Where my own knowledge or research has failed, I have sought the expertise of others: writers and wanderers, archaeologists, geologists and ecologists. Above all, I hope this book will inspire *you* – wherever you find yourself – to think about what lies beneath your feet and by doing so reveal new ways of looking at the world.

The map is almost complete. A muffled shout invades my candlelit world, followed by the clatter of metal. I have been up all night. Soon the sun will stream through the blinds into my flat and with it the noise of the market traders setting up their stalls in the street below. I fold up the map as best I can and pull on a hoodie.

I'm not going far – to an island of wilderness slap bang in the middle of London: a forgotten junkyard where the weeds grow wild and tall, and where the ground gives way to sudden, hidden depths.

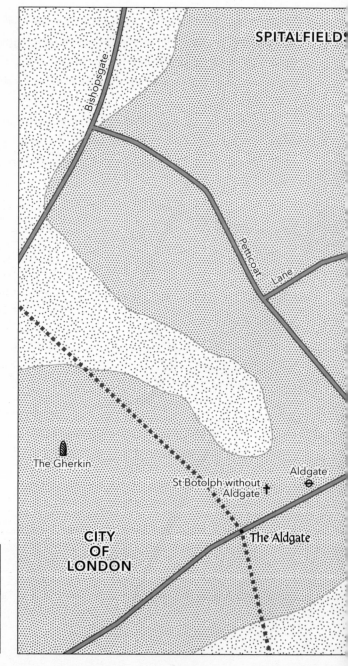

SPITALFIELD

Bishopsgate

Petticoat Lane

The Gherkin

St Botolph without
Aldgate †

Aldgate

The Aldgate

CITY
OF
LONDON

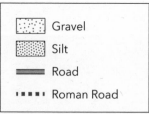

Gravel

Silt

Road

Roman Road

I: SINKHOLE

Unlocking the Secrets of Aldgate

A Hole in the City

'Ruins . . . are a reagent of memory, their incomplete, fractured elements demanding to be visualized or imagined whole again.'

KEN WORPOLE[1]

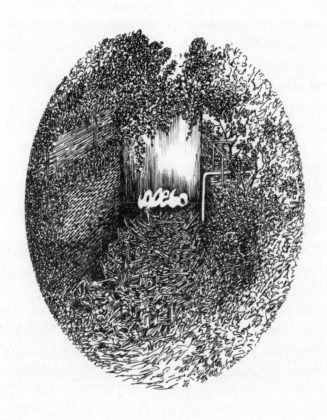

THERE IS A HOLE in the city to whose ruined energy field I am drawn like iron filings to a magnet, like a whorl of hair down the plughole – here in Aldgate, where the East End meets the old Roman city in a knotted mess of roads and empty pedestrian subways. The hole lies in a fenced-off island of waste ground measuring 150 by 80 feet, wedged between the Aldgate roundabout and Goulston Street. Its northern edge abuts United Standard House – a ten-storey concrete office block that has been derelict for as long as I have lived here. Its ground floor is open to the elements and employed as a makeshift car park. The crumbling walls and blocked doorways have become a canvas for graffiti taggers.[2] It is in this inauspicious, somewhat forgotten corner of Aldgate that my journey across London – and into the deep city – begins.

I have passed the hole most days in the nine years since I moved into a one-bedroom flat overlooking the nearby street market on Petticoat Lane. Back in 2008 I could even make out the hole from my office window; I was working from the top floor of the Hoop and Grapes, a seventeenth-century, timber-framed townhouse on Aldgate High Street that had survived the Great Fire of 1666. As the Credit Crunch descended on the City, I witnessed the exodus of jobless traders tramping east past the pub, some clutching a box of personal effects to their chest. The hole, to which they too seemed drawn, assumed the status of metaphor: a sinkhole for the City, threatening to swallow up the whole corrupt business of it – the banks and the bailouts, the dodgy deals and the liquid lunches.

Tomorrow the pocket of waste ground may be gone, and the hole along with it. The city is changing around us, performing an endless dance of construction and demolition. Steel and glass replace concrete, which once replaced brick and stone, and each material in turn survives as a layer, a deposit, as if the city were not land at all but a river flowing with the weight of what it has already destroyed. But today, on a bright morning in September 2013, the hole remains, for now, hidden behind a giant digital billboard promoting BVLGARI watches: a temporary screen designed to tidy away these scrappy edges.

I peer through the fence into a green haze; the interior of the island is bursting with plant life. Rampant, outsized weeds have colonized every inch of the empty plot; dense bushes on which discarded sweet wrappers have settled like budding flowers. Building rubble has grassed over, loose conglomerations bound into luminescent turf mounds.

In their application to Tower Hamlets' planning office, the billboard's owner claimed it would add 'vibrance, colour and interest to this derelict corner eyesore site'. In another, they described it as 'bland, vacant and degraded'.[3] I trace the fence all the way around, looking for a weak spot. I can barely see the hole, because it too is overgrown, obscured by a dark-green canopy. If only I could get inside, I think, I could attempt a descent; a quest to unearth whatever secrets lie hidden in the ground.

When I first arrived in Aldgate, at the start of 2005, the wasteland was unadorned with this wild growth. The hole – in effect a trench 15 feet below ground level and filled with junk – was open to the wind and rain. I could make out redbrick walls, the wrecked foundations of a building and, at one end, the blocked-off entrance to what appeared to be a tunnel running east beneath Goulston Street.

I take a step back, for a wider view. Today, buses, minivans and daring cyclists are tearing around the junction from the direction of Bishopsgate. Other vehicles are attempting to filter from the south, across the main east–west road into the City of London. On my modified Streetfinder, the roundabout appears within a wide band of Langley Silt that stretches from Bethnal Green to Cornhill. Commonly known as 'brickearth', this blend of silt and clay was once the source of London's trademark 'yellow stock' bricks.

I look around me. The derelict 1960s office block behind the hole is dwarfed by a larger, glassy rectangle called Aldgate House; it houses media group Thomson Reuters and construction services firm ISG, and is part-owned by Canada's state pension fund. Diagonally across the roundabout, several departments of the Royal Bank of Scotland are accommodated inside a Brutalist fortress whose concrete exoskeleton calls to mind the hexagonal pillboxes I have occasionally stumbled across on coastal rambles.

One door down, and propelling the eastward spread of tall buildings up to Aldgate East station, is the latest addition to the 'City Fringe': the sixteen-floor Aldgate Tower. A soaring blade of super-reflective glass, on sunny days the tower appears as a violent interruption of sky blue; in overcast weather it assumes the rough patina and foreboding spirit of a standing stone.

Amidst all of this jumble, pedestrians come and go, navigating the perilous tracks and traffic islands of an ill-conceived gyratory system. They come and go alone and in groups of two or three, with briefcases, rucksacks and shopping bags, in suits, in jeans, and Islamic abaya, creating their own pathways – 'desire lines' – into and across the affray.

These thrusting towers are not merely the organic expression of capital on the edge of Europe's premier financial district; they are the result of the deliberate transformation of Aldgate into a vibrant, business-friendly neighbourhood (to borrow the euphemistic vocabulary of town planning). It even has a sinister name: the Aldgate Masterplan. The site of the hole is earmarked for a hotel.

But more than that: the erection of gleaming office blocks constitutes a subliminal attempt to erase the history of Aldgate as a contested, in-between place, a neighbourhood characterized by impromptu development, ambiguity and the juxtaposition of unlike elements (high and low, rich and poor, official and unsanctioned). Even the principle material of the modern skyscraper, glass, with its transparent and reflective qualities, its surface effects, collapses the depth and complexity of the urban environment. The practice of 'zoning' makes non-places of the city, and non-citizens of those who live there. Aldgate has become an unreal space – beyond time and above geography.

Eald-gate. Old gate.
Eal-gate. The gate for all.

On the corner of Goulston Street and Whitechapel High Street opposite the hole, another remnant of a forgotten world stands defiant. Tubby Isaac's jellied-eel stall was founded by Isaac Brenner in 1919. Tubby's is an East End institution and has continued to serve up traditional seafood treats long after the area ceased to be the heart of Jewish London. But business is slow and Tubby's will not make its centenary. Proprietor Paul Simpson, a fourth-generation eel-seller, is shipping out. 'It's a sign of the times,' he says, resigned to his fate.[4] Across the street, another fast-food outlet is frying halal burgers and anaemic hot dogs for construction workers and local teenagers.

It is January, bitter cold, and the streets are full of shadows. I am staring at the same gap in the perimeter, where a single strut of black steel fencing has been worked loose enough for a body to squeeze through. This time I have brought a video camera and, given my intention to trespass, it is night. Sunday, 8 p.m.: the market stalls have been tidied away and, with the surrounding offices empty till the financial markets open in the morning, Aldgate is at its quietest. With the background hum of the roundabout and an occasional siren the only distractions, I pay my full attention to the terrain before me. Streetlight is bouncing off the irregular forms of its topography and in a glance I see three wooden pallets, a large tarpaulin blowing in the wind, one traffic cone, a pool of water rippling in an iron girder, and, in the water, the reflection of a digital hoarding that is fixed to the side of the derelict insurance building: *5% interest from the bank account that's different.*

The northern edge of the island is enclosed by this building's adjoining wall, which has been sprayed with a tag I cannot quite decipher in large, clumsy white lettering. I notice that the pallets have been stacked in such a way to offer access to a small, shuttered opening in the wall no more than two feet wide. The shutter is caught in the wind and is repeatedly hitting the window frame. *Bang. Bang. BANG.* I notice too a carrier bag stamped into the mud, and several empty cans of industrial-strength lager.

I step back to take a long shot of the fenceline down towards the fast food van, and immediately my right shoe meets the familiar squelch of a turd. I am wearing light-weight Gore-Tex walking shoes designed for clambering up fells, and here I am, stepping in dog shit at the porous edge of the City. I attempt to wipe the sole clean; first on a patch of dock weed bursting from the bottom of the fence, and then on the kerb. I am still on the safe side. I dare not go through.

And so instead I scout the edge back towards the main road. The turfed-over mounds in the centre of the waste ground are framed black against the light-polluted sky; I could easily be staring up at a Bronze Age burial chamber on some distant moor. All of London's past is here, I think. For all history is the history of waste, of what was left behind, excreted, discarded or lost. Watching the hole over these last nine years, I realize I have been witnessing an archaeological dig in reverse. London is always breaking apart, yielding up the junk of the long departed – oyster shells, broken pipes, Roman masonry and Tudor cess pits.

I wait for a pause in the hum of traffic and then slip through a gap in the fence. The ground is soft underfoot. Inside, I am invisible. Few bother to look this way. I pocket my torch and pick my way across the site in darkness until the level ground falls away into thick foliage. I peer into the hole itself. It is thrilling to be this close. The deep pit is filling up with bottles, cans, polystyrene cartons, building materials, coils of wiring, soiled nappies and other things too numerous to mention. These are the things we will be remembered by. These are the things that count.

Barely visible above all this waste I make out a faded *Exit* sign in old-fashioned type, revealing the site's true identity. For the hole, *this* hole, is all that remains of an abandoned Tube station: the first incarnation of what we now call Aldgate East.

Aldgate East station opened on 6 October 1884 to service the recently extended District Railway. A black-and-white photograph taken in 1895 shows a single-storey, flat-roofed brick structure built in the neoclassical style. It boasts five tall windows with pronounced keystones, a triangular pediment carrying the name of the station and, below that, a round archway leading to the booking hall. The station is dwarfed to the side and rear by chimneys and taller brick buildings, one of which identifies itself as EDWARD TOPLIS / TOBACCO MANUFACTORY.

It was the great age of rail. Newly formed private companies competed to build lines into the city from the rapidly expanding middle-class suburbs, ferrying clerks and bankers from their terraced villas in Clapham, Camberwell and Notting Hill. In the foreground of the photograph we observe the following scene of street life: three City gents are walking past in morning suit, hat and cane; a woman crosses Whitechapel High Street in a white bonnet and heavy winter coat; a moustachioed newspaper salesman is stationed by a lamppost; a boy stands by a street vendor whose goods are too blurred to identify; two young men in flat caps wait by the station entrance. One is dark-skinned and bearded, and is looking west. He is, perhaps, a recent immigrant to the city, a refugee from the pogroms of the Russian Empire. For Aldgate and Whitechapel once formed the heart of Jewish London. By the turn of the twentieth century the East End was home to some one hundred thousand Jewish people.

Three or four rusting girders are still attached to the sides of the pit – remains of the station structure. They hang over the void like a smashed ribcage.

*

1884: this date can be read another way. It was just four years before the notorious 'Leather Apron' began his reign of terror in the poverty-stricken streets of the East End. The Tube and Jack the Ripper: my mind struggles to synthesize the two. How can they possibly be contemporary? Every night in summer months groups of bewildered tourists file through the backstreets of Aldgate and Whitechapel on organized tours led by local historians, Ripperologists and out-of-work actors. Bored French teenagers chew gum outside Happy Days, the fish and chip shop on Goulston Street, as their guide brings to life the sadistic crimes of Saucy Jack with dramatic speech and grand gestures. Some even wear period dress.

I take no pleasure in this malevolent history, nor the salacious retelling of it. The Ripper was a murderer of women in streets still troubled today by prostitution and its attendant vices of drug-dealing and sexual violence. Still, there is one contemporary piece of Ripperology that has me perplexed: a sinister line that I found daubed in white paint on the derelict office block behind the hole.

<u>JUWES</u> I DO CARE 4U (B.H.B.)

Amid the sprayed tags and ripped posters, one scrawled note might easily be overlooked. But to students of the Ripper murders, that misspelt word – 'Juwes' – leaps off the wall due to its connection with the notorious Goulston Street graffito.

On 30 September 1888 the bodies of two women, Elizabeth Stride and Catherine Eddowes, were discovered with their throats slashed and, in the latter case, hideously disembowelled. At 3 a.m., Metropolitan Police Constable Alfred Long discovered a bloodstained piece of apron – later confirmed as belonging to Eddowes – in the stairwell to a tenement block on Goulston Street. On the wall above was chalked an enigmatic note: 'The Juwes are the men that will not be blamed for nothing'. The graffito was hastily erased on the orders of Superintendent Thomas Arnold, anxious to avoid escalating religious tensions between Jews and

Gentiles in the East End. Neither its author nor its objective has ever been established. As with all Ripperology, multiple theories have flourished in the absence of hard evidence. Some posit that it was designed to implicate a Jewish killer; others precisely the opposite. Others still believe it to have Masonic connotations.

But what of the *new* graffito, haunting these streets more than a century later? Like the original, it is a riddle that only raises more questions. Who would leave such a message? Is it anti-Semitic, some kind of occult cryptograph, or just a bad joke? Why does its author use textspeak? And who, or what, is B.H.B.?

A bloodstained apron, a disused Tube tunnel, two mysterious graffiti writers. Pieces of a puzzle I have no chance of solving. Could the Ripper have escaped on the new underground railway? Just how many secrets are hidden in this hole? I feel myself being sucked down inside.

Aldgate East survived for fifty-four years. When a new line was built from Liverpool Street, the resulting bend at Aldgate East was thought to be excessively sharp and so in 1938 the station was relocated to its current position on the corner of Commercial Street. This also allowed for the use of new, eight-car trains at both Aldgate and Aldgate East, and for the closing of another stop on that line: St Mary's on Whitechapel Road.* The original Aldgate East station shut its doors on Sunday, 30 October with the new site opening the following morning. The closure was timely, for the boarded-up station was flattened by German bombers in 1940.

It is not true to say that nothing remains. The tunnel itself registers the loss. In recent years a group of anonymous guerrilla explorers walked down the live tracks from St Mary's in search of the remains of the original Aldgate East. This is what they found. The old platforms reduced to

* The site of the former station building is now a Citroën car dealership.

stubs of their former selves. Original pillars, ever fresh in gunmetal-grey paint, still holding up the roof. The steel footbridges that once carried passengers over the tracks blocked off, but surviving; hidden above the modern trains that hurtle through the tunnel every ninety seconds.

> We popped up on to the Eastbound platform, and climbed up the filthy ladder, thick with brake dust residue . . . Even on the tracks below, our torches were picking up lots of unknown particles in the air. These are breathed in not just by track workers and explorers, but also commuters every day. There were no footsteps up here until we arrived.[5]

They also discovered, beyond the platforms and eerily lit by emergency lights, a passageway filled with railway detritus. The passageway led to a series of interconnecting rooms and access corridors – two empty halls, toilet and washing area, storage cupboards. All flooded with artificial light. The walls were cracked and peeling with age, and the only signs of modern use were fire extinguishers and a pair of plastic road barriers. It is this complex of underground spaces, seemingly frozen in time, to which the trash-filled passages of the hole belong. I want to know how they connect. How it all adds up.

A Mercedes saloon speeds past the hole with a sudden blast of head-lights and hip hop. The shutter swings back and forth in the wind, and I notice a faded yellow sign on the adjacent building: MCC LTD – CARPET SUPERMARKET – GOODS ENTRANCE.

I think of the workmen labouring in the tunnel on that long night in 1938. They are lowering the new tracks into place for the morning rush. It is hot, exhausting work. They will not have time to remove the metal hooks they have screwed into the ceiling for the job. The platforms of the new Aldgate East are wide and palatial, their walls covered in spe-cially designed tiles. The halls and corridors of the old station will soon be empty and grow dusty. And then they will be forgotten.

The Line of the Stage

I N THE NINE YEARS since I first moved to Aldgate, I have become
increasingly obsessed by the hole. I spend my evenings poring over
antique maps online, then buy my own in reproduction prints to hang in
the flat. On walks through the city I make unnecessary detours just to
pass the hole, noting its gradual transformation from naked building site
to island wilderness. I watch as billboards come and go, the railings damaged then upgraded, then damaged again, and hoardings raised to block
the view from one side. And yet the diggers never come. The city grows
around us, and whatever plans the owner of the hole had for it remain,
indefinitely, on ice.

I am learning the history of the hole piecemeal, excitedly tumbling
down arcane pathways, looking for gaps in the record, unlikely connections, yet never committing to a sustained period of research by which I
might build up a coherent story. I might make some profound discovery, only to forget it by the time I return to the messy folder of jpegs and
PDFs concealed deep in the file system of my laptop. I am learning that
this one small site was so full of *stuff* it could hardly be kept hold of; that
it was, like London itself, a total mishmash.

What was here before the coming of the railway station that now lies
bombed, ruined and buried in trash? I turn to my Ordnance Survey
maps. In the nineteenth century the plot containing the hole and the
derelict 1960s block behind it is shown as a complex of buildings, alleyways and courtyards labelled 'Boar's Head Yard'. It sounds familiar, but
nothing clicks. And so I start digging for names, dates.

Adkin's stable, *c.* 1880. A Calvinist meeting house, 1832. Hat-dyeing.
A tobacco pipe workshop. A synagogue. A dissenters' chapel. It was coming thick and fast. Levi Moses, 1759. Adrian Denise, Huguenot weaver,
1684. Mary Long, spinster of Walthamstow. John Oswin, baker of Spitalfields. Joseph Ager, apothecary and surgeon. William Thirtle, grazier.

And then I find it. Or, rather, *it* finds *me*.

The Boar's Head.

I am looking at one of London's first playhouses.

On 6 September 1557 a group of officials pulled in to a typical London inn on the very edge of the City's jurisdiction. They were there on the instructions of the mayor and the Privy Council to prevent the performance of a 'lewd play' entitled *A Sack Full of News* by the Earl of Oxford's players. We don't know exactly what transpired, but the players were arrested, slung into prison for the night, and banned from future performances for two months. Their play-books were seized and the text was lost for ever.[6]

1557. The long reign of Elizabeth had not yet begun. And it would be another seven years till a certain William Shakespeare was born in Stratford-upon-Avon. Out here, in the scrappy fringe of the City, we can discern the first stirrings of a theatrical movement that would transform London, and English culture, for ever.

A two-month ban became forty years of silence. The Boar's Head went dark, presumably reverting to the trade it knew best: the supply of strong beer and safe lodging. (Its location on the eastern edge of the City would have made it popular with travellers from Essex and beyond.) Or perhaps, *just perhaps*, performances of plays, 'lewd' or otherwise, continued; undocumented, unremembered, vanished from the corpus.

In November 1594 a haberdasher and money-lender by the name of Oliver Woodliffe bought a twenty-one-year lease to the Boar's Head. Within four years, it was up and running again: not as a simple inn conversion, but as a purpose-built playhouse with a stage 40 by 25 feet, a tiring-house for the actors to get dressed and elevated galleries for standing spectators. A year later, Woodliffe and his business partner Richard Samwell carried out extensive renovations – expanding and covering the stage, increasing gallery capacity, and improving drainage.[7] At its peak the Boar's Head could have held one thousand paying audience members.

It was the height of the Elizabethan theatre boom – the property bubble of its time – and speculation was rife. Profits could be huge but it was a precarious business: cash-hungry, dependent on the changing tastes of audiences, liable to damage by fire or closure due to the plague, and always at the mercy of the censors. Almost as soon as the Boar's Head was completed, its two shareholders sold their stakes in the playhouse: Woodliffe to a reckless speculator called Francis Langley; Samwell to Robert Browne, actor–manager of the Derby's Men. Discord arose immediately between the two parties. Langley, supported by Woodliffe, sued first Samwell and then Browne for their share of the playhouse, claiming that their lease granted them only right of access and not ownership. A hail of litigation ensued. Claims and counterclaims. Vandalism. Multiple arrests. Detention in Marshalsea Prison; not only for Samwell, but also his daughter-in-law, Winifred, with her infant, Rebecca, 'still sucking at her breast'. In this ever more bizarre story, Langley lives up to his reputation as an 'underworld figure'.[8] On four separate occasions in December 1599 he entered the playhouse with armed men with the intention of threatening violence on Samwell and his associates. On 16 December, Langley's goons 'did in the dark throw divers daggers and other weapons at [Samwell] . . . and his son, which weapons, hardly missing . . . did stick in the walls of the said house so as [Samwell] . . . and his son hardly escaped [with] their lives by shifting and flying away from their assaults'.[9] On Christmas Eve, the gang even interrupted the performance of a play, forcing audience members at knifepoint to cough up their small change.[10]

The accounts of the legal (and physical) wrangling between Samwell, Langley, Browne and others take up more than thirty pages of *English Professional Theatre, 1530–1660*, a book so compendious it kicks up dust when I close the thick cover on my desk. And we know of at least three companies of actors – Derby's, Worcester's and Prince Charles's Men – that played there. Yet there is no trace of a single play performed at the Boar's Head. Not one title. In his seminal study of the playhouse, *The Boar's Head Playhouse*, Herbert Berry proposes two anonymous plays that 'might have' been performed there, and waves a speculative hand at six others (including Thomas Heywood's *If You Know Not Me, You Know No Bodie*).[11] But there is no record. We have the bitter outer rind, but not the juicy innards. The play's the thing. Of nothing.[12]

For all the claimants, to me the Boar's Head was Robert Browne's playhouse. He was the true theatre man among them. He was buried, alongside Woodliffe and another impresario, John Brayne, in the White Chapel of St Mary Matfelon; its foundations barely visible today in the scruffy lawn of Altab Ali Park.

I am reading of Browne's death, during the plague epidemic of 1603, when suddenly, out of nowhere, a familiar name jumps off the page. On 21 October Joan Alleyn wrote a letter to her husband from their house in Southwark. 'My intyre & welbeloved sweete harte,' she greets him. 'Browne of the Boares head is dead & dyed very pore, he went not into the countrye at all, and all of your owne company ar well at there owne houses.' The company in question was the Admiral's Men. The recipient of the letter was Edward 'Ned' Alleyn.

Alleyn: the most celebrated actor of the age. The owner of theatres, bear pits, brothels and a vast estate from Herne Hill to Sydenham Hill. Philanthropist. Childless. The founder of the College of God's Gift at Dulwich for '12 poor Schollars'. Alleyn would have remembered Browne, for they were fellow players with the Worcester's Men some twenty years before, when Alleyn was just sixteen. Alleyn, who was born in Bishops-gate and died owning half of south London.

I close the book, thinking of my parents. My mother arrived at Alleyn's School – the sister school to Dulwich College – in the summer of 1979. It was there that she met my father, also newly qualified.

They were there to teach English and Drama to the sons and daughters of south London's middle classes. I think Alleyn would have approved.

I look back again at the battered sign for the carpet supermarket. Instinctively I put out my hand and place it flat against the brick wall. It is unexpectedly warm.

The playhouse is no more. Browne is no more. *This*, says Berry, is the line of the stage. This is the spot to fix a plaque.[13]

The Old Gate

'A! Go we see, caste up the latis wyde;
For thurgh this strete he moot to palays ryde;
For other wey is fro the yate noon
Of Dardanus, ther open is the cheyne.'

GEOFFREY CHAUCER[14]

THE HOLE IS ALL the more arresting for the growing conformity of its surroundings. An unmanicured, ruined slump within a high-finance utopia. In truth, the entire junction has been riddled with decay for years; beneath the streets of Aldgate lies a complex network of abandoned pedestrian subways.

When I moved here, fresh from university, in 2005, you could still navigate the entire gyratory using these subterranean pathways. I would dive down a stairwell at the south end of Middlesex Street and come up for air a few minutes later on the corner of Mansell Street and Whitechapel Road. Then dive again, and surface outside the west door of St Botolph's – the traveller's church. The experience of walking the subways, especially at night, was one of total submersion. The white and pale-blue tiles and the glare of always-on strip lights lent it the appearance of a municipal swimming pool. One passageway was decorated with colourful panels advertising local amenities, and you left full of promise for the wonders of Petticoat Lane Market.[15] Another was covered in graffiti and contained a locked door that was marked 'public toilet' but in my imagination concealed some sinister mystery.

As well as offering safe passage beneath the roundabout, the subway led to the ill-fated Aldgate Barrs Shopping Centre. Once home to around a dozen retail units, it is now entirely derelict; its entranceway used by itinerant, nocturnal drinkers whose stained and dusty sleeping bags are scrunched up against the boarded-up revolving door. It makes me think of other abortive attempts at sunless, troglodytic shopping: the bookshop and gents' barber underneath the Old Street roundabout; the stalls that once lined Brunel's Thames Tunnel.

The Aldgate roundabout, long considered a thorn in the urban plan, has been reshaped and the subways have simply lost their purpose; today the walkers, workers and lunchtime shoppers must take their chances above ground. All but a handful of the passages are closed up, shut off, the stairwells barred by steel security walls. *Ealdgate*. The old gate. I can't stop thinking how dark it must be, in the labyrinth beneath my feet.

A gate is a structure that both includes and excludes. A site of welcome or of rejection, offering a guarantee of safe passage and the inevitability of taxes. When London was still a fortified settlement – a *de facto* city state with its own governance and laws – its two-mile-long wall was punctuated by seven gates; an arc of monumental entrances on a chain of military defences first raised by the Romans at the turn of the third century. Constructed using rubble, concrete and layers of tiles on a sandstone plinth and set on a trench foundation of clay, the Roman wall is believed to have stood over four metres high. Each entrance to the city was also the terminus of a road: trading routes to Colchester, St Albans, York and beyond. In the Middle Ages, these gates provided access into one of Europe's great commercial spaces.

The Aldgate roundabout transforms the simple, linear dynamic of the gate into something altogether more ambiguous: a vortex from which you might as easily be thrown back out, pinball-like; or else ensnared, pulled in by centrifugal forces, condemned to circle for evermore.

Aldgate's function as frontier, as border checkpoint, has been downgraded to a botched traffic-calming measure. I sat out the long summer of 2008 watching confused minicabs reversing the wrong way down Leman Street from my temporary office. The casual driver, guided by coordinates punched into a dash-mounted sat-nav, might not even register the crossing from Tower Hamlets into the City. A silver dragon stands rampant but lost on a traffic island.* One claw grasps a shield

---

* The boundaries of the City are marked by cast-iron statues of the Tudor dragon, a heraldic symbol. The dragon is commonly misidentified, leading to a pejorative nickname for the Corporation of London: the Griffin.

bearing a coat of arms. A chubby, bright-red tongue flicks out from between his jaws like an obscene phallus.

It is only underground, in the now-mothballed subway, that this ancient boundary endures as a strip of metal, no more than three inches thick, set into the concrete floor between two crests. Walking home late from Aldgate Tube or from the bus stop on Mansell Street, I would descend into the cold light of the subway, and could not help but slow my pace on approaching the line. As I passed over the boundary, I would take a pronounced, slow-motion step, as if time itself had contracted to the width of that metal strip; as if the history of that place had become as dense as pressurized rock and I was falling through it.

> *The guarantee of safe passage.*
> *The inevitability of taxes.*

I am standing at the centre of a large traffic island at the western edge of the Aldgate gyratory, looking east, back out towards Whitechapel. Across the traffic, the Georgian church of St Botolph's is nestled in a little cushion of trees; and behind me the Gherkin pushes its brassy neck above the City. It is summer, 2012, and the sky is dark with thunderclouds. I am sheltering from pre-storm drizzle in a wooden structure that only two weeks before did not exist. Four slender columns support a canopy of struts and beams so intricately meshed that it resembles molecular modelling, or a map of the nervous system. The latticework is finely done, but with nails showing at the joints and the sky peeking through, the whole thing seems unfinished. Is that an owl – a life-sized wooden owl – perched on one corner? I step back, into light rain, and take it all in. Something like a house on stilts; or a piece of ornate scaffolding.

Four miles away to the east, the Olympic Games are in full swing in the reclaimed industrial land beyond the river Lea. (Though in typical British fashion, rainwater has been reported leaking into the velodrome and the men's trap shooting has been suspended due to 'lightning and dangerous conditions'.)[16] The structure I am scrutinizing and to whose partial protection I have hurriedly returned is the brainchild of Studio Weave, an architectural practice based in Hackney. Their *Paleys upon Pilers* was commissioned for High Street 2012 – a project to promote the route from the City to the Olympic Park in Stratford. For the first time in two hundred and fifty years Aldgate has a gate, albeit one that is ignored by all but the most curious or rain-soaked pedestrian.*

Like the hole, Studio Weave's larch-wood *Paleys* is conspicuous amid the glass, metal and concrete vernacular of Aldgate. Its unvarnished exoskeleton seems to glow even in this weather. I look closer and notice that the supporting columns are decorated with red and blue patterns and shapes: intricate interlacing, sprouting foliage, geometric fretwork, initials illuminated in gold like a medieval Book of Hours.

In June 1374 a young civil servant arrived in Aldgate – a vintner's son, trained in the law and fresh from foreign travel. He had been appointed comptroller of customs for the port of London, a position for which he received an annual salary of £10 and the lease to the rooms above the gate. Merchant's stock he may have been, but this Londoner enjoyed royal patronage; only two months earlier, on St George's Day, he had been granted a daily allowance of one gallon of wine by King Edward. As comptroller, his workplace was the Custom House, a ten-minute walk down to the river from the gate. His duties comprised the weighing and inspection of all wool, leather and sheepskin exported from the City, and the collection of taxes thereon. But at night he would return to the gatehouse, weary from work, and sit by candlelight with pen, ink and vellum (parchment made from animal skins). For he was a poet. And his name was *Geffray Chaucer*.

---

* Having been rebuilt several times over the centuries, the Aldgate was finally removed in 1761 and its materials sold for the princely sum of £91.

To live a stone's throw from this: imagine! Where the giant of early English literature laid his head. Where he dreamt up *Troilus and Criseyde*. *The Parlement of Foules*. Where he translated Boethius. Where, perhaps, *The Canterbury Tales* was first conceived. I was gripped. And no blue plaque to mark this site either; Chaucer was my little secret. A name to whisper to myself like a magic charm in the depths of the subway or while gazing out of my garret window above the Hoop and Grapes.

Chaucer lived, as Caroline Barron puts it, 'on the margin'.[17] At the boundary between two wards; neither outside the City nor entirely within. The gatehouse was a fortified structure, designed for use as a temporary prison. Yet it was from this unlikely vantage point that Chaucer surveyed his London. The beggars and the tradesmen. Merchants in their finery. Goldsmiths and victuallers. Travellers from the east. Flemings and Italians. Austin canons from the nearby priory of Holy Trinity shuffling past in black robes.

But Chaucer was no Dickens or Hogarth, chronicling the city with photographic precision. The subjects of his early (pre-*Tales*) poems were mythical, Classical or flights of fancy: the real world – yes – but refracted by the forces of imagination and language. He seems to have been obsessed with sleep, and with the potential of dreaming to trigger both the sublime and the surreal. Entering his poetry is, for the modern reader, a dazzling, joyously disconcerting experience. The language sounds uncannily like our own, and yet it is off-kilter, jolted out of time, corrupted by the twists and spins of English itself. Speak it in the air, and you could be speaking bungled French; speak again and a kind of Dutch comes out, blended with a Cornish twang.

> *Ye knowe ek that in forme of speche is chaunge*
> *Withinne a thousand yeer, and wordes tho*
> *That hadden pris, now wonder nyce and straunge*
> *Us thinketh hem, and yet thei spake hem so*[18]

Chaunge or 'change': it was perhaps Chaucer's central obsession. Change of love. Change of fortune. The change of *estaat* or class.

Aldgate. *Ealdgate. Ealgate.*

Chaucer, working late in his gatehouse rooms, did not write about London directly. Instead he turned his mind towards Troy, the archetypal city state, to pen his first poetic masterpiece. In *Troilus and Criseyde*, the city appears as a military fortress with 'toures heigh' and 'walles faste', besieged by a foreign army but ultimately destroyed from the inside out.[19]

It was not Greeks but Essex men who threatened the City of London on the afternoon of 13 June 1381. The rebels, armed with clubs, bows and hand-me-down swords, swept along the old Roman road from Colchester. They swept across the open farmland of Essex, past the tide mills at Stratford and the crossing of the Lea, past the workshops and scattered tenements of Stepney, past Panfield, Bradfield and Basefield, across the campground at Mile End Green, across the Galeysfield and on past Ashwynes Great Field and the whitewashed chapel of St Mary Matfelon. A contingent of Kentish rebels led by Wat Tyler was crossing London Bridge from the south when the Essex force – provoked by the poll tax, enraged by corruption, inspired by the chance to end their serfdom – approached the Aldgate.

It is not clear who opened the gate, or why – there were many in London who shared the rebels' grievances – but what followed is well documented.* The rebels streamed into the City from the south and east, forcing open the prisons and attacking Flemish immigrants. They

---

* Alderman William Tonge was accused of opening Aldgate to the rebels, but the allegation was never substantiated and is as likely to have been the result of squabbling between two factions of the City guilds. Tonge survived the revolt and went on to become a Member of Parliament.

destroyed the priory and manor house at Clerkenwell, and sacked first the Knights Hospitallers' precinct (the Temple), then John of Gaunt's Savoy Palace, gutting its interior and burning all the papers they could find. By the evening the rebels had assembled outside the Tower of London, where a fourteen-year-old King Richard was holed up with his senior noblemen and the detested Archbishop of Canterbury, Simon Sudbury.

But what of Chaucer, guardian of the Aldgate? Was he witness to events from above, his ear to the door as thousands of angry rebels flooded into the city? Might he even have been involved in opening the gate? Or was he, ever the pragmatist, concealed in some safe house? For Chaucer was a tax official *and* an associate of John of Gaunt.* He would have been wise to have left town altogether.

I look up again at the trellis-like structure above me. The weather is finding gaps in the fretwork. Fat raindrops land on my coat. A bus judders past. The whole thing is laughably precarious: a new gate where the old one stood. I think it might collapse at any moment.

In one of Chaucer's early dream visions, the dreamer searches for the 'Hous of Fame' and on finding it observes that its foundations are made not of rock but gleaming ice. 'This were a feble fundament / To bilden on a place hye,' he notes, before spotting the names of the famous melting in the sun. This was the fantasy that inspired Studio Weave's rickety gateway. Chaucer's dream poems are full of ethereal or unstable structures. He was haunted by human fallibility and the impermanence of things. *The House of Fame* was Chaucer's Tower of Babel, 'full of tydynges, / Bothe of feir speche and chidynges, / And of fals and soth [truth] compouned'.

* Chaucer's wife, Philippa, was sister to Gaunt's mistress and future spouse Katherine Swynford.

Perhaps he *was* at home after all, that fractious summer day in 1381, trembling in the upper room, carving his own name into the shaky fundament of the gate itself.

CHAUCER WAS HERE

Whose Streets

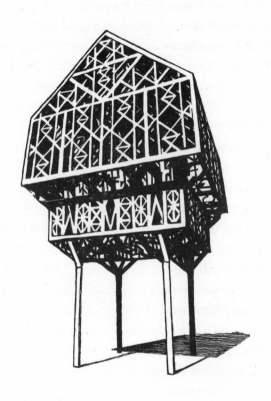

THE POLICE ARE PERFORMING exercises in the yard behind the hole. Fifty or so officers march in lines with riot shields held out in front, while a group of ten or fifteen guard the way into Aldgate. In their black, padded gear they resemble an amateur re-enactment society doing *The Empire Strikes Back*. Curious locals are being funnelled back towards Wentworth Street where a dozen Bengali teenagers are lounging around the empty market stalls in 'Muslim Council of Europe' hi-vis jackets.

It is September 2011. I have been circling the hole all week, looking for a way in, and now it is strictly off limits. Petticoat Lane is under lockdown. Lines of blackcurrant stormtroopers block the entrances to Wentworth, Toynbee and Old Castle Streets, turning the square of pavement outside my front door into no man's land.

The cause of this discord is a thousand-strong band of protestors who arrived that morning at Liverpool Street and Kings Cross stations before assembling at the north end of Tower Bridge. They call themselves the English Defence League. In truth, they are a rabble of far-right dissidents, Islamophobes and former football hooligans led by Tommy Robinson, a twenty-eight-year-old sunbed shop owner from Luton. I can hear distant chants of 'E! E! EDL!' and 'No surrender to the Ta-li-ban'.

Their plan: to march through the East End of London to protest against radical Islamism amid reports of Sharia Law being enforced in Whitechapel. The route would take them down Whitechapel High Street, past Brick Lane with its famous curry houses, to the door of the seven-thousand-capacity East London Mosque. But it was not to be. Three days before, Home Secretary Theresa May had issued a thirty-day banning order on marches in Tower Hamlets and four neighbouring boroughs. But still they were here, trapped inside the Aldgate gyratory, on the City side of the border. They would not take a single step into Tower Hamlets.

The riots that engulfed the city in August are fresh in the memory and the streets are tense. It's lucky I'm high up, then, wearing a crumpled Panama, eating Tesco's finest falafel and spying on the action from the rooftop. One copper, craning his neck to follow the trajectory of a news helicopter, spots me and nudges his colleague. I munch another falafel, and then descend to take a closer look.

A crowd of several thousand has gathered at the main police line across Whitechapel High Street. A mix of locals, both Asian and white, and anti-fascist demonstrators. Some are wearing the professional anarchist uniform of black hoodie, face scarf and rucksack, and break out into chants of 'Whose streets? Our streets!' There are small groups of young Bengalis, most in streetwear, a few in Islamic dress. I recognize faces from the estates around Petticoat Lane. They look bored and faintly embarrassed by the more vocal demonstrators. Behind us the main counter-demonstration is leaving from Altab Ali Park with banners and loudhailers. Beyond the police line, the road is deserted. From Aldgate East station to the roundabout, where the silver dragon of the City stands guard, where I can just make out another solid police line holding back the raised flags of St George.

The EDL rehearse old prejudices with sad predictability. Those with long memories recall Oswald Mosley's Fascist 'Blackshirts' marching through the East End in the 1930s, and the Jewish and Irish East Enders who stood against them on Cable Street. I think too of the men of Kent and Essex who stormed the gates of London in 1381 and whose legitimate grievances were set aside for the pursuit and murder of Flemish immigrants.

Forbidden to proceed horizontally *across* the city, the EDL are trapped within the vortex of the gate, an infinite loop, sanctioned to perform a 'static march'. I imagine them parading on the spot – an angry step aerobics – before descending corkscrew-like into the fabric of the city, down through melting tarmac, through water pipes and service tunnels, a millennium of rubble, and down through silt and wind-blown sand, to the very London Clay that lies beneath it all. This deep city.

Later a ten-minute video clip will emerge on YouTube. A crowd has gathered in the sunshine on Aldgate High Street. Spirits are high. Flags of St George are held aloft, some decorated with crudely scrawled place names: Lincoln, Croydon, Newcastle-under-Lyme. I can see only white men, many with shaved heads, some in hi-vis jackets. Some of the younger men have ski-masks and hoodies pulled over their heads. A figure dressed as an Orthodox Jew with fake beard and a wide-brimmed hat is introduced as 'Rabbi Benjamin Kid 'em on'. Cries of 'We love you, Tommy!' sound out as Robinson – real name: Stephen Yaxley-Lennon – stands, removes his disguise, and takes the microphone.

'The more Islam the less freedom,' he begins. 'We stand here today in Tower Hamlets. We stand for freedom. We stand for democracy. And we stand for democratic rights.'

He has the skilled orator's easy style. He attacks the police for issuing him with an ASBO, and promises to keep up the fight. 'There are thousands of Islamist lunatics running around the streets of East London. These streets do not belong to paedophilic Muslim gangs.'

Cries of 'Whose streets? Our streets!' start up before a police snatch squad moves in and the video ends. It's the same chant on both sides.

Whose streets. Our streets.

The headline reads LONDON CELEBRATES OLYMPIC VICTORY. I remember it word for word because as I passed the entrance to the Tube on my walk home a ragged copy of the *Evening Standard* almost flapped into my face, caught in a sudden gust of wind. Kelly Holmes with arms aloft as the magic word was said: London. It was 6 July 2005. The sky was unusually dark that evening, and the streets were deathly quiet. At dusk, the air was thick with exhaust fumes and little squalls of debris tracked across the junction. It was like walking through smoke. And there was that light you get when low sun streams through thunderclouds.

Sometimes, when you take the District Line from Aldgate East towards the City, the train will stop just outside the station to let a Circle Line train go past, and if you look to your right you can see the end of the platform at Aldgate, and for a moment the tunnel is lit by an eerie glow, long shadows are cast along the dirty brick walls and ancient cabling, and you see yourself too, looking out, caught between darkness and light, between the past and your final destination.

The next morning I left for work as usual, walking the half mile or so down Whitechapel High Street to my office behind the mosque. I thought nothing of the heavy shutters pulled across the entrance to Aldgate East station. I was at my desk when the first reports began to hit the news sites. A derailed train. Explosions caused by an electrical surge on the Tube.

By mid-morning the facts were falling into place: three simultaneous detonations on the Underground at Aldgate, Kings Cross and Edgware Road, and a fourth on a number 30 bus in Tavistock Square, its roof ripped clean off by the blast. The Aldgate bomber boarded a Circle Line train heading east. His device discharged 100 yards from the platform at Liverpool Street station, killing seven people and injuring hundreds. His name was Shehzad Tanweer. He was twenty-two. He would have been in my year at school.

The mobile networks were down and I received a tearful call on the office phone from my girlfriend, Sarah. She had overslept and hadn't made it in to work (yards from the Tavistock Square bus explosion). All day I listened to the wails of sirens as ambulances ferried the wounded to the Royal London Hospital in Whitechapel. Survivors were surfacing at Aldgate, shocked and covered in soot, bits of shrapnel, other people's blood, some with makeshift bandages or sucking at oxygen masks. They must have walked the 250 yards from the crash site to the station in almost pitch black, ghosting the line of the Roman wall, before emerging in the middle of the gyratory.

It was like a waking dream. I can barely remember what we said to one another, or if we spoke at all.

There was a hole in my stomach.

And as I walked back from work, the world felt complex and clear at the same time. The police had sealed off an area three streets wide around the station so I had to cross the cordon to get home. I sat down, alone, in my one-bedroom flat above an empty market, turned on the TV news and wept.

A ruined station. A lost playhouse. Terror, protest and poetry. A hole in the city slowly going to waste. This is the story of Aldgate: an island of erasure obsessively mapped and walked. The hole has sucked me down into the earth and now it spits me out, recharged and ready to begin again, to strike out across London in search of urban mysteries buried beneath the streets.

Aldgate station, 7 July 2015, 11 a.m. It is ten years to the day since the bomb. I guess there are a hundred of us here, standing in a circle outside the entrance. There is no signal. It just . . . begins. The traffic noise subsides. Our heads bow. A piece of litter skips across the pavement. And then it is done.

'The East End of London belongs to Cockneys,' Tommy Robinson had said, before being bundled into a meat wagon. I look at the faces around me. Faces of bankers, office workers, cleaners and Tube station staff. All colours and all creeds. Not here to be counted; but here to be present. To witness.

The *Paleys upon Pilers* has been dismantled. There is again no mark of that great gate. Tubby Isaac's is long gone, but now I spot that Rose Seafood has taken its pitch, with the promise of 'World Famous Jellied Eels'. I drift east to see the hole one final time, before it's cleared and backfilled for the footprint of some other grand design. It is as wild as ever, a deeper green now, bristling with bindweed and brambles: a jungle where once a playhouse stood. The gap in the fence has been repaired, but signs of entry linger on: a sleeping bag; two black bin liners spilling over with sweatshirts and denim jeans. Even on a summer's night, it is a desperate bivouac.

I turn a corner and freeze. They are filling in the subways. A team of workmen sit on a breezeblock waiting for the liquid concrete to dry. A lake of concrete where the entrance to the subway used to be. The tunnels I loved to navigate, where you could cross the invisible line into the City.

People are walking past me, so many people, walking this way and that, finding routes through the roadworks as best they can. Even ruins will one day be erased. There is an information board fixed to the railings. Promises of road improvements, new public spaces, a digital render of the future roundabout, and a hashtag: #aldgateischanging

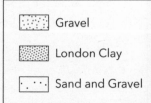

Gravel

London Clay

Sand and Gravel

II: RETURN TO THE SOURCE

In Search of the Ambrook

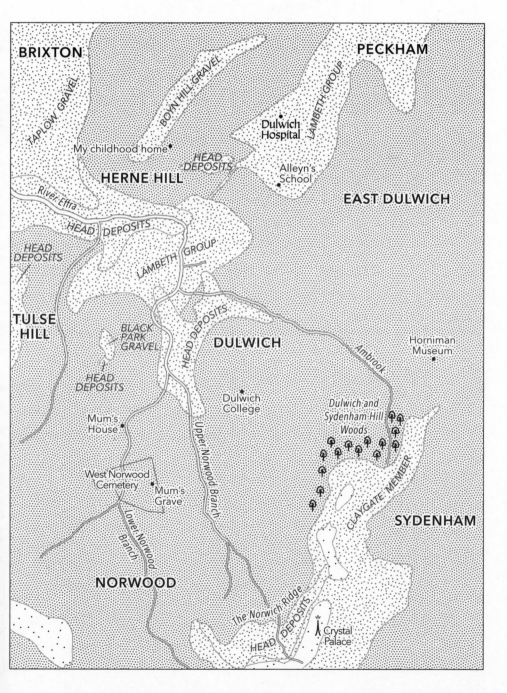

A dream of earth slipping. The churn of soil and clay.
Faultlines opening. A hillside collapsing from the inside.
And you are falling. Tumbling. Falling into darkness.
Darkness, then blue. Blue-grey. Greyish. A dream.
You are being carried down backwards.
You are sliding away and I am falling.

Herne

'I can still walk up and down the piece of road between the Fox tavern and the Herne Hill station, imagining myself four years old.'

<small>JOHN RUSKIN[1]</small>

I ENTERED THE WORLD inside the Gothic, redbrick edifice of Dulwich Hospital: a sickly, C-section baby. The maternity ward, with its dank, lonely corridors and stained walls, was said to be haunted. My parents had rented a number of modest addresses in Dulwich and Tulse Hill before settling into a three-bedroom Edwardian house in Frankfurt Road, Herne Hill that I would call home for the next twenty years.

Ours was one of numerous terraced streets projecting at right angles from the main thoroughfare over the hill. Each street was laid out on the line of an old field boundary or footpath from the time before the coming of the railway. Their increasingly steep inclines – perfect for steaming down on BMX or skateboard – describe the topography of the hill itself: a 50-metre ridge of London Clay capped with gravel. If you dug deep enough in our back garden, through the thin layer of topsoil, the clay would come out in large, waxy clumps.

Herne Hill is what my father calls an 'inner-city suburb' – an in-between place that possesses traces of both urban and suburban whilst never fully embracing either state. Just three miles from Charing Cross, it is bordered to the north by the dense inner-city neighbourhoods of Brixton and Camberwell; but a ten-minute stroll in the opposite direction will take you down wide, leafy avenues past the detached Victorian mansions and spotless playing fields of Dulwich Village. The boundary between the London boroughs of Southwark and Lambeth runs precisely along the crest of the hill and follows the road down towards the railway station where it splits the busy road junction in two. Blue bins on one side, black on the other.

Herne is a name with an uncertain history. From Old English *hyrne* meaning 'corner of a hill'? Or a corruption of *heron* – remembering the regular appearance of these large birds in the vicinity? (Spotted from my pram, Sunray Gardens, *circa* 1985.) Named after the Herne family, residents of Brockwell Hall in the eighteenth century? Or some darker, deeper etymology: the sign of the Hunter, horned god of the forest?

This contested locale suited me: a city kid with a taste for the wild. Herne. The damp smell of fox. Rudeboys riding the P4 from Brixton. Trevor, the local gent's barber and amateur archaeologist, drinking in the Half Moon with his shaggy dog fast asleep under a stool. A sycamore spilling its downy cargo by the bins behind the Chinese takeaway.

Herne. *Hyrne.* A corner. A crook. The crux. Where language and landscape collide. On my modified Streetfinder map the hill appears within a tangle of competing strata –

> *Taplow Gravel to the north*
> *a nodule of head deposits along Dulwich Road*
> *outcrops of bedrock from the Lambeth Group halfway down Burbage*
>   *Road*
> *exposed London Clay covering the west side of Brockwell Park all the*
>   *way to Brixton Prison*
>   *and on the flanks of the hill itself*
> *overlays of Boyn Hill Gravel on the crest*
>   *and in the former grounds of Sunray House.*

Put it this way. Where the terraces of the Thames rise up to meet the higher land, Herne is a geological crumple zone.

Against the complex landscape of the hill, formed over millions of years by forces unimaginably vast, the human story fades into insignificance. My own memories – these are the most ephemeral of deposits. They barely register.

When I was very young my parents used to play a trick on me to entertain guests. During lunch, my father would suddenly freeze and then turn to me, pointing his finger towards the garden.

'Look, Tom! At the end of the garden: a badger!'

Fooled every time, I would charge down the lawn to where three scraggy pine trees stood and spend the next few minutes searching the scrubby ground for signs of the enigmatic creature. On my return, dismayed by its non-appearance, my mother would join in with 'Thomas, there it is again! The badger! You *just* missed it!' and I'd scuttle off once more. Half an hour might pass in this manner, with me tearing back and forth from the end of the garden and the adults barely suppressing their laughter.

As soon as I was old enough to climb, I hauled a couple of leftover planks up into the pines and bound them to the flimsy branches as a precarious treehouse. I also began to make incursions into the alleyway that ran behind the pine trees. Our house being an end-of-terrace, a garden gate half off its hinges enabled access to this other world, enclosed by high wooden fences, hexed with impenetrable undergrowth.

One day, aged ten, I was joined by my best friend, Chris Cook, in an ambitious expedition to walk the entire course of the alleyway. Thanks to my mother's job as Head of Drama at Alleyn's School, I had a constant supply of period costumes. For some reason that I cannot presently recall, that day we were dressed as two of the Three Musketeers. The muddy floor of the alley was crawling with insects. However warm it was outside, the alley's interior was cool, chilled as a cold store. Sparrows detonated from their hiding spots as we passed. We discovered a fox's den, dug deep into thorn bushes; an enamel bathtub full of weeds; rags, bottles, newspaper-mulch and discarded plumbing (including a length of plastic tubing I would later convert into a rocket for a school project).

The further we went, the denser it became. We were journeying not only laterally but also vertically, descending into the deep past of the road, of the houses, of the hill itself. Our childish lives seemed suddenly behind us now: our schoolbooks and colouring-in, our comforts and routines. We surrendered to the philosophy of the alley, its freight of dark, compacted matter, until the sharp cry of a man surprised sunbathing in his garden sent us sprinting back home, breathless and howling with illicit laughter.

Years after leaving Herne Hill, I discovered that the Late Modernist poet Eric Mottram – author of *A Book of Herne* – had lived for decades on Half Moon Lane, at the southern foot of the hill. I must have passed him on the street a dozen times or more. Perhaps, like me, he used to drink in the Half Moon, where my fake ID would be accepted without question and where, in 1844, the tombstone of Edward Alleyn was recovered from the pub's skittle yard, where it was being used as a cover for the local sewer.

Mottram wrote in 'Herne's Descent': 'the dead layer presses / thrusts up from under / ground'.[2] Only now am I beginning to realize how profoundly the landscape of my childhood has infused my thinking with a sense of the city as a haunted, ambiguous place, where buried rivers, suppressed memories and the ghosts of forgotten histories threaten to emerge from beneath.

On early maps of Southwark, two streams are shown meandering through the landscape to their confluence near Herne Hill railway station, which is marked 'Island Green'. One stream, indicated on maps as late as 1872, approaches from the south-east, coursing underneath Winterbrook Road. The other follows the line of Norwood Road, skirting Brockwell Park; past the defunct Blockbuster Video; past Olley's (the best fish and chip restaurant in south London); past the whitewashed exterior of the legendary former nightclub Bon Bonne. This coagulation of watercourses has a name in these parts and it is *Effra*.

Effra

'a torrent carrying the waste of a dozen villages'
ALLEN FISHER[3]

O N 27 APRIL 2004, prolonged rainfall caused the sewers converging on Dulwich Road and Half Moon Lane to back up. In a matter of hours the low-lying centre of Herne Hill was under several feet of flood-water. The afternoon drinkers abandoned the Half Moon. Homes and businesses were evacuated.* Fire crews in waders loitered on the banks of what had become an urban lake, too late to save the cars parked up by the shops. A group of youths commandeered a rubber dinghy, and rowed to the off-licence along a newly formed channel at the end of Stradella Road. I was not at home – it was my final year of university. While I was cram-ming for Finals, fifty miles away, Herne Hill was once again 'Island Green', caught between two bloated tributaries of a lost river.†

Effra: from the Celtic *yfrid*, a 'torrent'.

Without knowing it, I had always lived on the banks of this half-forgotten waterway: first in Herne Hill; and then, with my mother, in West Norwood. The river entered my consciousness some time in my late teens, but I cannot put my finger on exactly when, or how. The reve-lation was transformative – a lightning bolt to my imagination. The Effra was my gateway drug. I soon acquired a copy of Nicholas Barton's seminal 1962 study, *The Lost Rivers of London*, with its iconic pull-out map of the city superimposed with a network of wriggly blue lines.[4] I was hooked. The rivers – dozens of them, tributaries of the Thames – seemed to me strange, exotic things with names out of a fantasy novel: Quaggy, Falconbrook, the Black Ditch of Limehouse. Some of these streams have entirely vanished from the modern city and can only be

---

* The flooded premises included Island Arts Studio, a tiny bar-venue in a converted railway arch where, between 2004 and 2006, I ran a poetry-reading series.
† A third tributary joins the main stream around the junction of Dulwich Road with Brixton Water Lane.

traced on historic maps or by studying street names. Many have been converted into underground sewers and run unseen beneath the pavement, carrying the waste of London's growing population. Others – such as the Wandle and the Brent – still flow above ground for most of their course. These rivers are 'lost' only in name, but they are degraded versions of their original forms, unfurling across the city in junk-filled concrete channels.

The Effra was once a willow-lined stream meandering through the water meadows of south London. In 1912 an old man recalled the river of his youth in Gipsy Hill, 'rugged in surface but bright in spring and summer with the flowers of coltsfoot, ragwort and sprays of furze blossom'.[5] In the seventeenth century, wells were sunk at Beulah Hill, Dulwich and Sydenham, drawing on the same aquifer that fed the Effra to serve iron-enriched water to visitors seeking rejuvenation. One is still remembered in the name of a Harvester pub, the Beulah Spa. Further north, where the gathered force of rivulets running off the land produced a stream once navigable by royal barge, the river lives on in street names: Effra Road, Effra Parade, Brixton Water Lane.*

By the turn of the nineteenth century the Effra had mostly been culverted (concealed in drains), an early victim of urban sprawl. In his eulogy for Herne Hill, John Ruskin complains of the river being 'bricked over for the convenience of Mr. Biffin, chemist, and others'.[6] In 1865 the Effra was one of many of London's waterways to be incorporated into Joseph Bazalgette's monumental sewerage system, with a series of intercept tunnels carrying its flow to Crossness, where it was pumped into the estuarine Thames. But this is a function the Effra had always provided in one way or another. The notable cartographer (and Huguenot refugee) John Rocque marked its course between Brixton and Kennington as 'The Shore' – an ancient word for sewer – in his maps of 1741 and

---

* Elizabeth I is reputed to have navigated the Effra by barge to visit Walter Raleigh's house at Brixton.

1763.* Today the river's presence can still be felt by the unusually wide pavement under which it flows on the east side of Brixton Road.

The Effra was an invisible energy line coursing through my childhood. Rising from springs in the hills of Norwood; cutting through the Victorian cemetery where we buried my mother; twisting underneath Croxted Road where my first school uniform was acquired; another branch from the west feeding the ponds in Belair Park; past the haunted schoolhouse and a stolen kiss; combining at the lido, Brockwell Park; rushing unseen past the Brockwell Tavern; past the basement flats and into Brixton; imitation jackets from the market; Electric Avenue; a nail-bomb outside Iceland; oregano in little baggies; Goth make-up for Marilyn Manson at the Academy; the right-angle turn at Kennington towards Claylands Lane, skirting the Oval cricket ground; another little stream from the vicinity of Cleaver Square; and into the Thames – a sorry pipe discharging south of Vauxhall Bridge.

Perhaps I have always been looking for the Effra, its mouth now concealed beneath luxury flats.† It came to stand for that whole hidden world beyond the human; the deep city, dark and nameless. The alleyway, feral, thick with junk, gone to seed. The buried river, sloshing at manholes.

I feel its pull now, to go back to where my obsession began. I have heard of a stream that still runs above ground through a pocket of urban woodland – a tiny capillary feeding the Effra mainline. The Ambrook. I pull on my walking shoes and stuff my Streetfinder into a rucksack. I am going to return to the source.

* Brixton Road has also, at various times, been called Brixton Causeway and the Washway. *See also*: Shoreditch.
† St George's Wharf, where a helicopter collided with a crane in January 2013, resulting in the deaths of the pilot and one passer-by.

Woods

*'And now I see as I look
That the small winding brook,
A tributary's tributary, rises there.'*

EDWARD THOMAS[7]

SOUTH LONDON IN MAY. Blossom is everywhere. Flares of white and pink flowers exploding from behind garden walls and wheelie bins, stroking the tops of bus shelters. People stop mid-flow on their way to work or the shops or to visit a neighbour just to take it in. Everyone says that this year is the best they can remember.

I am deep inside the woods and blossom is falling from the sky, shrapnel of catkins whirling in shafts of sunlight like theatre dust caught in a follow-spot. Now the wind drops and it is falling vertically in slow motion like sheet-rain; tiny, feathery parachutes gifted to the leaf-mulch. It is white and downy underfoot. A smell both sweet and earthy-damp rises from the path. High in the canopy a songbird trills the same three-note refrain, and below it another voice, less shrill, plays an insistent melody like a folk song. Somewhere deeper inside, short bursts of drilling give away a woodpecker's work.

I turn. A rustle in the undergrowth. Darkness as a cloud passes. Nothing. I focus my hearing. There is a low creaking sound as the trees lean in. Old oaks and hornbeams. I have the disorientating sensation of being on a wooden sailing ship at night.

A beat.

Then sun breaks through and the woods are revived again by dappled light.

I have come to Sydenham Hill, an enclave of dense woodland on the southern rim of the Thames basin. I am only eight miles from Trafalgar Square and less than one from the busy suburb of Forest Hill with its handsome Wetherspoon's and a new Costa. Together with the adjacent, and connecting, Dulwich Wood, Sydenham Hill is a survivor: one of the last remnants of the Great North Wood which once covered a vast area south of the Thames from Deptford to Selhurst. Its stock is oak and hornbeam, willow and elm, wild garlic, bugle and dog violet. Traces of Victorian intervention are felt in more recent arrivals: malevolent cherry laurel, a lone monkey puzzle. Exotic imports for the gardens of the big houses that once stood on the ridgeline. The largest tree in the wood is a giant cedar of Lebanon on whose thick trunk are recorded numerous teen romances. It is captured as a sapling in a photograph of The Hoo, the former Victorian mansion whose sprawling grounds have long been reclaimed for the wild. Inside the wood, the city melts away. At night, brown long-eared bats leave their nests in an abandoned railway tunnel to hunt moths in the moonlight.

This is clay land. You don't have to dig far into the topsoil around here to pull out moist, doughy chunks of the stuff. The Norwood Ridge, in whose slopes the woods are nestled, is capped, in geological terms, by the Claygate Member, the youngest variety of London Clay, which was formed in shallow seas 48 to 56 million years ago. The clay is dark and grey, a laminated and sandy clay with occasional concretions of iron-stone and 'septarian nodules' – mysterious egg-shaped objects which break open to reveal a network of colourful cracks radiating from the centre. Crystallogists call them 'dragonstones' and recommend them for the relief of stress and anxiety.

I pull out my Streetfinder and unfold it on the damp, moss-covered trunk of a fallen tree. Then I trace the outline of the ridge and write CLAYGATE MEMBER next to it in biro. Using old maps and obscure sourcebooks, I have already marked other lines on the map: seven or eight spidery pathways descending from the ridge before converging at Herne Hill and Brixton. These are the hidden tributaries of the river Effra. If the woods are south London's green lungs, then this network of streams is its bronchial tree, diverging like fractals into the springline.

The moss is cold to the touch. I raise my hand to the light; the sun filtering through the canopy catches on my fingertips and they shine like gemstones. From here, the horizon would once have been dominated by a huge plate-glass structure which stood at the summit of the ridge a mile to the south. The structure housed the Great Exhibition after it had been transferred from its original, temporary site in Hyde Park, and reopened in 1854 on an area of common land known as Penge Peak.* Three times the size of St Paul's Cathedral, its shimmering façade could be seen for miles around and gave it the nickname 'the Crystal Palace'. Inside, visitors could marvel at the treasures of human civilization in a series of themed 'courts' depicting art and artefacts from Ancient Egypt, Greece, Rome and the Renaissance, amongst others. The four-thousand-capacity concert hall hosted an annual Handel festival, while the central transept welcomed cat shows, dog shows, motor shows, circuses and the world's first aeronautical exhibition, as well as grand receptions for visiting dignitaries including Garibaldi and the Shah of Persia.

The Great Exhibition was a project of empire at its most confident. It positioned Britain at the epicentre of a newly globalized and industrialized world, with London as a new Rome and the exotic animals, trees and flowers imported as colonial tributes. There is nothing we cannot possess or tame, it proposed. For over eighty years, the Norwood Ridge broadcast the soft power of the British Empire until the Palace's destruction, hubristically, in fire in 1936. Today, only its brick foundations remain, along with a ruined subway and three pairs of concrete sphinx that have recently been repainted terracotta red. The name stuck too, lending itself to my local football team, Crystal Palace FC, and to the 219-metre-high television transmitter whose aircraft warning light flashed on and off, on and off, at night in my childhood bedroom.

*

* *Penge* is believed to be the only definitively Celtic place name in London. It was recorded in an Anglo-Saxon deed from 957 as *Penceat*, meaning 'wood's end' in Primitive Welsh. Margaret Gelling, *Place-Names in the Landscape* (Phoenix Press, 1984).

I am descending Cox's Walk into the heart of the wood. A cloud of midges appears then disappears ahead of me. I hear a baby's cry – it sounds close by, just off the path. Cut into the steep hillside, the wood has that effect, a vertiginous sensation of things being closer than they are: the glimpse of a hawthorn in brilliant white blossom caught in sudden sunlight; a walker calling after her dog; an elderly man in shirtsleeves and rucksack passing by an unseen upper level. I spot a green, fold-up Maclaren pushchair that has been stashed behind a bench at the bottom of the path. It is well camouflaged against the dark leaves of a bush spilling over the fence. A second path converges from the south when I see it, always startling – a large, iron footbridge, industrial in appearance, crossing the railway line that once bisected these woods.

I pass underneath a huge girder to the centre of the bridge. The ground on either side falls away, revealing the empty trackbed of the Crystal Palace and South London Junction Railway, opened in 1865 to transport visitors to the Palace from Victoria Station. I peer over the iron trusswork to where the railway sleepers once lay. A bumblebee is scanning the ground. A white baseball cap and a pair of grey tracksuit bottoms have been discarded by the brick pillars of the bridge to form a prone figure, like the chalk outline of a murder victim.

It was from this exact spot, in 1871, that the French artist Camille Pissarro painted his view of Lordship Lane railway station, an artwork now exhibited at the Courtauld Institute of Art. The critic Michael Glover describes it well: 'At the painting's dead centre is a small, soot-blackened steam locomotive releasing gouts of trailing, listing smoke, white edging off to smudgy greys, into the upper air.'[8] The view is virtually unrecognizable today. Where Pissarro's steam engine emerges from a cluster of redbrick houses and station buildings, with the land behind rising up towards One Tree Hill, now you cannot see beyond a solid wall of green woodland. Moss green. Spring green. Jade and forest. In the painting, the train and the landscape coexist quite naturally. For Glover, Pissarro has created for the viewer 'a new modernity' in which the railway is no longer an existential threat to the environment but an intrinsic part of it. 'The present, quite seamlessly, has replaced the past,' he writes, 'and the apocalypse has not happened.'

The trackbed recedes into the wood then vanishes. Apocalypse: from the Greek for 'revelation'. An uncovering. A vision of the future when the wildwood reclaims its debt and all shall be changed. For now, though, I am stepping through the ruins of Victorian industry – a railway sleeper here, a half-ribcage of twisted metal there – buried in the soil or hidden by rampant undergrowth. Still on the footbridge, I notice two cryptic lines of graffiti inscribed on one of the wooden supporting beams in an elaborate, cursive font. The first reads, *Lets get on it proper style alright boys.* And below: *Mum im sorry I get . . .* The rest is rubbed out.

I first came to these woods as a small child. My mother would drive the three of us from our home in Herne Hill, along Croxted Road, and park at the top of Grange Lane by the golf club. In December we would come to pick sprigs of holly and ivy to decorate the house for Christmas, my mother armed with a pair of secateurs from B&Q on Norwood Road. When I was old enough to spend whole days exploring my patch of south London with friends, I would scramble up the steep incline of Cox's Walk from Dulwich on my BMX. Later still, as a pupil of nearby Dulwich College, I used my knowledge of the woodland paths to cheat the annual cross-country run. After somehow evading the sports-master's surveillance, two of us, local lads, cut through an obscure part of the woods and found a quiet spot to share a cigarette before casually rejoining the tail of the race five minutes later.

In my teenage years, the woods became a hideout. It was my Arden, my Sherwood, my *forest dark*,[9] a refuge from a world I couldn't handle and sometimes wished I could escape for good. In sixth form I bunked off school and found secluded spots to sit and drink cheap spirits from the local West Indian off-licence. I had discovered poetry and carried slim volumes in my rucksack: William Blake, Edward Thomas and a first collection by a young poet called Alice Oswald.

> *my voice, a pollen dust, puffs out*
> *the reason I remain*[10]

Ignorant of the fauna and flora, I made up my own names for favourite haunts. A giant oak felled by the Great Storm of 1987 I dubbed the Honeycomb Tree on account of its insides, which were rotten and riddled with ants' tunnels. Another unidentified species I named the Wishbone Tree because its bifurcated trunk provided a comfy little crook in which to sit. I have been looking for these trees ever since, but they have vanished: removed or concealed or rotted down to mulch and absorbed back into the earth. I can no better find the Honeycomb Tree than reconstruct a faithful picture of my childhood, uncorrupted by exaggeration, misremembering and gaps in the record. The woods were a catalyst for my imagination. The little Victorian folly known as The Hoo, after the vanished mansion, I mistook for the ruins of an ancient chapel. It seemed the perfect location for the arrival of the Green Knight or the monster Grendel. I would sit beneath the artfully wrecked Gothic arch, put my hand on the moss-covered bricks and dream myself away.

I have come down from the bridge and am standing in the trackbed, near to the oldest part of the woods. Beds of wildflowers now flourish here, species that indicate ancient origins: sweet woodruff, wood-sedge and wood anemone. These woods have been managed sustainably for centuries; the coppicing of hazel here is thought to date to the Middle Ages.

Suddenly: the sickly-sweet perfume of wild garlic. I spot a familiar flower and a memory is triggered: I am walking on a carpet of English bluebells, their deep indigo heads all turned in one direction. It is June 2001. Brixton DJ Pied Piper's garage hit 'Do You Really Like It?' is number one in the Singles Chart and I have just turned eighteen. I am wearing my school uniform with battered skate shoes and reading aloud a poem by Barry MacSweeney from the latest issue of *Tears in the Fence* magazine. I say to the trees:

> *And everything from your eyes and mouth was sudden*
> *calculated gold pouring into the brilliant bucket of my*
> *bluebell heart*[11]

I am brought back to the woods – and to my search for the mysterious tributary of the river Effra – by the sustained note of a songbird high up in the canopy. I've completed a loop and I'm now underneath the footbridge. The cap and tracksuit bottoms are lying on the ground just where I saw them from the bridge, but next to them, pushed up against one of the brick pillars, and therefore concealed from above, is a metal camp bed. I look around, instinctively. No one. I look closer. On the bed is a flimsy mattress, ripped on one end to reveal the foam inside. On the mattress are a crumpled pair of black jeans and a comb, a blanket, a pile of receipts, an unopened can of Pepsi, an empty packet of cigarettes, a lighter and an iPhone in a salmon-pink plastic case. A patch of earth near by has been scorched by a small fire. More clothes, soiled and ripped, have been discarded there: a suit jacket, turned inside out, and a beige undergarment in the middle of which has been rolled out a long, black turd.

On 28 December 1802, the body of an elderly man was discovered in a cave in Dulwich Wood. His name was Samuel Mathews and he had been murdered. Known locally as the Norwood Hermit or Mathews the Hairyman, a newspaper illustration of the time shows him, clean-shaven, sitting on the floor of the wood, working intently at a branch with his whittling knife. Another shows him in identical pose tending his cooking pot over an open fire, and claims he was a 'Native of Pembrokeshire'. A gardener by trade, Mathews had excavated the cave himself when he had moved to the wood after the death of his wife. On Sundays he sold beer to curious visitors, and he was known to frequent local inns; the night before his death he was seen in the French Horn, Dulwich Village.[12]

> The body was discovered by some boys, who, at Christmas time had always made a practice of paying the old man a visit; he was covered with fern and under his arm was an oaken branch about six or seven feet long, which it is supposed the villains put into the cave in order to hook him out . . . it appears likely the hook had been hitched into his mouth, there being a hole of the size of it quite through the cheek.[13]

The woods are still full of abandoned shelters, from simple crawl spaces fashioned from bramble bushes to ambitious structures using fallen branches that bring to mind Mongolian yurts or the tipis of the Great Plains. But the precise location of Mathews's cave has always been a mystery. Perhaps it was backfilled after his death or simply lost beneath new growth. On Twitter @portalsoflondon posted a photo from the woods – a ruined brick wall behind a curtain of overhanging leaves, speculating, 'this can-filled grotto [is] a contender'.[14] Another tweeter posted an eerie, black-and-white photo of a den, described as a '[r]are photo of the Dulwich hermitage periodically rebuilt to appease the ghost of "old Matthew" [sic] foully murdered in 1802'.[15] He added, sarcastically, 'Legend has it that each new master of Dulwich College must spend one night in the hut to learn the secrets of the wood.'

Half an hour has passed. There's a moistness in the air now that forecasts rain. I can smell it. The wood breathes out. Wild garlic. Fox stink. Soil. I am walking the path that was the trackbed south towards the ridge. Through an arch of trees and into sunlight, and there it is, running in a gulley to my right, the Ambrook, barely there at all, a half-remembered thing, but still I shiver, seeing it, the Ambrook, *a tributary's tributary*, for the first time, which is also not the first time. Heraclitus said you cannot step in the same river twice. But I don't even remember this river, or stream, or runnel, from when I used to walk the woods as a child.

The Ambrook is about two feet wide here, very shallow, and crossed by a 'ligger' – three wooden planks reinforced by chicken wire. A simple wooden fence protects the stream either side of the crossing, where the water is the colour of stewed tea. The flow is barely a trickle. It emits no sound, but is discerned by the movement of light on the surface. A small tree has fallen right across the stream a little further up, its trunk split like a giant tuning fork. I crouch, then kneel. I need to get as close to the river as I can. The banks of the Ambrook are covered in moss and distinctly rounded at the bottom where they meet the water. Weeds and rotting leaves threaten at its edges. Downstream it disappears into a green avenue of dense vegetation. But here, at the crossing, the banks are washed right back to mud, bare earth, a dirty, black-grey tumour. I focus. It is clay. Of course it is. London Clay. I cannot help myself. I stretch my hand towards the bank and dig my thumb in. It comes out thick and yellow. The dark, sandy yellow of London stock brick. Clay. It's like a magic trick. I pull a small Tupperware pot from my rucksack and use the plastic lid to scrape a two-inch plug of wet clay from the bank. I hope no one is watching. This is probably illegal, I think. And definitely weird. I pocket the Tupperware and wipe my thumb on my shorts.

Ambrook. The Am-brook. No one knows where the name actually comes from. I have asked around. I have consulted my etymological dictionary. Nothing. No clues, no analogues. To me, it suggests something elemental. *Am. Om. Aum*: a held note, the primordial sound. *Am* is the Latin root word for love; *ammā* the Hindi for mother, from the Sanskrit *ambá*, also meaning wet nurse.

River. Milk.

Return to the source.

I follow the stream a few paces further south. A blackbird is taking a bath by the fallen tree. And then it stops. The Ambrook is no longer there. It has disappeared into the ground. I cannot cross the fence to get a better look. This can't be it, surely? The source I am looking for?

Suddenly, I taste cigarette smoke, as strong as if someone was standing next to me. There is no one around, but like a bloodhound I follow the trail away from the Ambrook and into the part of the woods known as Peckarmans Wood. It is deathly quiet, but I sense a presence. Through the trees, I see a clearing. In fact, it is a crossroads, where two paths intersect. There is a figure, a very large man, with his back to me, sitting on a tree stump. A cloud of smoke lingers above him. He is wearing a heavy overcoat and a woollen hat.

Woods have always been places of refuge for outsiders and recluses, as well as schoolboys playing truant. The hills of Surrey and Norwood were once famed for their encampments of Romani Travellers too. The most famous of them all – Margaret Finch, 'Queen of the Gypsies' – lived in a house on what is now called Gipsy Hill (although some reports claimed that she lived in a conical hut made of branches). When she died in 1740, aged about 109, stricter legislation for the eviction of 'vagrants' was already in the works. By the turn of the nineteenth century, most of the Norwood families had left the area, with only small numbers clinging on in the woods of Dulwich, where a young Lord Byron is said to have visited.

I check my watch. It is almost two o'clock. I have arranged to meet Rachel Dowse, Conservation Project Officer for Sydenham Hill Wood, to help me track down the source of the Ambrook. I find her back up at the Crescent Wood Road entrance, instantly recognizable in a black London Wildlife Trust T-shirt and combat trousers.

'So, which way do you want to go?' Rachel walks quickly and talks in a precise but easy manner, her eyes scanning the trees; she is, in effect, the warden of this wood. We take the left-hand path and descend the ridge back down to the trackbed. 'Oh, look,' she exclaims, pointing down at the ground. 'A centipede!' A curious brown thing scuttles out of the leaf litter. 'I notice little wriggly things,' she offers, by way of explanation. I realize, walking with Rachel, that she is constantly reading her environment in ways I never could.

We stop at a pair of shipping containers, and Rachel opens one to deposit some equipment. A curtain of ivy decorates its side. The tops of the containers have sprouted miniature wildflower gardens. 'Green roofs,' explains Rachel, 'colonized naturally by wind-blown seeds.' Beyond the containers is the great brick arch of the Crescent Wood tunnel. It is still astonishing to discover it here, in the middle of the woods – a derelict tunnel for the disappeared railway to the Crystal Palace. Today a steel barrier 15 feet tall conceals the entrance, but the tunnel retains an ominous presence. The top half is painted with a mural of brown bats flying through trees, the bottom emblazoned with graffiti: a ghoulish line-up of cartoon skulls, twenty in all, grinning out at us.

I naturally gravitated towards the tunnel as a teenager. I would peer through the gap in the huge iron gate and discern the outlines of burnt-out oil drums. I would imagine The Prodigy's menacing anti-hero Keith Flint dancing to their 1996 rave anthem 'Firestarter' in the gloom, his devil-horn haircut silhouetted against flames. Rachel tells me that now the tunnel is a registered bat roost. To get inside you must be accompanied by an accredited bat wrangler, and a council officer must also be present for unspecified health and safety reasons. 'I can let you through the outer gate, if you want.' Rachel is humouring my dreamy-eyed nostalgia. She unlocks the graffiti-covered steel door and we step into the space between the outer and inner gates. It is so packed with equipment I can hardly move: coils of plastic hosing, bags of gravel, fencing, a Honda utility buggy. Here too are stored various decaying objects from the wood's Victorian past alongside the results of recent fly-tipping. It is freezing cold. Rachel explains: the tunnel is on a slope, so as the warm air rises towards the higher, southern entrance, cold air is blasted out down here, into the wood. I put my hand on the rough metal surface of the inner gate. It is cold to the touch. I cannot go inside. Rachel shows me some shadowy photos on her phone instead. There are stalactites hanging from the ceiling of the tunnel where rainwater has leached through the masonry. Mysterious graffiti in white paint reads 'MORDOR', 'MORIA' and 'FRITZ'.

The Crescent Wood Tunnel is one of two bored through the Norwood Ridge in the 1860s to service the new High Level station at Crystal Palace. (The ornate pedestrian subway leading from the higher Paxton Tunnel is still intact and can be accessed on heritage open days. In 1996 it featured in the music video for 'Setting Sun' by south London electronic dance duo the Chemical Brothers.) Resourceful engineers set up an industrial kiln on site and used the clay excavated from the hillside to fire the bricks for the tunnel's construction. There is also an urban legend, dating to as far back as the 1930s, that a train packed with commuters was entombed in the tunnel by a roof collapse and was only discovered decades later.[16]

One summer Rachel observed smoke billowing out of the tunnel. Fearing the worst, she alerted the fire brigade. Three engines arrived at the southern entrance, located in a small wood behind the Hillcrest housing estate. The barrier had been breached. A campfire was discovered not far in and, when extinguished, revealed the smouldering remains of GCSE textbooks. It was the last day of exams and local schoolchildren had been celebrating with a ritual burning. You can hardly blame them.

Rachel locks up and we head north. I ask her about the Ambrook. I had assumed that the real source was higher up in the woods, but she assures me this is it: where rainwater percolating through the gravel capping of the ridge reaches an impermeable layer of clay and bubbles out. Even in the drought of last summer, she tells me, the stream refused to dry up. 'We believe the source is receding down the hill,' she adds.[17]

We follow the Ambrook in a straight line down to the Dewy Pond. The stream and the pond don't actually connect, as far as we can see.

Instead, the stream disappears into a dark hole a few paces to the east. The hole is obscured by the roots of a tree. Nothing is certain. 'We think the stream stops, pools and then percolates into the pond,' Rachel suggests. The Dewy Pond is bordered by lush vegetation, reeds and water plants, brilliant green, and encircled by tall trees. It's like something out of *The Adventures of Huckleberry Finn* or *Swallows and Amazons*. I remember conducting fieldwork for my 11+ Geography exam on the little island in the middle, panning for aquatic insects in pails of black, fetid water. Once known as the 'sulphur pond' due to the stench, the pool has since been dredged and fenced off and the water is now dazzlingly clear. Rachel points out a fallen tree that has formed a natural bridge across the water, and a section of fence that has been damaged by people jumping it to get to the island. The pond provides a rich ecosystem for dragonflies, beetles, frogs and newts.[18] On the island, Rachel tells me, 'with every step, things are crawling away from you'. She would like to remove the fallen tree, but she doesn't have her chainsaw licence yet.

Rachel is keen to show me something else: a network of dry gullies descending what she calls the 'Ambrook slopes'. I have to squint to detect these old streambeds negotiating the dark terrain of the woods, but yes, I say, you're right, they're definitely there.

Seeing the pond and the streambeds is instructive. The river is not singular but plural. Springs dry out, recede, appear and disappear. It's likely the Ambrook was diverted by the coming of the railway, Rachel explains, its multiple streams consolidated into one channel. There is no true source, just a procession of ghost-lines retreating in time.

'Do you mind going off piste?' Rachel looks at me conspiratorially. We have reached the wildest part of the wood, in its north-eastern corner. I have been telling her about my childhood adventures, about the Honeycomb and Wishbone Trees. 'Follow me,' she says. 'It's a bit of a scramble.' Rachel shoots off into the undergrowth, following a hidden path through dense brambles and over fallen trees. I follow close behind. The path climbs, then switchbacks, and we find ourselves in a small clearing. Rachel gestures ahead. 'And there it is.'

Before me stands a small, round, wooden hut no taller than a person. It has been constructed using branches of varying lengths – tall ones driven into the ground, shorter ones as crossbeams. A low earth wall encloses the space excepting for a wide entrance, and it is topped by a conical roof made of leaves and ferns. It is ingenious, a structure worthy of Mathews the Hairyman himself. 'You can't just build a hut in the wood without asking,' Rachel insists, then adds, 'but I couldn't help being impressed.' First finding it empty, Rachel had nailed a note to the doorway, addressed 'To the hut-builders', instructing them not to add anything more. A brief exchange followed and the builders revealed themselves to be local schoolboys from Dulwich College. They had made the hut according to instructions from a YouTube tutorial on bushcraft. Inside the hut I find a piece of slate on which has been written, in chalk, 'Thank you for coming'. The earth walls are dried and cracked, giving the hut the impression of antiquity. As we leave, Rachel shows me the shallow ditch from which the boys had excavated clay for the walls. Like the Victorian workers who constructed the brick railway tunnel through the Norwood Ridge, these schoolboy builders had found in the immediate landscape all the raw materials they needed.

Other discoveries have had less positive outcomes. One day, probing further into this corner of the wood, Rachel stumbled upon a ramshackle camp. A park bench had been requisitioned for seating, an oil drum as a bin, and as its centrepiece, a 'fire wok', all dragged up the slope through thick woodland. Little silver canisters of nitrous oxide – laughing gas – littered the ground. A stolen road barrier bore the camp's name, or that of its occupants: SNOWFLAKES.

We retrace our steps back to the main path. Rachel needs to check on the group of volunteers she is supervising. As we say goodbye back in Crescent Wood, I can't help myself.

'Your surname. Dowse. It's appropriate. After all, we've been looking for water.'

Rachel laughs, then reels off the names of people who have worked or volunteered in the wood: 'Helen Spring, Daniel Greenwood, Brian Whittle, Penny Hedge.'

She turns and heads back down Cox's Walk.

I am alone again. But I'm not yet ready to leave. I have been circling these woods all my life, so why not one last time? I need to return to the Ambrook, to see where it goes as it falls from the high ground of the ridge down to the meadows of Dulwich.

Beyond the Dewy Pond, I find a muddy run-off the colour of chicken soup. A toddler is attempting to dip his foot in it. As his parents goad him away, I turn and let my eyes trace an imagined flow north. There *is* a definite channel heading into the trees. I pause for a moment, then step down into the lost river.

Fallen leaves crackle underfoot. I enter a space between footpaths. It is dark in the interior. I see that the channel is not straight, like the stream by the Dewy Pond, but meanders, finding its own way, the desire line of water. Even though the riverbed is bone dry, it feels like I have found the real Ambrook, as if I might follow its course all the way to the Effra, to the Thames itself.

'Ralph! Ralph! Here, boy.'

Through the trees I watch a white terrier in a red collar chase a squirrel to the foot of a mighty oak, then turn back frustrated. I am standing in the riverbed. I look down. The ground is covered not with leaves but a carpet of fluffy, white blossom. It is beautiful, a gift. I take some in my hands.

The channel meanders around a small bluff, burrows under a wooden ligger and vanishes into darkness at the fenceline. This is where the woods themselves end; the manicured landscape of the Dulwich & Sydenham

Hill Golf Club stretches out beyond.* A trio of middle-aged women in polo shirts and chinos are playing a round. I take a photograph of the undulating terrain through the metal fence and one of them scowls in my direction. The pristine greens and synthetic bunkers of the golf course come as a shock after a day in the woods. In the middle distance two groundskeepers are riding a buggy across the course. With leaf-blowers strapped to their backs, they look like Ghostbusters, which strikes me as fitting.

The phantom river.

The sense of being watched.

The ectoplasm of blossom falling.

* Retired geography teacher Martin Knight suggests that the Ambrook follows 'an obvious valley (now dry)' across the golf course before entering Dulwich Park, where it drains into the boating lake.

Grave

*'He discovereth deep things out of darkness,
And bringeth out to light the shadow of death.'*

JOB 12:22 (KING JAMES BIBLE)*

---

* This verse is inscribed on the Doulton family mausoleum in West Norwood Cemetery.

WHEN I GET BACK home, I take out the Tupperware pot containing clay from the Ambrook and place it on a bookshelf, next to my grandparents' laminated memorial cards and a framed photograph dated 1977 showing my mother dressed as Mrs Allwit from Thomas Middleton's play *A Chaste Maid in Cheapside*. A cigarette is dangling, as was customary, from her right hand.

The next morning, I notice something peculiar. A fine layer of condensation has appeared on the inside of the pot, such that I cannot see its contents at all. I remove the lid. The saturated clay, black and moist when I scraped it off the riverbank, has leached water overnight and shrunk down to a grey-brown lump. The clay is breathing. I replace the lid and quickly put it back on the shelf. There is something reassuring in having it here, in the company of the dead.

Follow the Ambrook through Dulwich to its confluence with the main stream of the Effra falling from the Norwood hills. Follow *that* stream *back up*, swimming against the current along Croxted Road, until it too divides. Then take the western branch through terraced streets, still climbing in a tiny valley towards the source, and you will come, at last, to the boundary wall of a great cemetery.

There is no true source, only ghost-lines.

I am compelled back out.

On a blazing hot day I pack a bag and take the Overground line to Queens Road Peckham, where I pick up a deserted mainline train to West Norwood. The gates of the cemetery are smaller than I remember, but the Victorian mausolea larger and more ornate. It has been ten years. No, fifteen. My legs know where to go. They carry me up the long path that arcs around the southern perimeter, climbing the shoulder of the steep hill on which the cemetery rests. They bring me to the crest, above the chapel and crematorium, to where we used to leave the car, then down the little footpath – St Mary-at-Hill – and finally to a stop by a hawthorn bush. The woods, and the Ambrook, are two kilometres away to the east. I have come back south to find the *other* feeder stream of the Effra, to understand how it all connects. But first, there is this.

Two headstones are nestled here in a bed of grass and weeds, daisies and buttercups. The smaller, on the right, bears the symbol of freemasonry – the square and compasses interlinked – and the name Alphues Albert Copeland. An aeroplane passes overhead, leaving a perfect white contrail against the sky. I hear the distant buzz of a power tool, then birdsong. The larger stone is tipped slightly forward. It's a darker hue, the speckled grey of Scottish granite, uncommon in this landscape. On one side, a decorated cross in the Celtic style has been picked out in silver, but the text beside it has started to fade. I step through the foliage, kneel in front of the stone and use my fingers to trace familiar words.

EILEEN MARY
CHIVERS

BORN 23RD JANUARY 1952
DIED 15TH DECEMBER 1996

Sadly missed by her beloved
son Thomas, her family and
many friends

It was a cold, damp December when we put my mother into the ground. She was forty-four. On the slow drive to the cemetery, people stopped on Norwood Road to bow their heads or make the sign of the cross. At the funeral Mass at St Etheldreda's, Ely Place, the choir sang Tomás Luis de Victoria's *Missa pro defunctis* and 'Ave Verum Corpus' by William

Byrd. I sat with my father at the front on the left, wearing my school uniform.

The last time I saw my mother awake, she was being carried backwards on a stretcher down the stairs of the house in West Norwood where the two of us had moved after my parents' separation. Her skull was round and fluffy like a newborn chick's. She was smiling as she slid away.

In the hospital, there was an awful wheezing sound which I later discovered is called the death rattle. I was allowed to say goodbye, a few minutes alone with the curtains pulled closed around her bed, but I cannot remember what I said to her. I was thirteen years old.

In the months after my mother's death, I visited her grave every Sunday with my father to lay flowers or remove weeds with a trowel. He would always hang back a few paces before we left so I could say some words or just stand there with my own thoughts. I would also come up on my own, after school, combining it with a trip to Woolworths to browse the CD racks. But as months became years, the gush became a trickle. When I left home for university, and then for good, the visits stopped altogether. Undisturbed, weeds and wildflowers took root in the loose soil and grew tall. The headstone settled. Ten years passed. Then twenty. The place became unfamiliar.

I used to have a recurring dream: I am standing at the top of the cemetery at night and the whole hillside is collapsing in on itself. My mother's coffin is falling through a void as the earth slips and folds around us. The coffin tumbles through great masses of soil and clay, all moving and churning, and I am paralysed, unable to stop it. She plummets into the darkness below and I wake.

Like the river you cannot see, grief does not just disappear. It remains, the trace of a buried channel, and gives its form to the land that is your life after loss. I realize now that when, as a teenager, I took a blade to my arms and legs, it was my attempt to see those ghost-lines again, to open them up, to daylight what was once concealed.

*

West Norwood Cemetery opened in 1837, the second of London's 'Magnificent Seven' – a ring of large suburban cemeteries established in the nineteenth century to relieve overcrowding in the city's churchyards. Reputedly inspired by Paris's famous Père Lachaise, West Norwood soon became *the place* to be interred and was nicknamed 'the Millionaires' Cemetery'. Sugar magnate and philanthropist Sir Henry Tate is buried here in a terracotta mausoleum. Another fine tomb contains the remains of several members of the Doulton family, the manufacturing dynasty celebrated for its ceramic tableware. It is decorated with angels, the Lamb of God and other biblical characters.

Here lie the inventors of the automatic machine gun, a new steelmaking process, the prison treadmill, celluloid and Bovril. Entertainers, entrepreneurs, sportsmen and poets have all taken their places in the shade of poplars, sycamores, conifers and fourteen surviving oaks from the Great North Wood. The cemetery's occupants reflect multiple waves of immigration to south London: Irish, European, African and Caribbean. The city's Greek Orthodox community built its own, railed-off necropolis at West Norwood – a miniature city of the dead whose centrepiece is a magnificent chapel modelled on the Parthenon.

As I descend the hill by the path known as Lower Road, I find myself scanning the headstones, and my eye snags on recurring lines, the language of loss.

—who died
—who fell asleep
—who passed away
—who departed this life
—who was called away

Colin Fenn is waiting for me at the crossroads like the apocryphal devil, long-limbed and bespectacled. He is wearing a navy-blue baseball cap and greets me with an enthusiastic handshake. Local resident, community organizer, historian, author and erstwhile member of the Friends of West Norwood Cemetery, Colin has agreed to help me locate the lost course of the Effra through the graves. His knowledge – on subjects ranging from climate change to theatre – is compendious and he shares it with infectious delight. He calls West Norwood 'The Valley' and compares the south London hills to Switzerland. 'Each valley is specific,' he says, 'and it shapes the way you deal with things.'

The Lower Norwood branch of the Effra rises from springs in Westow Park. In recent years, wrote Jon Newman, 'one of these source springs, fenced by chestnut palings, could still be seen . . . leaking . . . down the hill from between a cluster of drain covers.'[19] It once flowed through the grounds of Virgo Fidelis Convent School, down the west side of Auckland Hill and entered the cemetery from what is now a low-rise housing estate. The Effra was first covered up and then, in 1865, diverted into a sewer along Norwood High Street. 'A polluted stream with a tendency to flood did not sit easily with the [South Metropolitan Cemetery Company's] prospectus for a pastoral garden enclave for the burial of the dead,' wrote Newman.

I follow Colin to a flat stretch of path next to a neo-Gothic tomb. He points to the tarmac and grins. 'Can you guess what it is?' I am looking down at an unexceptional square manhole cover. It is stamped BRUNEL. I resist the temptation to put my ear to the ground; I know that nothing flows here now. Colin takes a new bearing, then strides off into the long grass towards the boundary wall, looking for another manhole. 'I know it's here somewhere.' Colin walks likes he talks: digressively and at speed. 'We're looking for a slightly raised drain on a concrete base. It was definitely here last year,' he assures me. We are walking side by side, stalking the ground for clues. Colin is distracted by a large sandstone Celtic cross and stands for a moment with his hand on it, as if he could divine its origins by touch. 'This is the memorial of the surgeon James Battersby Bailey, father of Edward, the renowned geologist.'

I ask Colin about the geology of the cemetery. I've heard the urban myth of coffins falling into the Effra after heavy rain and being washed upstream by the floodwaters.[20] 'Sometimes,' he says, 'when a plot is opened up, the gravediggers will find that its occupant has moved ten feet down the hill.' He adds, cryptically, 'There are lots of different planes and shapes moving beneath our feet.'

Colin spots a rare white porcelain flowerpot. As he darts towards it, he suddenly looks up towards the wall and snaps his fingers. 'There it is!' The flowerpot was the signpost. We find the second manhole just as he had described it, slightly raised above the surface level, in a concrete surround that has seen better days. It is smaller and older than the first one. A crack has formed around it, clogged up with old spiderwebs and bits of grass. I crouch down to take a photograph through the crack with my phone, but what comes out is dark and indistinct. Colin tries prising the manhole cover with his fingers. 'I should have brought my crowbar,' he says.

Even after its diversion into sewers, the Effra made its presence felt in the local landscape. In June 1914, torrential rainfall caused the river to flood either side of the cemetery, causing 'Sunday joints [to be] washed out of ovens'.[21] More recently, Colin tells me, the re-laying of drains at the elevated southern edge of the cemetery caused flooding further down.

It is midday. I wipe away the beads of sweat that have sprung on my forehead in the heat. As we move on, defeated, I notice a small rounded headstone near by remembering OUR LITTLE DAUGHTER . . . CHEE-CHI. Only one date is recorded: 2 June 1999. I tell Colin about my mother's headstone, how I found it leaning a little forward, and he agrees to take a look. We climb the long path back up the hill, above the valley of the Effra. An electric maintenance vehicle appears over the crest and comes to a stop beside us. The driver – a middle-aged man in the green work clothes of a gravedigger – grins and offers his hand as Colin approaches: 'I thought you were dead!'

*

'The valley shapes the way you deal with things,' Colin had said, cryptically. And I am starting to suspect he is right. It comforts me to think of my mother here, in the land of my birth, in sight of the hidden river.

Dock and dandelion reclaiming the backfilled soil; buried things; the breathing clay: I remember so little of my childhood that all I can do is come here.

Colin is standing in my mother's plot. Behind us, a magpie hops down the path. A light breeze unsettles the leaves of a sycamore. Gently, Colin puts his hands on the headstone, then gives it a little wiggle. It stands firm; the steel screws driven through the concrete base into the earth are doing their job. Graves take time to settle. I know that.

Clay, Colin explains, is susceptible to movement on a slope. I remember that he trained as an engineer. 'At a thirty degree angle, clay can "slump" or "slough" at the bottom, causing the slope to become unstable,' he continues, relishing the words, the vocabulary of the geographer-poet. Then Colin turns to me. 'It's quite possible,' he says, 'that she's moved around a bit.'

I accompany Colin back to the crest of the hill and we shake hands. He is rushing to another appointment. I return one last time to my mother's grave. I walk back down St Mary-at-Hill in the dazzling sunlight. I sense something moving up ahead. I stop. And then my heart stops.

There is a shape on the path. And it is sitting right in front of the grave. An orange-brown blur. Something feral, untameable, a spirit of the place. I fumble in my pocket and it turns, sees me with its clever eyes and steals away into the trees: a fox.

In 2013, artist Steven Levon Ounanian created a sound piece for West Norwood Cemetery as part of the site-specific art trail Curious. In *A Device for Listening to the Dead*, visitors were invited to plug electrodes into the earth, listening for 'conversations and existential diatribes going on underground'.

I have a special memento that I keep in my bedside drawer: an old microcassette retrieved from my mother's answering machine. It is the only recording I have of her voice. She sounds grander than I remember, the Scottish lilt of her childhood in Dundee flattened to a clipped RP. The silence of the grave is deafening.

Later that day, energized by meeting Colin, I trace the Effra downstream by instinct alone and find myself back at the terraced house I shared with my mother in her final years. A loft extension has been put in, and the scrappy little garden much refreshed. Round the back, by a row of sullen garages, where I used to practise skateboarding every evening, I find a metal disc sunk into a pavement slab to mark the buried river. The front door my mother had installed has been painted black. I am sure no one is at home. On the tarmac outside, children have drawn a colossal imaginary creature in many shades of chalk, inspired, I imagine, by the famous dinosaur sculptures of Crystal Palace Park. Two doors down, a woman is taking her rubbish out. There, in the middle of Hexham Road, I see another manhole. The woman goes back inside. I walk into the middle of the road, check for traffic, and lie down on my front. I can hear it straight away: the rush of a river, like radio static, like the hiss of a tape that has come to an end. The tarmac is warm against my skin. And then, in the background, I make out a deeper sound: something banging in the darkness, a sluice perhaps, forced open by the weight of water falling downriver.

	Alluvium
	Gravel
	Clay

III: LIQUIDITY

Walking the Walbrook

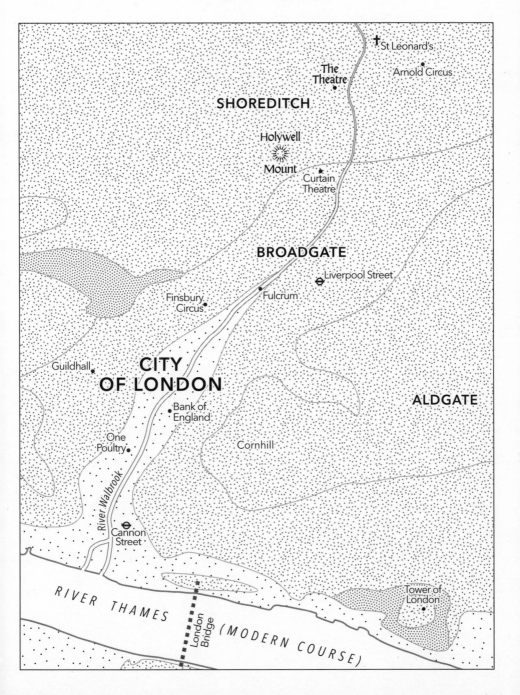

Panopticon

S NOW CREAKS UNDERFOOT AS I approach the mound. It is December and the city is suffering the coldest winter for years, battered by easterlies from the frozen wastes of Siberia. I turn the corner of Camlet Street and a gust of bitter wind nearly knocks me sideways. As I climb, I lay a trail of fresh footprints towards the summit.

Safely underneath the covered bandstand, I shrug off my rucksack and start to unfold two large maps. A table-tennis table installed here by the council bears the oily residue of last night's chicken dinner, so I get to work with my handkerchief before spreading out my wares. Today this frosty bandstand doubles as my map room.

Each map has been hand-modified using a combination of Sharpies, highlighters and fineliner pens. The buried rivers of London reanimated as squiggly lines of thick blue ink cutting through gravel terraces towards the alluvial floodplain of the Thames. I check my watch – it's almost time – then start to line up sets of headphones on the table. Have I mentioned the weather? My nose is developing the early signs of frostbite.

I am waiting at the top of an artificial mound at the centre of Arnold Circus, Shoreditch. Enclosed by seven mature trees, the mound stands at the nucleus of seven roads which radiate out across the former slum, or 'rookery', of the Old Nichol. It's like standing in a guard tower at the centre of Jeremy Bentham's impossible prison, the panopticon – an institution whose design would enable one guard to observe every cell – or at 'the still point of the turning world', as T. S. Eliot put it.[1] In fact, the mound is a spoil heap. It was built using the rubble produced during the construction of the Boundary Estate (one of the world's oldest housing estates) at the turn of the twentieth century.

I used to work on the edge of the Boundary, operating a tiny arts festival from a row of leaking brick sheds that once housed leather-workers and skinners. By my arrival in 2009, the occupants comprised an

Azerbaijani e-cigarette distributor, a collective of weed-smoking Bangladeshi security guards and a woman who made boiled sweets in the shapes of penises.

A mound may, in fact, have existed on this site before the construction of the Boundary. In his *Romano Lavo-Lil: Word-Book of the Romany* (1874), the travel writer George Borrow identifies 'Not far from Shoreditch Church . . . a locality called Friars' Mount, but generally for shortness called The Mount'.

> It derives its name from a friary built upon a small hillock in the time of Popery, where a set of fellows lived in laziness and luxury on the offerings of foolish and superstitious people, who resorted thither to kiss and worship an ugly wooden image of the Virgin, said to be a first-rate stick at performing miraculous cures. The neighbourhood, of course, soon became a resort for vagabonds of every description, for wherever friars are found rogues and thieves are sure to abound . . . The friary has long since disappeared, the Mount has been levelled, and the locality built over. The vice and villainy, however, which the friary called forth still cling to the district. It is one of the vilest dens of London, a grand resort for housebreakers, garotters, passers of bad money, and other disreputable people.

According to the antiquarian Alfred Watkins, this infamous hillock was the terminus of the Strand Ley, an ancient trackway connecting points of spiritual significance in the landscape.[2] Four of these points are now overlain by churches. Draw a straight line between St Martin-in-the-Fields, St Mary le Strand, St Clement Danes and St Dunstan-in-the-West and that line will extend through the medieval hospital of St Bartholomew, cross the Brutalist ruins of the Barbican and the dissenters' cemetery at Bunhill Fields, and bisect the saloon bar of the Old Blue Last in Shoreditch before, finally, lodging itself in the frozen hill on which I am now standing.

For ten years I have been chronicling the city in my spare time, publishing poems in obscure magazines and releasing a handful of pamphlets and books that practically no one reads. What had, in my twenties, felt vital – a creative imperative at the heart of my life – now feels like pissing in the wind. In truth, I had almost given up writing when I was approached, out of the blue, by the arts charity Cape Farewell to be their first poet-in-residence. Charged with exploring the impact of climate change through poetry, I soon gravitated back towards the city, to the buried streams and forgotten landscapes of my childhood. I had been given a second chance and set about my work with renewed passion. Experiments with sound soon led to the creation of a series of 'urban pilgrimages' – audio walking adventures along London's lost rivers.

And so it is that I find myself in Arnold Circus, handing out audio players and one-page maps to twelve hardy walkers, preparing them for a journey into the deep city; a pilgrimage from source to mouth.

As the group put on their headphones, they hear the quavering song of a violin and then my voice. 'This is a story about a river,' I begin . . .

🎧 *. . . a river that flowed under the wall. A sewer, a sluice, a ghost.*

Walbrook is the name assigned to a series of streams that flowed into the City of London from the higher land to the north. One branch sprang from the Islington hills and flowed south-east down City Road where it powered a lead mill at the Old Street turnpike (now a technology hub dubbed 'Silicon Roundabout'). A second branch began in the vicinity of Hoxton, and was fed by springs in Shoreditch. Water, claims the Reverend Paul Turp, can still be found oozing from the earth underneath the parish church of St Leonard's.

🎧 *This is Shoreditch. Everything is permitted.*

It's been fifteen years since the satirical fanzine *Shoreditch Twat* put this place back on the map, but Shoreditch is still London's newest party zone, an open-plan Soho of branded fashion bars, vintage shops, eighties nostalgia, strip clubs, fixed-gear bikes, street art, hair salons, art-rock bands, fashionable tattoos and fresh-faced City boys filling the vacuum the art students left when they migrated to Dalston, Hackney Wick and New Cross. The movement is so quick around here that it's never really changed – between the past and future, Shoreditch is a porous membrane, a pockmarked landscape of feral alleyways and unplanned development.

The earliest maps of London show the Walbrook passing into the City ditch at the church of All Hallows-on-the-Wall, but are unclear about its course through Shoreditch. But on John Rocque's map of 1746 the line of a stream can be followed along Curtain Road, past the Holywell Mount, as far as the modern junction with Great Eastern Street, where its two main branches united. If Rocque is to be believed, this confluence – somewhere between Pizza Express, the Old Blue Last and the American Carwash Company – falls directly on Watkins's Ley.

🎧 *Shoreditch. Sewer-ditch. Sewer from the Saxon* scor, *meaning 'a ditch'.*

I am pacing up and down the aisles of Cowling & Wilcox art supplies, blowing into my hands. They are beginning to turn blue. 'Are you all right?' asks a concerned sales assistant. I nod and look interested in some pencils. From the warmth of the shop I can observe the line of walkers – my urban pilgrims – turning into Rivington Street, before making their way underneath the railway arch. It's better to keep my distance on this journey, to let them navigate the city without the assurance of a guide. Two of them stop to photograph graffiti by prolific street artist Ben Eine: the word *SCARY* in giant capitals. As you approach from the east, the *Y* is obscured by the curve of the brickwork so it reads, instead, *SCAR*.

☙ *A tally, a mark made to keep a count. Also: related to the words*
'to score' and 'scar'.

I glove up again, exit the shop and track the group past Cargo nightclub and music venue, a glass-fronted art gallery, Franco's Take Away and then across Curtain Road. The street level drops as they turn into Charlotte Road; its sloping course clearly describes the valley of the lost river. A young woman is adjusting her headphones and scribbling furiously into a Moleskine notebook. An elderly man glances anxiously back. What has he let himself in for? My voice in their ears, my eyes on their bodies; ghosting their journey through the city, awaiting my chance to resurface.

In the nineteenth century, this was the heart of London's furniture trade, bustling with carpenters' workshops, warehouses and showrooms. I catch sight of a straggler darting into the darkness of Mills Court, where the sign of the ironmongers W. A. Hudson can still be glimpsed above a cobbled yard that has changed little since the 1930s – at least if you ignore its garnish of upturned office chairs and ruptured council rubbish bags. Tangles of dock weed and hoary buddleia spew over a boundary wall from a pocket of wasteland – a miniature, I think, of the Aldgate hole. The snow here is wet mulch dissolving into dirty rivulets tracing the line of the Walbrook.

In spite of its proximity to the financial heart of London, Shoreditch retains a wild, untamed energy. Graffiti artists throw up great beasts on walls, shutters and hoardings: wolves, rabbits and giant rats; a many-trunked elephant. Holed up in railway sidings by day, gangs of urban foxes steal into alleys and side streets after dark in search of unsecured waste. Once, stumbling home from a late-night drinking session in the Whistling Shop, I came face to face with a particularly mangy character nosing a discarded kebab behind Plough Yard.

With its numerous bars, clubs and 'adult entertainment' venues, Shoreditch is London's 'suburb of sin', a reputation it has maintained since Tudor times. In a vacant lot on New Inn Broadway lie the remains of the Theatre, one of London's first purpose-built playhouses. Constructed in 1576 by James Burbage, the Theatre hosted early plays by Shakespeare including *Romeo and Juliet*. While the Boar's Head in Aldgate lay dormant until the 1590s, the Theatre flourished as the venue for the Leicester's, and later the Admiral's, Men. A plan based on the extant lease of the site shows the playhouse as an octagonal structure nestled among the gardens and agricultural outhouses of the former Holywell Priory.

The success of the Theatre was short-lived; by the mid-1590s a dispute had arisen between Burbage and his two sons, on the one hand, and the landlord, the disapproving Puritan Giles Allen, on the other. In 1595 the Lord Chamberlain's Men, the Theatre's third and final resident company, were forced to relocate to the nearby Curtain playhouse (recently excavated on the corner of Curtain Road and Hewett Street). One cold night in December 1598, the two Burbage boys assembled a crack team of carpenters to dismantle their entire playhouse in the dark before transporting it, plank by plank, across the city to Peter Street's yard in Bridewell (at the mouth of the river Fleet). The timbers would be ferried across the Thames in the following spring to be reused in the building of the Globe at Bankside.

In the land behind the Theatre lay the Great Horse Pond. Today its footprint corresponds with the UK headquarters of Amnesty International. The pond was fed by a stream flowing north to south on the western edge of the playhouse, marked on the plan as the 'Ditch or Common Sewer'. A well is also marked: the original 'holy well' that gave the priory at Holywell – or Halywell, or Haliwell – its fluid name.

The wells and springs of London are the city's forgotten energy points, phantom nuclei around which the axes of human life once turned. Revered for their iron-rich, 'chalybeate' waters, springs were first made sacred as sites of pilgrimage and healing. Later, many were rebranded as spa resorts by quack doctors and entrepreneurs with an eye for the gap in the market. Here, in the backstreets of Shoreditch, the liquid history of the holy well has re-emerged in the guise of Market Sports – a state-of-the-art health and fitness club with a twenty-five-metre, chlorine-free swimming pool. Its marketing reads like an advertisement from the golden age of the spa.

> PoolSan is hypoallergenic and does not cause breathlessness, eye irritations, asthma attacks, eczema or other ailments associated with chlorine use. The water in a PoolSan pool is odourless, leaves no unpleasant smells, residue on the skin or damage to swimming costumes and is often referred to as 'like swimming in Evian'.

I watch the pilgrims crossing the treacherous junction of Great Eastern Street and Curtain Road. A triangulation of estate agents. Tarmac buckling along the course of the Walbrook. Watkins's Ley. The Old Blue Last pub, where I once convinced the actor Paul McGann that we were distant relations from the old country. And in the distance, over the tops of buildings, the sun flashing off the silver blade of Broadgate Tower. One of the pilgrims adjusts his headphones, then looks up to the sky.

꩜ *The city is changing. You cannot keep pace.*

Urban planners call it the Eastern Cluster – this new high-rise zone centred on the Gherkin. The City is growing upwards, proffering its hands towards the light. Bishopsgate, Kingsland, Whitechapel and Mile End Roads are dead-straight avenues radiating geometrically away from the swollen Roman *civitas*. For people in the cacophonous suburbs of Hackney and Tower Hamlets, the Eastern Cluster appears as a ritualized space; an architectural henge, simultaneously distant and immanent, each new skyscraper raised like a great standing stone.

Walking the southern limits of Curtain Road, the great silver blade of Broadgate Tower is a constant presence in the peripheral vision, an early warning sign for the fierce collision with the City that awaits. As Shoreditch burns out, the anarchic spirits of its streets fire a final shot. The walls are bursting with apocalyptic visions, hallucinations of gnashing jaws and incredible beasts. A Hell's Angel with a badger's head. A cowboy with Stetson and a handlebar moustache. A monkey flying a dragon; a bare-breasted Amazon bathing in a blue lagoon.

On his map of 1746, Rocque marked a large, oblong mound or tumulus in the open field abutting Curtain Road; the site now overlain by Gatesborough, Luke and Christina Streets. The precise origins of this 'Holywell Mount' are unknown, though it was probably incorporated into the Lines of Communication – the ring of forts and earthwork defences constructed around London during the English Civil War. One etching shows the corpses of plague victims being deposited in a mass grave at the top of the mount in 1665.[3] A gravedigger levers an upturned cadaver into the pit by means of a long stick, while his pipe-smoking mate stands by with a blazing torch. During the plague bodies had become hazardous waste to be disposed of under the cover of darkness. By the eighteenth century the site had become a notorious hiding place for thieves and rapists. It was eventually flattened in 1787 and housing built on its footprint.

Shoreditch ends with an absence – an abscess – in the street plan. A vast wasteland extends across the north side of Worship Street. Formerly occupied by an impromptu shanty town of five-a-side football pitches, driving ranges and paintballing facilities, the site has recently been cleared for development. The main line out of Liverpool Street station rumbles past in a deep cutting to the east, but behind the tall hoardings of this derelict plot nothing is moving. Without a confirmed tenant, construction on the £290 million Principal Place has stalled; the empty site remaining as an eerie reminder of the volatility of the markets.

The pilgrims turn into Worship Street (formerly Hog Lane) by the Queen of Hoxton – a fashion pub with a dislocated name – and walk tentatively towards the base of Broadgate Tower, where the course of the

Walbrook is lost beneath new development. The snow is dissolving on the smooth stone pavements. The pilgrims are leaving Shoreditch and leaving the London Borough of Hackney. The sixteenth-century Agas map – also known as the 'Woodcut' map from the method of its printing – even marks a small gateway here. I look back, towards the borderlands. The redbrick flank of an old warehouse comes into a view. It is daubed with a slogan: STOP THE CITY.

Fulcrum

Up a hidden flight of stairs, past a sign outlawing cycling, smoking and skateboarding, and I emerge into the vast, empty plaza beneath Broadgate Tower. I scan a line of silver maples for the pilgrims. There they are: at the far end, their heads craned skywards above a canyon of steel and sheet glass. Some hold their phones aloft like radio transmitters. I follow their gaze towards a colonnade of super-sized metal beams that looms above the plaza like the pistons of some monstrous engine.

Completed in 2008, the dynamics of this luminous space stage the victory of architecture over nature. As I approach, I realize that the spindly maples have been sunk directly into the stone floor of the plaza; it is as if they have grown out of the building itself, organic life forms fed by a mechanized interior.

Broadgate is the architectural equivalent of a black box theatre. Like a digital projection of a real place, it could be located anywhere in the world. In the Bond movie *Skyfall*, the summit of the tower stands in for the Shanghai skyscraper where Daniel Craig's 007 witnesses a hit, and where a mercenary falls to his death.

🎧 *You're stepping into an unreal space.*

Ludgate, Newgate, Aldersgate, Cripplegate, Bishopsgate, Aldgate – these were the six principal entrances to the walled Roman city of *Londinium*. A seventh, Moorgate, was constructed after 1415. There was never actually a gate at Broadgate, just a railway terminus – Broad Street – now long buried. In the eighteenth century, this was a suburban backwater riddled with squalid alleyways with a yard known as the Hovel at its heart. No one lives here now. Broadgate is a corporate zone with heritage branding, its name invented by resourceful property developers in the 1980s.

The pilgrims are climbing the wide staircase into Broadgate Exchange, another plaza lined with office blocks. From this new, elevated position they look down to the platforms of Liverpool Street station. I do not follow. Instead I descend to Appold Street (formerly Long Alley) and return to the line of the lost river. From here, the Walbrook passed into the jurisdiction of the Corporation of London, the city's ancient governing body whose lineage can be traced to Saxon times. Originally constrained by the city walls, the Corporation's authority has leached outwards over the centuries, incorporating the edgelands and ancient 'liberties' (those anomalous places outside the city's control) as municipal buffer zones. Since 1994, the 32 acres of the Broadgate Estate have been Corporation land, watched over by the two heraldic dragons emblazoned on its crest. During the week these streets and squares are bustling with more than thirty thousand office workers, traders, analysts, accountants and media buyers. But today is Saturday and Broadgate is a ghost town patrolled by bored security guards.

I have rushed ahead on alternative paths and am now looking back towards the first pilgrims as they descend from the raised deck of the Exchange. I must conceal myself behind the parked cars to avoid detection. I've a mole in the group. I text, *Everything OK?* And the answer pings back: *On time and on course.*

Back at street level, the pilgrims begin to examine a cluster of tall black objects at the base of the lost river's valley. *The Broad Family* by Catalan sculptor Xavier Corberó comprises four shaped basalt rocks. Formed in the fires of a volcano, the rocks are rich in iron – carbon traps sucking in CO_2 from the atmosphere. They could be giant arrowheads or petrified giants; tribal icons marking the invisible banks of the Walbrook.

Where Appold Street turns sharply to the west, the way is blocked by hoardings and the river's course is lost beneath a vast construction site. I look up and see a lattice of stilled cranes, two naked concrete towers settling against the darkening sky. On completion they will house Swiss banking giant UBS. Once, walking the Walbrook on a weekday, I paused at an open gate and persuaded the guard to let me watch the foundations of the building being piled deep into the earth. The site was a giant, flat-bottomed crater crawling with diggers. I half expected workmen to be frantically pumping out dirty river water from its base.

I slip through a gap in the hoardings and proceed into Finsbury Avenue Square, past Gaucho – a cocktail bar that is entirely contained, like an exhibit in a museum, within a transparent glass box. At the far end another space opens up, revealing the second great sphere of the journey. The pilgrims proceed, locked into a soundtrack, my voice whispering.

🎧 *Your body is in orbit.*

Broadgate Circle consists of a large plaza ringed with offices. At its core a concrete semicircle houses shops and bars on several levels. In this cold December, an ice rink has been installed in the centre.

Circus and circle. Ring and rink.

They're close behind me now, probing for the route. And now, all of a sudden, the valley of the Walbrook opens up below and it feels like standing on a lonely headland, facing out to sea. In a sunken yard, an angular monument points towards the sky. It is a rusting lighthouse.

The artist Richard Serra was born in San Francisco in 1938, the son of a Mallorcan pipe-fitter and a Russian Jew from Odessa. After initially studying painting at Yale, Serra began to experiment with the raw materials of industry – steel, lead, fibreglass and rubber – to make large-scale abstract works. In 1987 he was commissioned to make a sculpture for the new Broadgate Estate. The result was *Fulcrum*, a 55-foot monolith that stands outside the western entrance to Liverpool Street station. Composed of five plates of COR-TEN steel, *Fulcrum* is self-supporting, like a standing stone or a cairn. There are no joins in the steel. It appears in the landscape like the ruins of a future city.

In an interview, Serra described how his work was influenced by visiting shipyards as a child.

> – [My father] takes me to the launching of a ship that he's worked on . . . He's proud. And it's frightening because it's so enormous, like a skyscraper on its side. They undo the shackles, the dunnage, and all of a sudden this enormous object is going down a chute . . . and when it first goes into the water, the bow goes under and the stern lifts and there's an apprehension that it's not going to make it. And then it raises. And it's adrift, it's afloat . . . and for me that's a transformation. It was like an object can become something light; that amount of tonnage can become something lyrical. It became a recurring dream for me.
> – *A dream?*
> – It still is.
> – *A dream?*
> – A dream.[4]

I step into the dark interior. It is like entering the burial chamber of a Bronze Age barrow. There is the sharp odour of fags and urine. I crane my neck to the aperture above. Even on this frozen, overcast day, the light penetrating the space from above gives it the appearance of an observatory, a giant telescope looking out to deep space.

🎧 *Put your hand against the metal. Let your fingertips brush against the rough surface. Feel the patina of the weather on it.*

In 2011, archaeologists digging the site of the new Crossrail station at Liverpool Street discovered evidence of Roman occupation on the banks of the Walbrook. Finds included writing tools, a key, a poppy-head beaker and a silver denarius from the reign of Severus Alexander

(AD 222–35). A minor Roman road had previously been uncovered on nearby Eldon Street; it is believed to have crossed the stream not far from *Fulcrum*. But as archaeologist Nick Elsden told me, 'the channel has proved elusive ... [W]here and how [the road] crosses the Walbrook has yet to be found, so it is only conjecture whether it was by a ford or bridge.'[5]

The first pilgrims appear – and then so do I, from the shadows, signalling to remove headphones. We draw ourselves, one by one, into the heart of the structure, out of the wind and intermittent flurries of snow.

'The Walbrook runs beneath our feet,' I say. I am thinking of *Fulcrum* as a way into the deep city. 'Turn a borehole inside out,' I say, 'and you've a telescope.'

True to its name, *Fulcrum* represents a turning point in our journey down the vanished river. Beyond this point the Walbrook valley can be mapped in the geological record. It appears on my Streetfinder as a tongue of alluvium cutting through the gravel terraces of the Thames. Before the founding of London by the Romans, the stream was fringed with reed beds and alder trees. A tributary joined from the west where fragments of prehistoric spelt wheat have been recovered from archaeological digs, suggesting that cereal crops were being cultivated on its banks.

Before we leave, I glance towards the station. One of the pilgrims has walked to where the glossy floor of the shopping arcade begins. He turns back towards *Fulcrum*, kneels for a moment, and then puts his head to the ground. From where I am standing, he appears to be praying.

Wall

THE PILGRIMS HAVE NOT yet entered the walled city that gave the river its name. They linger on the outskirts, in the suburbs (literally 'below the city'), where the language of the periphery sinks deep into cartographic memory. Curtain Road may derive from the exterior or 'curtain' wall that extended from the main fortifications of medieval London. Early maps record certain fields or meadows here as 'No man's land'.

The original suburbs were places of marginality, madness and death. The Romans laid out their cemeteries here, in the edgelands of Spitalfields and Bishopsgate. Toxic, noisome industries such as leather-working were often pushed out here too, beyond the boundaries of the city, along with plague pits, playhouses, brothels and asylums. In 1602 Sir Stephen Soame called the liberties of London 'the very sinke of sinne, the nursery of nawghtie and lewd places'.[6]

The concourse of Liverpool Street station was dug out on the site of the thirteenth-century Bethlehem Hospital, the *ur*-madhouse which has bequeathed to us the contracted name 'Bedlam'. It is remembered today by a blue plaque on the wall between McDonald's and the Andaz hotel. This accretion of uses – asylum, rail terminus, fast-food restaurant – manifests as a kind of double vision, a hallucination in which the frenzy of rush-hour commuters appears as a scene from the terrifying imagination of Hieronymus Bosch.

I am walking south towards London Wall – that stretch of highway between Bishopsgate and the Barbican that follows the line of the original Roman boundary. The left side of Blomfield Street is dominated by building works for the new Crossrail station, but its gentle meander is unmistakably the course of the Walbrook; the pronounced camber of the road and the numerous manholes sunk into its surface are further signs of our hidden waterway.

I'm holding back again, allowing the pilgrims to find their own path forward. They follow the slight incline into Finsbury Circus and find themselves in a crescent of tall, neoclassical buildings surrounding an enclosed garden. Today the garden has been colonized by works for the new railway. With its whale-grey Portakabins and giant mechanical diggers, it has all the grace of an abandoned terraforming installation.

In the 1980s a Roman cemetery was discovered on the north side of Finsbury Circus: 132 burials, including some cremations. Osteoarchaeologist Natasha Powers once described the scene to me as 'CSI Walbrook'. Two bodies were found crouched in pits, as if they had been interred alive. One body was unearthed without its head, presumed decapitated. Two corpses were found with leg rings, and evidence of de-fleshing (the removal of flesh and organs from a body before burial). In one burial, a woman and a young man were lying prone, as if they had been holding each other when they went in. It seems a strange place to bury the dead, in the soggy northern margins of the city. When the Walbrook flooded, as Powers explained, the cemetery would have turned into a swamp. The bloated stream carried such force that stone sarcophagi were raised from their beds and scoured clean of their cargo, sending fractured skeletons and decomposing corpses cascading downstream like so much unwanted river-junk.

In the 1860s the pioneering archaeologist Augustus Pitt Rivers discovered a massive hoard of crania in an alluvial channel of the Walbrook near Cannon Street. Conditioned by his long career in the British Army, Pitt Rivers thought these skulls the remains of Roman legionaries decapitated by Venedoti fighters from Gwynedd (an alternative theory has them as victims of Boudicca's annihilation of London in AD 60/61). Powers disagrees; the skulls, she contends, were washed downstream from the Roman cemetery at Finsbury Circus. According to her research, bodies disturbed by flooding might easily have been carried by a swollen stream, breaking up in a predictable sequence: first go the hands and wrists, then the feet. Next comes the head, and the mandible (the lower jaw). The legs and arm begin to separate, and you're left with a floating torso. The river sifts each body into its composite parts, much as it does to any flotsam and jetsam, depositing each body part in a different spot along its course. The skulls, she told me, being round and heavy, were carried the furthest. They 'bounced' along the riverbed all the way through the city, where they gathered in an underwater spoil heap – awaiting Pitt Rivers's grand reveal.

As the pilgrims complete their circuit of the old burial ground, they pass an obelisk of polished Portland limestone. I am already ahead, sneaking behind a colonnade on London Wall. The obelisk is a sham monument; its thin façade conceals a ventilation shaft for an underground gas storage tank. These stink, or stench, pipes can be found all over London and are more commonly used to allow noxious gases to escape from the sewers.

On the north side of Finsbury Circus abutting Moorgate, a sewer *does* run. The London Bridge Sewer is one of the city's oldest, constructed in the 1840s on, or very near, what was left of the Walbrook. It was later incorporated into Bazalgette's sewerage network. Despite its age, it is one of London's lesser-known drains; even the professional flushers with their headlamps and waders rarely walk its dank, dark course. Some claim that the tunnel has run dry, but others report that it is being flooded from the surrounding earth, as if the Walbrook was trying to reinhabit its old course, seeping back through the brickwork.

This is the realm of urban explorers, renegade cartographers who disappear into manholes in broad daylight. Descending into the bowels of the city is like a military operation. Stoop's Limit, the Last Bastion: even the names they have given to parts of the sewer are more fitting for a theatre of war. But there are prizes to be found down there in the 'steamy, turdy' underworld.[7]

In retreating, we found some smaller side-passages. Along the sides of these, a crystalline deposit had built up on some of the old brickwork.

I don't know what mineral it was, but it was gorgeous, especially as it suddenly glittered out of the complete darkness in the light of our headlamps. As I was taking pictures of it, I noticed a tiny, nearly transparent spider that crouched on the crystals.[8]

I have crossed at last into Corporation land, London's barricaded core. The City pulls its own history around itself like an invisibility cloak, hoping we won't notice the moral void at its heart. Black Stone, Northern Rock, Peak XV, Stonegate Wealth: the financial-services industry frequently reaches for the language of geology and the natural world to provide weight to the intangible business of micro-trading, derivatives and credit swaps. Arrowgrass, Amethyst, Citadel: currency ripped from its material roots as the exchange of precious metals.

The Walbrook seeks gravity's relief, seeps beneath All Hallows-on-the-Wall, the Carpenters' church. When the Roman wall was constructed, after AD 190, it restricted the river's flow such that water began to back up against it, creating an expanse of wetland north of the city. Moorfields, as it became known, remained open land until 1800 and is now home to the world-famous Eye Hospital. For the Walbrook, it was the beginning of the end.

I follow the river's shadow into Copthall Street and head towards a red telephone box. The street has the form of a meandering gully and I can feel the pilgrims' eyes on the back of my head.

Must walk faster.

A 'copped' or 'copt' hall is a hall adorned with a crest; the word 'cop' derives from the German *kopf*, meaning cup or head. This copthall was owned by the Drapers' Company, who acquired it in the sixteenth century from Thomas Cromwell. (Cromwell, in turn, had bought the land from the Augustinian or Austin Friars.)

The Middle Walbrook is a waterlogged zone, so damp it remained open gardens as late as the nineteenth century. Manholes pepper the tarmac, sewers flowing beneath. Once, scoping the route after heavy rain, the dirty water swilled so high I could have reached through the grille and touched it.

In the early Roman period this was an industrial zone of leather-tanning, copper-beating, horn-working, butchery and the burning of animal bones in pits to make glue. Pottery was big business in the Walbrook valley. A group dubbed 'the Moorgate Potters' even stamped their names on their wares: Catullus, Lucius, Maximus and the one who left the mark of a herringbone on every urn and amphora. Among the treasures dredged from the ground here are Romano-British face pots: anthropomorphic water containers decorated with grinning or gurning faces.

At the end of Copthall Street, the roadway bends sharply to the east, while the valley continues due south through a line of disrupted street furniture: three bollards that have tilted off their axes, as though compelled by an invisible current.

Here, an ancient face looms down from a stone façade above the telephone box. I first saw him on a bright autumn day, the sunlight catching on his feral locks; a hirsute river guardian. If the Greek sea god Poseidon lived in London, he would be called Old Father Thames. They share the same unkempt beard and brooding aspect. In some depictions, Poseidon's trident is morphed to a mudlark's shovel. The beachcomber-deity rises from the murk with a half-drowned cat in his rucksack; one part protector to two parts miscreant, staring dead-eyed from the wall like a watery gargoyle. Great Swan Alley, Whalebone Court: even the street names have assumed an aquatic character. T. S. Eliot called the river a 'strong brown god'.[9] In his *Four Quartets* the Thames and the Ganges are bound together by their shared cargo of sacred water, the ghosts of a fading empire. Walbrook, capillary to the fat vein of Thames, deserves at least some minor deva as its presiding spirit.

I catch sight of the pilgrims and turn into a narrow alley. They haven't seen me. I have taped a tarot card to the inside of the phone box. One of them will have to enter to collect it; an urban curio designed to evoke forces from beneath the landscape. A winged angel hovers above the reed-fringed banks of a stream, pouring liquid between two golden cups. *Temperance*. Like the depiction of the Hindu god Shiva as Lord of the Dance in a ring of fire, the angel has only one foot on the ground; the other is submerged in the waters of the stream.

The way ahead is signposted by a depression in the pavement; it is damp with the trace of standing water. I enter a covered passageway that tunnels beneath solicitors' offices and emerge into Tokenhouse Yard. Centuries ago, small lead coins or 'tokens' were traded here by London merchants – payment in lieu of authorized currency. Years later I will witness a scraggly-bearded mudlark pull a medieval token from the anaerobic mud of the Thames at Rotherhithe. He will hold it up between grimy fingers – this shiny disc that looks as good as the day it went in – and he will grin from ear to ear, exclaiming: 'Mint condition.'

☈ *The city deals in obfuscation: futures, forwards, hybrids.*

Moving down Tokenhouse Yard, the way appears to narrow, like the aperture of a camera lens, with the high wall of the Bank of England rearing up in the distance. I feel like Alice, tumbling down the rabbit hole. During construction work at the Bank in 1805, a stream, long enclosed, was temporarily released. Current, currency; income and out-flow: the history of money is the history of a flowing idea.

A few months ago, I joined a group from Museum of London Archaeology (MOLA) to visit an excavation on the west side of Token-house Yard. Figures in hard hats were squatting in the dirt, scraping and brushing the dark brown surface or photographing the remains *in situ*. Others manned plastic trays full of small finds. In the compacted mud of the valley they had uncovered the ruins of timber buildings, three chalk-lined walls and a tessellated brick floor – all dating to Roman London. The river channel itself was exposed as a strip of black silt run-ning tantalizingly along the eastern boundary of the site. This trace deposit was the closest I had been to the 'real' Walbrook and I craned to take a picture on my phone. The dark soil had yielded coins bearing the faces of Claudius and Nero, fragments of a board game and a copper alloy phallus. Just as the bogs of Northern Europe coughed up leathery, intact bodies from the Iron Age, so the ink-black shadow of the Walbrook has proved a natural preservative for treasures from the city's Roman past.

The Romans were not the first people to inhabit this landscape, but they were the first to build a permanent settlement here, in the valley between the two gravel bluffs of Ludgate and Cornhill. They were also the first to bridge the Thames – initially with a military pontoon and then with a stone bridge connecting the solid ground of the north bank with the provisional, tide-blown terrain of the south. The Thames was not then the embanked and fast-flowing torrent that it is today, but instead a much wider and shallower waterway connected to an extensive hinterland of tidal creeks and marshes. At Southwark, a series of gravel islands reached across the flooded land like stepping stones.

The history of London before the Romans has long been plagued by imaginative guesswork and conjecture. Recent archaeological discoveries are slowly revealing a picture of a marshy landscape worked by bands of semi-nomadic farmers. Wooden causeways have been uncovered in the flatlands of Bermondsey and, at Vauxhall, the remains of a bridge or pier projecting into the Thames; perhaps the site of ritual offerings to the river. Many believe that Watling Street – the great paved highway that sliced through the landscape towards the Roman *civitas* – was constructed on the line of an Iron Age trackway which originally crossed the river in the vicinity of Westminster. But the evidence is slim, the alignments lost.

I hurry east up Lothbury, past the Bank of England. Great iron gates decorated with serpents creak open to reveal an empty courtyard manned by a portly security guard from another century. I turn into a gap in the wall and wait, hidden, for the first pilgrims to appear.

Bank

ON THE EDGE OF the Sabine Hills near Rome lies the small town of Tivoli. It is best known for its ornamental gardens, which were laid out in the sixteenth century in the grounds of the Villa d'Este. So celebrated were these gardens that Tivoli lent its name to a public park in Paris, and subsequently to gardens in Copenhagen, Tokyo and Ljubljana, Slovenia. Tivoli has since gone viral, spawning clones all over the world – theatres, football stadia and even housing estates – becoming a global brand name for leisure, pleasure and entertainment.

In 1805 Sir John Soane, the architect responsible for the rebuilding of the Bank of England, completed his own, typically idiosyncratic, contribution to the craze: a spherical enclosure at the junction of Lothbury and Princes Street which he named Tivoli Corner. It is a tomblike, functionless space appended to the main structure of the Bank and enclosed with thick columns. It can be entered from the north or west. Its roof is open to the sky, a circular oculus around which is carved a dedication to THE CITIZENS OF LONDON. A CCTV camera is now stationed ominously above the opening.

Soane was an obscurantist. His design was not modelled on the gardens of the Villa d'Este, but on the nearby Temple of Vesta, which he had visited as a young man. A circular shrine to the Roman fire goddess, the temple was built early in the first century BC and stands above the town on a high promontory or acropolis. Far below, the Aniene River pours out of the Sabine Hills in a series of dramatic waterfalls. The falls are now dammed, their energy harnessed to light households across Rome. Vesta, the fire goddess, would like that confluence of fire and water. Perhaps Soane was thinking of the Walbrook as an Aniene stand-in – two rivers barely contained by the earth. Like many of the famous monuments of Rome, the original temple was shaped from travertine, a type of limestone produced by hot springs and quarried from the hills around

Tivoli. It was also used to tile the floor of Broadgate Tower and for the circular altar of St Stephen Walbrook.

Tivoli Corner is an enigmatic structure. According to one biographer, Soane 'delighted in "lesser" spaces – vestibules, corridors and alcoves'; seeking 'illumination from hidden sources, harking back to the Roman subterranean regions . . . Soane saw Tivoli Corner neither as entrance nor passage'.[10] The pilgrims enter. One lights a candle to honour the goddess Vesta. Another shivers in the cold. Once, entering this space, I discovered that a pyre of half-smoked cigarettes had been constructed on a ledge; another day, three empty bottles of vodka, arrayed like wonky cricket stumps. A locked metal box is set into the wall like a safe, a secret door into the Bank. It is impossible to resist the temptation to try your house key in the lock.

To step inside the frozen time capsule of Soane's London home (now a museum by Lincoln's Inn Fields) is to enter a mind wired by the neuroses of making and unmaking, of the raised and the ruined. Artworks he commissioned include a landscape painting populated by every one of his buildings to be constructed: a city of his own making. More surprisingly, a companion piece gathers every structure that was *not* realized: monuments, mansions and palaces that remained as lines in the architect's sketchbook. A city of the undone, like Wren's designs for a new London street plan, all laid out on geometric lines. The Bank of England receives its own weird memorial: a bird's eye view of the entire complex reduced to a crumbling ruin. 'The ruin traffics with more than one timeframe,' wrote Brian Dillon. 'It conjures a future past, the memory of what might have been.'[11] This, I think, is the real meaning of this odd structure. Soane was, at once, paying homage to and undermining the forms of classical Rome. The Temple of Vesta stands, reconstituted, inside his new temple to a new empire of trade. Tivoli Corner is a Roman pastiche at the centre of a Roman city; a folly at the heart of capital.

The pilgrims leave by the western exit. I am already far ahead, at the south end of Princes Street. They pass, on one side, an elliptical sign fixed into a recess on the wall. It is the only marker of having passed through the invisible boundary of the Ward of Walbrook. On the other side of the street, they squint to make out the remains of another sign. The letters H-S-B-C traced as off-white lines against smog-darkened stone: a reverse branding where a metal logo has been ripped clean off the wall.

☊ *The street records all losses.*

The crossroads at the south end of the Bank of England, where the passageways of the Tube station riddle the ground like unravelled intestine, marks the *col* between the miniature peaks of Cornhill and Ludgate Hill. Here the culverted stream once passed beneath the Wren church of St Mildred's, a renovated medieval structure that was eventually demolished in 1872 to make way for the imposing office buildings that now dominate the junction.

It may only be the slightest of gradients but the view of Cheapside rising towards St Paul's in the west is unmistakably that of a hill seen from a valley bottom. A market for chicken and geese was once held here and the lower section of Cheapside is still known as Poultry. I head towards a pink-and-yellow-striped building jutting out into the confluence of highways. Its tubular clock tower resembles the funnel of a steam ship and as I approach I notice that its sandstone flanks are peppered with circular windows like portholes. It is time for a pause, to get out of the sloshed weather, to reset before the final descent.

In September 2008 the recession descended like a toxic cloud over the Square Mile. In the early days we gave it a name like something out of a tabloid headline – the Credit Crunch – then later, euphemistically, the Downturn. I had moved my tiny publishing and performing-arts company to a new office above the Hoop and Grapes on Aldgate High Street in the month the bad news came. Lehman Brothers, Fannie Mae: the alarum was raised three thousand miles away on Wall Street and in the ghost towns of the Rust Belt.

Anjool Malde was an Oxford graduate and a successful employee of Deutsche Bank. On 5 July 2009 he jumped from the rooftop restaurant at One Poultry. He dropped seven floors through the empty centre of the building like a stone thrown into a well. He was clutching a glass of champagne as he fell. According to a friend, 'He never slept and lived on Red Bull.'[12] He was twenty-four.

In October 2012 investment specialist Nico Lambrechts followed suit. He was forty-six and lived in a £2-million house in Cobham, Surrey.

> There was a huge thump and bang. Everyone started running into Starbucks. He was wearing a dark top, coat, grey trousers and black shoes, one of his shoes fell off. Someone felt his neck for a pulse.[13]

In the years following the recession, five people jumped to their deaths from this building. The restaurant, Le Coq d'Argent, is accessed by a private lift set into the atrium, and offers a convenient launch pad into the central well, although safety rails have now been installed to discourage would-be jumpers.

Death and decay shadow the river. The sacred stream is always haunted by its double, the open sewer – degraded, filthy, bearer of infection – or reversed as Styx, the river of the dead. The life-giving waters of a spring emanating from a fissure in the rock face can be reinterpreted as an entrance to the underworld. And they often were; there are as many devil's holes as holy wells.

During the construction of One Poultry in 1996, archaeologists peeled back the earth to reveal the medieval cemetery of St Benet Sherehog: 274 bodies, all aligned east–west with their heads pointing towards the Walbrook. Those who jumped to their deaths fell, unaware, into once-consecrated ground. And then, beneath the cemetery, the diggers hit Roman: 'an unparalleled sequence of buildings, roads and open spaces' abutting the main east–west highway through London. It was a road, like the one at Liverpool Street, that bridged the Walbrook.[14] A rare document emerged too, a miracle, still legible, from the mud: a second-century writing tablet made of silver fir which recorded the sale of a slave.

> Vegetus, assistant slave of Montanus the slave of the August Emperor, has bought the girl Fortunata, by nationality a Diablintian [from near Jublains in France], for 600 denarii. She is warranted healthy and not liable to run away . . .

Fortunata. 'Lucky.' A child sold as a slave to the slave of another slave. Roman Britain was not all underfloor heating and amphitheatres. According to the social hierarchy of second-century London, people could be traded as easily as stocks and shares – the human cargo of a once-great empire.

One of the pilgrims removes his thick ski mittens and casts a handful of petals into the well in memory of those who fall from the sky. In the windless space of the atrium the petals drop unceremoniously into the basement. They will lie unseen and undisturbed until Monday morning when they will be crushed into the floor's glossy lacquer by the well-heeled shoes of bankers collecting their nine o'clock lattes.

The group is hushed – engulfed by the negative atmospherics of the building – and so I usher them forward, out and across Queen Victoria Street and on to the cobbles of Bucklersbury, before disappearing again into the city.

Communion

As janus, the roman god of beginnings and endings, looks out with two faces, so London is governed by two heads, each operating within a discrete sphere of influence. Since the year 2000, the democratically elected Mayor of London has governed the greater metropolis from a squat glass carbuncle at the south end of Tower Bridge, while his ceremonial doppelganger, the Lord Mayor of London, is enthroned over the river, in the city within the city: a robed don in a tricorn hat. The Lord Mayor's official residence is the Mansion House, at the south-west corner of the Bank intersection. During its construction in the mid-eighteenth century, works were halted at the discovery of natural springs; buried river-juice percolating through the soil.

From Mansion House to Cannon Street, the phantom river names the way. The street sign reads simply, WALBROOK EC4. Surface and substrate converge; we are walking on water. I let the pilgrims go first and they descend sharply towards the Thames, past the square stone tower of a Wren church. They hold their MP3 players loosely in their hands like rosaries.

St Stephen Walbrook was listed by Nikolaus Pevsner as one of his top ten most important buildings in England. Its dome was based on Wren's original designs for St Paul's and its spherical interior gives you the impression of entering a large well or basin. Abandoning the conventional cruciform structure of the Western church, St Stephen Walbrook is more suggestive of an Orthodox basilica or even a Neolithic henge. Like twinned radar beacons, the smaller church, down here in the valley, networks with its larger cousin on the crest of Ludgate Hill across the sacramental landscape of the city. Concentric rings of curved wooden benches surround a circular slab of roughly hewn travertine by the sculptor Henry Moore; an altar that recalls the stone table on which Abraham intended to sacrifice his son, Isaac. Above the west door an elliptical porthole – like the ones at One Poultry – affords a direct view of the cathedral. Wren's vision of London appears as a complex geometry of lines and circles. I am reminded of the urban theorist Kevin Lynch, whose work conceives of the city as a system of 'pathways', 'edges' and 'nodes'.[15]

The pilgrims continue down Walbrook, following the piped directions of their absentee tour guide. I have taken a different route to avoid being seen.

Descend the gravel terraces to the mouth of the river. Let yourself be pulled along by its flow.

Across Walbrook from St Stephen's, a long wall of hoardings conceals a giant crater, where the footing of a new office block is soon to be pile-driven into the soft earth. At the bottom of the crater, a crack team of archaeologists is tapping the ground, exploiting a brief window of opportunity between excavation and construction to sink themselves into the river's treacle: to dredge, to brush, to wash, to map.

Displaced from the completed dig behind Tokenhouse Yard, the MOLA crews are constantly on the move. They are the nomads of the city, working from field offices in borrowed Portakabins and improvised marquees. As London shoots up, fulfilling its endless cycle of destruction and renewal, these scrapers and sifters move across – and beneath – its surface in search of the next construction site, the next dig, the next big thing. But here, on the banks of the Walbrook, they are breaking ground that has already been broken.

In 1954 W. F. Grimes, assisted by the pioneering female archaeologist Audrey Williams, obtained permission to excavate the bombed-out ruins of Bucklersbury. Like me, they were searching for the Walbrook channel; an exercise in geo-archaeology, topography mapping. For the first few days investigations proceeded well enough, the former river revealed in ghost-traces of black silt, but little else of value emerged from the mud. Then, on the final day, the archaeologists stumbled across the stone head of a young man. With trademark Phrygian hat, the head was instantly identified as Mithras: the Persian deity born from a rock and worshipped throughout the Roman Empire in underground temples, known as Mithraea, between 100 BC and AD 300. Mithraea were male-only places and were especially popular amongst the military. Devotees to the cult were known as *syndexioi* – 'those united by the handshake'.

The discovery of the head gave Grimes and Williams's excavation a new lease of life. Before long, the entire temple complex was unearthed, including a complete 'tauroctony' – a marble relief showing the iconic scene of Mithras slaying the astral bull – and dated to AD 240. The discovery was front-page news and thousands of people were soon patiently queuing along Walbrook for a glimpse of the remains. One black-and-white image from the *Daily Mail* shows two archaeologists, a man and a woman, holding the stone head of Mithras. The woman wears a woollen hat and clasps his Smurf hat, smiling. What looks like a lit cigarette, but might just be a scratch on the photograph, dangles from the man's lips. In post-war London, the stone head was so much more than mere treasure. Mithras was a phoenix rising from the ashes of a ruined city, a newborn baby boy.

Under Grimes and Williams's supervision the remains of the temple were removed brick by brick and rebuilt a road away, where they sat – unloved, out of place and open to the elements – for five decades. In the 1960s a concrete office block, Bucklersbury House, was built over the original site, where it remained until 2011, when it too was demolished. A new temple will soon rise from the crater: the European headquarters of multinational financial services firm Bloomberg.

By the time I began my explorations of the river valley, the ground had already been reopened and MOLA brought in to finish the job, to recalibrate Grimes and Williams's studies. What was found, just south of the Mithraeum site, stunned historians: a hoard of treasures amounting to some ten thousand finds from Roman London. Coins, pottery, leather shoes and lucky charms; hundreds of wooden writing tablets, some complete with styli; a tiny amber amulet shaped to resemble a gladiator's helmet; and a network of wood-lined drains, evidence of industrial sites discharging waste into the Walbrook. Timber structures rose to the surface; mosaic floors; a well into which coins and cow skulls had been thrown in some unspecified ritual. Having covered the original excavation almost sixty years before, the *Daily Mail* led with 'London's Most Important Ever Archaeological Dig' and quoted MOLA's own nickname for the site: the 'Pompeii of the North'.[16]

I am rushing past Cannon Street station, where the geography of the river valley is unmistakable. The road climbs away in both directions: towards Ludgate Hill and St Paul's to the west and across the gravel flanks of Cornhill to the east. At the lowest point of the road, a pool of slush ice has gathered in a nook in the tarmac; it leaks meltwater like a miniature glacier.

Near by, the mysterious London Stone can be found set behind a grille in the wall underneath a shop selling greetings cards. The stone is a slab of oolite limestone masquerading as a Neolithic monument. No one knows its true age, nor its provenance, though Brutus, King Arthur and the Elizabethan alchemist John Dee have all been associated with its occult energies. Ask for the London Stone around here and you're more likely to be directed to the pub adjacent, which bears its folkloric affiliations in foreboding Gothic minuscule.

The Walbrook once split in two before its outfall: a twin-mouth for the city of doubles, of Mayor and Lord Mayor, Gog and Magog. The main stream descended due south down Dowgate Hill, while the other made a right-angle turn along Cloak Lane. I step back into the shadows and watch the pilgrims cross the junction and then follow this second path. They walk Cloak Lane in the gathering darkness.

Cloak: a corruption of the Latin *cloaca*, meaning 'sewer', from *cluere*, 'to cleanse'.

Shoreditch: sewer ditch.

Cloak Lane: sewer lane.

The route slaloms along College Hill, past the house of Richard 'Dick' Whittington. From a hidden spot behind trees I watch the pilgrims pass the western door of St Michael Paternoster Royal. Some stop to inspect the blue plaque. A trickle of snow-juice meanders the cracked tarmac as Walbrook simulacrum. They turn back east along a kinked pathway then pause before the high brick wall of Cannon Street railway bridge. I am already far ahead, a secret agent observing from the shadows.

On a topographical map, a stream whose waters run only in the rainy season is marked with a line of blue dashes and dots. These intermittent, or ephemeral, streams are known as 'winterbournes'.* Here, at the outfall of the Walbrook sewer, the language of the transient river seeps into the offices and trading floors as Winterflood Securities Ltd – a financial services firm based in Cannon Bridge House. Founded in 1988 by Brian Winterflood, the company is one of London's leading providers of liquidity. Winterflood seems bound for ever to the sodden word-hoard of the buried river. It specializes in a form of electronic trading known as 'dark pools', in which traders buy or sell large orders secretly and outside of public exchanges.

'Liquidity as an end seems to have trumped the need for transparency and fairness,' said US Senator Ted Kaufman in 2009.[17] Financial regulators have been slow to grapple with the new technologies revolutionizing banking. 'The market,' he continued, 'should work best for those who want to buy and hold in hopes of a golden retirement not just for high frequency traders who want to buy and sell in milliseconds.'

Beyond the tarmac speedway of Upper Thames Street we walk on provisional ground – on land reclaimed from the river for wharves and

* In Herne Hill, a channel of the Effra flowed across Winterbourne Road.

warehouses. At the corner of Cousin Lane, within sniffing distance of the Thames, I pass a strange niche in the brick wall. Look closely. This red granite anomaly is like a model of a house or, with its tiny Gothic arch and gabled roof, a doorway to a miniature church. A small basin protrudes from the bottom; it is filled with an inch of dirty water with a chaser of soggy fag ends clogging the plughole.

This is one of the many drinking fountains installed in the nineteenth century to provide clean water to the inhabitants of a polluted and cholera-plagued city. From 1859 the Metropolitan Drinking Fountain Association erected hundreds of fountains across the city, as well as troughs for horses and cattle. To this day the organization funds the building of wells in the developing world. It is hard to imagine a time when the only source of sterile water for many citizens was beer – although perhaps the pervasiveness of pubs and drinking in the national psyche demonstrates that the link has not yet been severed. Above the fountain, a maroon board advertises a nearby Fuller's hostelry, the Banker, promising 'Traditional Ales and *Great Fresh* British Food'.

London was once a city of breweries. From the Anchor in Southwark to the Alma in Whitechapel, Meux & Co.'s Horse Shoe, Hoare & Co., Charrington and Watney. In the 1830s, the Truman in Spitalfields (now a complex of art studios and event spaces) was producing over two hundred thousand barrels of London Porter every year. Breweries were greedy consumers of water, which was usually pumped directly from the ground; even small establishments boasted a private well, sunk deep through gravel, sand, silt and clay to the vast chalk aquifer beneath the city. Young's still brags that its London Gold cask ale is 'brewed with natural mineral water from the brewery's very own well'.

Such was the demand for this natural resource that by the 1960s the water table – the level at which water can be found in an aquifer – had fallen by as much as 100 metres in some parts of central London. The city was literally being drained from the bottom up.

Modern London is a service city, no longer the industrial powerhouse it once was. The breweries, tanneries, factories, foundries and distilleries have all but vanished, leaving behind a vast, unused system of water-extraction. Deep wells were sealed off or covered over, springs abandoned. The aquifer has recharged and today the water table is not falling but rising – and by as much as three metres a year.

The pilgrims approach, cautious at first. Then one steps forward, a woman in trench coat and boots.

◐ Extend your hand towards the niche. The wall feels closer, and suddenly pliant, as if it might yield to touch.

In other fountains I have seen, a metal cup hangs from a chain above the basin and the chain itself is fastened to a back panel. But in this dank spot beneath the railway bridge, the cup – with its suggestion of shared communion, a vernacular grail-lore – is long gone. In its place, there is a fissure in the granite, maybe three inches across, where the chain has been ripped clean out; a gap just large enough to squeeze a hand.

◐ Flatten out your palm. Turn it sideways as you might a key. Insert your hand into the stone.

These fountains, pumps and troughs are structures whose very meaning and function has been lost or redirected, just as the natural streams were culverted and rechanneled, buried in Bazalgette's vast sewerage system. No longer serving any practical function, they have become urban curios; minor monuments to be catalogued by the few historians still interested. But to me, the fountain is a roadside shrine to water and it provides a useful waymarker for the urban pilgrims who have come this far.

The lights change on Upper Thames Street. Apart from the traffic, the City is empty. Who would want to venture out in this weather?

◐ Reach through to a darkened, mossy place: a fault in time.

Mouth

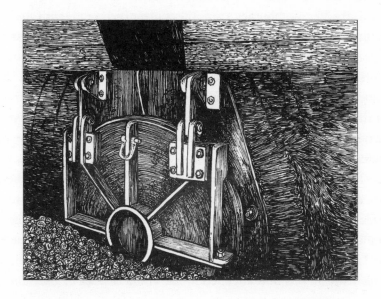

THE RIVER IS SENSED before it is seen; sensed as a gap, an absence in the unrelenting sprawl of the city. And before even that, the river is tasted. Thames salt-chutney stains the cold air and blends with chlorine fumes discharging from the swimming pool on Cousin Lane. At the bottom, by the Banker pub, I climb a set of concrete steps and there at last the foreshore is laid out beneath me, swathed in half-light. I have pushed through the overcoats at the back of the wardrobe and out into the dream space beyond. It has started snowing again. As I descend, a pleasure boat passes and its wake hits the beach like a foamy gasp, and another, and another.

I have seen car tyres, perched on the rocks; animal bones weathered to driftwood. I have seen a child's shoe one day; the next, a wrench. A traffic cone. An unopened bag of coal. Electrical wire and black rubber tubing sprout from the glistening rubble, as if the foreshore has need of good plumbing and lights. This pilgrimage – my walking ritual for the hidden stream – is now engulfed by the grand reveal of a much larger river. The Thames is that great, breathing expanse of tidal waterway whose edges, embanked and scrappy, are perhaps the archetypal shifting landscape; sodden margins whose wrecked cargo of stones and shells, smashed bottles and hub caps, is sifted twice daily like so much re-arranged furniture.

The foreshore is a place where the laws of physics seem to have been suspended. Two waste barges from Walbrook Wharf are grounded on the rubble; their colossal, rusting hulks tower above the pilgrims as they descend towards me. At high tide, the Thames erases this provisional ground – its turbulent, grey soup barely contained by the embankment – and the barges are unsettled from their rubble beds, lifted up by the swell.

I recall the words of Richard Serra, witnessing the launch of a ship. 'An object,' he said, 'can become something light. That amount of tonnage can become something lyrical.' I am beginning to understand what captivated him as a boy visiting the shipyards of San Francisco – perhaps even what drove him to make *Fulcrum*. For Serra, both ship and sculpture are a magician's trick, monuments to the mystery of the physical world.

The pilgrims appear on the bank, then descend the river stairs, one by one, to the beach. United, we pick our way across the rubble and then along a narrow strip of causeway between barge and river. In the dying light we reach the Walbrook outflow. Its mouth is a circular hatch set into the base of the embankment wall; an entrance, maybe four feet wide, that is locked by a thick metal door. The river is an unopened can. A dry concrete channel, partially blocked by debris, projects from the wall like a slumped tongue. We pause for a moment, in reverence for the choked-up storm sewer, for this desolate spot, for our effort in finding it.

I tell the pilgrims how the sewer is not, in fact, locked; how, in storm conditions, the heavy lid will be forced open by the sheer weight of water flowing towards it. I tell them how I came down here with my wife, Sarah, one New Year's Eve, armed with a bottle of champagne and two flute glasses in my inside pockets; how we listened to the ordnance booms of the fireworks, the city glowing red and orange and purple, with the incoming tide narrowing the causeway that was our only way out. I was thinking of Eliot's 'strong brown god', how a river is reduced to this: the Walbrook's final destination. Liquidity. Loss and renewal. Water and waste. A new year by an old river.

Going Dark

IN 2014, I MOVED back south of the Thames after almost a decade living on the fringes of the Roman city. Aldgate was changing. And so was I.

In the years since I had begun to walk the valleys of the Walbrook and the Effra, a sense of London as a 'liquid city' had been clarifying in my mind; of water as a prime agent of geology and the lost rivers as memory paths connecting us backwards through time.[18]

We landed, Sarah and I, in a 1990s block next to a converted Victorian granary on the northern edge of the Rotherhithe peninsula. Rotherhithe (or 'Redriff') is where old ships were once brought to be broken up for parts. Clapboard houses and the squawk of gulls lend the streets a maritime atmosphere. The foreshore here is studded with timber piles, iron chains and submerged dock structures. The name of the local pub, the Mayflower, commemorates the area's connection to the converted cargo ship which set sail from Rotherhithe in 1620, heading for the New World.

While often considered contiguous with its better-known neighbour Bermondsey, Rotherhithe stands alone as an almost-island in the provisional landscape south of the Thames. The interior of the peninsula is covered by low-rise housing blocks, suburban-style cul-de-sacs and scrubby woodland planted in the ruins of the Surrey Commercial Docks. We had moved, against all reason, to one of the lowest parts of London. The only high ground is a turfed-over slag heap called Stave Hill, which is popular with fitness enthusiasts and stands at the apex of a tree-lined corridor with all the ritual suggestion of an Aztec pyramid.

In my twenties the unforgiving speed and aggression of the City fringe had manifested as a cracked mirror to my own emotional life; to the explosive anger and unresolved grief that was gnawing at my insides. Here on the Rotherhithe peninsula we settled into slower, gentler rhythms. The noise and perpetual motion of the East End was replaced by wide open vistas and the natural movement of the tide. I could watch the sun go down behind the Eastern Cluster from our new vantage point on the south bank. Like the panoramists of the sixteenth and seventeenth centuries, I had attained the kind of critical distance by which I might attempt further incursions into the deep city.

One afternoon, a few years later, I return to the Walbrook valley to visit the remains of the Temple of Mithras, which have finally been reconstructed in a purpose-built basement beneath Bloomberg's European headquarters. That icy December, when I walked the Walbrook from Shoreditch to the Thames with a band of hardy urban pilgrims, seems like an age ago. Today I come alone, in T-shirt and shorts.

I enter through a glossy atrium housing artefacts from the Roman city in a giant display cabinet. The London Mithraeum, as it has been rebranded, is guarded by athletic security guards in quilted gilets emblazoned with the Bloomberg livery. On arrival a young women in a business suit ticks off my name on a clipboard like a hostess at an upmarket nightclub.

I descend a flight of stairs to a darkened room, where a series of interactive digital displays present the history of the site: the walled city, the river and the mystery cult; Grimes and Williams's excavation and the discovery of the stone head. The walls are polished black stone; I feel as if I have travelled down a fault in the earth. Video projections appear – phantom figures emerging from clouds of luminous pixels. And now we're being led down a second staircase to the original ground level of the temple: three German tourists; two hipsters in matching coats; and me.

A uniformed usher is waiting at the bottom. She speaks into a radio – coded instructions to someone on the surface.

We are seven metres below the modern city.

A tall black door swings open, like the 'door in the mountain-side', and we step through into the darkness of the Mithraeum.[19]

I find myself on an elevated walkway at the edge of a large, rectangular chamber; maybe 80 feet in length and half as much across. Shadows bloom then shrink away to nothing. Two parallel walls of rough-hewn Kentish ragstone describe the sunken nave of what appears to be a small, ruined chapel, with a raised platform or altar at the far end.

Inside the Mithraeum, it is dusk, then moonlit, then midnight black.

'Darkness might be a medium of vision,' wrote Robert Macfarlane, '[and] descent . . . a movement towards revelation.'[20]

The sound of drums and bells and piercing horns fills the chamber with a strange, feral music. Shafts of light appear through clouds of haze that plume and roll like incense, like smoke from a thurible. Then voices come, a solemn liturgy in a mix of Latin and Persian.

Nama Patrī, tutela Saturnī.

'Hail to the Father, in the protection of Saturn.'

The shafts of light cohere into a spectral outline of the temple; translucent, vertical walls rising from the ground plan. It is so much like the fragmented world of the video-game series *Assassin's Creed* that I recoil from reaching through the light lest I fall, 'desynchronized', into a rift in time.

This is the cave where Mithras killed the astral bull, his knife plunged deep into the creature's neck, his eyes inclined towards the sun god, Sol. Four hundred extant Mithraea from Syria to Scotland: four hundred bulls; four hundred caves.

Through ritual practices whose precise features remain unknown to historians, Mithraic worship collapsed time and space by restaging the central acts of the mystery in these underground spaces: Mithras's birth from solid rock, his banquet with Sol and so on. Temples were frequently located next to springs or streams for the easy conveyance of fresh water; a vital component of the re-enactment of the 'water miracle', in which Mithras is said to have fired an arrow into a rock, causing water to pour out.

The drums grow louder and now a single beam of light lands upon the altar, where a sculpture of Mithras in twisted metal stands in for the marble tauroctony. We are held in the moment. By light. By voice. By the pressure of rock.

Blackout.

It would be easy to dismiss Bloomberg's Mithraeum as an exercise in corporate PR, a one-of-a-kind events space for entertaining clients. But the truth is: this place is magic and I am happy to submit.

As the light show subsides, I make my way clockwise around the temple. Here is the wood-lined well or basin used for the 'water miracle'. It was sunk into the permeable ground of the Walbrook valley. Here are the bases of columns and, here, the remains of stone benches on which initiates reclined for the communal feast. Here is the apse and, here, the altar.

I find a seat at the back, sink into the shadows and close my eyes. 'How clear everything becomes when you look from the darkness of a dungeon,' wrote Umberto Eco in *Foucault's Pendulum*, his brilliant satire of conspiracy theorists and dabblers in the occult.[21]

After all these years, the lost river has led me here, to a place where time is thick and the air is charged.

When I wake, the chamber is empty. Even the usher has left her station. Something is flickering at the edge of my vision. I look up. The ceiling is studded with recessed LED lamps. To believers, the cave was the cosmos. The lamps sparkle like stars in the night sky.

I need to go down further. To go dark again. To descend.

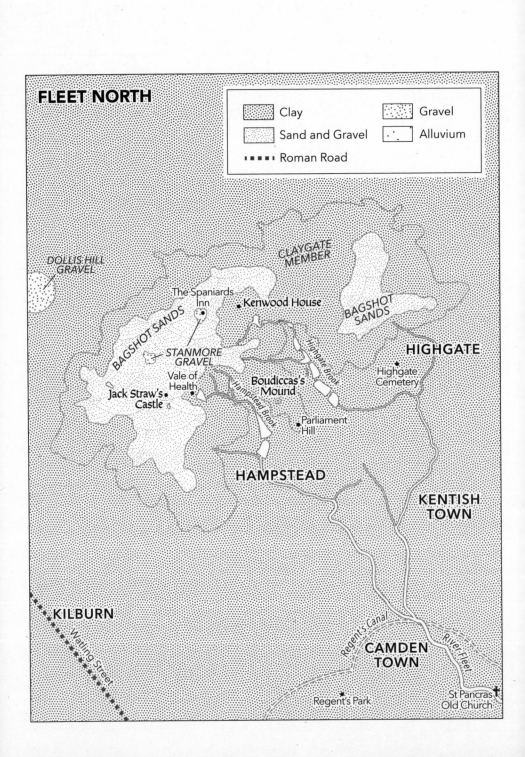

FLEET NORTH

Clay

Sand and Gravel

Gravel

Alluvium

Roman Road

DOLLIS HILL
GRAVEL

CLAYGATE
MEMBER

The Spaniards
Inn

Kenwood House

BAGSHOT SANDS

BAGSHOT
SANDS

HIGHGATE

STANMORE
GRAVEL

Vale of
Health

Boudicca's
Mound

Highgate Brook

Highgate
Cemetery

Jack Straw's
Castle

Hampstead Brook

Parliament
Hill

HAMPSTEAD

KENTISH
TOWN

KILBURN

Watling Street

Regent's Canal

CAMDEN
TOWN

River Fleet

Regent's Park

St Pancras
Old Church

IV: DESCENT

Into the River of Wells

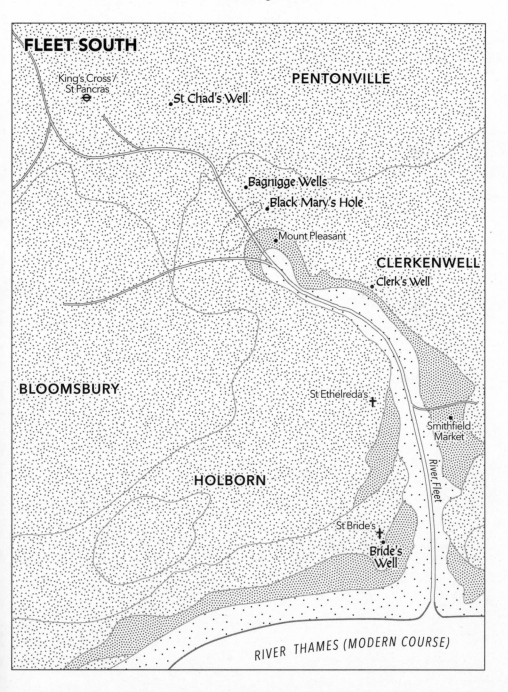

FLEET SOUTH

King's Cross /
St Pancras

PENTONVILLE

.St Chad's Well

.Bagnigge Wells
.Black Mary's Hole

.Mount Pleasant

CLERKENWELL

.Clerk's Well

BLOOMSBURY

St Ethelreda's †

Smithfield
Market

River Fleet

HOLBORN

St Bride's †
Bride's
Well

RIVER THAMES (MODERN COURSE)

Sewer

'The majority of the inhabitants of the cities and towns are frequently unconscious of the magnitude, intricacy, and extent of the underground works, which have been designed and constructed at great cost, and are necessary for the maintenance of their health and comfort.'

J. W. Bazalgette[1]

I AM DRESSED HEAD TO toe in protective clothing: white hooded boiler suit, thick rubber gloves, long black waders with integrated steel-capped boots and a hard hat. My chest is bound in a DayGlo harness. A portable gas monitor hangs by my side. I step forward and someone clips my harness to a safety line. The line is secured to a tripod standing directly above the hole. I look down, see the ladder, take the first step and then the next . . .

I'm the first civilian into the hole. We're here at the invitation of Tideway, the company behind the so-called 'super sewer'. With planning permission for the £3.8-billion project hanging in the balance, Tideway are on a PR offensive and we – two journalists, a historian and a poet – have been recruited for the defence.

At the bottom of the ladder, a sewer man unclips me and the line goes up again. The light from his head torch bounces off the brick walls of the tunnel. A wooden sign – black paint on white.

→ FLEET MAIN LINE ←

This labour past, by Bridewell all descend
(As morning prayer and flagellation end)
To where Fleet Ditch, with disemboguing streams,
Rolls the large tribute of dead dogs to Thames;
The king of dykes! than whom no sluice of mud
With deeper sable blots the silver flood.[2]

The walls are sweating. My boots crunch a red-brown gravelly silt. Rags.

The Fleet: the river of wells.

> Thames Water Utilities, *Confined Spaces Resources Manual* (Section B):
> Permission to Visit a Sewer or Other Confined Space:
> 1. Sewers and many other confined spaces contain atmospheres, which may be unpleasant.
> 2. Entry may be via deep shafts involving long runs of ladders or steps. Lighting may be poor and in some cases, such as sewers, the route may change direction and shape, and conditions may become restricted – all requiring agility and fitness.
> 3. Confined spaces have been known to induce claustrophobic fears or distress in inexperienced persons.[3]

'If you look down there, that's the flow going through the Low Level 1. That's a two-and-a-half-metre diameter sewer and today we're just coming up to one of our peak flows,' says Rob Smith, grandfather, native of Essex, former oyster dredgerman and Thames Water's chief sewer technician or 'flusher'.

Let me tell you about the smell. One part urinal to two parts wine cellar. A warm and fetid perfume that prompts a memory from nowhere: I am eighteen, hauling crates of lager in the mouldy basement of Threshers off-licence, an eerie cell that seems to have been sunk directly into the clay ridge of the hill I grew up on.

> The objects sought to be attained in the execution of the Main Drainage works were the interception of the sewage (as far as practicable by gravitation), together with so much of the rainfall mixed with it as could be reasonably dealt with, so as to divert it from the river near

London; the substitution of a constant, instead of an intermittent flow in the sewers; the abolition of stagnant and tide-locked sewers, with their consequent accumulation of deposit; and the provision of deep and improved outfalls, for the extension of sewerage into districts previously, for want of such outfalls, imperfectly drained.[4]

I enter a small chamber housing an elaborate mechanism called a penstock. With its huge metal gears, it resembles the inner workings of a giant clock. Everything glistens with a thin brown film of sewage. It looks like it's not been used in decades. The penstock controls the flow of water from the Fleet sewer into the Low Level 1 interceptor by means of a sluice gate balanced by a 10-tonne counterweight. 'This one would normally be operated by hydraulic power,' says Rob. 'We bring a power pack down and couple it up to the winder and drive it down.'

'Where's the river from here?'

In December 2012 Thames Water released a parody of viral hit 'Gangnam Style' on YouTube. 'Sewerman Style' starred Rob Smith and his team of flushers and was intended to educate the public about the dangers of pouring the fat from their Christmas turkey down the drain.

A question about the penstock comes. 'How many men does it take to close the gate by hand?'

A sewer man answers. 'The weight is minimal, it's so easy, not being rude, but a woman could wind this down, that's how easy this one moves, one hand like that, it just winds, nice and easy, nice and easy.'

'Mind your head.'

> A very large number of ancient animal remains, curiosities, and coins
> were found in different portions of the work; many of these were sold
> by the workmen and were not given up to the Board. Most of them
> may be seen at the British Museum. They consist chiefly of the bones
> of elephants, whales, and the horns of deer and oxen, with some flint
> implements of war and ancient human skulls, stone and leaden coffins,
> and a number of Roman coins of various reigns.[5]

Another ladder. I close my mouth as I descend. My gloves are smeared
with sewage.

Darkness.
'Can we have another light down here please, mate?'
The message echoes through the tunnels, from sewer man to sewer
man.

Darkness.
A lamp is passed down.

The Fleet rushes towards us, ghostly pale in the lamplight, then
drops into a hole in the floor of the tunnel. White noise. The steady
bleep of a gas monitor. I remove my outer gloves, careful to avoid touch-
ing anything, and take out my audio recorder. The stream is flowing at
one and a half times walking pace. I want to take its music with me.
'So, if you flush the toilet in Paddington,' a posh voice speaks, 'your
production will arrive in Beckton about four or five hours later.'

'That's very good news,' says another, a newspaper columnist. 'I'll reflect on that.'

'It's cheaper than taking a taxi,' a sewer man says. 'And there's no traffic.'

Old English *flēotan* 'to float; drift; flow, run (as water)'

    from Proto-Germanic **fleutan*

        (source also of Old Frisian *fliata*, Old Saxon *fliotan* 'to flow', Old High German *fliozzan* 'to float, flow', German *fliessen* 'to flow, run, trickle (as water)', Old Norse *fliota* 'to float, flow') from Proto-Indo-European root **pleu-* 'to flow'.

A steel-mesh walkway carries us over the sewer into the cavernous out-fall chamber. It is filled with dark water. Rob's lamp reveals an arched ceiling in handsome Victorian brickwork. The walls are covered in grey scum. A band of tiny white particles I later discover are fragments of polystyrene indicates the level of the high tide.

'This water here you can see – when we came down this morning, the tide was just up at the top of that brickwork up there. It's gradually dropping down. We've got this set of flaps behind us here and out by the river wall you've got another set of flaps. They're one hundred and fifty years old and they let a certain amount of flow through.'

I grip the handrail separating us from the water. Rob's light makes spectral shapes on the surface. Faint forms are hanging from a chain under the archway. Rags, a mooring ring. We pose for a photograph – four civvies and two sewer men.

'Hear that?'

A deep note, then static rush.

'That's a boat just gone past up the river. The wash from the boat is hitting the flaps, and the flaps are rocking backwards and forwards, and we'll see that water, it won't come up here, it'll just go up and down a couple of inches.'

The whole room seems to be moving.

The salt hit of the river.

The hot air in my lungs.

Minutes later, I am squinting in the glare of the city. The manhole cover is being levered back into place. Across the busy road junction, office workers are filtering out of the Tube station. A lone drinker outside the Black Friar – an elderly man in a brown leather bomber jacket – appears, just for a moment, to raise his pint and nod.

Rats. Crabs. Eels. Wet wipes. Condoms. Tampons.

Human bones. Guns. A live hand grenade.

Black swine running wild in the slimy feculence.[6]

When I get back home, I strip down and put all my clothes straight in the washing machine, then run a very hot shower. I won't feel clean for days.

Years later, I visit the Museum of London to see a piece of the Whitechapel Fatberg, a 130-tonne slab of congealed oil, fat and human waste discovered under Whitechapel Road. Set concrete-hard, it took a team of eight sewer men nine weeks to remove the fatberg using high-pressure water jets and then shovels.

The exhibition is heaving with Londoners and tourists alike. Despite its toxic threat to our health, human waste retains a curious, magnetic quality. The fatberg might be moon rock or kryptonite. One commentator compared it to an 'old, complex cheese' and also noted its similarity to ambergris, 'the sundried and sea-seasoned sperm-whale bile coveted by perfumers'.[7] The only perfumer *I* know, Sarah McCartney, once told me that many popular scents contain an organic compound, called *skatole*, that occurs naturally in human faeces.

A small girl in a pink raincoat with nut-brown ringlets presses her face to the glass. Like the plug of clay I dug out from the Ambrook, the fatberg is breathing fine mist on the walls of its double-skinned vitrine, an ancient thing pulled from the deep earth whose cut face reveals a stratigraphy of wipes and nappies, pubic hair and the fossilized remains of cotton buds.

My descent into the Fleet sewer was a malodorous but necessary undertaking. To understand London's lost rivers, I had to experience first-hand a small section of the subterranean world through which so many of them now flow. Once you have been down into this shadow place – been down and then returned – the city never seems the same again.

But the Fleet is also the river of wells, once renowned for its healing waters. I want to find this *other* Fleet, to track its course upstream from sewer to source. I have the perfect place in mind from which to start. Tucked away on an unremarkable side street above the Fleet valley stands one of London's true hidden treasures: the ancient chapel of St Etheldreda's, Ely Place.

Holy Water

'For now we see through a glass, darkly'

1 Corinthians 13:12 (King James Bible)

FATHER TOM DEIDUN MOVES slowly down the central aisle. With a deft flick of an aspergillum, he shakes a spray of water to his left, and another, and another, then turns at the choir screen and repeats. As he passes each aisle, congregants make the sign of the cross: right hand to forehead, chest, left shoulder, right. The choir sings the plainchant antiphon, *Asperges me*. 'Thou wilt sprinkle me, O Lord, with hyssop and I shall be cleansed. Thou wilt wash me, and I shall be washed whiter than snow. Pity me, O God, according to Thy great mercy.' Effigies of the English martyrs in painted polystyrene stare down solemnly from the walls: Swithun Wells (hanged, Gray's Inn, 1591); Margaret Ward, the 'pearl of Tyburn' (hanged, 1588); John Forest, Franciscan (burned at the stake, Smithfield, 1538).

St Etheldreda's is reputedly the oldest Roman Catholic church in Britain, constructed in the thirteenth century as the chapel of the Bishop of Ely's Palace (his official residence in London). The church is the last remnant of a complex of buildings that was once grand enough to host royalty. In 1381, the Duke of Lancaster, John of Gaunt, rented the palace after his own, the Savoy on the Strand, was destroyed during the Peasant's Revolt. In 1531, Henry VIII and Catherine of Aragon attended a lavish, five-day feast in the crypt (although they dined in separate rooms). In 1620 St Etheldreda's was given to the Ambassador of Spain, Gondomar, ostensibly for his personal use only, the old faith being forbidden in post-Reformation England. Recusant Catholics flocked to hear Mass at the Ambassador's chapel in what was effectively a protected enclave. The area later became one of the 'liberties' of London and was considered outside of the city's jurisdiction.

St Etheldreda's today retains something of that privilege; you will find it halfway along a private road, Ely Place, whose iron gates are supervised by a beadle (though he no longer wears a top hat, as far as I can tell). Until very recently, the local boozer, the Mitre, was subject to Cambridgeshire's licensing laws – a curious anomaly of geography owing to the connection to the Bishop of Ely.

Early drawings show the church surrounded by undulating meadows leading down to the river Fleet, whose fertile banks were once fringed with vineyards and orchards. Their produce lingers on in modern street names: Plumtree and Pear Tree Courts, Saffron Hill, Herbal Hill, Lily Place and Vine Street Bridge. The garden of the palace itself was famed for its strawberries and is mentioned in Shakespeare's *Richard III*, when the Duke of Gloucester says to the Bishop of Ely:

> *When I was last in Holborn,*
> *I saw good strawberries in your garden there;*
> *I do beseech you, send for some of them.*[8]

I hear the distant siren of an ambulance racing across Holborn Circus towards the Victorian viaduct spanning Farringdon Road, where the Fleet sewer now flows beneath the ground. Father Tom returns to the sanctuary and hands the aspergillum to a server, a middle-aged man with the walrus moustache of a 1970s police detective. '*Gloria Patri et Filio et Spiritui Sancto*,' he intones. To the right of the altar stands a statue of Etheldreda herself, the Anglo-Saxon saint who was born Æthelthryth to East Anglian royalty and founded a monastery on the fenland island of Ely in AD 673. A jewelled casket set into a niche in the stone wall is designed to contain a relic – fragments of her uncorrupted hand – although it is now kept under lock and key in the sacristy.

It is Sunday, 11 a.m., and I am here in my usual spot: towards the back, on the left-hand side. The familiar faces of the congregation are supplemented today by a group of Catholic students from the US. I can tell that because the boys are wearing matching chinos. The interior of the small church is dominated by J. E. Nuttgens's dazzling east window, one of London's largest examples of stained glass, showing Christ the King surrounded by the Evangelists. The sprinkling of holy water is part of today's *Asperges* rite and was recommended by Thomas Aquinas – the watery-named Doctor of the Church – for the remittance of venial sins and the inclining of the will towards charity.[9] It is one of numerous ways in which water is deployed for its transformative power in Catholic ritual, from the dipping of fingers in a font or bowl at the church entrance to the beautiful ceremony of the Washing of Feet on Maundy Thursday. In these moments of contact, the Catholic remembers their own baptism, that fundamental symbol of purification and rebirth.

I arrange to meet Father Tom in the rectory after Mass. 'When I pour water on a baby's head,' he tells me, 'I think of their wonderful future, their wonderful salvation, and the line, *Let the wilderness rejoice!*' He reminds me that the world of the Old Testament was 'framed by the wilderness'. In a desert landscape characterized by thirst and barrenness, water was the ultimate salve.

St Etheldreda's is located in a liminal zone, close to the intersection of three metropolitan boroughs and just outside the City of London. It is, as Father Tom puts it, 'an amorphous situation'. The parish has few residents, being located within a business district, so the congregation at Sunday's sung Latin Mass is a strange mix. People often travel far due to a longstanding connection or an affinity with the liturgy. In my case, it is both. My mother's funeral and my marriage were both conducted here, under the unblinking gaze of the English martyrs, a stone's throw from the Fleet.

After my meeting with Father Tom, I climb down worn steps to the crypt of the church – the second descent underground on my journey up the Fleet. It is cool and dark. A simple stone altar stands at one end before a fresco of the Risen Christ. Another proclaims the first line of the Gospel of John: *In the beginning was the word.* A warm glow emanates from niches set into the thick walls, in which appear the elongated figures of the Madonna and Child, the Sacred Heart, and St Joseph with the boy Jesus.

The foundations of the crypt are said to date from the sixth century and may contain fragments of Roman masonry, suggesting the presence of an even older structure on the site.[10] A crude limestone font discovered buried in the centre of the crypt indicates some form of very early Christian worship here.[11] It is still in use at the entrance of the chapel as a container for holy water. Today the crypt has been set up as a venue for private dining – all white linen tablecloths and upholstered chairs. As I crouch to examine the stonework, a prospective hirer enters with an events manager from the restaurant next door, the Bleeding Heart. She looks around, then asks wryly, 'I suppose I can't put anything up on the walls?'

I let my hands trace the rough surface, a rubble masonry composed of undressed Kentish ragstone; nodules of smooth black flint; seams of reddish material that may be brick or sintered clay; and chunks of white chalk that turn to powder on my fingers. Could St Etheldreda's have been the site of a Romano-British church? A pagan temple? Or some other, indeterminate structure outside the walls of Londinium? St Etheldreda's does not give up its mysteries easily. Like the slab of fatberg in its display case, the walls of the crypt seem to evoke deep time, as if their contents are not the result of human endeavour but geological strata laid down over millions of years.

I have heard a rumour of a sealed-off tunnel leading from the crypt to the pub, but I can find no evidence to back it up. 'As far as I know,' said Father Tom, dryly, 'my congregation reaches the Mitre overland.' A stapled pamphlet on sale for 50p in the cloister mentions 'evidence of a well'.[12] Again, Father Tom denied any knowledge, although he added, with characteristic self-deprecation, 'I would walk past the most stupendous Roman temple and not notice it because I was thinking about Sunday's sermon.'

As I head to the bus stop on Farringdon Road, I cannot help but see

St Etheldreda's as part of a sacred landscape, standing there on a bluff of gravel above the valley of the Fleet. A vision is beginning to form in my mind: the river as a deep cleft in the tarmac fed by a stream of holy water falling down Charterhouse Street from the chapel. The water sparkles in the sunlight with pearls and gemstones loosed from the diamond vaults of Hatton Garden. But from the east cascades another torrent, of filthy blood and animal waste slopping out of the butcheries of Smithfield, the two streams intermingling, sacred and profane, life-giving and diseased, blood and holy water.

Ditch, sewer, river of wells – the Fleet has a split personality and many names. Passing the City, it's the *Hol-born*, the stream in the hollow; in Farringdon, the Turnmill Brook. Upstream, at Kentish Town, it divides and is called, respectively, the Hampstead and Highgate Brooks. The mouth of the Fleet was once 100 metres wide, a tidal inlet utilized by the Romans as a harbour and for powering water mills. A painting in the style of the Venetian artist Canaletto shows the entrance to the river from the Thames *c.* 1750 as a grand waterway flanked by town-houses and crossed by an elegant stone footbridge.[13] But no one is fooled; the Fleet was already being used as an open sewer, filled with 'Sweepings from butchers' stalls, dung, guts and blood' according to Jonathan Swift.[14] Its covering-over began as early as 1732. By the nineteenth century, slum housing crowded its banks. The sluggish, choleric stream was overhung by haphazard wooden props and fed by human and industrial effluent, which then spewed out into the Thames.

Londoners had had enough. In the long, hot summer of 1858, a foul miasma descended on the city. Raw sewage clung to the foreshore, six feet deep in places. The newspapers declared a 'Great Stink'. At Westminster, the curtains of the Houses of Parliament were soaked in lime chloride to disguise the stench. Dickens described the Thames as 'horrible', adding, 'I can certify that the offensive smells, even in that short whiff, have been of a most head-and-stomach-distending nature.'[15] Joseph Bazalgette's ambitious plans for an integrated network of sewers could not have come too soon. Work began on the interceptor tunnels in 1859 and was completed by 1865. The Fleet was entombed in Portland cement, along with most of London's smaller streams, its flow diverted downstream to Beckton, where it was held in balancing tanks before being dumped into the estuarine Thames at high tide.

It's a muggy July day when I return to the Fleet, a little downstream from St Etheldreda's. It's not quite the 48°C reported in 1858, but warm enough that when I take off my rucksack to consult the map or take a swig of water, my shirt is wet through and clings to my back. I am standing outside a Wren church – St Bride's on Fleet Street. I'm going underground again, but I won't be needing waders this time. I'm here to test my theory: that, long before Bazalgette's sewer, the valley of the Fleet, with its healing springs and holy wells, once constituted a sacred landscape.

In the medieval period, the banks of the Fleet hosted important religious institutions: at its mouth, the Dominican priory of the Blackfriars and the Carmelite friary of the Whitefriars, and in Clerkenwell, the headquarters of the Knights Hospitaller and the Benedictine nunnery of St Mary. Further north, the river flowed past St Pancras Old Church, which, like St Etheldreda's, claims pre-Conquest origins (a tradition tracing the site to a Roman temple is tenuous but possible). A short walk either side of the Fleet would have taken you to the round church of the Knights Templar, the Carthusian priory at Charterhouse or the Augustinian priory of St Bartholomew (now Barts, Britain's oldest hospital).

According to the sixteenth-century chronicler John Stow, the Fleet had been known as 'the river of wells' since the time of William the Conqueror.[16] Stow mentioned several by name: 'Clarkes well . . . Skinners well, Fags well, Tode well, Loders well, and Radwell.' Many more have now been identified, including Sadler's Well and St Chad's Well. Some, such as Bagnigge Wells, produced chalybeate (iron-rich) water and were developed into fashionable spas, the 'destination resorts' of their day. Others were attached to Christian sites and ascribed holy properties.

The interior of St Bride's is bright and Baroque, with a white, barrel-vaulted ceiling, polished wooden choir stalls and gold flourishes. It's a world away from the Gothic mystery of St Etheldreda's, but there is an interesting connection between the two. The image of the Irish saint Bridget or Brigid of Kildare, *Bride* being the anglicized form of the same name, appears in the east window of St Etheldreda's.[17] I am hoping to find some trace here of Brigid's Well, or *Bridewell* as it was known. In the sixteenth century Henry VIII built a palace immediately to the south of St Bride's and it became known as Bridewell. The palace later became an orphanage, then a correctional facility for women and finally a prison. Today, the site is home to the St Bride Foundation, a charitable institute comprising a library, print workshops and a studio theatre.

I have heard that the well is located in the south-east corner of the church. A staircase by the gift shop leads down to the crypt, where I follow a narrow passageway lined with gravestones. A low rubble wall claims to be part of a Roman ditch, some jumbled stone remains of Saxon foundations. At the end is a reward: a tiny fourteenth-century chapel that has recently been restored as a memorial to journalists killed in the world wars. Retracing my steps, I find my way into a larger chamber, which functions as both museum and another chapel. Masonry structures of various ages can be seen behind the vitrines and display boards. There have been seven churches on this site, I learn, the earliest dating to the sixth century, making it very early Saxon. As well as the ditch, archaeologists have uncovered a mosaic pavement, stone foundations and a red-tiled wall, indicating the presence of a Roman villa.[18] Bride/Brigid has been identified with the Celtic goddess Brigantia, with at least one historian speculating that the Christian church was built on the site of a 'Romano-Celtic temple or shrine'.[19] A map shows the outline of the small Saxon church and marks the position of the well near by; it was incorporated into the building itself in the thirteenth or fourteenth centuries, but is currently inaccessible. The only trace I can find is the cast-iron spout of a pump. Once set in the retaining wall of the church on Bride Lane, it now lies inactive in a glass display case.

Back upstairs, a pukka gent in an expensive suit is hovering around the gift shop. I guess correctly that he's a verger and take the opportunity to quiz him. 'I'm afraid there is nothing to see,' he explains. 'The well dried up in the nineteenth century and if there was anything left after that, it was obliterated by a German bomb.' Sensing my disappointment, he offers to show me the spot from outside. 'During royal processions through the city, holy water from the well would be sprinkled on the monarch as they approached St Bride's.' He gestures towards the back of the churchyard, by a pile of black bin bags. A colossal plane tree has burst through the ground, its sinuous branches uncoiling above Bride Lane like the tentacles of the kraken.

A report from July 1821 describes the last public use of Bride's Well. An unexplained 'sudden demand' led to 'several men ... filling thousands of bottles'. Happily, sufficient 'sainted fluid' was drawn from the pump to be used at the coronation of George IV a few days later.[20] In 1915, a surveyor, Mr Sunderland, claimed to have tasted the water, commenting, 'the spring had a sweet flavour'.[21] Curiously, the neighbouring Bridewell Theatre was built over a Victorian swimming pool, now disused. Its white, tiled basin can still be seen underneath the floorboards and is occasionally uncovered for art installations and site-specific performances. Complaints about the quality of the pool have been dredged from St Bride Foundation's archives and describe the water variously as 'foul', 'pale green' and 'slimy'. One swimmer noted, 'Every visit brought another verruca!!'[22]

Before I leave, I buy a small gift from the shop: a set of silver earrings for Sarah in the shape of Brigid's cross, a square cross traditionally woven from rushes that bears a passing resemblance to the Hindu swastika. In the Roman tradition, Brigantia is a goddess of victory, but in Ireland Brigid or Bríg is associated with fertility, healing and poetry. In some depictions she is shown milking a cow. The saint's feast day on 1 February corresponds to the pagan festival of Imbolc – the beginning of spring.

I am thinking, too, of my mother. Before she died, she traced our family, the McGanns, back to Tullamore, the county town of Offaly, just seven miles from the ruins of St Brigid's abbey at Kilbride, Clara. Above the portrait of Brigid in the east window of St Etheldreda's is a smaller image depicting the construction of this *cill* (church) at Clara.

Saxon, Roman, Celt . . .

Brigantia, Brigid, Bride . . .

The well has begun to feel like a riddle, an intricate pattern of interweaving stories and urban myths designed to suck me in or push me off course. I need to reconnect with the Fleet itself, to climb upstream, against the current, to Clerkenwell and beyond.

Drift

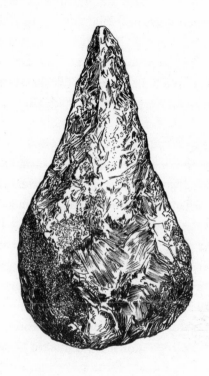

FOLLOWING ANY 'LOST' RIVER is a fool's errand. In a city as busy as London, it's a risky venture. Be prepared to invite the queries of tourists, the suspicious gazes of locals and the casual mockery of workmen. No entry. Private property. Do not loiter. 'Have you lost something?' asks a woman who sees me crouching over a manhole outside the Coach on Ray Street. Be aware of oncoming traffic when inspecting drains or lining up a photograph. Keep your belongings close. Take a compass. Stay hydrated.

I am clutching Tom Bolton's *London's Lost Rivers: A Walker's Guide*.[23] I consult it frequently for interesting titbits of history but try to avoid looking at the maps. I would rather let the city itself be my guide, looking for clues in the landscape, always seeking the lowest point of the valley. Sometimes the road itself replicates the sharp turns and sudden drops of the hidden stream. Often, an alignment of manholes signals the correct way forward, like a trail of breadcrumbs embedded in the tarmac. In several places, the Fleet can be heard rushing six feet under and even glimpsed, like a flickering screen, in the darkness of the sewer.*

The first well on Stow's list is the only one on mine that is still accessible, albeit by private appointment via Islington Local History Centre. The Clerk's Well can be found behind the window of a smart, redbrick building facing out across Farringdon Road. I must have passed it a hundred times or more, stumbling back drunk to the Tube from raucous poetry nights at the Betsey Trotwood. I bluff my way inside and end up in the reception of 'award-winning creative agency' Intermarketing. 'I've never actually seen it myself,' says the affable woman who meets me on the stairs. Even inside the building, the well is blocked from view by a glass partition; the bottom half is frosted so you have to crane your

---

* Ray Street, Warner Street/Eyre Street Hill, Leeke Street, St Pancras Way, etc.

neck to see it. Sunk about a metre below street level, the Clerk's Well is set in an ovoid stone surround and sealed with a pair of wooden shutters that gives it the appearance of a theatrical trapdoor. Today the shutters are open and I am surprised to see that the well is filled with a turquoise-green water that reminds me of mouthwash. A layer of scum sits on the surface. 'We should organize a company trip,' she adds.

The trapdoor is a fitting image. In the Middle Ages, plays based on Bible stories, called 'Mysteries', were performed here by local clerics on the feast of Corpus Christi. In York, where an entire cycle of Mystery plays survives, the Devil was seen emerging from (or falling into) a trap-door in the stage. Perhaps the parish clerks of London used this well in a similar way, the deep shaft sunk into the banks of the Fleet becoming, for the duration of the performance, a portal into the underworld.

Clerkenwell is full of subterranean spaces. I have visited the ancient crypt of St John's, the Hospitaller church, and glimpsed the derelict plat-forms of Snow Hill station from the train between Farringdon and City Thameslink. The cavernous cold store underneath Smithfield Market, where secret experiments were conducted during the Second World War under the codename Project Habakkuk, I have yet to explore; so too the vaults of the former Clerkenwell House of Detention, which are known as the 'Clerkenwell Catacombs' and reputed to be haunted by the ghost of a little girl.

The well is marked on the Agas map of 1561 as 'Clarken Well'. The map shows a stream of water flowing into a cistern from the south-west wall of the Priory of St Mary. The Priory is the last building on the map, at the northern limit of the medieval city. Fields and rolling meadows stretch out to the horizon, where the hills of Hampstead can be seen in the far distance. The Fleet stream weaves its course beneath Holburne Bridge, Chick Lane, Clerkenwell Road, then it too melts away, at Hockley-in-the-Hole. I have my path to follow. I cross back to Farringdon Road, above the deep railway cutting from the station. Its scale is immense: industrial terraforming at its most ambitious. Here, roadway, railway and sewer are bound together like the fibres of a rope, an optical cable carrying light through the gloom of Victorian London.

The city is all frenetic surface, doing its best to conceal its true form beneath car parks and postal depots, behind temporary hoardings and abandoned corner shops. West of Farringdon Road I find my way through the damp lowlands of Hockley-in-the-Hole, once notorious for blood sports such as bear-baiting and dog-fighting, before getting lost in the alleyways and hidden yards around Coldbath Square. A medicinal spring was discovered in fields here in 1697. Its waters were harnessed for a public bath by a Mr Baynes, who marketed the venture as 'the Cockney Pool of Bethesda', claiming that a dip in its icy water would cure a cold and improve digestion.[24] The eighteenth-century Swedish mystic Emanuel Swedenborg lodged in Coldbath Square and at the Red Lion on Warner Street and is reported to have performed what Iain Sinclair called a 'baptism': 'rolling naked in the deep mud (and worse) of "a place called the Gully-hole".'[25]

Coldbath Fields later became the site of an infamous prison, originally founded in the reign of James I, and is now dominated by the unforgiving ziggurat of Mount Pleasant Mail Centre, one of the largest sorting offices in the world. The tarmac-covered depression in the middle of the site is still referred to as 'the bathtub' and is used for vehicle parking, equipment storage and the loading and unloading of mail. The name Mount Pleasant seems to have been ironic, given its reputation as a dumping ground for cinders and other refuse. The area retains something of that malodorous character, despite its proximity to fashionable Clerkenwell.

I climb the clay bluffs of the Fleet valley and on to a plateau of Hackney Gravel. Pockets of wasteland appear at the edges of my vision. Then, at the crest of Mount Pleasant, I notice an obvious slump in the roadway. I check my map. I'm bang on the Fleet. There's even a giant blue arrow pointing upstream. Across the street, the doors of a converted Victorian schoolhouse suddenly swing open to reveal a hive of young designers glued to flatscreens. The arrow is actually a road sign and it's directing traffic around a deep trench. I wait for a gap, then look in: a broken tarmac skin; stone and rubble; then sandy clay, terracotta-red; a tangle of plastic cables; and, at the bottom, a pool of soapy, grey bathwater.

Opposite the Union Tavern on King's Cross Road, three street drinkers are sitting in a sunken, rubbish-strewn yard. In the middle of the yard, three plane trees have erupted through the concrete. A knackered bicycle leans against one of the trees. The redbrick Crowne Plaza hotel rises from the corner plot opposite a mini-mart, hair salon, laundrette, etc. The housing is a familiar mix of Victorian terraces, 1930s council blocks and low-rise maisonettes. On the surface there is nothing especially unusual about this place; it could be almost anywhere in suburban inner London. But there is mystery here, in the no man's land between Clerkenwell, Pentonville and St Pancras. The contemporary chronicler John Rogers described the area as a 'dark pit [that] keeps drawing me in, night and day'.[26] I hear a voice from the shadows. It says, 'Come, let us go to Black Mary's Hole.'[27]

Black Mary's Hole. The name erupts like a hex.

Black Mary's Hole or Well: 'a solitary hovel'[28] surrounded by pools of standing water, one feeding a conduit. It is marked on Rocque's map of 1746 as a hamlet of ten houses strung along the Fleet.

Black Mary's: known cruising spot. A mineral spa on the edge of the map. 'The first place where a Londoner, crazed by crowding and choked from coal-smoke, could break out into the open.'[29]

Bolton tracked the exact site of the well to a small garden in front of Margery Street Estate.[30] The hole itself has long vanished. By 1815 it was being used as a cesspool for the new houses. A workman in a bright orange vest sneers as I line up a photograph of Spring House, then another of Bagnigge House.

Everyone wants a piece of Mary; it's a site without a definitive history, only competing origin myths. *The Gentleman's Magazine* traced its genesis to 'one Mary, who kept a black cow, whose milk the gentlemen and ladies drank with the waters of the conduit', but also suggested that it could have been a deliberate corruption of a pre-Reformation name, Blessed Mary's Well, 'the name of the Holy Virgin having . . . fallen into disrepute'. [31] One journal ascribed its origin to a well attendant, Mary Woolaston, another to a 'Blackmoor woman' who lived in a circular stone hut around 1730.[32] An association with the black-veiled nuns of St Mary's Priory has also been proposed.[33]

Could the hole, or well, be connected to the tradition of the Black Madonna, dark-skinned icons or figures that are revered throughout Catholic Europe? They are often found in caves or dug out of the ground. In some cases, their veneration may have replaced the worship of an earlier, pre-Christian goddess. I have seen such a figure in the monastery of Lluc on the Balearic island of Mallorca – an ornate, burnished statue of the Blessed Virgin Mary. Our Lady of Lluc was reputedly discovered half-buried by a young Moorish shepherd in the thirteenth century; she now sits above the high altar on a turntable, so she can be revealed to the congregation by the pushing of a button – like a bowl of steamed rice on a lazy Susan.

No such figure has been discovered on the waterlogged banks of the Fleet, but something just as curious was unearthed here on 11 December 1673 by John Conyers, apothecary of Shoe Lane.

> A British weapon, found with elephant's tooth, opposite to black Mary's near Grayes inn lane. It is a large black flint, shaped into the figure of a spear's point.[34]

Conyers misdated the weapon to the time of the Roman conquest. It is much older. In fact, it is the earliest recorded discovery of any prehistoric tool anywhere in the world. Writing of the find as late as 1886, Brother Fabian gushed, 'science cannot point to one single monument of the existence of man on our planet which is known to be older than this worked flint found opposite Black Mary's'.[35] Conyers also discovered the skeleton of an elephant or mammoth near by. The two finds were first exhibited in a pub in Newington, south of the Thames, and according to one obscure report, this is how the Elephant and Castle got its name.[36]

Conyers's flint weapon has since been identified as a late Acheulian hand-axe[37] and the site of the Travelodge on King's Cross Road proposed as a prehistoric 'kill site', where humans hunted and butchered animals.[38] The weapon is on display on the ground floor of the British Museum. It is beautiful, complex; amber-gold to smoke-black, the irregular angles of its worked face catching the light like polished glass. It is not of earth, I think, but fire – a sun-crystal. In a novel of 1840, Black Mary is imagined as a witch, an 'ancient sibyl' who lives in a cottage at the bottom of a disused clay pit.[39] More recently, a medium brought to Black Mary's Hole sensed that it was a sacrificial pit to a female deity.[40]

I follow the road to the 'kill site', tracing the boundary between the boroughs of Islington and Camden. It is a particularly grim-looking Travelodge, a dark-brick battlement clad in concrete armour; it's not hard to imagine prehistoric Londoners clubbing reindeer and woolly mammoth to death here. A trio of football lads are smoking outside reception; its proximity to King's Cross and Euston stations makes it a convenient overnight stop for travelling supporters. Reviews are mixed. 'Breakfast was so-so,' says one. 'Blood on the floor and unsecure rooms,' another. 'Bacon overcooked and the buffet lacking in variety.'[41] The hotel conceals a dramatic flight of stairs, memorialized as Riceyman Steps in Arnold Bennett's novel of the same name.[42] The steps rise from the valley floor to an elegant, tree-lined square. This terrace above the Fleet was once dominated by a church, St Philip's, described by Bennett as an 'ignoble temple [out of which] came persistent, monotonous, loud sounds, fantastic and nerve-racking'. A 63 bus pulls up opposite the hotel, brakes hissing. It has followed me here, along the Fleet, all the way from Blackfriars Bridge. I look back from the top of the steps and notice, tucked behind the

Travelodge, a fenced-off concrete yard containing a single blue reception chair. The cracked floor is sprouting buddleia and knotweed, which I cannot help but see as signs of hidden water – a river flowing underground.

As the 63 moves off, I spot something behind the bus shelter and cross the road to inspect. For a moment, there is no traffic. The football lads have gone back inside. Silence in the city. There is a stone face set into the terraced house, a goggle-eyed Green Man with a grassy beard and demonic smirk. THIS IS BAGNIGGE HOUSE, reads the plaque below. *Bagnigge*: another name that sounds like it's been dredged from the primordial soup; a name that is missing from any dictionary of toponymy. The Fleet was called the Bagnigge River here, its sodden floodplain Bagnigge Marsh or Wash. More springs were tapped and by the late eighteenth century the western side of the road had become known as Bagnigge Wells. The fashionable flocked from the city to try the purgative waters and enjoy a stroll in the formal gardens. There was a 'domed and columned pump house . . . clipped-hedge lined walkways, leaden statues, fish ponds, fountains [and a] castellated grotto'.[43] A satirical poem of 1760 by one Grub Street hack presents Bagnigge Wells in splendid Technicolor, as this passage demonstrates:

> Here ambulates th'Attorney looking grave
> And Rake from Bacchanalian rout uprose,
> And mad festivity. Here, too, the Cit
> With belly turtle-stuff'd, and Man of Gout
> With leg of size enormous. Hobbling on,
> The Pump-room he salutes, and in the chair
> He squats himself unwieldy. Much he drinks,
> And much he laughs to see the females quaff
> The friendly beverage.[44]

At Bagnigge Wells, the Fleet was not yet sewerized but flowed through a bucolic landscape crossed by ornamental footbridges. A novelty waterwheel was installed, powering a barrel organ by way of 'connecting rods driven by a crank, pumped air using bellows';[45] and so at last the Fleet might sing.

I'm curious about the name. I perform an internet deep dive and locate a peculiar theory. 'The ubiquitous Bagnigge,' muses Harold Bayley in *Archaic England*, 'was in all probability *Big Nigge* or Big Nicky.'[46] Bayley conjures us 'the fairy Nokke, Neck, or Nickel . . . said to have been a great musician who sat upon the water's edge and played a golden harp'. He connects the name to Old Nick, the alias of both St Nicholas and the Devil, and to *nicor*, the Old English word for water-monster. The word appears five times in *Beowulf*; Grendel's mere is described as *nicorhusa* ('water-demon's house'). In Sussex, there is a tradition of 'knuckerholes' – deep pools or caves where water-monsters dwelt. Could the Big Nicky or Nixie of Bagnigge represent the suppressed folk-memory of a female water sprite, perhaps the kind that was endowed with witch powers according to the Brothers Grimm?

Elephant bones. Water sprites. The Black Madonna. There is a deep magic at play here; an unease that is felt in the guts. 'Dissonance,' wrote Robert Macfarlane, 'is produced by any landscape that enchants in the present but has been a site of violence in the past.'[47] As I prepare to leave, I happen to pull the Streetfinder from my rucksack. The swirling patterns of London's geology feel suddenly reassuring in this landscape of urban myths. My index finger traces my journey from the mouth of the Fleet, along the alluvial deposits of its lower reaches, across the exposed clay at the edges of the valley and on to the gravel terraces of the Thames. Then I see it. A 300-metre-long teardrop bisected by Calthorpe Street, from Gray's Inn Road to Black Mary's Hole. Why had I not noticed it before, this glitch in the system? I coloured it in myself. I stumble for my phone, then look again. No, not a teardrop; more like a velociraptor's claw. I tap the screen and bring up the British Geological Survey's website. The glitch is completely surrounded by a sea of London Clay overlain by Hackney Gravel. It too, contains gravel, but instead of clay, the bedrock is identified as the Lambeth Group, the stratum usually found *beneath* the clay. The formation is unmistakable; I have stumbled across one of London's mysterious drift hollows.

A contact, geo-archaeologist Mary Ruddy, set up a Dropbox folder for me. I click and open a rich hoard of maps and technical articles, jpegs of core samples, dig sites. Mary suggested I read F. G. Berry's seminal article on 'Late Quaternary scour-hollows' first.[48] Berry identified twenty-six anomalous features hidden beneath the streets of central London. Discovered during engineering works for sewers, roads and Tube tunnels, these 'drift hollows' are cut deep into the clay and filled with loose deposits of gravel, silt or reworked clay. Some have 'cliff-like walls' and descend as far as 30 metres below the surface of the city. Most were found near stream junctions and may be related to buried channels. The hollows, wrote Berry, 'represent sediment traps ... the time-equivalents of erosion surfaces and sedimentary lacunae'.

The site is coming into focus.

Black Mary and Bagnigge Wells as *lacunae*:

gaps

in the text,

cavities or

empty   spaces.

The hollow below Calthorpe Street was revealed in 1915–16 during tunnelling works for the Post Office Railway, a narrow-gauge, driverless railway designed to carry mail between sorting offices. As the boring machine encountered 'disturbed' strata and water-saturated gravel, the tunnel began, without warning, to collapse. When it had been fully uncovered, the hollow was estimated to be over 300 metres in width, filled with gravel and lined with 'black deposit'. Later excavations, in 1969–71, revealed the presence of freshwater molluscs and ostracods (seed shrimp), fragments of moss and the seeds of aquatic plants. The discovery of two fossilized species of pea mussel, a bivalve extinct in Britain, sealed the deal; the hollow, argued Berry, was formed during the

Pleistocene, what used to be called the Ice Age, when the Thames valley was covered in thick permafrost and glaciers reached as far south as Finchley Road. The hollow is of such antiquity it makes the river Fleet look like an awkward teenager, uneasy in its shifting skin.

The precise cause of Berry's 'drift-filled hollows' is uncertain. Could they be scour holes, carved out by the furious waters of an earlier Thames? Or perhaps periglacial phenomena, formed by the freezing and melting of ice? Landslips have been discounted. So too the theory that they are portions of buried river channels (as Berry pointed out, they have 'no apparent outlet'). If the origins of these anomalies are unknown, their impact on subterranean engineering cannot be denied: 'If an advancing face encounters such a deposit, gravel and water may rush into the tunnel and create a major subsidence cavity at the surface.'[49] The Post Office Railway, whose construction was halted by the discovery of the hollow, closed in 2003 but has since reopened as a visitor attraction. 'Take a ride on Mail Rail and experience 15 minutes of immersive underground exploration,' promises the website. 'There's even a surprise or two. Are you ready?' I make a mental note to return another day. I'll invite my dad along for the ride. For who could resist such a journey into darkness?

Like a poem enriched by rereading, the magic of this landscape is not dispersed but deepened by the discovery of the hollow. It is clarifying in my mind into a major occult site, dwarfing the mythical energies of St Pancras Old Church or even nearby Pentonville, with its alignment to ley lines and spurious connection to Merlin. A picture is forming in my mind, a bird's eye view. The glaciers are retreating, withdrawing their white-gloved hands from the Thames valley like a snooker referee from the baize.

We zoom in: here, where the ground falls suddenly away and a swamp is forming, filled with rich, black mulch, reed beds, the toxic green of moss and algal bloom. Look: there are pools of standing water, like the ones on Rocque's map, and here, wild animals emerging from the shadows to drink – reindeer, bison, mammoth and sabre-toothed tiger. Man, too, arrives, with flint axe and empty belly. Blood spills. Fire and sun. The first words are spoken. Man offers back his weapon to the swamp, a simple ritual of thanks. Or perhaps it is lost, slipping from his hand as he gasps his final breath. Decades pass, then centuries, millennia, until another hand reaches into the earth and pulls out flinty treasure, smoke-black to amber-gold.

'Excuse me? Are you from here? We are looking for the Baptist church.' A family – mum, dad and two kids – wearing traditional West African dress are on their way to a wedding. I've been here too long. My words splutter out. I haven't spoken to a soul for hours. We're going the same way, following the Fleet upstream towards King's Cross.

Media agencies and coffee chains give way to warehouses and workers' caffs, then to hardware stores and printers, and finally to youth hostels and chicken shops, before the whole cycle begins again at the colossal glass temples to Google and YouTube. I track the river past King's Cross station, the city suddenly ablaze with crowds of tourists, then past St Pancras Old Church and St Pancras Hospital, darting down side roads, probing alleyways, listening at manholes for the gurgle of the sewer.

I can't get Black Mary's Hole out of my head. I feel like I've been enchanted by some strange energy. I'm probably dehydrated. I turn a corner. A bearded man in a stripy polo shirt is gliding through the air, his lower half obscured by a high wall. As I get closer I realize that the man is attached to a handsome red barge and the barge to the water of the Regent's Canal, which appears, through some optical illusion, to be floating above the roadway. The truth is, I need company. I make a phone call. The Fleet does not meet the canal, but instead dives beneath it; the two waterways flow one on top of the other in a manner that reminds me of the vertical burials in West Norwood Cemetery. Arrangements are made. I will return tomorrow, to complete the journey and find the source of the river high up on Hampstead Heath.

Heath

'The earth hath bubbles as the water has,
And these are of them. Whither are they vanished?'

SHAKESPEARE, *MACBETH*[50]

THE HEATH FORMS THE apex of the Hampstead Ridge, a belt of high land that stretches for almost 20 kilometres from the valley of the Brent in Ealing to the Lea at Tottenham. As south London has the Norwood Ridge, with the ruined Crystal Palace at its peak, so north London boasts its own extensive uplands, crowned by the beacons of Hampstead Heath (137m), Highgate (129m) and Parliament Hill (98m). The geology of the Hampstead Ridge echoes Norwood too. In both, the bedrock of London Clay is overlain by the younger, sandier clays of the Claygate Member. But here, the very highest points of the Heath are capped by outcrops of fine-grained sand from the Bagshot Formation.* These sands were formed around fifty million years ago in shallow water and today provide the perfect conditions for the heathland vegetation of gorse and broom.

It is at the joins between geological strata – where permeable sand meets impermeable clay – that springs naturally form. The Heath is full of them, feeding tiny streams that, in turn, supply four of London's rivers. But the Westbourne, Tyburn, Fleet and Brent are haunted by the trace memory of a fifth channel, mysterious and ancient. Smooth flint pebbles are unearthed from the yellow sands here, loosed long ago from the chalk of the Wessex Downs by the Great Bagshot River – a massive, prehistoric watercourse as vast as the Ganges that once flowed from Dartmoor, across Salisbury Plain and the London Basin, before disgorging into the North Sea.[51]

When I arrive at the Heath, a film crew is shooting the Netflix mini-series *Behind Her Eyes*. The footpaths are buzzing with production staff

---

* There are also two local deposits of Stanmore Gravel overlying the Bagshot Formation.

in hi-vis jackets, yammering instructions into walkie-talkies. A four-by-four rumbles past me in the direction of a clump of trees where the main crew has set up camp. It is mid-morning and the July sun is already beating down on the dry grassland of Parliament Hill. I break into a sweat as I climb. The view from the summit takes my breath away. Or it would do, if it were not instantly recognizable from so many other films and TV dramas. The land to the south falls away down a steep gully, revealing a wide panorama of London. I take a seat on the bench where Dame Judi Dench portrayed the infatuated history teacher Barbara in *Notes on a Scandal* (2006). The city shimmers in the distance – a blocky range of towers rising and falling like the graphic equalizer on a hi-fi. The Shard, the Gherkin and the pyramid-topped skyscraper at Canary Wharf are all easily identified alongside boxy new-builds and the spindly arms of innumerable cranes still working the horizon. A large storm cloud hangs in the middle distance, casting the southern slopes of the ridge in shadow. St Paul's is there too, if you squint; the view of the cathedral from Parliament Hill is protected by law. And behind it all, the hills of Norwood and the unmistakable antennae tower of the Crystal Palace transmitter.

The hi-vis theme is continued up here; a group of about fifty primary schoolchildren, all decked out in luminescent yellow vests, has colonized the summit. They are, variously, clutching miniature clipboards, inspecting wildflowers, balancing on fallen trees, dancing, pointing, running, screaming, doing handstands, wandering off, falling over and playing kiss chase. 'Woah, look over there,' one little boy shouts to his mates as he surveys the skyline. 'A playground!' I close my eyes and listen to the sound of a brass band practising, carried on the wind from a school at the base of the hill.

I have spent two hours carefully tracing the geology of the Heath on my Streetfinder. A weird amoeba emerges in north London. From this angle, it's a shrivelled prawn or a seahorse. Another way round and it's a deformed Bat-Signal thrown up against the city. Inspecting my handiwork, it's easy to see Parliament Hill as an *interfluve*, a narrow promontory of high ground between two river valleys – in this case, two tributaries of the river Fleet. With commanding views of the surrounding landscape, these promontories were considered sites of strategic importance and some even assigned ritual status. The Anglo-Saxon tribes who settled England from the fifth century named them *hoh/hoo* ('hill-spur', 'heel') or *ness/næss* ('headland', 'nose') and raised great burial mounds, such as those at Sutton Hoo in Suffolk, at their summits. Parliament Hill has one of those too, but it's set far back from the viewpoint, away from the marauding school-children and the film crew, away even from the Lycra-clad runners, in a meadow of long grass and thistle beds rustling in a gentle breeze.

I have arranged to meet my friend Nick at Boudicca's Mound, a fenced-off knoll that is reputed to mark the grave where the Iceni warrior-queen was laid to rest after her forces were defeated by the Romans in AD 60 or 61. As I approach, three large carrion crows are scuffling on the fenceline. I hear them before I see them, their corvid croaks low and insistent, giving this isolated spot an ominous atmos-phere. I feel like Macbeth coming across the Three Witches upon the heath. A protected historic monument dating to the Bronze Age, the site is encircled by a berm (platform) and ditch. The mound itself is over-grown with trees and tall grass, more like a dark grotto than a shining beacon. A drawing from 1725 by the antiquarian and Druid revivalist William Stukeley depicts a causeway across the ditch and identifies the mound as '*Immanuentii tumulus*' (Imanuentius being a king of the Trinovantes, allies of the Iceni during the Boudiccan revolt).[52] Later excavations in 1894 revealed a small hole filled with charcoal, but no body or grave goods. This hasn't stopped the myths from spreading. On the summer solstice of 1994, a crowd of white-robed figures assembled on Parliament Hill to inaugurate the Council of British Druid Orders. Proceedings commenced with the blowing of a herald's horn by Dylan Ap Thuin, self-styled Arch-Druid of Portsmouth. Healer and therapist David Furlong claims on his website that Boudicca's Mound is the apex of two triangles of ley lines connecting the major sacred sites of pre-historic London including Greenwich, Westminster and the Tower of London.[53]

Nick Murray approaches from the south, waving and smiling. He has a new angular haircut – shaved on one side, long on the other – that gives him the appearance of an electro-punk guitarist. The comparison is not unmerited. Nick is a multi-talented musician, writer and composer with a particular interest in obsolete technology. He opens his rucksack to reveal various bits of audio equipment, 'just in case we want to do some field recording'. Nick is, in all respects, the perfect walking partner. He's also a local boy, raised in Cricklewood, just beyond the western slopes of the Heath. 'My school friends lived in different parts of north London but everyone knew the Heath. We used to meet right here at the mound, drink cider and play Frisbee. I didn't know about Boudicca until much later.' A crow squawks loudly and starts probing a discarded sandwich wrapper. 'You know, crows can use tools,' Nick remarks. 'And these are specialist Heath crows.'

I follow Nick down the eastern side of Parliament Hill towards the tree line. I'm glad of his local knowledge, although as he admits himself, it's been years since he's explored the Heath properly. 'I'm going on muscle memory,' he says, and his remark reminds me of my experience of climbing through West Norwood Cemetery after fifteen years away. The first sign of a river comes soon enough: a simple wooden plank bridging an empty channel. I leap down to investigate. The streambed is full of dead leaves and twigs, the soil dark but dry, crumbling in my fist. I notice a giant brown fungus growing in the roots of a tree that stands, improbably, in the middle of the channel. 'You're not going to touch that, are you?' asks Nick, sardonically. A small grey terrier appears and crosses the bridge, nose to the floor, followed by a middle-aged woman in slacks and a Panama hat. I feel ridiculous. 'So *this* is the Highgate

Brook? One of the sources of the Fleet?' I turn to Nick. 'No, just a feeder,' he answers. 'We need to follow it down to the ponds.'

We track the channel downhill and emerge on the footpath above the Men's Bathing Pond, the second in a sequence of eight reservoirs formed by the damming of the Highgate Brook on the eastern side of the Heath. It's Friday. Half a dozen bathers can be seen standing on the jetty or bobbing around in the dark water. It's an idyllic location, surrounded by mature trees and fringed with reed beds. A sign reads:

WARNING:
Deep water
Deep silt

I ask Nick if he ever swims in the ponds. He shakes his head. 'Only once, years ago. I hated it. The water was so thick I couldn't see a thing. Who knows what's down there?' The pond *is* surprisingly deep – more than six metres in parts – and while accidents are rare, there have been two drownings in recent years.

The ponds sit on a chain of terraces descending the Heath and are separated by artificial embankments. The Highgate Brook flows between them through pipes and culverts, so each pond has both an entrance and an exit. The whole thing is an elaborate water feature worthy of the great aquaformers of the Mughal Empire. In 2016, works to upgrade the ponds and prevent flooding faced opposition from swimmers and local residents, united under the banner 'Dam Nonsense', but went ahead anyway at a cost of £22 million to the City of London Corporation, which owns the Heath. The embankments were raised using London Clay – 30,000m^3 of it – excavated from the site itself. Engineers used a new suction method to remove excess silt from some of the ponds without the need to empty them.

Nick and I scramble up the embankment and down the other side, following a desire line through thistle beds. The Model Boating Pond is still and quiet, but on certain days it's frantic with the movement of miniature craft, their owners furiously mashing remote controls from the water's edge. On the far side, a couple of anglers are fixing bait. During the improvement works, the Boating Pond was drained and the wreck of a Mark III Ford Cortina was discovered half-submerged in the muddy bottom. I spot the drain leading back to the Men's Pond at the base of the embankment and get down on my knees to get a closer look. The drain is a wedge of concrete covered by a menacing steel grille. Greyish water pools around its teeth without any discernible flow, a light consommé of heath-juice through which a clump of flowering buddleia has thrust four obscene, purple lances towards the sun. Nick lines up a photo and I oblige, reaching out a hand to touch the grille in a small but somehow necessary gesture of contact.

As we circle the pond to the west I notice a small, unnamed island, brimming with wildflowers: purple thistle, golden buttercup and the bristly white heads of false oat grass. An elderly man strides past us in Speedos and a bathing cap. At the northern edge I find the 'water-in' drain set directly in the stone embankment. The water flows unhindered from a ceramic pipe, falling an inch or two into the pond with a satisfying trickling sound. It reminds me of the decorated fountains found in Mediterranean villages which are often considered holy and associated with local saints. I lie prone on the ground and dip my hand in. It is cold and clear. Fingers meet a little furry tuft of green algae. 'This is Fleet water,' I say to Nick, who is negotiating a narrow stone walkway to get a better look. 'Don't fall in.'

We find the next pond, a bird sanctuary, then track the river west through two metal pipes into thick woodland. I'm starting to think we should have waited for the rainy season; we're following another dried-out streambed. We shadow the course as best we can for half an hour on footpaths that seem to trail off into nothing. As we climb into the heart of the Heath, the stream becomes more pronounced, with rounded banks and bluffs of dirty yellow clay exposed to the muggy air. Dark patches begin to appear in the streambed. Nick sources a serviceable stick, which I sink into the sodden earth. It comes out black as tar. The Highgate Brook is here, somewhere, underground, leaching downstream. I scoop a plug of sandy clay from the riverbank and hold it in my palm. It cannot hold form and crumbles away, drier than the clay I removed from the Ambrook. I tentatively ID it as the Claygate Member. Finally, the stream itself vanishes. Immediately above us, the boundary of the Kenwood House estate is marked by high black railings. I pull out the street map. We have reached the springline, where rainwater percolating through the Bagshot sands meets impermeable clay and oozes to the surface. We trace the stream back to a muddy dip beneath a bowl-shaped area of intense green undergrowth. Nick makes a breach from above through dense brambles, then signals for me to follow. He rocks back and forth on the heels of his boots, grinning. I feel it too. The ground is suddenly spongy. It gives like a sprung dance floor.

There is nothing quite like the feeling of finding the source of a river, even such a pitiful stream as this. I take a swig of bottled water and turn to Nick. Should I offer a high five? A man hug? He is squinting at his phone. He pinches at the screen. 'I think we turned off too soon,' he says. 'According to Google Maps, we're actually *here*.' He jabs his finger at a green wedge, then scrolls. 'The main stream is further north.' Nick and Google are right. I realize now that, since the Bird Sanctuary Pond, we have been following another feeder stream. The lure of a channel through the woods is irresistible. We have let our enthusiasm guide us here, to the wrong place. Further north, four more ponds lead to the primary source of the Highgate Brook, though even that draws on two separate springs. It's past lunchtime so we decide to leave the Highgate Brook for another day and tackle its sister stream, the Hampstead Brook, instead.

The Heath is perforated land. There is no definitive source. I locate us on the Streetfinder. I have drawn a little yellow spur of Bagshot sands which I realize now must represent the watershed between the Hampstead and Highgate Brooks, a replica in miniature of the Parliament Hill interfluve. If we head due south we should be able to connect with the western branch of the Fleet and complete our expedition.

After pizza and ice-cold beer in the garden of the Freemasons Arms, we begin to climb the shallow terraces of the Hampstead Ponds in search of the Hampstead Brook and another source of the Fleet. Nick takes the lead this time, stalking from drain to drain with an anxious energy. We pass the tall houses of South Hill Park – once home to the film director Anthony Minghella and the poet Adrian Mitchell – and then the celebrated Mixed Bathing Pond, where I witness a parakeet ascending into the trees with a bright-green flash.

In 2012, Hampstead Heath was the unlikely site of an alien invasion. Red swamp crayfish, native to Louisiana, had colonized the ponds, with reports of nude bathers being 'nipped' by their sharp claws. The local newspaper led with 'Killer Crayfish', while the *Daily Mail* stuck to its anti-immigrant agenda with an exposé on the Polish 'gang' found poaching from the angling pond at night (the three young men were fined £790 for their misdemeanour).[54]

By the time we find the final outflow pipe, the bright sunshine of the morning has vanished. A humid, itchy fug has descended on the Heath. The bed of the Hampstead Brook is wetter than its eastern counterpart, a soggy ditch fringed with young reeds, new growth, broad-leafed ferns and knotweed. The woods are darker here and the footpaths ambiguous; we have to double back twice, probing the undergrowth for a way through. The stream disappears in heavy foliage then resurfaces at the muddy confluence with a channel from the north, a channel that drains (we calculate) the Viaduct Pond. Here, I find an enormous fungus growing on the underside of a tree that has fallen across the stream, two gnarled brown saucers hovering inches above a puddle of orange, iron-stained water. Nick swipes in vain at the midges attacking his legs. I start to notice, here and there, sprays of blotchy leaves, covered in a powdery mildew. Shafts of light reveal whirls and eddies of spores in the air. Red earth everywhere. I am sweating profusely when we come across the gully of another rivulet feeding the brook. Astonishingly, just a few feet from this second confluence, the gully disappears into a cleft in the earth from which a dark liquid oozes. I straddle the gully to get a closer look. The liquid is the blue-black colour of squid ink and has the consistency of spat phlegm. I have no intention of repeating my earlier ritual, I tell Nick. The cleft has the unmistakable appearance of a pair of buttocks.

The association of pools, wells, springs and caves with a female deity – an Earth-mother – is common to many ancient cultures. I think of Sheela-na-gig, baring her exaggerated vulva from stone carvings across Britain and Ireland. And of Shakti, the Great Divine Mother of Hinduism, who is represented by the yoni ('womb') icon and worshipped at Kamakhya Temple in Assam, where a rift in the bedrock is fed by an underground spring. The prehistoric Danaan people (reputed tribal ancestors of the Greeks) believed the Black Sea to be the womb of the Earth-mother, and even devised a theology of the female body to describe the sea-passage from the Mediterranean, with the Bosporus signifying her vulva and the entrance to the Dardanelles her labia.[55]

We struggle to track the brook much beyond this point, forced along paths that lead nowhere. The channel dives beneath reed beds and lurks behind impenetrable brambles. We hack our way through nettles and the overhanging branches of poplars and are about to turn back when I am suddenly aware of a sickly-sweet smell. There is something draped on the branch of a sycamore. Dozens of long sinuous plants have been ripped up from their roots and now hang limply like rags. I find another branch. And then another. But before I can fully register the strangeness of what I'm seeing, Nick points towards the reed beds. 'What on earth is that?'

In a little clearing no more than a metre wide, the ground gives way to a quagmire of black mud. A belt of light, orange-brown material can clearly be discerned moving across it, before vanishing beneath a fallen tree. I see now what Nick is looking at. My stomach lurches. There are objects impaled in the bog: a large wooden stake, fragments of a metal crowbar and three twig crosses bound together with grass. The atmosphere feels suddenly oppressive, as if the river is pulling me in. Who has made this makeshift shrine? And why? I crouch at the edge of the mud, careful to stabilize myself with one hand, and crane my neck. 'Be careful,' says Nick. The ground is wet through and chalybeate-red. In the dark crevice under the fallen tree, something is bubbling through the mud, taking form as a gobbet of white foam. It could be mistaken for frogspawn or cappuccino froth.

There is something malign about this place. It feels like a secret we should not have discovered, a doorway to the Underland. The earlier associations of the river with purity and the sacred seem to have been left far behind, down in the valley. I don't look back. We rejoin the footpath and climb out of the darkness of the woods. When we reach the ridge, the sky is bright, the air is clean, and we are rewarded with the magnificent sight of open water fringed by oaks, willows and lush green banks – the final pond on our journey to the source of the Fleet.

We have reached the Vale of Health, a remote hamlet of fifty or so houses surrounding the pond which is entirely encircled by the Heath. The name is the result of nineteenth-century rebranding and, like Mount Pleasant downstream, was probably intended to be ironic. The wife of the sculptor Joseph Nollekens called it 'a stagnate bottom; a pit in the heath, where, if a bit of paper is whirling in the air, it can never rise above the high ground about it'.[56] Originally a malarial wasteland known as Gangmoor,* the area was later dubbed Hatch's or Hatchett's Bottom after the harness maker Samuel Hatch, who had built a workshop there by 1720. In 1777 the Hampstead Water Company drained the boggy

---

* Cf. Old English *gang/geng*: going, journey, step, way, path, passage, course.

ground to create the large reservoir on whose southern shore we now find ourselves. Clear water laps against a narrow strip of sandy beach. I spot the outflow drain, culverted underneath a footpath.

The Vale is deserted, save for three anglers in branded sportswear. It is every bit the archetypal English country village, with old-fashioned streetlamps and a red, pillar-style post box. I half expect it to be revealed as an elaborate hoax, a painted backdrop from the Golden Age of Hollywood. The grand town houses proudly display the names of former residents: Byron, Tagore and D. H. Lawrence. The poet–physician John Keats frequented the Vale to visit the cottage of his friend Leigh Hunt (now demolished). Hunt was enchanted by what he described as the 'Sweet upland' of Hampstead, with its 'green lanes' and 'brown dells'. Keats himself wrote of being 'Nested and quiet in a valley mild' in his long poem 'Sleep and Poetry', composed while reclining on a daybed in Hunt's study.

Keats first moved to Hampstead after training as a surgeon and apothecary at Guy's Hospital. His house on Well Walk was yards from the famous Chalybeate Well, which still sits in its ornate stone surround on the west side of the street. Keats was no doubt drawn to the health–giving properties of its iron-rich water. In spite of his medical training, he took poisonous doses of mercury to 'cure' an unspecified condition (probably venereal disease). Neither the mercury nor the chalybeate water worked. Keats succumbed to tuberculosis aged twenty-five and was memorialized by Shelley as 'a pale flower . . . the loveliest and the last'.[57]

Heath. Health.

Valē, John; farewell.

Today the Vale of Health is one of north London's most prestigious residences. Back home I find myself browsing property websites and discover a three-bedroom house on the market for a cool £2.6 million. The Vale maintains its artistic lineage, being home to comedians Rowan Atkinson and Sacha Baron Cohen, Monty Python star Terry Gilliam and, until 2010, Oasis frontman Liam Gallagher. We pass a house called Upfleet with an electric-blue front door. A locked notice board in what must be the centre of the hamlet advertises a community choir, the Fleet Singers, and the Vale of Health Society's summer party, to be held in Fleet House. 'Please bring a plate of "Finger Food",' it instructs.

As the big houses peter out, we make an unexpected discovery worthy of a Keatsian epiphany: a caravan site. Known as North Fairground, this scrap of edgeland has been owned by the Abbotts – a family of fairground workers – for one hundred and fifty years. I count a dozen or so mobile homes as well as several vans, trailers and a packed-down Ferris wheel. Nick recognizes the Friendly Falafels food stall from its usual pitch on South End Road.

In the 1961 children's film *The Monster of Highgate Ponds*, a prehistoric creature named Beauty is smuggled out of Hampstead from North Fairground. A smartly dressed showman assists Uncle Dick (played by Sherlock Holmes actor Ronald Howard) in covering Beauty with a tarpaulin, before wheeling her on a barrow through the Vale of Health like a Madonna of the Ponds.

We have almost made a full circuit of the Vale. I follow Nick over a fence and down to the water, which shimmers with a glassy image of the sky. We crouch at the edge. This is about as far as we will get. I collect a little sample in a Tupperware pot and hold it to the light. Tiny particles swirl and eddy. The true source of the Hampstead Brook – of the Fleet itself – lies hidden near by, perhaps in the scrubby, sun-baked hillside rising to the west where we will find, buried deep in nettles, the faintest hollow where the ground is soft and the soil comes out black.

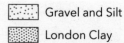

:·.	Alluvium
	Gravel and Silt
	London Clay
▪▪▪▪▪	Roman Road

V: FLOODLANDS

Crossing the Westminster Delta

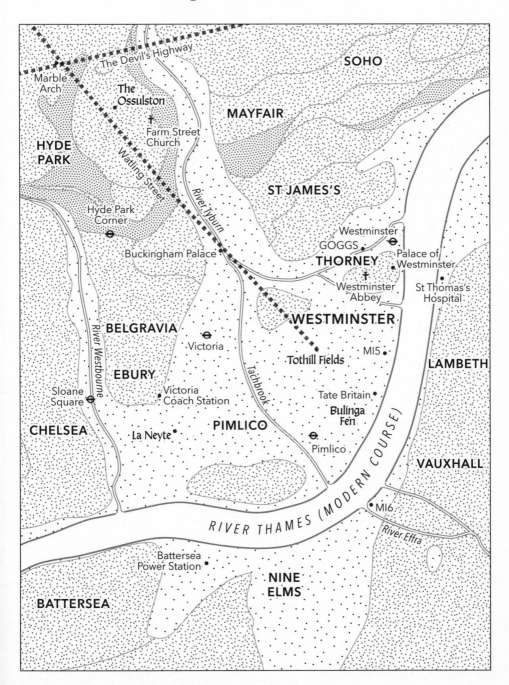

Dawn

BABY GIRL of
SARAH CHIVERS
DOB: 2/5/2016
17.21

Dawn, the first day. The world feels sharp and out of focus at the same time, as if I am looking through heat haze or a gauze; or as if the city were a simulation, a digital rendering of itself, and we were just ghosts passing through. I am holding a takeaway cup in one hand and a little bag of pastries and fruit in the other. The river is completely still, not even a ripple troubling its surface. It must be slack tide, that brief interlude between the incoming and outgoing tides when the river appears to be motionless, a held breath. I feel my phone in the pocket of my jeans pulse with the arrival of another text and take a hit of coffee: earth-rich. On the embankment wall facing the water, the name J. W. BAZALGETTE appears in embossed capitals, although I do not notice it this morning, of all mornings. It is not yet six o'clock. The components of the city seem to have been condensed into a two-dimensional screen I might reach out and touch. On the bridge, the first commuters are crossing from the south bank; a red double-decker bus moves off; a jogger's nylon vest catches the light. The outline of the Palace of Westminster clarifies in the pale dawn.

I have been awake all night, in a pull-out bed on the seventh floor of St Thomas's Hospital, in a room with sweeping views across the Thames. It is 3 May 2016. As the sun went down, it spread the last of its glow through the room like a follow-spot. The little golden lights of the Palace came on one by one and the black water of the river showed them back to us diffuse. The traffic waned, then, for a while, stopped altogether. Fade to black. Silent craft moved downstream, huge barges carrying waste from Cringle Dock. I listened for new sounds in the room: the tiny coughs and muffled mouth-breathing of a newborn child. Our daughter, Martha, arrived at teatime on the May Bank Holiday with a mop of dark-brown hair plastered to her head. When she first appeared, she was still submerged in the womb's deep-dreaming and made no sound, before retreating back inside, out of sight. *It's not my time. Let me rest some more.* When eventually she emerged into the cool air she wailed and shook her fists, her face contorted in blind rage until a mother's touch soothed her back to sleep. After I had cut the umbilical cord (my white cotton shirt remaining miraculously spotless), the midwife handed Martha to me and then left the room. I wrapped her in an NHS-issue swaddling blanket, her plump cheeks blossoming with new blood. For weeks she would keep her curled hands up at her face like a boxer.

That night, Sarah fell into the deep sleep of total physical exhaustion, with Martha beside her in a Perspex bassinet. Across the river, the bells of Westminster marked each passing quarter-hour with a four-note melody. I downloaded *A Moon Shaped Pool* by Radiohead to my phone and lost myself in a waking dream. On the hour Big Ben himself rang out his famous tone, a cracked E natural. In the Palace, a small army of cleaners was preparing the two houses of Parliament for the coming day. That afternoon, Business Secretary Sajid Javid would field questions on apprenticeships, small businesses, the digital economy and the crisis in the steel industry. The MP for Batley and Spen, Jo Cox, would raise an urgent question on the situation in Aleppo. I would lift my day-old child into a taxi and take her home.

Island of Thorns

'Now pees,' quod Nature, 'I comaunde here;
For I have herd al your opinioun,
And in effect yet be we never the nere'

GEOFFREY CHAUCER[1]

Here I am, three and a half years later, in a subterranean hall of concrete and stainless steel, my fingers resting on the rubber handrail of an escalator. The escalator is one of seventeen that traverse the vast, man-made canyon through which I am ascending. A framework of giant pillars and intersecting struts gives the space an unfinished, postmodern look, as if it were scaffolding yet to be dismantled. The walls are unfaced concrete – a rough, scarred surface that has retained 'the marks of the earth into which it was poured'.[2] A shaft of light falls from above and dissolves into nothing. Like a figure on a stairway from the mind of M. C. Escher, I wonder if I will ever find my way out of this impossible architecture. Three policemen are taking the down escalator, their hands wedged into the tops of their stab vests. As they pass and I line up a photograph, one of them eyeballs me. A voice speaks over a tannoy: 'There is a good service on all other lines.'

The London Underground was only five years old when Westminster Bridge station opened on Christmas Eve, 1868. Steam locomotives ferried passengers in wooden carriages from the western terminus of the District Railway at South Kensington, a journey of a little over two miles through a 'cut-and-cover' tunnel.* When, more than a century later, the Jubilee Line was extended across the city towards the mushrooming financial hub at Canary Wharf, Westminster station (as it was by then called) underwent a complete transformation. The new station was built inside a colossal void known as the 'station box'. At 39 metres, it is the deepest underground excavation in London; the westbound

---

* This is a simple method of constructing shallow tunnels in which a trench is 'cut' into the ground and then 'covered' by a load-bearing roof. Although cut-and-cover tunnels were widely used in the nineteenth century, deep-level bored tunnels are now predominant in London.

Jubilee Line platform lies at 25.4 metres below sea level. Only Waterloo is deeper (the ground level being lower there, in the alluvial flatlands of Lambeth Marsh). The station's construction was a triumph of engineering over geology. Due to the proximity to the Palace of Westminster – with its iconic clock tower – it was decided that the deep-level Jubilee Line platforms would be stacked directly on top of each other, with the ticket hall and relocated platforms of the District Line positioned above, and the whole thing capped by a new building for MPs' offices called Portcullis House. Deep trenches were excavated for the walls of the station box and filled with reinforced concrete. As the earth inside the box was removed, massive horizontal steel braces were fixed across the cavity to prevent the walls from collapsing. To mitigate the effects of the tunnelling on the Palace, two innovative techniques were employed.[3] Firstly, additional concrete struts were bored into the clay beneath the excavation and fitted with jacks that could be adjusted in response to ground movement. Secondly, a network of steel tubes, called *tubes à manchette*, was installed underneath the foundations of the clock tower and a stabilizing grout composed of cement, sand and water was injected through tiny holes into the clay. The precise position of the clock tower was monitored to ensure that its tilt was controlled within the range 15–25mm. Had these methods not been employed, it was estimated that the clock tower would have tilted by at least 12cm, causing structural damage to the Palace of Westminster.

I emerge to blue skies and the hubbub of tourists. Big Ben is shrouded in scaffolding. It is the morning after the government announced its intention to trigger prorogation. This obscure mechanism normally concludes one session of parliament in order to prepare for the Queen's Speech, but in this case its deployment was clearly designed to shut down debate and avoid accountability in the lead-up to the United Kingdom's scheduled exit from the European Union at midnight on Hallowe'en. Dissent is in the air. Protests are hastily arranged from London to Llandudno. Twitter is in meltdown, a malevolent vortex of snowflakes and gammons,

Remoaners and Russian bots. In the weeks that follow, three separate court cases will lead, eventually, to the dramatic return of parliament and an eruption of anger from MPs on all sides. Former Mayor of London and now Prime Minister Boris Johnson, a tousle-haired pub-clown in an ill-fitting suit, will dismiss concerns of death threats to Remain MPs as 'humbug'. While left-wing and centrist forces flounder, failing to unite, the pro-Leave right will marshal the language of war and nationalism, dismissing opponents as 'traitors' and 'unpatriotic' and dubbing legislation designed to block a no-deal Brexit as the 'surrender act'.

I have dropped Martha off at her new nursery. She is three and a half. The slick helmet of baby hair is now a glorious mane of nut-brown ringlets. Martha's favourite things are scrambled eggs, going on the swings and Princess Anna from Disney's *Frozen*. This morning, as we walked in along Rotherhithe Street, she scuttled behind me incanting her bastardized version of the *Wizard of Oz* theme: 'Follow the brick road, follow the brick road.' That sleepless night on the seventh floor seems so far away that I wonder if it really happened to somebody else. Parenthood is playing havoc with my memory. I constantly feel like I've just woken up from an implausible dream. Today I'm the scarecrow, flinging my sackcloth arms in both directions; tomorrow, the tin man, squealing for oil.

I have been thinking about Martha's birth: how strange to have entered this world in the shadow of Westminster's iconic towers, with the chimes of Big Ben – once broadcast across the British Empire – swimming in real-time in the gummy shells of your barely formed ears. I want to get behind the noise, peel back the surface and dive in. 2016 was the year everything changed. Brexit, Trump and you, my little bean. Now, the room you were born in seems like an island, adrift in tidal waters. Night terrors. Division. Solid ground gives way. The Brexit dream evaporates like the mirage it always was, working loose the foundations of democracy, the bonds we thought had united us. Like everyone else, I've been trying to work out what has happened – and how to move forward.

I need to return to ground zero, to the mother of all parliaments, where a sainted king of England turned a small island-monastery into the most powerful place on Earth. This journey will begin in the heart of Westminster then lead me out, via flooded basements and ancient causeways, across the marshy hinterlands – what I call the Westminster Delta – in search of mysteries that leap off the geological map.

I have set up shop on a metal bench behind the 650-year-old Jewel Tower, surrounded by the contents of my Karrimor hiking rucksack: books, notepad, print-outs from the internet. I carefully begin to unfold the Streetfinder. The edges are ragged, corners dog-eared; it almost comes apart in my hands. A large scrap of Hammersmith tears off with the cover, floats away from the rest of the city. The map smells of putty. Clapham collapses into New Cross. A German teenager poses in front of the tower then does the splits. A Japanese couple lines up a selfie in front of a row of European Union flags that have been cable-tied to the railings opposite the Palace. The flags flutter in the breeze, a dozen circles of twelve gold stars on fields of azure blue. Every few minutes a passing vehicle blasts its horn and the driver shouts an obscenity/slogan/message of support. *Out means out! . . . Bollocks to Brexit!*

The Jewel Tower was raised around 1365 during the reign of Edward III and is one of only two buildings to survive from the medieval Palace of Westminster. Today it lies in a sunken yard, detached from Charles Barry's neo-Gothic 'new' Palace by a busy roadway. Beneath the lavishly sculpted golden limestone of the later building, the tower now assumes a modest identity, a stubby outhouse in good old Kentish ragstone. Originally designed to house Edward III's personal treasures, the tower retains traces of its defensive function in the empty moat that still surrounds it on two sides. I notice that the moat appears to extend underneath the road and towards the Palace, disappearing into shadows behind a fearsome set of black steel railings. A small door is set into the

wall beside it. I cup my hands against the frosted glass and make out a
staircase descending beneath the street. It looks like it hasn't been used
in decades. I try the handle. Locked. I want to climb down into the ditch
but there's a high police presence in Westminster today and I have no
intention of getting arrested. A young man in an English Heritage polo
shirt emerges from the tower. I ask him about the ditch. 'The moat,' he
explains, 'was once connected to the Thames, but that portion has long
been blocked off and backfilled.' He gestures towards the railings. 'A
medieval docking platform was discovered just there in the 1980s. That
was when they replaced the foundations of the tower with steel and concrete piles. The original timbers came out as good as new, preserved in
the waterlogged ground. Did you know, the tower is slowly sinking?' A
group of blue-clad protestors passes overhead, carrying EU flags and the
Union Jack.

'What about the door?' I ask. 'Where does that staircase lead?' My
mind fills with images of secret tunnels, flooded chambers beneath the
House of Lords.

'Oh, that's just the back way into the underground car park. No one
uses it any more.'

'The staircase or the car park?' I ask.

'Both,' he says. 'It's £11 an hour.'

He spots my map, crumpled on the bench. 'That's cool,' he says, then
makes an exit; a group is arriving for a guided tour. I smooth out the
map with one hand: Westminster in the naked, undeniable truth of geological science. I locate the Jewel Tower – there it is, a bright blue speck;
the Palace, in purple, flush to the river; the large Abbey complex to the
west: three points on a map gathered on an ovoid disc of sandy gravel
floating in alluvial marsh. Westminster before Westminster. This is
Thorney, 'isle of thorns', one of at least three *eyots* or *aits* (small islands)
that once stood proud of the waterline here, where the river bends and
the tide once washed across the flatlands of Victoria and Pimlico.

Thorney was both remote and encircled by impassable marshes and

streams: '*terribilis locus*' (a terrible place) according to one ancient charter. This small island was the ideal location for the founding, around
970, of a Benedictine monastery dedicated to St Peter – later dubbed the
'west minster' to distinguish it from the ancient cathedral of St Paul in
the east. It was the great age of monastic reform in England, led by King
Edgar with his energetic Archbishop of Canterbury, Dunstan. A contemporary portrait of Dunstan – probably embellished by the man
himself – shows him genuflecting before a looming, giant-sized
Christ. One hand is outstretched in supplication, the other placed on his
forehead. 'Watch over me, Dunstan,' he prays. With his monkish tonsure
and five o'clock shadow, Dunstan looks like a regional bank manager
who has just lost the keys to the vault. His *monasteriolum* ('little monastery') on Thorney housed just twelve monks and was a modest enterprise,
situated a mile and a half away from the old fortified Roman city of
Lundenburh.[4] With the Thames lapping its eastern edge, the island was
further delineated by two channels – the bifurcated mouth of the river
Tyburn, now lost beneath the streets.[5] A third outlet (later known as the
King's Scholars' Pond Sewer or the Tachbrook) flowed through present-
day Pimlico, disgorging to the south. The whole territory was bounded
to the west by a fourth river, the Westbourne. On the geological map, the
landscape of early Westminster is instantly recognizable as a river delta:
a shifting environment of migrating streams, islands and tidal creeks.

It is not known for certain if a church existed on Thorney before the
tenth century. Legend reports the reconsecration of a church at the time
of the first Bishop of London, Mellitus, at the beginning of the seventh
century, but there is no archaeological evidence to support this. Located
near to an obvious fording point of the Thames, Westminster may have
been the northern bridgehead of the Roman military pontoon built to
cross the Thames during the Claudian invasion of Britain in AD 43.[6] But
only 'slight evidence' of Roman activity on the island has been identified:
masonry; a fragment of hypocaust (underfloor heating system); and,
most notably, a limestone sarcophagus made by the sons of Valerius

Amandinus for their father.[7] The sarcophagus was exhumed from a pit on the north side of Westminster Abbey in 1869 and dated to the fourth century AD. There was no sign of Amandinus; he had been removed some six or seven hundred years later to make space for the body of a Saxon. Coffins recycled like tin cans. The empty sarcophagus is now on display in the Queen's Diamond Jubilee Galleries – suspended, as it were, 52 feet above the Abbey floor in the medieval triforium (interior gallery).

In his beguiling book, *Unearthing London*, Simon Webb repeats Geoffrey of Monmouth's assertion that Westminster Abbey itself was built over the remains of a temple to the Roman god Apollo. Webb goes further, claiming Thorney as a sacred site for the Druids, the mysterious priestly caste of pre-Roman Britain.[8] 'This strange region was invested with power,' he writes. 'It was the nexus; the focal point where many aspects of the sacred came to a point.' Islands, marshes, the confluence of rivers, an ancient ford – for Webb, these are the 'liminal zones' suggestive of a ritual landscape dating back thousands of years. It is true that prehistoric pottery has been dredged from sandbanks buried beneath Westminster station, along with flint blades and 'a fragment of a polished Neolithic axe'.[9] And indicators of human cultivation of the landscape have been discovered elsewhere on the island: cereal pollen, charcoal from burning and 'ard marks' – traces of Bronze Age ploughing. But little is certain. Webb's is a speculative history. Filler phrases pepper his text, marking the gaps between historical fact and the allure of imaginative guesswork: 'there is little doubt', he says (*there is much*); 'almost certainly' (*probably not*); 'it is a reasonable assumption' (*is it?*). Before the embanking of the Thames, Webb contends, Thorney was at the tidal head, 'where the salt sea meets the freshwater river'. But the tidal head was a movable feast; evidence from recent archaeological excavations on and around the island reveal a 'complex pattern of change in the tidal and flooding regime'.[10] Where others sense disruption, change, Webb sees only continuity – a solid line from ancient to modern. 'The holiness which was associated with Thorney from the time of the Stone Age has transferred to the monarchy,' he declares. 'Thorney Island is the heart of all power in Britain, just as it was 3,000 or 4,000 years ago.'[11]

It was not Druids, though, but a Saxon king, Edward the Confessor, who injected Westminster with royal authority when, in 1042, he ordered the refounding of the small religious house on Thorney. Edward's great stone Abbey was built in the new Romanesque style favoured by the Normans and was designed to serve as his personal mausoleum.* This was statement architecture, conceived on a vast scale in Reigate stone with a nave of six double-bays, a domed central tower and wide Roman arches (a few of which are extant in the undercroft of the present Abbey). It took at least ten years to complete the build. When the Abbey was finally consecrated in 1065, Edward was gravely ill, possibly having suffered a stroke. He died a week later. The funeral was recorded in the Bayeux Tapestry. The king is pictured wrapped in a shroud, like a butterfly that has returned to the chrysalis, and is being carried aloft by eight gangly footmen to his Abbey church of St Peter. In this rendering, the Abbey looks more like a mosque than a church. A workman is fixing a weathervane to the roof: a cockerel. A divine hand appears from above, *deus ex machina* breaching the frame.

Edward's investment on Thorney was not limited to the Abbey. The previous panel of the Bayeux Tapestry shows Edward seated in his new royal palace, receiving news from the future king Harold Godwinson. Edward's Palace of Westminster was built on the eastern edge of the island facing the Thames, probably on the site of an earlier timber structure raised by his stepfather, Cnut. By moving his court from Winchester, the traditional capital of the Wessex kings, Edward had effectively repositioned the London region at the centre of national life. And by

* Although known as the penultimate Anglo-Saxon king of England, Edward was in fact half-Norman through his mother, Emma, and was clearly influenced by Norman culture and aesthetics.

reconsecrating the Abbey as a royal tomb, he had bound together the power of God with the body of the monarch. Of course all ancient things were once new, but it is still curious to think of Westminster in this way – as a purpose-built capital, like the planned cities of Brasilia and Nur-Sultan in Kazakhstan or the sanitized ghost town of Naypyidaw, constructed from scratch in 2005 on a greenfield site in Myanmar at the cost of $4 billion.

My phone buzzes. It's Sarah. She's waiting for me at the Abbey, where we have arranged to meet. A bank of dark cloud is working its way across the city. Cat Stevens blasts out from a passing car. I pack up my gear and leave. College Green is teeming with journalists and TV crews covering the unfolding drama in the Commons. Each station has its own little gazebo, like a miniature army setting up camp before battle. Inquisitive tourists watch through the railings. A nervous man in a long grey raincoat is delivering a piece to camera. A young reporter is walking up and down the fenceline practising her spiel to the air like an actor waiting for their call. The stage is set. Let the play begin. The light fades and it starts to rain.

Holy Theatre

'A man walks across this empty space whilst someone else is watching him, and this is all that is needed for an act of theatre to be engaged.'

PETER BROOK[12]

I FIND SARAH SHELTERING IN an archway in Dean's Yard, where the boys of Westminster School claim to have invented the game of football. She has taken the day off work and is excited to see the wax funeral effigies of famous royals that have recently gone back on display in the triforium galleries. We enter the Abbey through the cloisters. The white noise of the city recedes into the murmur of hushed voices. A Chinese tourist photographs the delicate fan vaulting, then steps back for a wider angle. An elderly couple with North American accents are inspecting a commemorative stone tablet.

'Is that Vancouver?'

'No, sweetie.'

Sarah spots a wide, Roman-style arch leading into one of the oldest parts of the Abbey, a sunken strongroom known as the Pyx Chamber that was built around 1070. The heavy wooden door is fitted with no fewer than six metal locks. The Chamber was used to store valuable items, *pyx* being the name for the small round containers designed to carry the consecrated host but repurposed at Westminster for the storage of gold and silver pieces. A member of the Abbey staff glides past, her plush red mantle flying behind her. We follow a group of African visitors into the nave. They are wearing creaseless blue shirts and dog collars under their raincoats. The nave is crammed with visitors, but surprisingly quiet; almost everyone is hooked up to the multimedia guide, which they carry like a votive offering, the voice of the narrator whispering directions softly in their ears. My eyes are drawn upwards, tracing pointed Gothic arches and columns of Purbeck marble towards an immense, rib-vaulted ceiling. At 31 metres, the Abbey boasts the highest vaulted ceiling of any Gothic building in England (the west towers adding a further 38 metres). The huge west window floods the Abbey with natural light. It takes my breath away; the nave rises almost as far into the heavens as the Westminster station box plunges deep into the earth.

A service of Holy Communion is about to start. Instinctively, I pick up an order of service and we find ourselves guided through the crowds of tourists by a network of vergers on walkie-talkies.

'Two more coming, Bill. Green jackets.'

We shuffle across the checkerboard floor of the choir, negotiating a bottle-neck – a group of Italians on a guided tour. Another verger appears and gestures past the High Altar, the site of royal coronations since the Norman Conquest.

'This way, sir.'

I hardly have a moment to take in the sumptuous Cosmati pavement or the gilded *reredos* (ornamental screen), restored by Gilbert Scott in 1867. The verger is unhooking a rope barrier and ushering us up a small flight of wooden stairs and we step, the two of us, a Roman Catholic and a Muslim, into the space behind the altar.

'The Lord be with you.'

'And also with you,' we reply, as one.

I am standing before the shrine of St Edward the Confessor, last but one of the Anglo-Saxon kings of England, in a makeshift chapel raised above the Abbey floor. The shrine comprises a rectangular marble pedestal covered by a painted wooden canopy and stands twice the height of a man in the centre of the space. I make out swirling patterns of interlocking circles and diamonds, like the knotwork of Celtic tradition or the complex geometries of Islamic art. In fact, the present shrine was built in 1269 by a Roman craftsman named Petrus (Peter); it was the centrepiece of the renovations commissioned by Henry III.[13]

'Please be seated.'

A group of thirty or so has gathered at the shrine, drawn away from the splendour of the nave to this inner sanctum, the heart of the Abbey, its holy of holies. There is a feeling of the curtain having been drawn back. The service is led by a single priest in a white surplice; a small altar has been installed for the purpose at one end of the shrine. The congregation is a mix of visitors and regulars. I'm not the only Catholic; a South American couple next to me cross themselves vigorously and kneel on the hard stone floor for the blessing of the Sacrament. Candles throw their wavering light on the rough surfaces. The shrine glows with a weird, extraterrestrial energy. It's about the right shape and size for an electrical substation, I think. In another moment, it appears as the *Kaaba* – the sacred, granite-walled cube at the centre of the Great Mosque in Mecca. The sides of the shrine are punctuated by shadowy recesses, 'three trefoiled arches that served as *foramina* or "squeezing spaces" into which worshippers could insert sick or wounded body parts in the hope of a miraculous cure'.[14] The priest's words leave his mouth as waves of sound collapsing in a field of static, invisible matter. Just being here is making me better.

At the Sign of the Peace, I kiss Sarah on the cheek. The South Americans shake my hand. They are beaming. This moment of simple connection, of being present, together, in this space: this.

In 2005, ground-penetrating radar (GPR) picked up a series of sub-terranean anomalies in the vicinity of the Confessor's chapel, 'grave cists' that archaeologists have identified with burials of royal children.[15] Beneath the shrine itself, the radar revealed what some believe to be the Confessor's original burial site – a 'substantial chamber with an arched or vaulted roof' along with a backfilled access passage. The Rorschach inkblots of the GPR radargram are all we have. No proof of life, just an empty space beneath the stage. 'To comprehend the visibility of the invisible,' wrote Peter Brook, 'is a life's work of a holy theatre.'[16]

Imagine a body after death. A saint. A king of England.

You wrap the body in gold cloth then lift it into a stone coffin. You place aromatic herbs and spices inside, a pair of purple slippers by the feet. The heavy stone lid slides on. Then the tomb is sealed. One hundred years go by.

Another you unseals the tomb, removes the lid. A sweet aroma fills the air. You unwrap the body. Take new cloth. Take silk. Then lift the body into a wooden coffin. Darkness.

One hundred years again. The body lighter now. You are many. You carry the coffin on your shoulders, place the body in a new tomb, a space that has been set aside.

The Confessor's shrine is the heart not only of the Abbey but of Thorney itself, a macabre trig point marking the centre of the island. The royal cult that grew around that first tomb soon spread across the complex like Japanese knotweed, inflating the Abbey to the status of national mausoleum and Thorney to a simulacrum of the whole country – an island for an island kingdom. In the Lady Chapel, dedicated to the usurper Henry VII, the Protestant monarch Elizabeth I is buried on top of her Catholic half-sister, 'Bloody' Mary, with her cousin and rival, Mary, Queen of Scots, on the opposite side of the nave. Has British history ever been more than an elaborate series of family feuds played out at the expense of the rest of us?

After the service I walk clockwise around the shrine. The tombs of monarchs and their consorts radiate from the centre of the chapel like spokes of a wheel.* Three smartly dressed men around my age – Anglican traditionalists, I guess – are lining up for a group photo by the altar, all chinos and cheesy grins. 'Tradition itself,' wrote Brook, 'in times of dogmatism and dogmatic revolution, is a revolutionary force which must be safeguarded.'[17] I check that no one is watching, then place my hand on the corner of the shrine. Edward's body, what is left of it, still lies in a cavity inside. The stone is warm to the touch, or perhaps it is my hand that warms the stone.

* Clockwise from the south-west corner: Edward I, Henry III, Eleanor of Castile, Henry V and Catherine de Valois, Philippa of Hainault, Edward III, Richard II and Anne of Bohemia.

Flood

'I felt as if the power had been granted me of opening a trap-door in my chest, to look upon the long-hidden machinery of my mysterious body.'

JOHN HOLLINGSHEAD[18]

THE NEXT TIME I'M in Westminster, I've managed to arrange a tour of the Treasury building thanks to my civil servant friend – let's call her Anna. I have a tip-off about the easternmost branch of the lost river Tyburn and am eager to investigate. I surface from the Tube into a squally, autumnal afternoon. Brexit rumbles on, each new day bringing fresh controversy or the exhuming of yet another obscure parliamentary procedure. The pedestrian subway underneath Parliament Street is closed due to flooding. A council cleaner is mopping out the public toilets. 'It was coming up through the drains,' she tells me, then draws me closer. 'Shit, I mean.'

Anna hands me a security lanyard and I'm in. Government Offices Great George Street, or GOGGS for short, is an imposing Baroque Revival building clad in white Portland stone. Completed in 1917, it has been headquarters of Her Majesty's Treasury since 1940, though it now houses a range of other government offices including HM Revenues and Customs and the Department for Culture, Media and Sport. I remove my raincoat and try to look like I belong, which is hard when you're wearing knackered jeans and merino-wool running shoes.

Anna is an art enthusiast. She takes me behind the sweeping, polished marble staircase and shows me a giant etching hanging there: *The Prospect of London and Westminster Taken from Lambeth* by the seventeenth-century draughtsman Wenceslaus Hollar. The Abbey, even without its totemic towers, dominates the skyline like a dark prison hulk. The Jewel Tower is there too, its crenellated square roof distinctive among the high eaves of the wooden buildings jostling on the riverfront.

GOGGS is a labyrinth of carpeted passageways and offices. I needn't have worried about the dress code. T-shirts and casual shoes are standard attire in the corridors of power. 'On Fridays the ministers go back to their constituencies,' Anna explains, 'so it's a bit more relaxed.' She waves to a young man in a red lumberjack shirt and jeans who is walking quickly in the other direction. 'That's my boss.'

We climb to the top floor, Anna pausing only to show me a series of brooding etchings of suburban alleyways by George Shaw that she loves. Anna works in a light-filled, open-plan office with breakout spaces and an array of wacky furniture in primary colours. It could be a Shoreditch media company, not a major department of Her Majesty's government.

'I want to show you the view from the top,' Anna says. A wrought-iron spiral staircase takes us into a small room inside one of the ornate turrets. 'This is a good place for a quiet meeting.' There are sweeping views of the island: the Abbey's north flank; the snooker baize of Parliament Square; Big Ben swaddled in scaffolding. 'I came up here during the terror attack,' Anna says. She is referring to the events of 22 March 2017. That day, at twenty to three in the afternoon, a fifty-two-year-old Kent native, Khalid Masood, drove his Hyundai Tucson into pedestrians on Westminster Bridge, killing four people and injuring over fifty, before crashing into the perimeter fence of the Palace and running into the grounds, where he stabbed to death an unarmed police officer, PC Keith Palmer. 'We couldn't leave the building,' Anna tells me. 'The whole of Westminster was in lockdown.' We look down towards the bridge; workmen in hi-vis are installing defensive barriers across the road. From this angle I can just make out the river, grey-green under storm clouds, and there beyond it, rising thirteen storeys from the opposite bank like a Soviet office block, the North Wing of St Thomas's Hospital.

Anna knows what I'm really here for. We head back down, all the way down. I had heard rumours that the easternmost branch of the lost river Tyburn still runs underneath the building, and my research backs it up. Even the Treasury's own historians talk of the 'constant trickle of water through the sub-basement'.[19] Anna is less hopeful. 'We can go and have a look if you like, but it's probably off-limits,' she says, then adds, wistfully, 'I have always wanted to find out where the generator is.'

The basement of GOGGS smells of body odour and rising damp. The floor is gunship-grey linoleum, the ceilings rigged with strip-lighting and air ducts. We pass a table football room – '20p PER GAME' – and a pair of vending machines emblazoned with an advert for Lucozade Sport. Through an open door, we hear pumping dance music and a voice barking instructions. A laminated schedule of lunchtime activities is taped to the wall. Today is High Intensity Interval Training. Alternative classes on offer include Pilates, Yoga, Box Fit, Spin Bike and 'Legs, Bums and Tums'. Before the Second World War, the part of the basement directly under the Treasury was converted into a temporary emergency government centre. The secret complex boasted a map room, transatlantic telephone communications, dormitories for staff, an office-bedroom for the Prime Minister and, at its heart, the Cabinet War Room – 'the room,' declared Winston Churchill in May 1940, 'from which I will direct the war.' During the Blitz, a layer of concrete five feet thick and known as 'the Slab' was installed above the basement to protect against aerial bombardment.

It is easy to get lost down here. We seem to be walking in a rough circle, Anna and I, but who can be sure; the corridors all look the same. We pass a series of doors marked 'Restricted Access'. Here and there, unwanted furniture has been stacked up against the whitewashed walls: dark wooden table tops; leather-backed armchairs; threadbare sofas; upside-down bar stools and swivel chairs, their feet poking up like the barbs of some ancient instrument of torture. We turn one corner to discover a dumping ground of metal cabinets and safes, some fitted with old-style rotary combination locks and labelled 'Authorized personnel only'. What secrets they once held are long gone – shredded, pulped and encrypted as bytes of data on a protected server, intangible as stardust.

I notice a small trapdoor in the floor and take a blurry photo when Anna is not looking. Then, around another corner, we come to a set of steps leading down to the sub-basement. Anna seems suddenly nervous, as if *this* was the real secret and she its guardian. We peer down and, through the darkness, we see ourselves shown back. The passage is flooded with water.

Is this—could it be—the thing itself—the lost river Tyburn?

The water is still, its surface unbroken. I guess it is at least two feet deep. I can feel the cold air coming off it.

'In one place,' records the Treasury report, 'a channel was dug and the water was witnessed to flow like a stream through the concrete.'[20]

Suddenly someone appears behind us – a workman in utility trousers and a black polo shirt. 'Are you lost?' It is not really a question. 'The exit is that way,' he adds, before we can respond. Anna mutters some excuses and makes to leave, but I want to know more. I ask the man about the standing water, the lost river. 'Yeah, I don't know about that,' he replies, evasively. 'The whole sub-basement is below the water table, so it bubbles up when it rains. You can't stop it.'

The workman disappears and Anna leads me to the exit. Her lunch break is almost over. As we climb back to ground level, I take one final look back down the stairwell that connects every floor of the building. There, at the bottom of three flights, I see it again – my reflection flickering in a pool of cold, black water.

Like the Fleet and the Westbourne, the Tyburn – or 'boundary stream' – rises in the hills of Hampstead, forced from beneath the ground by the impermeable London Clay. Its source was once the Shepherd's Well on Fitzjohn's Avenue, described in 1827 as a 'beautiful spring' covered by an arch and surrounded by 'green turf'.[21] The spring was tapped for drinking water by local residents and, so it was claimed, never froze in winter. From Hampstead, the Tyburn flows south past Swiss Cottage, across Regent's Park, where it aligns with the western edge of the boating lake, and through the old manor of Marylebone, its meandering course still marked by the arc of Marylebone Lane. From here, the river appears in my customized Streetfinder as a finger of alluvium – the tell-tale sign of a once broad channel – cutting through the gravel terraces of the Thames. The vanished stream pours beneath the bargain-hunters of Oxford Street, snakes its way through Mayfair – beneath the super cars and afternoon tea – and across Green Park towards Buckingham Palace.

In the 1860s, the journalist and playwright John Hollingshead walked the length of the Tyburn with a gang of sewer men, reporting the journey in his book *Underground London*:

> We had not proceeded much further in our downwards course, when Agrippa and the rest of the guides suddenly stopped short, and asked me where I supposed I was now? I thought the question quite unnecessary, as my position in the sewer was pretty evident.
>
> 'We don't mean where are you in the sewer,' said Agrippa, 'but what's above your head?'
>
> 'I give it up,' I replied.
>
> 'Well, Buckingham Palace,' was the answer.
>
> Of course my loyalty was at once excited, and, taking off my fantailed cap, I led the way with the National Anthem, insisting that my guides should join in chorus. Who knows but what, through some untrapped drain, that rude but hearty underground melody found its way into some inner wainscoting of the palace, disturbing some dozing maid of honour with its mysterious sounds, and making her dream of Guy Fawkes and many other subterranean villains?[22]

Beyond the Palace, in the former marshlands bordering the Thames, the Tyburn divided in the manner of a river delta. The western branch continued due south across Pimlico, where it was known variously as the Tachbrook and the King's Scholars' Pond Sewer. The eastern branch veered south-east then divided again, its twin mouths discharging either side of Thorney island.

Could the dark water filling the sub-basement of Government Offices Great George Street really be the lost river? By all accounts, the Tyburn channels have been entirely sewerized for over one hundred and fifty years.

So here is a riddle.

When is a river not a river?

When it has been dammed and diverted or imprisoned behind walls of concrete, metal and brick, cut off from its source? What do we call that which remains?

Like the vanished earth imprinted on the concrete walls of the station box, some 'lost' or 'former' rivers can only be detected as absences, as topographical lacunae. These invisible channels are truly the 'dark matter' of the city, whose existence is implied only by observing their effects on the surrounding landscape. 'You can't see it, you can't feel it,' wrote Jodi Picoult of dark matter, 'but you can watch something being pulled in its direction.'[23]

I am starting to believe that my Streetfinder may not be enough.

We have entered a new geological epoch: the Anthropocene. The deep time of geological change can no longer be kept at a distance or conceptualized as an abstract force. The human impulse to control and dominate our environment; our insatiable appetite for the Earth's limited resources; our disregard for biodiversity: these are the grounds for the sudden, undeniable shift – sudden in geological terms – in global climate. Humans have become, in Gaia Vince's memorable phrase, 'the change-makers'.[24] In Hawaii a new type of rock has been identified: a mix of sedimentary grains and organic debris bound together by molten plastic. These 'plastiglomerates' are but one of many markers of this new age of the human; synthetic deposits that will be laid down as geological strata long after we are gone. 'What will survive of us,' wrote Robert Macfarlane, 'is plastic, swine bones and lead-207, the stable isotope at the end of the uranium-235 decay chain.'[25]

When, in 2012, I was commissioned to write about the climate crisis, the few conventional poems that surfaced were brief, evasive affairs. 'How can I begin to speak of change?' I asked. 'We cannot see beyond the next financial year.'[26] Thinking of the Anthropocene ignites our worst fears of global catastrophe and species extinction. Its cultural by-product is the apocalypse movie, the world reframed as flooded (*Waterworld*, *2012*,

Flood), frozen (*The Day After Tomorrow, Sunshine*) or both (*Geostorm*). Meanwhile, stories of intergalactic travel and planetary terraforming conjure implausible visions of life after Earth. Better, I thought, to retreat from the world: 'You'll find me, head down, in a mulberry bush.'[27]

It was only later that I began to conceive of London's lost rivers as early markers of the Anthropocene, and also as the means to write my way out of inertia.

Most are not really 'lost' at all, just waiting for their chance to resurface. There are tales of diverted rivers returning to their original beds, of construction crews breaching perched aquifers like unwanted guests at a house party. From Lewisham to Shepherd's Bush, the buried streams are breaking out of their sewers. On Christmas Eve 2013, the residents of Westhorne Avenue in Eltham, south-east London, woke to the sound of water rushing into their living rooms and kitchens. The culverted river Quaggy (a tributary of the Ravensbourne) runs behind the terraced houses here. But 23 December was different: a month's worth of rain fell in twenty-four hours and high winds blew branches and even entire trees into the river. A grille or 'trash gate' installed by the Environment Agency failed and the Quaggy burst its banks. It was a 'living nightmare' for residents like sixty-three-year-old Rosemary Clay (her real name), whose ground floor was inundated with dirty water. 'The grille was blocked,' she told the local paper. 'If that had been cleared I don't think this would have happened. We have lived here for many years and it has not flooded. Something went wrong and we need to know what.'[28]

In Westminster, the threat of destruction has often come from beneath. According to tradition, the temple to Apollo that may once have stood on the site of the Abbey 'fell down by the Violence of an Earthquake' during the reign of Emperor Antoninus Pius (AD 138–161).[29] Some nine hundred years later, in around 1050, a 'large flooding event' covered most of Thorney Island, perhaps disrupting Edward's efforts to renovate the Abbey.[30] In 1605 disaster was narrowly averted when, in the early hours of 5 November, a man giving his name as 'John

Johnson' was discovered in a cellar of the Palace of Westminster, a room directly below the House of Lords that had once been used as a kitchen. The man was in possession of matches, touch-paper and thirty-six barrels of gunpowder and was later identified as the Catholic recusant Guido (or Guy) Fawkes.

On 16 October 1834, Fawkes and his co-conspirators' vision became a reality when the Palace was largely destroyed in a huge conflagration – the largest in London between the Great Fire and the Blitz. The fire began in the heating furnaces beneath the Lords, wherein labourers had been instructed to dispose of two cart-loads of tally sticks, an antiquated form of tax receipt used by the Exchequer.* The furnaces were unsuited to wood burning and their chimneys, clogged with soot, soon began to smoulder. At 4 p.m. two gentlemen visitors, Messrs Snell and Shuter, entered the Lords, later recalling that the chamber was so thick with smoke that they could not see more than a foot in any direction. 'Bless me!' exclaimed Mr Snell. 'How warm it is in here! I can feel the heat through my boots . . . I should almost be afraid this would take fire!'[31] The first flames were spotted two hours later by the wife of a doorkeeper, Mrs Mullencamp. 'Oh, good God! The House of Lords is on fire!' she exclaimed. At 6.30 p.m. a giant ball of flame erupted from the heart of the Palace, lighting up the night sky.[32]

On 8 January 1928, a violent storm surge raced up the Thames, whose channel was already swollen with meltwater from the Cotswolds. River defences were breached from Woolwich to Hammersmith. The moat of the Tower of London filled back up for the first time in centuries. Black-and-white photographs show children being rescued from first-floor windows in Rotherhithe, the flat-capped rescuers balancing on floating planks of timber like deal porters from the nearby docks. Westminster was worst hit. The Palace was submerged beneath a foot of

* The House of Lords was relocated within the Palace in 1801; the furnace room and Fawke's cellar were therefore distinct spaces.

water, islanded again by the flood. At Millbank and Lambeth, Bazal-gette's embankments collapsed. The Tate Gallery was engulfed and freezing water poured across Pimlico, cascading into basement flats. Ten people lost their lives in the lowlands of the Westminster Delta that day: nine drowned and one dead from shock.

Something went wrong and we need to know what.

The latest Brexit deadline – midnight on Hallowe'en – has been missed. I spent the night, appropriately, leading after-hours walks through an East End cemetery, miles away from the political living dead in the House of Commons. The hopes of Leavers smoulder in the bonfires of autumn, their masks crumbling like the caved-in faces of abandoned jack-o'-lanterns. A woman in Meltham, West Yorkshire witnesses mysterious lights in the night sky: nine 'orange balls of flames' hovering in formation above the Iron Age ruins on Castle Hill.[33] The eye of the storm keeps moving, so fast that no one can predict what will happen next. Johnson calls a snap election to break the deadlock. We will know the outcome by the morning of Friday, 13 December. A new day.

I want to make one final journey to Westminster; but this time I will head away from Thorney and cross the alluvial floodplain itself in search of another mysterious island, a disappearing village and an ancient stone at the centre of it all.

Eye

'Jesus saith unto him, Thomas, because thou hast seen me, thou hast believed: blessed are they that have not seen, and yet have believed.'

JOHN 20:29 (KING JAMES BIBLE)

THE RAIN BEGINS AT midday and doesn't stop till after nightfall. At first it's a gusty mizzle, then torrential, monsoon-heavy, soak-to-the-skin. On a day like this, I'm finding lost rivers everywhere. They bubble up between paving slabs, gurgle from raging manholes, pool in the gutters. They run down my waterproof jacket and into my shoes, persistent rills of rainwater from London's toxic skies.

Flooding is in the news again. In Yorkshire, the river Don has burst its banks, wrecking more than a thousand properties. The village of Fishlake, near Doncaster, has been evacuated, its lanes becoming rivers navigable by dinghy. I light up my phone and see photos of a white Volkswagen submerged bonnet-up in a flooded field, coffin lids floating in a water-logged funeral parlour. Chinook helicopters are sent in to shore up defences. There are rumours of looters breaking into empty houses. The following week, the Prime Minister will visit the region – every inch the gentleman farmer in his wellies and quilted jacket – and receive a typically mardy Yorkshire welcome. 'You took your time, Boris,' scoffs one local resident. 'I'm not very happy about talking to you,' says another, 'so, if you don't mind, I'll just mope on with what I'm doing.'[34]

Fishlake: the language itself conspires. Rosemary *Webb* stands in front of her abandoned home, talking to the camera. The Environment Agency dispatches flood manager Adrian *Gill* to *BBC Breakfast* to defend its river maintenance strategy.[35]

I am walking along Millbank in the drizzle. High tide – and the river is the colour of poured concrete. A massive piece of driftwood is being carried downstream, out to the estuary. It looks like it's been ripped from the base of a tree. The pavements are littered with crushed, yellow-ing leaves. I pick one up and sketch its outline in my notebook – a sycamore – and a verse from the Jesuit poet Gerard Manley Hopkins comes to mind.

No wonder of it: shéer plód makes plough down sillion
Shine, and blue-bleak embers, ah my dear,
Fall, gall themselves, and gash gold-vermilion.[36]

Head south from the Houses of Parliament and you will hardly notice that you have left Thorney and crossed the threshold from gravel eyot to river delta. Do I detect a subtle dip on Great Peter Street? A shift in the atmosphere? Today being Saturday, the streets are practically empty, save for a small army of professional window cleaners servicing the many government offices.

By the time I hit Thorney Street, I'm already 300 metres south of the island it describes. An open-top bus judders down Horseferry Road, the way to an ancient crossing of the Thames. A lone tourist in a bright pink poncho eyeballs me from the upper deck. It's raining hard now. *Weirdo*, I think, then step away to inspect the flooded lightwell of an office block. The hypocrisy is obvious. I have become one of *them*, haven't I? Those men – and they usually are – who wander our cities in search of the 'urban weird'. Guardians of arcane trivia. Weekend explorers, obsessively travelling the edges of authorized culture. Some call themselves 'psychogeographers', though I can think of other names. The Scottish nature writer Kathleen Jamie coined a term that might fit: the Lone Enraptured Male.[37]

I suddenly realize that I'm standing behind Thames House, headquarters of MI5. A security camera swivels towards me. My shoes are sodden, my hood pulled up tight against the cold. I am wearing fingerless black gloves. *Don't be ridiculous*, I mutter. *It's not about me.* I move into a stairwell, out of the rain, and reach into my rucksack. I'm here to look for a place that has disappeared, erased from the city's collective memory. Erased, yes, but not entirely unrecoverable. For like a palimpsest revealed by ultraviolet light, this place might yet be conjured by a little creative detection.

*

When I first began marking out the subsurface of Westminster on my Streetfinder, stretched out on my belly in my one-bedroom flat above Petticoat Lane, my eye kept returning to one name – a half-recognized word hovering at the margins, where a gravel headland projects into the alluvial marsh. The name was *Ebury*.

There it was in *Ebury* Bridge and *Ebury* Bridge Road.

Ebury Street.

Ebury Mews.

Ebury Square.

I could not believe it at first. It was so obvious. The first syllable of the name must be *ey*, the Old English word for *island*, as in Thorn-*ey*. And 'bury' derives from *burh*, a fortified settlement. Yes, it was certain; I was looking at an occupied peninsula, an 'almost-island'.

The peninsula is the shape of a snake's head (or a flat-head screwdriver) and correlates roughly with the area known now as Belgravia, from Victoria Coach Station on its southern tip to Hyde Park Corner. It is bounded on either side by the valleys of the Westbourne and Tyburn streams as they make their way down to their confluence with the Thames. Could this be *Ey-bury*? The island-burg? The discovery of a fortified site on the edge of the Westminster Delta would transform our understanding of early medieval London.

Determined to learn more, I scoured the web and ordered the only books I could find on the subject from Amazon: *The Westminster Corridor* and *The Westminster Circle* by David Sullivan.[38] There it was, in black and white . . .

> . . . the estate of Eia, immediately adjoining Westminster to the south, part of which was known in later centuries as Eye or Ebury.[39]

Sullivan died in 2015. He wrote in the fine tradition of the amateur historian. His meticulously researched books were produced in his retirement, after a long career as a QC. He was also known for his part in saving Burgh

House in Hampstead from a council sell-off in 1978, along with the actress Dame Peggy Ashcroft.[40] Sullivan's Westminster studies combine geographical knowledge with a thorough reading of Anglo-Saxon and medieval charters to trace the early history of the Abbey and its lands. The first book also includes a series of hand-drawn maps.

Eye first appears before the Conquest as belonging to Earl Ralph, nephew of King Edward, and then to Ralph's young son. (Eia is just the Latinized spelling used in land charters.) By 1082, it was in the hands of the Norman baron Geoffrey de Mandeville, who described Eye as a *maneriolum* or 'little manor'. Its inhabitants were sometimes referred to as *de insula* – 'of the island'. In 1086 the Domesday Book recorded twenty-four families – serfs, smallholders and tenant farmers – living on lands in Eye with a taxable value of ten hides. Around the turn of the twelfth century, de Mandeville donated the manor to the Abbey, a down payment on eternal salvation.[41] The estate was enclosed by three rivers – the Tyburn, Westbourne and Thames – and, to the north, by the Roman road to Silchester (now Oxford Street). According to Sullivan's forensic work on early charters, the manor consisted of 'four distinct areas': the Field of Eye (present-day Belgravia); Ossulston (Mayfair, between Hyde Park and the Tyburn); La Hyde (the Park itself); and La Neyte (the meadowlands stretching down to the Thames through what is now Pimlico).[42]

But questions remain. If Eye means 'island', then where exactly was this island? Can we describe its bounds or find any trace of it in the modern city? Where is the *burh* to which the name Ebury refers? Could there really have been a fortified settlement here, on the edge of the marshland? And what of the village (or 'vill') of Eye that is recorded in medieval documents?

I fold up the Streetfinder and wedge it between the Sullivans. Bits of map keep falling off and working their way to the bottom of my rucksack, to the place where biros go to die. I am standing outside Tate Britain, the art gallery established by the Victorian sugar magnate Sir Henry Tate on the site of the former Millbank Prison. (Tate, I remember, is buried, not far from my mother, in West Norwood Cemetery.) Today the gallery is showing exhibitions of William Blake and Mark Leckey, visionary artists separated by two centuries. The Leckey is entitled 'O' Magic Power of Bleakness'; a poster shows a motorway flyover in fluorescent light, under which the artist claims to have seen fairies as a child. I consider stopping for a visit – to get out of the rain – but I have to push on. I end up following a quartet of twenty-something Goths around the perimeter of the gallery. They are wearing oversized white Fila trainers with long black coats, like a cross between Sisters of Mercy and the Spice Girls. The strange thing is this: they were on the C10 bus when I left home this morning. We must have been following each other all the way from Rotherhithe.

I turn into Bulinga Street. This peculiar name is the only visible trace of the mysterious Bulinga or Bulunga Fen, a marshy place mentioned in a charter of around 970 but soon after drained for pasture. I skirt the edge of a scrappy garden where a man is smoking a roll-up in the rain. A broken bench has been covered in red-and-white hazard tape like a crime scene. Rocque's map of 1750 still shows great pools of standing water here, in what became known as Tothill Fields. The Goths have disappeared. They must have trailed off back towards Thorney.

The Saxon energies are strong here; I take a right into St Oswulf Street and follow a row of pollarded trees past a redbrick housing estate whose blocks are named after famous artists. Then something stops me in my tracks: a concrete ditch sunk between the estate and a terrace of houses. Could this be a lost river, hiding in plain sight in the streets of Pimlico? A diverted section of the Tyburn? Or a culvert from the draining of the marsh? A dog goes sniffing at my leg, a bull terrier with an eyepatch. The ditch has been turned into a community garden. Herbs and vegetables are growing in wooden planters, wildflowers in terracotta pots. A deckchair.

A washing line strung from railing to railing. I sneak into the estate and track the ditch as far as it goes. The dog's owner, an elderly man with a laundry bag, is watching from the pavement. Is he in on the secret?

When I finally emerge on to Vauxhall Bridge Road it's raining heavily, so I duck into the nearest café – a large branch of Pret a Manger – for lunch. The café is rammed. I squeeze into a corner seat with a ham and cheese sandwich and a cuppa. A large group of Labour Party activists has colonized the tables: earnest young white men with beards. In their unbranded knitwear they could be junior lecturers, I think. Two older women are poring over a red folder – names and addresses of potential voters. One sports a shock of dyed pink hair. The other is the spit of Diane Keaton. I feel sorry for them all, really. What a miserable time to be in politics, on either side of the divide. Jeremy Corbyn seems to have galvanized a portion of the Labour core, but questions remain over his position on Brexit and his response to claims of institutional anti-Semitism in the party. I munch on my sandwich and make some notes. *Bulunga. Oswulf. Millbank.* I google the ditch. It's neither river nor culvert, but a remnant of the perimeter ditch of Millbank Prison. Jeremy Bentham's plans for a panopticon here were never realized. But from above, Millbank's pentangular footprint can still clearly be seen in the street plan. Bentham's panopticon has become the all-seeing eye of satellite surveillance, CCTV and social media. In their own way, the Labour activists are mapping the streets just as I am, chasing lost causes in the rain. It is only surprising to see them here, so near to Parliament. But then Pimlico is not Westminster; there is still plenty of social housing in this part of London, alongside the luxury apartments of the super-rich. After lunch I walk to the river. I want to locate the mouth of the most western branch of the Tyburn – the King's Scholars' Pond Sewer or Tachbrook – then trace its course back upstream towards the mysterious island of Eye.

Outside the Grosvenor pub, a middle-aged man in a flat cap and Chelsea FC polo shirt is bellowing into his phone. Inside, on the big screen, his team is leading mine (Crystal Palace) by two goals to nil. I cross the busy road and reach the Thames behind an exclusive residential block, Eagle Wharf. A commemorative slate by artist Paul Mason is set into the wall here and records the course of the Tyburn all the way from the Shepherd's Well in Hampstead. The actual outfall is through a brick archway underneath the adjacent properties of Tyburn House and Rio Cottage. A plaque on the latter reads: *Built 1832 as part of King-schoole Sluice.* Tom Bolton wrote that 'the lowest part of the creek was still open in 1963 when Eric Newby found "a fine unmounted pair of antlers" and "a folio bible in the Welsh language" floating in the river'.[43] The marshy edges where the Tyburn meets the Thames was part of the fertile meadowland of Eye which, by 1086, sustained eight teams of oxen and produced an annual hay crop worth sixty shillings.[44]

Today the entrance to the sewer is hidden by the high tide sloshing against the embankment. I will have to come back another day. I retrace my steps and turn into Aylesford Street, which curves between a terrace of stucco-fronted townhouses and the Tachbrook Estate in the manner of a meandering stream. The name is alluring; upstream, the Tyburn was once known as the *Aybrook* or *Eye-brook*.* The rain is bucketing down and I can hear the sound of rushing water from somewhere below. A wild-eyed ginger cat stands poised in a gulley behind the railings of the estate like Rousseau's *Tiger in a Tropical Storm.*

Beyond Pimlico station, I follow the course of the Tyburn along Tachbrook Street, where a buried channel might easily be imagined in the recessed backyards of Lillington Gardens, the award-winning 1960s housing estate that rises above the traffic like a redbrick ziggurat. I make a detour into the maze of walkways to find the church of St James the Less – 'the lily among the weeds' – that is embedded in the centre of the estate. But instead I get lost and stumble across a later appendage to the complex, the

* The connection is fanciful. The street was probably named after the 3rd Earl of Aylesford, who lived at 44 Grosvenor Square.

unremarkable 1980s blocks of Longmoore Gardens. Longmoore. A sudden jolt of recognition. David Sullivan wrote of this as *Longmore*, 'a long narrow field . . . containing apparently some one-acre plots and meadow land' and mapped it along the eastern bank of the Tyburn as part of the fields of Tothill – one of many 'fields within fields'.[45]

Language is like rock; it comes in many forms. Some can be eroded, chipped away, others changed by heat and pressure. Here language is durable as diamond. A millennium has passed and yet this name, Long-more, persists. I am struck by a sense of history reaching out to speak to me and I wonder whether anyone else is getting this uncanny feeling – the woman taking out her bins on the estate, the builder with his feet up on the dashboard, the market trader packing down in fading light, or perhaps the small boy running home with his hood pulled up and a Paw Patrol rucksack bouncing on his shoulders . . .

It's gridlock at the junction of Tachbrook Street with Warwick Way, where once the Tyburn was crossed by the Abbot's bridge.* I'm back in High Street Britain: Snappy Snaps, Domino's, charity shops and road rage. A Deliveroo moped cuts up an SUV. The driver slams on the brakes, winds down his window and shouts, 'Wanker!'

Warwick Way was once a tree-lined path through the meadows known as the Willow Walk; and before that, a causeway raised above the marshes, marked 'footway to Chelsey' on a map of 1676. I leave the Tyburn valley here and set off west in that direction. Warwick Way really does feel like an elevated track; the ground on its northern side falls away sharply and I find myself being pulled forward by the steady flow of vehicles and pedestrians. Eventually the shops and pubs are replaced by stucco-clad hotels that have seen better days: Limegrove, the Tudor Inn, Best Western Victoria Palace. The road suddenly feels provisional, as if it might detach itself, untethered from the land. I hear the rumble of the railway in an unseen cutting. Down a side street, demonic plumes

* On Horwood's map of 1799 it is marked as 'Crace Bridge'.

215

of steam are belching from the open-plan kitchens of basement flats. Umbrellas open. A man in a hooded Puffa jacket exits a newsagent's, working furiously at a scratch card, then throws the card to the ground and releases a guttural scream. In the distance, a tower block rises into the colourless sky. White-out.

In around 1223 the Abbot of Westminster, Richard of Barking, purchased land in the manor of Eye for his, and future abbots', private use. Stretching from the gravel headland at Ebury down to the Thames, this new estate contained a manor house known as La Neyte. Puzzlingly, La Neyte was *also* referred to as *insula* – 'the island'. Sullivan speculated that the house was surrounded by a defensive moat. He offered no explanation of the name, although it survives in later maps and records as *The Neat House(s)*, an obsolete term for a cattle shelter. In the seventeenth century, as market gardens sprang up in the suburbs to provide for London's growing population, the fertile fields of La Neyte occupied 100 acres and produced cauliflowers, asparagus, artichokes, spinach, radishes and even melons.[46] Samuel Pepys wrote in his diary that he bought a 'millon' here on 5 August 1666, one month before the Great Fire. After 1723, the area was claimed for the Chelsea Waterworks and was transformed into 'a strange suburban fenland, with creeks, sluice-gates and footbridges, frequented by water-birds and anglers'.[47]

The tower block is no longer distant but looming above me, the twenty-three storeys of concrete, brick and foam-filled aluminium cladding of Glastonbury House. It is impossible, in 2019, to look at a building like this and not think of Grenfell, the tower block in North Kensington destroyed by fire two years before, with the loss of seventy-two lives. Glastonbury House is a retirement community managed, along with the rest of the Abbot's Manor Estate, by Westminster City Council. Following the Grenfell fire, the Council commissioned an independent fire risk assessment and promised to install a new cladding system. But as of today, 9 November 2019, the works have still not been carried out; they are 'on hold whilst alternative insulation options are considered'.[48]

I circle the base of the tower, then crouch under cover to remove my rucksack. Inside, an elderly woman is manoeuvring her mobility scooter into the lift. I lay my Streetfinder on the ground next to Sullivan's book, open on his map of medieval Westminster, showing the location of La Neyte. I'm not sure. It could be further south. The maps won't quite align. Abbot's Manor Estate was built in two phases across a derelict bombsite. The whole plot is riddled with gloomy subways, storage basements, damp passages behind locked gates. Behind the tower, where the estate borders the huge railway cutting leading to Victoria station, residents have culti-vated a patch of unused concrete as a 'wildlife garden'. There, in the centre of the hollyhock beds, rain-soaked but resplendent in its coat of gold-and-black-painted resin, is a figurine of a snarling tiger.

This is it, or so I choose to believe. Caught between the railway and the road, the tower block is just like the moated compound described by Sullivan. The Abbot's house: La Neyte. It's got to be.

Streetlamps are flickering on. In the half-light, I leave the estate and cross the railway cutting over Ebury Bridge. There's no river here though. The only thing I can hear is the mechanized music of a train leaving the platform at Victoria, heading home with a

    clickety-clackety
        clickety-clackety
            clickety-clackety . . .

Look here: a steel ramp leads down to the tracks, to Pugs Hole Siding.* *No unauthorized personnel.* I descend in the dwindling light through a forest of buddleia. Railway sleepers are stacked like Jenga blocks. Rag-wort probes at the fenceline. The railway arcs south towards the Thames, ten tracks combined, carving through the city. And this *was* once a waterway, the Grosvenor Canal, crossed by a wooden bridge near to

---

* 'Pug' was a nickname for short steam locomotives used for shunting.

Jenny's Whim, where a visit to the tavern might be enhanced by the 'queer *spectacle*' of grotesque automata appearing from shadowy recesses or a mechanical mermaid surfacing in a pond.[49]

More trains are approaching now, their carriages lit up like Chinese lanterns. In the distance, I can just make out the white towers of the disused Battersea Power Station, a landmark of my youth. The music of the trains is deafening and joyful, a Delta blues for the disappeared island.

I climb back to the railway bridge and don't look back. From somewhere, the sound of metal on metal. Then, a percussive blow. Headlights on slick tarmac. A young mother and child walking at speed towards Victoria. They are walking an imaginary line, a line on a map between gravel and silt.

Ebury, Westminster's lost island, lies beyond the junction, where the ground rises to the north. The border is marked by a sentry post of sorts: a Victorian drinking fountain whose elaborate stone megalith is decorated with recessed enamel mosaics by the Venetian glassmaker Antonio Salviati. I've seen these swirling designs before – in the Cosmati pavements of Westminster Abbey and on the black box of St Edward's shrine. A forlorn statue of St George slaying the dragon stares down from another redbrick housing block, Fountain Court. Now lacking arms, I'm not sure how he would fare in the rematch. Could there once have been a natural spring here, emerging from the edge of the island?* Today the fountain runs dry, but water still pools in its granite basins, fag ends swimming in acid rain. The way in is via Avery Farm Row, a stubby little street whose name retains a corrupted version of Ebury, itself an elaboration on the original Eye or Eia. And so it goes: the alchemy of naming.

Night falls in Ebury Square, where London plane trees and acacias block the last of the light. It feels like a secret, this place, tucked behind

---

* A map of 1750 shows a small pool on the site. In 1800 a 'New Spring Gardens' is recorded near by.

Victoria Coach Station. It is not quite a grand square, despite its Belgravia postcode. The eastern side is dominated by Semley House, a fortress-like residential block that was once the London headquarters of Pan Am. Insipid green light spills from the illuminated sign of a car rental agency. A group of lads in matching bomber jackets piles into Rileys sports bar. A Megabus turns in, its engine releasing a horrible, choking rattle. The presence of the coach station gives the square a strange, uncertain atmosphere, as if it exists outside of ordinary time. The surrounding streets are full of people waiting – waiting for their coach to leave, or, having already arrived, working out where to go next. The station itself seems to be in a semi-permanent state of disrepair, staff and travellers high on diesel fumes. As I cross the square, through an enclosed garden with four paths radiating from a central fountain, a shadow passes in front of my eyes: not a ghost but the realization that I have been here before, as a teenager, waiting for the night coach to Oxford.

O, blue-bleak embers.

O' magic power of bleakness.

In the far corner of the coach park, a Shell petrol station stands alone in an empty lot, islanded in a former bombsite that must have escaped developers' plans. Shell: the pilgrim's mark. It glows like a golden beacon in the darkness.

I enter Belgravia proper with more questions than answers. Is the gravel headland around Ebury Square the 'island' that gave Eye its name? Or, as Sullivan has suggested, might there have been 'another island . . . its size or character . . . unknown'?[50] And what about La Neyte, the Abbot's rural retreat, enclosed by a moat and accessed by causeway? Was *that* the island?

I have more immediate concerns. Sarah texts: *Where r u now?* She has been in town with Martha all day – lunch with an old friend from university and her daughter, followed by a trip to the London Transport

Museum. She must be knackered. Looking after a toddler is exhausting at the best of times, let alone in central London in the rain. I reply: *Phone dying. Meet at Bond Street?* We both need to get home. Tonight one of us will be babysitting our neighbour's son, while the other puts Martha to bed. For the rest of the journey I will be walking against the pressure of time – and the weather.

A crowd of people has gathered outside Peggy Porschen, the luxury cake shop on the corner of Ebury Street. Its windows are adorned with glowing snowflakes and illuminated sprays – an early Christmas display. A teenaged girl poses in the doorway, head tilted for the perfect Instagram post. Rileys, Europcar and Victoria Coach Station are less than 100 metres away, but they seem to belong to a parallel world. In the eighteenth century, Belgravia was a notorious crime hotspot known as Five Fields and frequented after dark by footpads and highwaymen.* Ebury Street itself was called Five Fields Row, although on earlier maps it was marked variously as 'the way from Chelsey [to] Westminster' and 'the old way from Westminster to Ebury Farme'.[51] Take a ruler to the modern street map and you will find that Ebury Street aligns directly with Buckingham Palace. Overlay the geological deposits and it appears as a dead-straight track following the eastern edge of the gravel headland between the valleys of the Westbourne and the Tyburn. For Sullivan, the alignment was no coincidence, but supported his theory for the location of a medieval settlement, the disappearing 'vill' of Eye or Eye Cross, at or very near what is now the London residence of the Queen.

No material evidence of a village in the vicinity has ever been found. Nor does one appear on any extant maps. Sullivan had only land charters and property transactions to go on. With these modest resources, he uncovered a linear settlement in the Field of Eye, a collection of

* On Rocque's map of 1746 the five fields are identifiable in the land north of Ebury Street. Each field is clearly delineated by hedgerows.

houses and gardens clustered around a high street running north to
south parallel to a 'brook'.[52] It is here, in the middle of the thirteenth
century, that 'Alan the son of Alexander of Eye gave up all claims on one
messuage [a dwelling house with outbuildings and land] in the vill'.[53]
Here, too, that Robert Brown of Eye bought a plot of land from Walter
the carter and his wife Alice, and another from Alan of London. In Sullivan's account, a 'merry-go-round of activity' follows: Brown flips his
plot to Ralph of Corf, 'marbler', then finds a buyer for his own house –
John Benyn of Aldeburgh. Richard Wombe of Westminster purchases a
plot from Alan of London's daughter, Agnes. Alan, son of Alexander, lets
one of his three houses to another Ralph, son of Gilbert of Knights-
bridge. And on it goes, a flurry of property speculation which suggests
that the 'vill' of Eye was a significant new area of development west of
Westminster Abbey. An array of crops flourished here too: wheat, rye,
barley and oats; beans, peas and vetch. A herd of cows – as many as
sixty-six in one year – grazed in the Abbot's fertile lands to the south,
and from around 1296 its management was contracted out to tenant
farmers living in the village.

The pavements of Belgravia are glistening with the glow from
shops still open this late. A headless, armless mannequin in a white
wedding dress stands in the window of an Italian bridal boutique. An
elegant young woman in a mustard trench coat steps out of a café. The
lights are on too in the living room of a handsome, stucco-fronted
house and I glimpse an empty wing-backed armchair, a series of etchings of English castles in gold frames, newspapers on an occasional
table. Sullivan was unequivocal in locating the site of the village of Eye
or Eye Cross at the eastern end of Ebury Street, in what are now the
grounds of Buckingham Palace.* But how did the village disappear,

* A televised investigation of Buckingham Palace by Channel 4's *Time Team* and
Oxford Archaeology in 2006 failed to uncover any materials predating the eighteenth
century.

and when? Was it destroyed in some calamity, ploughed over for arable or simply consumed by the urban sprawl of Westminster? The answer, I discover, is far stranger.

In 1609 James I ordered the creation of a 'mulberry garden' in what had become, after the dissolution of the Abbey's properties under Henry VIII, royal land. James was a keen supporter of the silk trade and believed the garden would encourage the growth of a silkworm colony. The site is clearly marked on a 1614 map of the manor of Eybury, a rough square laid out in quarters on the west bank of the Tyburn just before it splits in two. But James's silkworm project failed; he had bought the wrong variety of tree. The mulberry garden became, instead, a commercial pleasure garden, a place of 'new-erected sodoms and spintries' (a male prostitute), according to one critic, before being developed for a succession of aristocratic mansions.[54] It was not until the accession of Queen Victoria in 1837 that Buckingham Palace became the principal royal residence.

So it was that the humble silkworm devoured an entire village. In what condition Eye or Eye Cross existed in 1609 – or indeed in 1536, when it was detached from the properties of the Abbey – is not known. It had perhaps already fallen into decay and was barely visible – just lines in a field where once houses stood.[55]

Sullivan believed that James's mulberry-garden project did not only result in the erasure of the village, but also in the radical realignment of local roads. The map of 1614 shows a new road between the mulberry garden and Ebury Farm, running parallel with but to the south of Ebury Street.* Its route is now followed by Buckingham Palace Road, the deafening thoroughfare between Victoria Coach Station and the railway terminus. Ebury Street was demoted to the 'old way' and then, at its end,

---

* It was recorded in 1614 as 'Road to Chelsea' and on a map of 1663 as 'now the way from Chelsey to Westminster'.

deflected away from the mulberry garden – away, that is, from the former site of the village and the crossing of the Tyburn at Eybridge. According to Sullivan's research, the abandoned high street may even have been relocated to the opposite bank of the Tyburn. The vill had become, in his words, 'a no-go area'.[56]

Stone

M Y HEAD IS SWIMMING. Images emerge then dissipate: the ruined village; a silkworm turning in its white cocoon; the ghosts of islanders wandering the gardens of Buckingham Palace at night like confused junior estate agents, tracing pathways that no longer exist.

I walk the final stretch of Ebury Street half-dazed by the cold and rain. On Grosvenor Place cabs are hailed by gents in Crombies with velvet collars. I track the brick-built perimeter wall of the Palace north towards Hyde Park Corner. The Palace itself is constructed from oolitic limestone, which consists of tiny balls of carbonate sediment that were recently identified as the fossilized remains of microbes from the Jurassic Period. The *Express* led with 'Dinosaur Fossils in Buckingham Palace: Boffins in Spectacular 200-million-year-old Find'.[57] My phone flashes on; the battery is almost dead. I'm carrying white gold in my pocket – lithium, from *lithos*, the Greek for 'stone', mined from beneath the Tibetan plateau or exhumed from the salt flats of Bolivia and Chile. Wellington Arch comes into view through night-mist – stranded on a traffic island, vast and white. A new five-star hotel is under construction, its name stamped across gunmetal-grey hoardings: The Peninsula. It's too good to be true.

And now I am climbing, ascending to the higher terraces beyond Hyde Park Corner, then down suddenly into a subway, like opening a door in the hillside, its tiled walls decorated with sycamore leaves, and the sickly-sweet smell of weed around every corner, where, in the artificial light of a waking dream, two men without a place of their own are playing cards on a bed made from corrugated cardboard.

By the time I surface, on Park Lane, I have already crossed, unconsciously, into Ossulston. I am standing, rain-sodden, beneath the Hilton. Revellers are stepping out of carriages in ballgowns, dinner jackets and silk scarves. Ossulston. One of the four fields of the manor of Eye. My hood sticks to my skull. My shoes are dripping. For carriages, read: two black Ford Galaxys with 'Addison Lee' emblazoned on their rear windows. *This* London is alien to me – as alien, perhaps, as the *idea* of London itself is alien to those outside the city's fierce orbit. 'All the country is gotten into London,' said James I, in 1616, 'so as, with time, England will only be London, and the whole country be left waste . . .'[58]

Sullivan parsed Ossulston as either Oswald's or Oswulf's stone.[59] I text Sarah: *Running late, see u at home.* And then my phone powers down. It sits in my palm, inert, like a polished flint. How can I be grounded in this place? To walk here feels like trespass. Was that me near-colliding at pace with a tall figure under a golfing umbrella? Was that me, hood down, muttering obscenities to the empty street? To the night? Am I that man? Is that me? In the BMW showroom, a white supercar gleams under spotlights, its gull-wing doors raised like a raptor preparing to kill.

What time is it?

My phone is dead and now my watch has stopped. A bead of rainwater is working its way across the face.

I turn into South Street.

To find the Ossulston. To find Oswulf's stone.

In the 1614 map of the manor, Ossulston appears as an egg-shaped circle within an oblong enclosure at the corner of a field adjoining Park Lane.* This site was once a folkmoot, a public assembly or meeting place from the time of the Anglo-Saxons. It gave its name to the Ossulstone Hundred, a now obsolete subdivision of the shire of Middlesex covering most of what is now central London north of the Thames – from Brentford to the river Lea.† As late as the mid-fifteenth century, the Middlesex county

---

* The site was labelled 'Osolston' and the field as 'Mr. Colbanks his hay hills'.
† Excluding the City of London.

court was still convened here at Ossulston, in rotation with two other locations in the shire.[60] In the eighteenth century the area was identified in legal deeds as 'a common or waste . . . called Ossulton Common'.[61]

I have followed Sullivan's instructions to the junction of South Street and Park Street. I half expect a giant *menhir* or a sacred *lingam* to appear. I take off my glasses and wipe them with an already-damp handkerchief to little effect. I take in a block of serviced offices, mansion flats, an upmarket estate agency and a chauffeured Bentley, parked up, engine idling. There is nothing to suggest I am in the right place.

On the evening of 10 January 1870, the antiquarian William Henry Black announced to the London and Middlesex Archaeological Society that he had located the Ossulston at Marble Arch, some 600 metres to the north of where I am standing. Black's findings were the result of an 'infallible' method (his words) based on geometric principles.

Ossulstone is figured in Sir John Roque's [*sic*] great map of 1741–1761, sheet xi. in the very spot to which my process on other maps had led me; and it is there called the 'Stone where soldiers are shot,' situate near the north-east angle of Hyde Park. It was afterward covered with an accumulation of soil, and is now dug up and lies against the Marble Arch . . . [62]

Black was a Seventh Day Baptist, a skilled palaeographer and keen poet. Ossulston, he proposed, marked the western vertex of an isosceles triangle, with two other relics – a Roman stone found in Panyer Alley, near St Paul's, in 1865, and the sarcophagus currently on display in the triforium of Westminster Abbey – completing the trick. Marble Arch is only the latest structure to occupy the crossroads, where the ancient route of Watling Street (Edgware Road) meets the Devil's Highway from Silchester (Oxford Street). On a nearby traffic island, the site of the infamous gallows known as the Tyburn Tree is remembered by a roundel set in the pavement. Like Iain Sinclair, the poet of *Lud Heat*, Black conjured a psychic map of the city as 'a system of energies'; historical fact held less weight for him than the ecstatic buzz of connection.[63] I think also of Sullivan, who saw at work across the history of Westminster the 'binding threads of water'.[64] Not even the most diligent of scholars is immune to such lyrical flourishes.

Was Black's mysterious pre-Roman stone the Ossulston? If, as Sullivan suggests, it was relocated to Marble Arch from the original site, when exactly did this take place and why?[65] And what happened to it after 1870? Was it stolen, lost or, as some have claimed, broken up, with one piece recycled for the Tyburn milestone?

A motorbike courier stops to check his route. He wipes the rain from his sat nav with a gloved hand. One last clue draws me back. Since the nineteenth century, the area south of Marble Arch has been set aside for public speaking and debate. At Speakers' Corner today, you can find firebrand preachers arguing the finer points of Qur'anic scripture with tourists, street drinkers, white nationalists and conspiracy theorists. And so the folkmoot at Ossulston lives on; perhaps a parliament more fitting, I wonder, than the one we have now, down there, on the island in the marshes.

I wanted to have found something tangible, some small trace I could touch, or see, to complete my journey. But Ossulston has turned out to be a dead end. I am reminded of a line by Jessica J. Lee on walking through mist with her mother in the mountains of Taiwan: 'The longer we walked, the less we could see'.[66]

I cut across Mayfair, through streets I have never walked down, hoping to be spat out somewhere near the Tube. I'm tired and cold. Sarah will be home by now, Martha playing in the bath with Mermaid or pulling on her Bing pyjamas. I take a wrong turn, then circle back, past a shop selling countrywear and hunting rifles. Another turn, then raucous laughter spills from a pub, the Punchbowl on Farm Street, and something stops inside.

*

Time, writes the poet Denise Riley, 'was always layered'.[67] A golden light pours into the rain-soaked street. I *have* been here before. But I have no memory of this place, no images to recall, just a name, Farm Street, and a year – the year of my birth. I push open the glass door for the first time and step into the soft glow of the Jesuit Church of the Immaculate Conception. The high altar, by Pugin, is aflame in amber light; I am pulled forward, past empty pews veiled in shadow.

In her lyrical essay on the death of her son, Riley writes of the sensation of time having been 'suddenly arrested':

> [A] sudden death, for the one left behind, does such violence to the experienced 'flow' of time that it stops, and then slowly wells up into a large pool. Instead of the old line of forward time, now something like a globe holds you. You live inside a great circle with no rim.[68]

Inside the church, time has not stopped but seems, instead, to *fold back*, or *in*, on itself. Summer 1983: I was brought here, to Farm Street, at three months old, to be baptized. It was my mother's idea – it must have been; she was the Catholic – though why *this* church, five miles from our own parish, I will never know. As a drama teacher, I like to think she was attracted to the liturgical theatre of its renowned Latin Mass, the high camp of incense and cassocks.*

The atmosphere in the church is so thick it's like walking through an energy field. I hear the blood rushing in my ears and think of what Jodi Picoult wrote of dark matter; that it pulls things towards itself. In one of the side chapels a life-sized bronze statue of a man lies sleeping on a park bench, a homeless Jesus with nail-holes in his bare feet.[69] That day, thirty-six years ago, I wore a long gown of white cotton lace – or was it silk? My father in a dove-grey suit. Grandparents and uncles.

---

* Evelyn Waugh was a congregant at Farm Street and the church appears in his novel *Brideshead Revisited* (1945).

The Welsh poet–priest R. S. Thomas described his church as a 'stone trap' designed to lure God 'as though he would come like some huge moth / out of the darkness to beat there',[70] an image reprocessed by Iain Sinclair in *Lud Heat*: 'Each church is an enclosure of force, a trap, a sight-block, a raised place with an unacknowledged influence on events within their nome-lines.'[71]

What are these words that keep tumbling out?

Everything flows;

the river falls;[72]

then suddenly, a noise like radio static. I spin around. Behind a pillar, an old woman in a woollen hat is rustling a polythene bag. Why hadn't I noticed her before? She looks up, vacantly, without acknowledging my presence. My heart sounds a dampened drumbeat. Has she even seen me?

I turn to face the Madonna, stationed above the sanctuary. She wears a crown and a robe of blue and gold. Her hands are clasped in prayer. Her eyes are lowered in humble obeisance.

Hail Mary, full of grace.

Her face – her face is my mother's face. The same look of serenity and concentration, lips slightly parted, that I remember from my childhood.

Blessed art thou amongst women.

When something disappears, or is erased, we find ourselves tracking back in ever-diminishing circles, like aircraft stacking in the troposphere, waiting for their turn to land.

For years, after their separation and then my mother's death, I kept a tiny photograph of my parents in their thirties – tanned and beaming in the south of France – in the zipped compartment of my wallet. A relic from my own deep time, the image grew warped and sun-bleached from handling before finally disintegrating in the ice-cold water of a glacial lake.

I have walked the Westminster Delta from Thorney to Ossulston through a landscape where danger rises from beneath and secrets are stashed underground, in ancient crypts and flooded basements, where the powerful dither and deceive on an island of gravel in the river's soapy backwash.

Perhaps the Westminster Bubble will finally burst. The Palace is sinking. Politicians on left and right have lost the public's trust. There are calls for a new parliament – in Birmingham or Belfast or 'a big top that moves from town to town'.[73] In the future it may be wise to move to higher ground.

Farm Street completes the journey. The holding pattern melts away like a vapour trail. As I leave, the woman with the rustling bag is nowhere to be seen. I think I dreamt her, a reverie from the vill of Eye, from Ossulston.

A stopped watch;
the silkworm moth;
this stone trap.

I step into the night and head for home, back south, across the river.

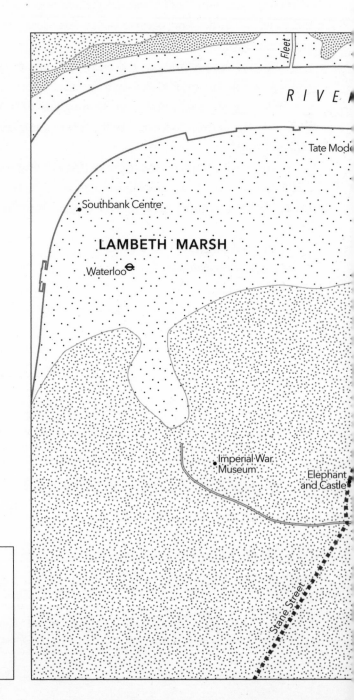

Fleet

R I V E

Tate Mode

Southbank Centre

LAMBETH MARSH

Waterloo

Imperial War
Museum

Elephant
and Castle

Stane Street

Alluvium

Clay

Gravel

Peat

Roman Road

VI: DEAD RIVER

Tracking the Neckinger

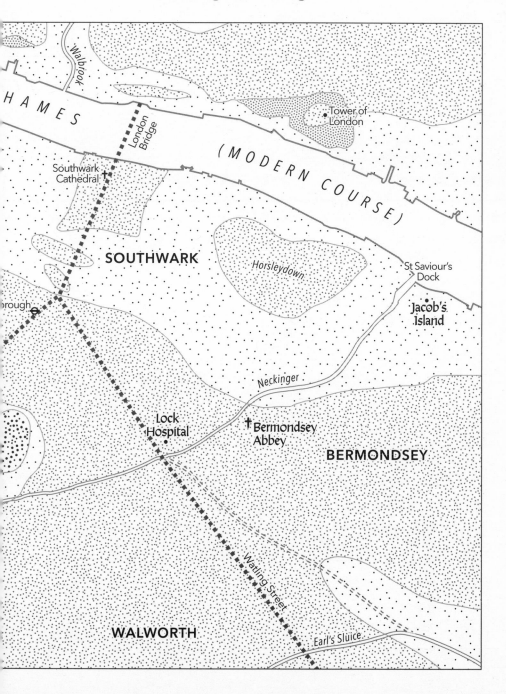

THAMES

Walbrook

London Bridge

Tower of London

(MODERN COURSE)

Southwark Cathedral

SOUTHWARK

Horsleydown

St Saviour's Dock

Borough

Jacob's Island

Neckinger

Lock Hospital

Bermondsey Abbey

BERMONDSEY

Watling Street

WALWORTH

Earl's Sluice

Tabula Rasa

*'There are tell-tale signs of the
truth of the collapse of the truth'*

JOHN GIBBENS[1]

FARNBOROUGH, FLEET, WINCHFIELD, HOOK – the departure boards flash up destinations like a Home Counties *poème concrète*. It's early afternoon and already the concourse of Waterloo station is buzzing with office workers heading home for the holiday. Accountants and insurance brokers wield Christmas shopping in oversized gift bags from Hamleys, Oliver Bonas and Hotel Chocolat. Above our heads, a latticework of dirty white girders supports a vast roof comprising twenty-four thousand individual panes of glass. A muffled tannoy sounds and the concourse shifts below. We could be birds in a giant aviary, I think, or workers in a Soviet tank factory.

I'm back in south London, in search of the source of another vanished channel. But the stream I'm looking for begins without a name or definitive source. The whole lost river has come to be known as the Neckinger, but this peculiar word used only to refer to its lower reach and is a relatively recent coinage. It derives from slang for the gallows that stood near its mouth, just east of Tower Bridge, in the seventeenth and eighteenth centuries: 'the Devil's neckerchief', where pirates were hanged. In its middle course, it was called the Lock Stream, after the Lock hospital, a medieval foundation for the quarantine of lepers whose grounds it crossed.* In the backwaters of Lambeth, it went unnamed.

In *The Lost Rivers of London*, Nicholas Barton traced the Neckinger to 'near the site of today's Waterloo station', but added, 'there are no maps that show its upper parts clearly'.[2] Tom Bolton has mapped the stream back to the Thames at Barge House Stairs (near the Oxo Tower), a work of 'informed conjecture' that presents the Neckinger as a creek or tidal loop of the Thames with no freshwater source of its own.[3] His route

---

* The name derives from the Old French *loques*, for the linen rags applied to patients' sores.

follows the meandering boundary between the boroughs of Lambeth and Southwark, tracking a drainage ditch along the Broadwall. My friend the poet Chris McCabe swears he has smelt the toxic vapour of a buried river outside The Stage Door on Webber Street. 'An aroma of heavy tannins,' he explained, two pints in at The Mayflower. The prolific blogger 'diamond geezer' even speculates that the Neckinger 'might possibly have been the leftover remains of an oxbow lake'.[4] It all seems implausible to me: like a good story, surely a river must have a beginning, a middle and an end? But perhaps they are right; recent geological modelling of prehistoric Southwark depicts the Neckinger as a 'braided channel creating a number of fragmentary eyots, rather than a true tributary of the Thames'.[5] We have, as the poet John Gibbens says, only 'tell-tale signs / of the truth'.[6]

I want to trace the source of the Neckinger before following its course through south London; but here in the flatlands of Lambeth the conditions for locating a lost river are uniquely unpromising. Where the Walbrook, Fleet and Tyburn are celebrity streams flowing through the mainline of London history, the Neckinger is an unknown quantity – mysterious, disappearing, undocumented. So how to begin? With a clearing of the throat? A mark on the page? The first line is always the hardest.

I open my laptop and the white space at the edge of the map glares back. In early panoramas of the city, Lambeth Marsh or Moor appears as a *tabula rasa*, a blank slate, providing mapmakers, as Bolton has pointed out, with a 'handy space for titles and credits'.[7] Originally a tidal wetland bordering the Thames, Lambeth Marsh was a herbalist's paradise – a rural backwater brimming with frogbit, willowherb, rocket and heart's ease.[8] The marsh was protected from the river on three sides by the Narrow Wall and the Broad Wall, raised earth banks of Roman origin that doubled as causeways. Another raised track once cut through the centre of the boggy ground, taking a ruler-straight course from London Bridge to the old river crossing at Stangate (a name preserved today by a 1950s tower block opposite St Thomas's Hospital). The alignment of this causeway was reproduced by the later road known simply as Lambeth Marsh (now Upper and Lower Marsh), which Rocque's map of 1746 shows as a ribbon development transecting a landscape of meadows, gardens, fields and bogs. Since the Middle Ages, the wetlands south of the river had been scored and sliced by drainage ditches, giving Rocque's rendering an almost diagrammatic quality, as if the marsh were a circulatory system or a city-sized microchip.

I have abandoned my perch above the concourse and am now climbing down the grand staircase to street level beneath the iconic Victory Arch – a memorial to station staff killed during the Great War. This elevated entrance gives Waterloo the outward appearance of a Baroque cathedral, an effect I have always interpreted as a sardonic commentary on the dank, murky tangle of sliproads, railway viaducts and alleyways in which it is situated. The station was constructed in multiple stages on a site described at its opening in 1848 as 'vacant ground, to a great extent occupied as hay-stalls and cow-yards and by dung-heaps, and similar nuisances'.[9] At the bottom of the steps, a teenaged girl is slumped on the pavement, hoodie pulled up, an empty paper cup in her lap. An enthusiastic *Big Issue* seller greets each passer-by. 'Good afternoon, madam, sir. No problem. God bless.' A middle-aged woman in a trouser suit sucks on a vape.

The waterlogged terrain of Lambeth Marsh had required the engineers of Waterloo station to raise the railway and its terminus building above ground level on a network of brick arches, creating a shadow world of tunnels and vaults, plant rooms and emergency bunkers. Some of these cavernous spaces have since been repurposed as bars, clubs and even theatres. In 2010, I witnessed a performance of *Unearthing* by cult comic-book writer Alan Moore in one of the recently opened tunnels. The Magus of Northampton incanted the feverish text in his East Midlands *basso profundo* as sound-makers Crook & Flail tuned in to the frequencies of abandoned Victorian industry, returning them as drones, scraped metal and electrical buzzes.

A daytime drinker slips out of the Hole in the Wall and joins the back of a group of tourists in matching anoraks waiting to cross the frenetic speedway of York Road on their way to the London Eye or the Southbank Centre. There is something melancholic about Waterloo and today I have the mood to match. My stomach has been cramping for a week – a background noise of bodily discomfort to a succession of minor crises at work. Walking provides temporary release but no cure to the fog of pre-Christmas depression into which I find myself slowly sinking. Meanwhile, the country is being pulled further into the mass psychosis of Brexit; Pandora's box has been opened and there's more than just one racist uncle inside.

I head south down York Road, past mini-marts, betting shops and car-rental firms. I'm looking for a dead river and I'm already lost. Across the street, a glassy, box-fresh development of shops and luxury flats is about to open under the predictably generic name Southbank Place. I was expecting the Shell Centre, headquarters of the petroleum giant, but it appears I'm too late – the site is now part-owned by the oil-rich state of Qatar. Clad in Portland stone, the Shell Centre was Europe's largest office block when it opened in 1961, with two wings known as the Upstream and Downstream Buildings. The complex was constructed on a massive reinforced concrete raft, a type of foundation used to overcome 'difficult soil conditions' by spreading the load over a greater area than traditional footings.[10] Special 'under-reamed' concrete piles added further stability in the soft, alluvial ground; their shafts were excavated by hand and lined with precast rings to avoid subsidence from the Bakerloo Line tunnel below. The original Shell tower has been retained in the new development, given a multi-million-pound facelift by architects Perkins & Will. And if you peer into the Thames at low tide, you can still see the turbulence where the block's air conditioning system sucks in cold water from the river.

The tubular steel vault of the former Waterloo International station comes into view, elevated above York Road like the exposed skeleton of a reticulated python, its massive ribs licked clean by the marsh winds. Still partially unused, this curious appendage to the main station housed the platforms for the Eurostar from 1994 until its removal, to St Pancras, in 2007. Waterloo always seemed to me a terminus unbefitting of such a prestigious international rail service; a passenger embarking at Gare du Nord in Paris would alight in the dreary fag ends of Lambeth at a station named after a famous French military defeat. I remember, as a teenager, waiting on the platform at Herne Hill for the next slam-door train to Victoria or Blackfriars, when the tremendous drone of an engine would herald the passing of the Eurostar through south London, its huge, shiny grey nose like the head of a beluga whale, gliding towards the coast, not even yet at half-speed. It was like something from science fiction. Sometimes, I would glimpse, through tinted windows, the ghostly faces of passengers: a small child, eager at the glass; businessmen sipping coffee or scan-reading *Le Monde*. What must they have seen, that instant, from a passing train? A hill, a tower block, the unruly siding where foxes skulk, a boy in baggy skater jeans waiting for the future to happen.

In the summer of 1996, my grandparents took my mother and me on a week's holiday to Paris. It was to be her last. She wore long, practical dresses and a sandy-coloured bob, her own, darker hair having fallen out during chemo. When we arrived at the check-in desk at Waterloo, my grandfather, ever the benevolent Scottish patriarch, had a surprise up his sleeve; he had booked us all first-class tickets. We would be travelling in style. I remember, with perfect clarity, discovering the complimentary pastries in the first-class lounge and stuffing an entire tray of chocolate croissants into my rucksack for the trip. I was wearing a blue checked shirt and shorts and had my blond hair in curtains like a tiny, chubby boyband member. On the platform, I posed for a photo in front of the Eurostar, this strange creature that would carry us under the sea to France through a stratum of chalk marl laid down in the Cretaceous period.

Another tunnel beckons now, decades later; I approach the entrance, set back from York Road, a gateway into the shadowy underworld beneath Waterloo station. A dazzling gold skull with grinning teeth in the style of the Mexican *Día de Muertos* has been sprayed on the brick wall, its forehead stamped with SCRAP BREXIT. A cartoonish sigil for the dead – dead river, dead mother and all.

Skull

A BEARDED MAN IN CARHARTT jeans and a baseball cap is working on a complex calligraphic design. A small boy, whom I assume to be his son, sits cross-legged beside him in the gloom, rattling cans of spray paint. An Instagram model in an embroidered bomber jacket strikes a pose. One assistant holds up a portable light reflector, while another plays tinny pop music from her phone. A greenish light catches on her contoured cheeks. Further down, another artist makes wide gestures in fluorescent colours. He is wearing latex gloves, a white boiler suit and face mask, and has brought his own sound system: a vintage ghetto blaster.

Leake Street is where graffiti writers come to play without fear of penalty or arrest. Known colloquially as The Tunnel, it has been designated an 'authorized graffiti area', although a list of rules at the entrance does prohibit some practices ('No Sexism. No Racism. No Adverts.') Every surface is covered – even the wheelie bins outside the hip new restaurants that have appeared in the once abandoned archways. Cartoon characters – Bugs Bunny, Donald Duck – leap off the walls in primary colours, alongside *Star Wars*' Jabba the Hutt and a fearsome samurai in the Japanese anime style. Scrawled tags – AREA 51, NURSE, GROPE, HOT OWCH – appear in the edges between garish throw-ups and complex compositions that must have taken weeks to paint: a green-eyed woman with an enigmatic smile; a huge black-and-white mural inspired by West African textile design; an ominous Tube train; a figure in a gas mask glaring down from the roof.

When I first explored the tunnel, back in 2013, it was practically deserted, but today I am joined by office workers clutching Styrofoam lunch boxes from the market on Lower Marsh and tourists posing for photos with their wheelie cases. A 'Vietnamese tapas' joint has opened in one of the arches, a 'board game café' in another. Coloured spotlights hang from metal trusses fixed to the roof. Autotuned R&B spills from one of the arches. Lambeth Council has even added Leake Street to its cleaning rota; a worker in hi-vis is carefully brushing the dirt from the gutter. I stop to photograph the coils of a giant snake that have been painted on the floor when something clips my elbow and a hooded figure on an electric scooter shoots past, swerving through the pedestrians at break-neck speed. I shout some obscenity, but he's long gone. A group of lads in winter coats approaches in a cloud of vapour and I smell strawberries.

At the eastern end, the tunnel divides. On the left, a pedestrian ramp leads up and out of the tunnel, to the shops and cafés of Lower Marsh. On the right, the roadway plunges down and then turns sharply, into the light. I take this lower path, where a man in a denim jacket is spraying the outline – or 'shell' – of a new design directly over another. This practice is known as blocking, or capping, and is sometimes considered disrespectful, a deliberate 'crossing out' of another artist's work. In Leake Street, it's routine procedure; the walls have become palimpsests, dense with hundreds of layers of paint. Nothing stays the same for long. Further down the tunnel, a youth in a hoodie is using a bucket and roller to cover a three-metre section of wall salmon-pink, a roll-up hanging from his mouth. A grey-haired accomplice in paint-splattered overalls is already working up his design, an intricate 'wild style' of interlocking letters and tracery that would not look out of place in the margins of the Lindisfarne Gospels. At the lowest point of the tunnel, a pool of water has collected, a stagnant puddle covered with an oleaginous film.

In J. G. Ballard's novel *Concrete Island*, an architect driving home down the Westway interchange loses control of his Jaguar and plunges down a grass embankment into the wasteland between three converging motorways, a 'forgotten terrain' of dumped cars and ruined buildings from which he cannot escape.[11] Now closed to vehicles, Leake Street once fed the turbulent gyratory circling the Park Plaza hotel; an access ramp at the far end still rises towards the traffic. As I approach the steel security fence, I feel like Maitland, Ballard's urban castaway – trapped by the concrete walls of the slip road.

In 2013 I visited the tunnel to photograph the fly-tip that had accumulated at the dead end of the ramp, an enormous mound consisting of soiled clothing and smashed timber, laundry bags, bin bags, spent cans of spray paint, a woman's high-heeled shoe, a plastic bumper and what looked like the carcass of an entire tree. A pair of black jogging bottoms had snagged on two branches that rose from the centre like two fingers or the horns of a goat. The crude outline of a skull had been daubed in white paint by the roadside. The mound seemed to radiate a wild, malevolent energy, as if it were a monster guarding the tunnel. But now, six years later, it is gone, a patch of scuffed tarmac the only sign it had ever existed. Like everything else in the underworlds beneath the city's railway infrastructure, Leake Street has become sanitized, its messy edges tidied away and sold on. The night economy is flourishing in these spaces, offering revellers a journey into London's underbelly but with the comfort of flushing toilets and well-mixed drinks. At number 26, the cavernous bar and music venue, you can even buy a pint of Neckinger, a 'pale gold [lager] with a crisp, persistent bitterness that simply leaves you wanting more'.[12]

I've had enough and retrace my steps. As I climb out of the tunnel, following a construction worker towards Lower Marsh, I spot one final graffito, an unembellished scrawl in large black capitals: HAPPY NEW YEAR YOU CUNTS.

An Eastern European man dressed in black military fatigues is walking an angry Alsatian on a leash stamped BOY. The air is thick with falafel wraps, grilled chicken and vegan curry. The man stops to chat with the owner of the Chunnel Bar, an Italian greasy spoon that looks as if it hasn't changed in thirty years. I can't quite hear, but it sounds like he is saying the words 'hardware' and 'prison' over and over. Despite its proximity to

Waterloo station, Lower Marsh seems to have resisted the tide of corporate chain restaurants that threatens to engulf the rest of London. Alongside the ubiquitous charity shops, it boasts an art gallery, a beauty salon (Angela's Nails), a branch of Ryman the stationer, a shop selling model-making kits and another specializing in wind instruments.

It's hard to believe this pedestrianized road is the ancient causeway that once crossed the marshes of Lambeth at the time of the Romans. But true enough, the alleys on its northern side fall away sharply to the level of the tunnel. An atmosphere of independence persists, as if Lower Marsh were somehow disconnected from the rest of the city, but this sensation is abruptly dispelled by the thundering intrusion of Westminster Bridge Road. Beyond the traffic, the causeway continues under a railway viaduct and is called Upper Marsh. I notice a sticker for the pro-Remain People's March and a simple graffito: EU 1 – UK 0. The black arches are dripping with mysterious fluid. If I follow this route I will be spat out at Stangate, St Thomas's and the Thames. There is a better path, a path that will get me back on the course of the Neckinger and, in doing so, reveal something of Lambeth's radical poetic history.

A pigeon flies down from its roost in the girders above Carlisle Lane, its wings riffling like the pages of a thrown book. The brickwork of the tunnel roof is exceptional, sweeping in golden arcs that seem to defy gravity. At the apex, where rainwater has bled through, it is stained in rich greens and browns, a mineral wash that belongs on the walls of a limestone cave. Rocque's map of 1746 shows Carlisle Lane as a crooked path between neatly arranged market gardens. It was known then as Back Lane and led to another road called The Green. Today Carlisle Lane and two adjoining roads form an open-air gallery for a series of mosaics inspired by the poet, painter and printmaker William Blake, who lived near by. A woman sits with two children beneath a fruit tree in the frontispiece to *Songs of Innocence* (1789). A terrifying serpent hisses in *Europe, a Prophecy* (1794). Its tongue is a fork of lightning.

For the first time on this walk, I find myself alone. In the middle of the tunnel, a rough sleeper has laid out a thin mattress and duvet. On the wall behind he has written TOCK BOY SLEEP IN with a large arrow pointing to the ground. His digs are surrounded by discarded takeaway boxes and bottles of fruit juice. An arched niche in the wall is filled with more detritus – old milk cartons, orange peel, fag ends, the sole of a shoe. It reminds me of the roadside shrines to the Madonna that are common in Catholic countries and I approach for a closer look. It is only then that I realize the niche is hollow; behind the litter there is a crawl space, pitch black inside. I can just make out another wall and a fragment of graffiti: SAVE THE RAINFOREST. I turn on the torch on my phone and push my hand through. In the darkness I see more wall, a low passageway, a shadow moving. I can't be sure I heard a noise, but I quickly withdraw my hand, aware that I could be disturbing someone's sleeping space, perhaps Tock Boy himself, enclosed within the wall like a medieval anchorite. Suddenly the tunnel is filled with the roar of an engine. A sports car with blacked-out windows accelerates past me. At the end of the lane, a large crow picks up a plastic food container in its beak, drags it into the road and then stands next to it staring right at me. The mosaic behind the crow reads:

> Reason or the ratio
> of all we have already known
> is not the same thing that
> it shall be when we know more[13]

I find the plaque on Hercules Road marking the site of Blake's old house, the cottage he shared with his wife Catherine between 1790 and 1800. It is set high on the side of a redbrick estate, next to a child's bedroom window. For Blake, Lambeth represented the antithesis to the corrupt, industrial city from which he had escaped: a prelapsarian paradise of fields, meadows and orchards. His new home provided space for a print workshop and infiltrated his poems as 'the place of the Lamb', a new

Jerusalem for the mythical land of Albion. When a friend, Mr Butts, interrupted the Blakes reading Milton's *Paradise Lost* naked in their Lambeth garden, William is reported to have said, 'Come in! . . . It's only Adam and Eve, you know!'[14]

I continue along Hercules Road, then swing right at Cosser Street. A heavy-set man emerges from an end-of-terrace house and shouts, 'Hello? Hello? Hello!' after a woman. She ignores him. 'Hello! You want it?' She turns. 'You sure you don't want it?' He is grinning. He is holding a giant black dildo, which he raises towards her like a sceptre. She continues walking and he cackles with laughter, then drops the dildo in a recycling bin.

Field

I T IS A RELIEF to find green space after the claustrophobia of the Lambeth tunnels. A group of children in maroon blazers are playing tag on the grass. Another group, in moss-green sweaters, is mustering by a knobbly tree – a baobab plane. They are holding miniature clipboards and stubby pencils. A young couple encourages a very small dog to climb a wooden exercise ramp. The huge west wall of the Imperial War Museum rises above even the tallest trees like a prison hulk in neo-classical clothing.

Named after the mother of the newspaper mogul, the 1st Viscount Rothermere, Geraldine Mary Harmsworth Park is the last remaining portion of a vast area of open land known as St George's Fields. On Rocque's map, its territory stretches from the southern boundary of the Paris Garden almost as far south as the Kennington Oval. Although safely located on a gravel terrace above the alluvial flatlands of the Thames, St George's Fields shared the same boggy, waterlogged character of the surrounding marsh. For centuries – while the city swelled, breaching its medieval limits, spilling west along the Strand and over London Bridge to Southwark – the Fields were left uncultivated, a rural wasteland through which the Neckinger may once have flowed.

The first building of note appeared in the first half of the seventeenth century: a tavern on Lambeth Road called the Dog and Duck. The name derives from the grotesque sport of duck-baiting which took place in ponds near by. Just as at Bagnigge Wells, on the banks of the Fleet, the tavern owners took advantage of natural springs that flowed from the ground, selling its purgative waters for '6d per gallon' according to an advertisement of 1773.

> The Waters of this Spaw . . . are recommended by the most eminent phy-
> sicians, for the cure of the rheumatism, stone, gravel, fistulas, ulcers,

cancers, sore eyes, and in all kinds of scorbutic cases whatever; and are remarkable for restoring a lost appetite.[15]

My mind turns to the KitKat stashed in the front pocket of my rucksack. In the late eighteenth century, the tavern was enlarged and then rebranded St George's Spa (or *Spaw*), becoming a fashionable resort for Londoners seeking elegance and entertainment in a bucolic setting. But like Bagnigge, its star did not shine brightly for long and it was soon the subject of satire in print and on the stage. In a comic play of 1774 by Gentleman Johnny, the Dog and Duck appears as a rustic Arcadia gone bad, whose 'frowsy bow'rs' and 'midnight damp' host 'Fauns half-drunk, and Dryads breaking lamps'.[16] A print of 1783 by the caricaturist Robert Dighton depicts a voluptuous woman squeezing between fence posts in St George's Fields while two creepy men look on grinning, a scenario clearly designed to play on the area's reputation for debauchery.[17] In 1810, after a spate of speculative (and unlawful) building on the undrained land, the tavern's licence was not renewed.

The corner of the park nearest to the junction where Lambeth and Kennington Roads cross is brimming with lush vegetation. I trudge across the damp grass for a closer look. There are no frolicking fauns to be seen. Instead, at a picnic bench a man with a white goatee is playing an electric guitar without amplification, his hands ghosting the strings in fingerless gloves. The pioneering botanist John Gerard was a frequent visitor to St George's Fields and recorded his discoveries in his seminal book, *The Herbal Or General History of Plants*. Here he found hedgehog grass, burre reed, arrowhead or water archer, white saxifrage, water dropwort and horsetail.[18] As I approach the corner, I realize it is set ever so slightly lower than the rest of the park – a tiny, accidental wildflower meadow. I crouch by the fenceline and scan the surface: orange starbursts of *calendula*; the glossy, broad leaves of wild spinach; love-in-a-mist, its fine filaments like green capillaries; the golden warmth of marsh marigolds.

It is a wonder anything grows here, amid the clouds of exhaust fumes drifting across the grass from the crossroads. When, in 1779, William Curtis opened a botanical garden in Lambeth specializing in 'aquatic and bog plants', he complained:

> I had an enemy to contend with in Lambeth Marsh . . . and that was the smoke of London, which . . . constantly enveloped my plants . . . [as well as] the obscurity of the situation, the badness of the roads lead- ing to it, [with] the effluvia of surrounding ditches, at times highly offensive.[19]

In 1812, the Dog and Duck was demolished to make way for the founda- tions of the new Bethlem Royal Hospital, the psychiatric institution which could trace its origins to the medieval asylum on the banks of the Walbrook. One of the prospective architects, John Gandy, complained that the swampy ground of St George's Fields would not allow for the building to be sunk any more than three feet below the surface.[20] None- theless, three years later, in the damp summer of 1815, the first patients arrived in a fleet of hackney coaches from the old site in Moorfields. The hospital was enormous – 580 feet in length – and consisted of a central block (the present museum) and two, three-storey wings (now demolished). For over one hundred years, 'Bedlam' housed the mentally ill, the vulnerable and the criminally insane, some of whom were kept chained, restrained, often naked, the incontinent lying on beds of straw in cells little bigger than dog kennels.

In Blake's illuminated book *Jerusalem*, a prophetic journey through London leads him back, in the spirit of the drift, to the new asylum on St George's Fields, to 'Bethlehem':

> *where was builded*
> *Dens of despair in the house of bread: enquiring in vain*
> *Of stones and rocks he took his way, for human form was none.*[21]

I move across the plot, stepping carefully between plants. Here, an outcrop of tough green plantain. Here, a spray of milky-white yarrow or bloodwort, a herb known to staunch wounds. It would have come in use in many of the conflicts commemorated by the museum behind me. Two police vans are suddenly steaming down Kennington Road, sirens blaring. It is then that I notice a manhole cover between the wildflowers. Then another one. And another. In total, six manholes are set into the ground of this unkempt triangle. There is something underneath my feet.

In 1746 Rocque recorded a number of small ponds by the Dog and Duck – no doubt the ones used for duck-baiting. One, a little amoeba-like mere, sat just below Lambeth Road, right at the borough boundary. By the turn of the nineteenth century the three ponds had been consolidated into one large lozenge of water, probably the swimming bath built in 1769.[22] Rocque's map shows clearly that the ponds were drained by a series of channels to the south and collected in what appears to be a natural stream. Could this be it – the source of the Neckinger, the dead river I have been searching for?

The antiquarian William Henry Black included this location, or somewhere very near it, in his occult vision of the city as a network of invisible connections. According to Black, lines of identical length (2,700 metres) linked the Ossulston first to Westminster Abbey, then to a point of uncertain relevance on the Fleet near Smithfield, then again to the boundary between Aldgate and Whitechapel, and finally here, to a now disappeared landmark called the Lord Mayor's stone. The stone was itself probably a boundary marker, situated, said Black, 'at the ancient watercourse bounding the borough of Southwark and the parish of Newington, near the Elephant and Castle.'[23] In his 1915 history of the Bethlem Hospital, E. G. O'Donoghue revealed that he had discovered 'a slab of blue slate' marking 'the limit of the hospital property and of the jurisdiction of the city in Southwark.'[24] O'Donoghue asserted that the stone was installed here in 1818, during the mayoralty of Christopher Smith, but earlier histories, from 1753 and 1766, had already located the Lord Mayor's stone 'near the

Dog and *Duck*'.[25] Curiously, O'Donoghue also claimed that it was called 'London Stone' in old maps.[26] I can find no other original reports of the stone, nor any explanation for its name (more commonly ascribed to the ancient slab of limestone opposite Cannon Street station), but there is no doubt – *this* is the spot.[27] It is not inconceivable that whoever chose this place for a boundary marker was consciously replicating an existing association – the source of a river. I scour the ground again, hoping for the appearance of some artefact; but any sign of the site's history has long disappeared beneath parkland. And yet, I feel the spirit of St George's Fields – and the herbalists who recorded its rich flora – living on in this rough wedge of wildflower meadow by the crossroads.

The park has emptied out. I head south-east, following the course of the stream across the same open land that Rocque mapped out using compass and chain, theodolite or perhaps a perambulator – a wheeled contraption used by surveyors. I feel buoyant, walking in his footsteps, finally on the right track. The tension in my stomach has released. I'm in Southwark now, the borough of my birth. Sometimes, at Christmas or Easter, my mother would drive us up from Herne Hill to hear Mass at St George's, the Roman Catholic cathedral on Lambeth Road. The council has been busy planting trees, thirty-four species that colonized Britain towards the end of the last Ice Age. As I cross the park, I move from sessile oak to wych elm, from ash to broad-leafed lime. I pause for a moment by a crack willow, little more than a sapling, and read that it usually grows in marshes and by streams.

A chubby toddler lurches towards me like a drunk at a wedding. I grin then give his parents a knowing nod. I find the boundary wall of the park at the rear of the museum, by the maintenance office. A delivery driver is mashing his thumb on the doorbell without success. The high brick wall stretches in a south-east direction, separating the park from the back gardens of the houses on Brook Drive. Is it getting dark already? I have to squint to find my way. The wall was built in 1835 to enclose the grounds of the Bethlem Hospital. I pass a swaggering bulldog and its owner, then a skip full of plasterboard. The back of the museum is covered in scaffolding and hoardings. In the gloom I almost miss it completely. Fixed to the boundary wall and choked by ivy: a stink pipe.

The last time I had encountered a stink, or stench, pipe was years ago, following the Walbrook stream towards the City of London; it was encased in a replica stone obelisk in Finsbury Circus – a concealed ventilation chimney for an underground gas storage tank. *This* pipe is a Victorian original and is caked in rust. The opening at its top through which toxic vapours would once have risen from an underground sewer is now plugged, in obscene fashion, by a thick creeper. I place my hand on the metal and it wiggles, no longer connected to anything below. I follow the wall and find two more identical pipes, alongside garish cartoons of Danger Mouse and Penfold, the Gruffalo and the fish from *Finding Nemo*. Fat, blue water drops have been painted as if they are gushing from the top of one of the pipes. Next to the other, I make out the unmistakable shape of a skull, daubed in white paint, just like the one I found at the end of Leake Street six years ago. The paint was applied too quickly and has dripped, as if the artist had been in a hurry or on the run. I take out my phone but I can't keep it steady and the photo comes out blurred, the colours leaching between the skull, the pipe and the wall. It feels too strange, the locations too well chosen, to be a coincidence. Is someone really marking the course of the Neckinger with the same macabre graffiti; a skull for the buried stream?

I hear someone approaching from behind. It's a man in a Puffa jacket with a dog. The dog squats to shit in an orchard. Apple, pear, mulberry, quince. The orchard was planted in the footprint of an abandoned children's lido, built in 1938 but filled in less than ten years later. Another demolished structure close by, the House of Occupations, once contained subterranean baths for its residents – the orphaned children of London – although, as O'Donoghue pointed out, they were 'manifestly unsuitable' for bathing and were soon converted into storehouses.[28] The dog slopes off and the man bags up its production. Today the groundwater is rising and the surface of the park is often wet and marshy. Plans are in place for the construction of a 'swale' – a ditch or basin to collect rainwater – on the course of the old stream.[29] I look for a way through the hoardings. It's another dead end. So I double back, then turn into Brook Drive, where the Neckinger once flowed behind the houses. A street sign suddenly lights up:

NO THROUGH ROAD
TO ELEPHANT AND CASTLE

Roundabout

'To the Elephant'

SHAKESPEARE, *TWELFTH NIGHT*[30]

THE ELEPHANT AND CASTLE has always occupied a singular place in my imaginative map of the city. Mostly I would pass through on the 68 bus on my way to town. After the slow passage of Walworth Road, the Elephant would suddenly appear in the window, a monstrous gyratory system surrounded by grey tower blocks. The iconic 1960s shopping centre at its core always seemed to me prefabricated, as if it were a temporary structure; it was painted bright pink in the 1990s and has been recoloured several times since. Raised on a plinth outside the front entrance is the bronze statue of an elephant, with the stone keep of a castle strapped to its back like a creature from Tolkien's Middle-earth.

Brook Drive has led me here, to the Elephant, on a curving path from the old Bethlem Hospital in St George's Fields. There was an eerie silence on that street, as if something was gathering itself. Christmas lights twinkled in the windows of Edwardian terraced houses. Sometimes I thought I glimpsed a trace of the buried river Neckinger in the alignment of an alley, a garden wall, a doorway. A young girl on a purple bike shouted at me from across the street. It sounded like, 'Eat pigeon.'

As a teenager, the Elephant possessed a fearsome reputation. To descend into the gloomy subways beneath the roundabout was to run the gauntlet of menacing, knife-wielding thugs, or so I believed. This wasn't mere childish fantasy; in the 1990s Lambeth and Southwark regularly topped the violent-crime charts. I have lost count of the number of times I was threatened on the street before I hit twenty. Peckham, Brixton, Herne Hill and Stockwell . . . the memories dither at the back of my skull. Once, during the long summer before university, I was drinking in the Falcon in Clapham with a girl I liked when the pub was stormed by masked youths brandishing bats and kitchen knives. I managed to smuggle my date into a cubicle in the gents, where we duly snogged.

Behind its concrete façade and the air of being perpetually 'under

construction', the Elephant and Castle is an ancient junction – the centre
of a network of paths radiating from Stane Street, the Roman road from
London to Chichester.* Its outlandish name derives from a coaching
inn which stood on a triangle of land in the middle of the junction. The
site was previously occupied by a blacksmith's forge, which is believed to
have displayed the heraldic symbol of the Worshipful Company of Cut-
lers: an elephant bearing a castle in the manner of an Indian *howdah*.†

Before the eighteenth century, the settlement that grew around the
junction was known by another name: Newington. The northern tip of
Stane Street is still called Newington Butts, after the triangular piece of
land – the 'butt' – that once separated the roadways. The small park and
children's playground opposite the southern interchange is all that
remains of the burial grounds of Newington's parish church, St Mary's,
which was pulled down in 1876 to widen the road. The park is still consecrated ground. The Jacobean playwright Thomas Middleton was
buried here, and I wonder if his was one of the graves left undisturbed
during the latest renovations. The council has installed a small pond and
fountain, and formed a stone circle from twenty-five concrete spheres.

On Rocque's map, you can just make out the Neckinger stream
approaching Newington from the west, then ducking out of sight
beneath the Fishmongers' almshouses before reappearing on the eastern side of the highway in a little yard marked *Pump*. During the
redevelopment of the leisure centre on Brook Drive, engineers discovered groundwater in the shallow gravel aquifer, as well as alluvium
associated with 'the historical stream known as the River Neckinger'.[31]
In his survey of 1756, William Maitland described the land west of the
almshouses as 'Moorish [marshy]' and identified 'a small Watercourse,
denominated the River *Tygris*, which is Part of *Cnut*'s Trench, or

* The dead-straight orientation of Stane Street is preserved by the A3 as far as Clapham.
† An alternative theory, that Elephant and Castle is a corruption of 'La Infanta de
Castilla', has been widely discredited.

Canal'.[32] The nickname *Tygris* (or Tigris) was presumably sarcastic, given the comparison with that important ancient river, but the legend – that the Neckinger formed part of a channel cut by the Danish king to sail his warships around London Bridge – persisted in later histories of the city. The Fishmongers' almshouses are now the Metropolitan Tabernacle, a large Reformed Baptist church whose grand portico gives it the appearance of a Greek temple. The pump yard is long lost beneath the shopping centre, but its position is marked by a bus shelter and, behind it, two leafless trees. It almost looks like a gateway.

A young woman hurries past, eating a slice of unbuttered white bread. I think about buying a coffee from one of the chain cafés that have recently opened to service the new-build apartment blocks. The Elephant is in the grip of a major urban regeneration scheme that has already resulted in the closure of the pedestrian subways, the demolition of the colossal Heygate Estate and the erection of Strata SE1, a forty-three-storey residential tower dubbed the 'Electric Razor'. The neon signs of estate agencies sit alongside Latin American restaurants and mini-marts. *Live in Zone 1 with just 5% deposit*, proposes one advertisement. *Dinner! Dancing!* another.

I cross the dual carriageway as close to the course of the Neckinger as I can get without being run over. A double-decker bus pulls up with a groan and a passenger leaps on, exclaiming, 'Yo, Big Life!' The shopping centre has been painted blue, but already the cladding is streaked with milky-white water stains. The ground floor is sunk below street level and set back a few metres, creating a kind of concrete moat packed with tin-roofed market stalls offering African and Caribbean food, computer parts, carpets, fruit and veg, and vinyl records. Entering through the double doors is like stepping back thirty years. Many of the shops look unchanged even from the 1960s – greasy spoon caffs with Formica tables, a hair salon full of old girls getting their perms fixed, a hardware store you could get lost in. The flecked, tiled flooring looks like something geological. There is an old-fashioned arcade machine or giant gobstopper dispenser around every corner. It makes my local shopping centre, the much-maligned Surrey Quays, seem positively futuristic.

I buy a coffee at Sundial, a restaurant selling fried chicken and all-day breakfasts. 'I'm excited,' says a young boy whizzing past in a pushchair. A morose middle-aged man wearing AirPods is browsing second-hand video games, a statuesque woman examining her false nails inside Andrea's Hair and Beauty Bar. The big corporate chains are notable for their absence, with the exception of British staples Boots, Greggs and WH Smith. A young mum with a baby strapped to her chest talks into her phone: 'Hello? You're breaking up *bare.*' Many of the shops here are independent, small businesses run by first- or second-generation immigrants. A stall selling phone accessories proudly displays posters in its window of 'Great Men and Women of Colour' and 'Kings and Queens of Africa'. Upstairs I find a Colombian restaurant and delicatessen, La Bodeguita, and a branch of the Jamaica National Bank. Outside, an elderly woman is explaining the origin of the phrase 'to spend a penny' to a dreadlocked security guard. 'I'm still learning!' he replies, and they both fall about laughing.

I take a seat on a bench back downstairs. An elderly man on crutches, wearing dark glasses and a NEW YORK baseball cap, joins me and we immediately strike up a conversation. His name is John. He lives in Spring Gardens, Vauxhall, and has been coming to the Elephant and Castle since he was twelve. He is blind in one eye (he takes off his glasses), relies on an oxygen tank to breathe (he opens his rucksack to prove it) and has no toes on one foot (he points).

'Not being rude, but . . .'

John begins every other sentence in this way, but I needn't be worried: he is excellent company. I tell him why I'm here, about my search for the dead river, and he nods sagely. 'I saw it once, you know, that river. There was a burst water main on Brook Drive and they dug it up. Not being rude, but . . . it was quite a small pipe.'

A woman appears with a plastic cup containing a bright orange beverage and he hands her a pound coin. 'Thanks, John,' she says. John remembers the lido too – the one behind the Imperial War Museum. He must have swum in it as a very young boy, just after the war.

Since his mother died, John has visited the shopping centre every day – even after he had a fall on the escalator. ('They offered two grand compensation,' he said, 'but I held out for six.') We exchange stories about growing up in south London, several generations apart, and I comment on how much the Elephant has changed, even in my lifetime. 'They tried to knock this place down, but we won,' John tells me, proudly. 'I give it two more years.' But many businesses have already moved out. The bowling alley and legendary bingo hall are out of bounds behind hoardings. Later, I read that the bulldozers are due to arrive in just six months' time. John is either optimistic or in denial.

The Elephant has been dubbed gentrification's 'ground zero'. It's hard to comprehend the pace or scale of change here. The shopping centre will make way for property developer Delancey's vision of a new town centre, with luxury flats, retail units and facilities for the London College of Communication. People like John do not appear in the artist's impressions of this future London.

'Have you seen the American Embassy?' he asks. 'In Nine Elms?' I tell him I haven't, not yet. 'You have to see it, Tom. It's got its own moat.' I make my apologies and as we shake hands, John leans in. 'Now, not being rude,' he says, 'but if you want a cup of coffee, don't buy it from outside – it's too dear.' Then he points. 'Go over there and say you're a friend of John and you might get a discount.' As I head towards the exit, he calls after me: 'Good luck with the book!'

What is it that draws John back, day after day, year after year, to this same spot on the ground floor of the shopping centre? I feel it too, this magnetic pull; it's like the Elephant and Castle holds some mysterious power over the landscape, a charge we are both unable to resist. As a child I attributed the sensation to the influence of a sinister silver cuboid structure that sat on an overgrown traffic island in the middle of the northern roundabout, adrift in exhaust fumes.

As I make my way along the 'moat' around the shopping centre, I discover one of the pedestrian subways, not yet filled in but blocked off by metal gates. I think immediately of the labyrinth of tunnels beneath the Aldgate roundabout, now backfilled with concrete. This tunnel is strewn with rubbish: plastic bags, takeaway boxes, shoes and bottles, a stranded shopping trolley. Yellow security lights flicker in the darkness. A white sleeping bag lies by the tiled wall like an abandoned cocoon. On the wall of the moat someone has scrawled TORIES OUT.

The roundabout has been remodelled and the traffic island is now connected to the shopping centre by a wide pavement, the dense vegetation I remember stripped back to bare tarmac. I approach beneath a dark-grey sky; a flock of pigeons startles, a hundred pairs of wings beating the air, then circles the cuboid. A billboard reads: *Welcome to the money wellness revolution.*

The silver cuboid is not, as I had once imagined, an interplanetary spacecraft or Soviet missile silo, but an electricity substation – a giant transformer supplying power to the Tube. Officially it is called the Michael Faraday Memorial, a fitting monument to the influential scientist of electromagnetism who was born in Newington Butts in 1791. The cuboid's exterior is composed of hundreds of individual panes of stainless steel. They are cold to the touch. A constellation of peeling stickers is spreading, fungus-like, across the shimmering surface: *Urban Nerds*; *Brixton's Baddest*; *The Satanic Temple, London*. In 2001, the electronic musician Aphex Twin claimed that he had bought the cuboid and was planning to live inside it, an urban myth that persisted for years (in fact, he lived near by in a converted bank).[33] A modified electrical hazard sign has been fixed to an access door and reads: *Zeus strikes.*

Years ago, I invited the musician Leafcutter John to accompany me on an ill-fated trip to the Faraday Memorial. John is one of a kind, a sonic innovator whose records and performances range across genres – folk, jazz, contemporary classical and electronic. An appropriately wiry figure, John always seems to be hovering on the edge of a joke or ironic observation, delivered in perfect West Yorkshire deadpan. I wrote to him, explaining my theory about the Elephant, and he replied enthusiastically; a plan was forming in his mind to capture the electromagnetic energy of the roundabout and transform it into music using a home-made pick-up. We would present our collaboration at an event I was curating on 'alternative landscapes'.

So it was that on a warm June day in 2013, I found John standing behind the Faraday Memorial holding what looked like a modified coat hanger with wires attached to it. As he moved carefully around the cuboid, probing there, pausing here, I took out my own microphone and pressed record . . .

Footsteps on grass.

The background drone of vehicles.

A sneeze.

'Are you picking anything up, John?'

'Huh? No, nothing.'

Sirens, more footsteps, then silence.

'Oh no, it's making loads of noises, but I think it might be *this* though . . . OK.'

Wind buffer, a muffled voice, distortion.

'I'm convinced this isn't working. I got, I got, kind of, the various hums and bits and pieces out of it . . . but nothing that would make a fifteen-minute piece of music. Back to the drawing board.'

'Yeah, I think so.'

'Never mind. It's *slightly* annoying.'

A seagull wheels above the cuboid, heading north along Newington Causeway. Despite its peripheral location, the Elephant has always attracted thrill-seekers from across the city. One of London's first playhouses was established at Newington Butts in 1576 and may have staged early performances of *Hamlet* and *Titus Andronicus*. The property was bounded by a common sewer, presumably the Neckinger, on its southern edge, placing it roughly on the site of the Coronet Theatre.[34] Today the Coronet is swathed in the same tatty blue cladding as the shopping centre and earmarked for demolition, but the Frank Matcham-designed venue once played host to major performing artists – from local boy Charlie Chaplin to pop superstars Justin Timberlake and Alicia Keys.

Across the New Kent Road from the Coronet once stood another auditorium, the gigantic Trocadero. It was here, on 1 March 1958, that Buddy Holly opened his tour of Britain, playing two shows to a combined audience of four and a half thousand adoring fans. Photographs from backstage show the young rock 'n' roll sensation clowning around with bandmates and posing with his support act, the Tanner Sisters. According to the *Melody Maker*, Holly and his band, the Crickets, 'unload[ed] all their disc hits with feverish speed'.[35] Perhaps he had good reason to play fast; less than a year later, he was killed in an air crash outside Clear Lake, Iowa.

Today, the entertainment business is represented by Southwark Playhouse, newly transferred to Newington Butts, and Ministry of Sound, the legendary superclub off Newington Causeway. Established in 1991 in a derelict bus garage 'with a roof covered in pigeon poo', Ministry now boasts one of the world's finest sound systems, using Dolby's three-dimensional Atmos technology.[36] The main room is entirely contained in a soundproof box made of magnesite, the same calcite mineral that is used to line blast furnaces and incinerators. 'It [is] like a nuclear bunker,' said co-founder Justin Berkmann. 'If there's ever a nuclear strike on London, everyone at the Ministry of Sound will probably survive.'[37]

I retrace my steps past the boarded-up Coronet, looking for any sign of the dead river – the Tigris of south London.* I'm convinced that the line of the stream is lost somewhere beneath the railway station, where an access ramp corkscrews down to an underground car park. In a map of 1828 its course appears to correspond with a small street called Nile Place. Bolton maps the river across the New Kent Road, then along County Street where it flowed through the fields of the former Lock hospital.[38] Suddenly there is a change in the atmosphere. Across the roundabout, the cuboid is glowing, cycling through the colours – turquoise, violet, amber – like a gemstone held to the light. It is late; the streetlamps fizz on one by one. I will have to return another day to complete my walk. If I catch a bus from Newington Causeway I can be home in time for Martha's tea.

I'm on the back seat of the C10, racing through Bermondsey, when I remember my emergency KitKat. I rummage around in my rucksack and pull out instead the old, dog-eared street map I've been carrying with me all this time. It has been little use so far on my journey through south London; the landscape is too flat and the river has left little trace of itself in the geological record. Nonetheless, the vivid colours I had ascribed to the different rock strata are oddly comforting and for a few minutes I find myself immersed again in this invisible world. I'm half a chocolate finger in when I see it – a shape I must have drawn myself, by hand, but which arrives now, in the sodium blaze of the bus, as wholly unexpected, like a cigarette burned into the map.

There, in a triangle of land between the New Kent Road and New-ington Causeway, the gravel terrace has been ruptured by a mysterious, dark blot encircled by an oval disc of alluvium.

I have it, then – my next target.

The dead river has led me right to it.

---

* A few streets away, on Rodney Road, I discovered, by chance, the Tigris convenience store. The manager – a young man wearing a gold chain and AirPods – attributed the name to the previous owner, who was originally from Turkey.

Anomaly

I RETURN TO THE ELEPHANT after Christmas. I have had turkey at least five different ways and am ready for the new year, Brexit and all. It's one of those brilliant winter mornings when everything shimmers with a cold, thin light.

The site of the Trocadero is now part of Metro Central Heights, the Grade II-listed residential complex designed by the Hungarian-born Modernist architect Ernő Goldfinger. Originally named Alexander Fleming House, the last tower was completed in 1967 and the site leased to the Ministry of Health until the 1990s. Today, it is a desirable private development for young professionals, boasting a gym, swimming pool, underground parking and a twenty-four-hour concierge.

I peer through the main gates, just off Newington Causeway. The towers are clad in white with blue trim; a severe but functional aesthetic replicated in countless hospitals, schools and office blocks across the country. I can make out the central *piazza*, where a fountain bubbles and a quaint wooden bridge crosses a fishpond filled with koi carp. Or so I have heard; like the Faraday Memorial, Metro Central Heights seems the kind of place where urban myths rise like noxious vapour from the sub-basement. Architecture creates 'magic places, entirely works of the mind', wrote Goldfinger, who really did inspire the name of the chrysophilist Bond villain and Trump-alike.[39] A young woman exits the gates, dressed head to toe in Lycra running gear. She stops to set her watch, then shoots off towards the roundabout.

Before its conversion into flats, Metro Central Heights was said to suffer from 'sick building syndrome' – a nebulous, unexplained condition affecting office workers which presents variously as headaches, fatigue, nausea and respiratory problems. Perhaps, as one local writer suggested, 'the psychological disjuncture' of the roundabout 'began to seep in like a malignant damp'.

Might these office-bound civil servants filing records and other bureau-
cratic memoranda have been struck down by the malaise of appearing to
be silo-ed in their interminable routine as the fast-moving world rolled
on and on and on past them?[40]

I have been thinking of the Elephant and Castle as London's Bermuda
Triangle, a place where things (and people) get lost or stuck. The roundabout, the silver cuboid and the ominous subways tunnelled beneath
them; a sick building and a shopping centre trapped in a time warp: these
have become, in my mind, the outward signs of some invisible energy
source. And now, it seems, I might just have the evidence to prove it.

Metro Central Heights stands, fortress-like, at the south-west corner
of an area dominated by the Rockingham Housing Estate; an area which
is known to geologists as the Rockingham Anomaly. Here, the continuous terrace of Thames gravel is disrupted by a large depression, nearly
300 metres wide and over 19 metres deep, filled with peat, which I have
marked black on my map.[41] The peat, in turn, is surrounded by a caul of
fine-grained alluvium stretching south towards the shopping centre,
where it is crossed by the buried channel of the Neckinger.

I turn off Newington Causeway and follow Rockingham Street
beneath a railway viaduct and into the heart of the Anomaly. It is like stepping through a doorway. The clamour of the roundabout melts away.
Everything, for a moment, is still. My shoes on tarmac. The low sun
throwing shadow. Movement without intention. And then the road
descends, not sharply but with a pitch I sense in the balls of my feet; as if,
in fact, I was walking barefoot, my soft toes stretching out to meet the
ground, the rough, cold surface which I see, now, is not one surface but
many – a patchwork of slabs and cobbles, warped asphalt and flown
debris. Outside a row of redbrick maisonettes, the ground falls away again.
I watch the reflection of a train shuttling north in a pool of standing water
so deep I dare not walk across it. A face is watching me: a small boy sucking on a carton of juice in the window of Costa Azul, the Ecuadorian

restaurant squeezed into a converted railway arch. A cyclist in a red beret flies past and for a second I think she is a poet I used to know.

The Rockingham is Southwark Council's fourth largest housing estate, with a combined population of almost one thousand. According to government figures, it is also one of the most deprived communities in England. The development consists of twenty-two brick-built housing blocks, arrayed along three parallel roads – Bath Terrace, Rockingham Street and Falmouth Road – with the long arc of Harper Road forming its northern boundary. Most of the blocks are four or five storeys tall, which would have been considered 'high-rise' when the development was built in the 1930s; but today the estate is overlooked by the towering, half-completed skyscrapers that are rising from the new Elephant.

The spaces between the blocks are filled with yards, garages and gardens – scrappy lawns enclosed by metal barriers and low, crumbling walls. A single blue plaque attached to one of the blocks commemorates the estate's most famous resident: the human rights campaigner Peter Tatchell. In a vacant plot on Tarn Street, I stop to admire a large fly-tip – just like the one I had discovered at the end of Leake Street tunnel. On the wall next to it, someone has daubed KEEP CLEAR in white paint. In 2006, a pub on the corner of this street, the Duke of Wellington, was demolished to make way for flats. Archaeologists dug two trenches in its ruins and uncovered a 'dark brownish-grey peaty organic layer, very anaerobic, with preserved wood and roots'.[42] Astoundingly, the peat contained 'Roman pottery and building material dating to AD 240–300' including a 'combed Voussoir flue tile from some kind of vaulted roof structure, probably a bath-house or similar building'.[43]

Everywhere I look there are signs of disturbed ground: tarmac ruptured by tree roots, buckled kerbstones, a manhole raised like pinched skin. In a side street behind a row of garages, I find a shallow depression covered in grass and chickweed, and, next to it, a crack in the road surface so wide I could fit my hand inside. A security guard is observing me suspiciously from the corner of a private apartment block, one of the

new-builds that has crash-landed on the fringes of the estate. I'm playing out the conversation in my head. *I'm with the council*, I tell him. *I'm
here to investigate reports of seismic activity.* A flurry of seed pods settles
by a kerb. Beneath a sewer grille, a deep channel flows with dirty, black
water.

In early leases, the land now occupied by the Rockingham Estate
appears as a marsh called Stewfen. As late as the end of the eighteenth
century, the area remained uncultivated, 'an ozier ground [a meadow
where osier willows grow] "bounded all round by a Common Sewer"
and for the most part under water during nine months of the year'.[44]
Rocque's map of 1746 depicts at least one watercourse flowing through
the site: a tree-lined stream which followed the modern line of Rockingham Street and joined the main Neckinger channel south of the New
Kent Road. Around this time, waste material was already being dumped
on the site 'to consolidate the marshy terrain'.[45] A tenter ground (for drying dyed cloth) was established to the north and the wasteland formalized
into separate plots. A map of 1802 by John Fairburn shows the first,
tentative developments on the edges of the area, as well as a circular
structure at its core marked 'New Halfpenny Hatch' and cautiously identified as a riding school. By the end of that same century, the drained
marshland had been swallowed up completely by densely packed terraces and industrial yards (the Hatch newly occupied by basket and
glass factories). These were streets walked by the Victorian social
reformer Charles Booth for his famous 'poverty map' and he spared no
details in his portrayal of their inhabitants: 'many gossiping women & ill
clad children'; 'ragged children'; 'terrible women, mostly pregnant'; and
'bus men of the lower grades'.[46]

Stewfen: the name invites comparison with the brothels – or *stews* –
of Bankside, Southwark's red-light district. Or perhaps, at some
undocumented time, there was a *stew pond* here, where live fish were
kept ready for the pot. A third etymology stakes the boldest claim: a
direct connection to Tíw, the Anglo-Saxon god of war: 'The early forms

of the name show that [Stewfen] was originally "Tiw's Fen" and in the sixteenth century it was sometimes corrupted to *Tuffen*.'[47] The claimant provided no further evidence, but did add that a fen was not a likely focus for pagan worship.[48] Just as in the case of Bulunga Fen, near Westminster, the origins of Stewfen resist interpretation, lost in the murky waters of local history. The poet and musician John Gibbens, who died in 2015, knew these streets and celebrated their strange energy in liner notes that read like poetry:

> If you turned down here three hundred years ago, you'd be splashing in
> a stewfen, an osiery – only good for eels and willows. Or a little later,
> with pick and spade, to ditch the sucking clay and sink foundations, so
> that some thousands more could cram the last, least habitable land in
> Southwark.[49]

In the middle of the estate I find myself surrounded by dragons, spaceships, elephants, mermaids and a yellow submarine. These are the exotic creations of graffiti artist mORGANICo in a mural designed with local children and young people for the Rockingham Community Centre. A woman in a light-brown headscarf is waiting at the door of the adjoining crèche and nursery, tapping at her phone. A memorial incorporated into the mural lists the names of two young people: seventeen-year-old Jozey, killed in a car accident; and H, twenty-one, shot dead at Jozey's funeral in Camberwell Old Cemetery. The Rockingham has a history of gang-related violence, with fatal stabbings on the estate in 2008 and 2019. In 2011 a police officer found himself in the middle of a mass brawl between rival gangs on the estate, involving around thirty youths armed with knives, baseball bats, petrol bombs, a hockey stick and a bayonet. Gang members have even approached young worshippers of the local mosque to join their ranks.[50]

Today, the estate is eerily quiet. I follow an elderly man up Falmouth Road, little clouds of flavoured tobacco smoke rising from a shisha pipe that he holds in the crook of his arm. A large crow lands on the deformed boundary fence of Longridge House. In some parts of the estate, the steel railings are made from repurposed Second World War stretchers. Here, the grass is acid green and lumpy, the ground rutted with holes filled with leaf mulch. One section of the fence has collapsed entirely. The concrete platform at the base of Longridge House has half caved in, exposing dark voids beneath the brickwork. A man wearing a white skullcap passes on a mobility scooter; then a woman in a black niqab. They are heading to the mosque on Harper Road.

The Rockingham Anomaly was first uncovered during the construction of a storm relief sewer in 1906–8, but its existence has long remained a secret known only to a handful of specialists. In 1979 F. G. Berry associated the Anomaly with the group of 'scour-hollows' or 'depressions' formed in the bedrock either side of the Thames, a group that also included the anomalous feature at Black Mary's Hole.[51] It has been suggested that the depression is so deep that it has 'penetrated the impervious London Clay' and the gravel at its base lies 'directly' on the underlying rocks of the Lambeth Group.[52] Berry recorded 'appreciable local subsidence' centred on the junction of Rockingham Street and Meadow Row and also noted the proximity of the Neckinger or Lock Stream, proposing that its waters may have drained into a 'large mere' within the Anomaly.[53] In 1980 J. N. Hutchinson argued that these scour hollows are the collapsed remains of landscape features known as *pingos* that formed under the permafrost during the last Ice Age.[54] *Pingo* means 'small hill' in the Inuvialuktun language of the western Canadian Arctic. These circular, earth-covered mounds resemble miniature volcanoes and are created by the freezing of groundwater; they have cores of solid ice. As the climate ameliorated and the glaciers retreated north, Hutchinson argued, the pingos collapsed, their frozen cores melted into nothing, and the resulting craters left vulnerable to the scouring action of water.

Three years later, in 1983, Patrick D. Nunn outlined an even bolder theory – a grand plan for the northward migration of the Thames which might also tell me something about the Neckinger and the Rockingham Anomaly.[55] Imagine a straight line cutting across south London from the mouth of the Wandle at Wandsworth to Deptford Creek; this, Nunn proposed, was the course of the Thames around ten thousand years ago. The sharp bends at Lambeth/Westminster and Rotherhithe/Limehouse were yet to be formed. But as climate – and sea levels – changed, the river slowly progressed north, like a snake coiling and uncoiling, before reaching the meandering form we know today. According to Nunn's model, the Thames left behind a series of 'relict channels' and some of these subsequently flowed as tributary streams – the so-called lost rivers. The Neckinger, he argued, was once part of a much larger system of drainage incorporating the lower stretches of the Tyburn, Fleet and Walbrook. As the Thames moved north towards its current alignment, between two and three thousand years ago, its former channel – along with the southernmost parts of these tributaries – became occupied by a new stream: the Neckinger. And so the dead river once possessed another, cannibalizing the shed skin of the great serpent Thames; a Frankenstein's monster of old body parts. The abandoned channels, continued Nunn, also became 'a focus for marsh development'.[56] He identified the marshy area of Stewfen with an earlier stretch of the combined Fleet–Walbrook, a stream which became cut off from the main river system. He also associated an 'approximately north–south channel' passing through the Anomaly with this relict stream.[57]

Scour hollow, collapsed pingo or truncated stream – the Rockingham Anomaly resists classification.[58] Its relationship to the Neckinger – the stream I have been following across south London – is unclear. And yet I feel the mystery drawing me deeper inside.

In the years since I first began exploring the geology of London, new fieldwork has been conducted on the Anomaly. In 2017, a team of earth scientists used a hand-operated auger to extract soil from two metres below the surface of a garden next to Martin House on Rockingham

Street. Beneath a metre of stubborn 'made ground', the auger eventually encountered a deep layer of 'moist, dark, brownish black' peat, 'with occasional woody fragments'.[59] 'It was a euphoric moment', wrote geologist Di Clements.[60] Analysis of pollen preserved in the peat determined that it had been laid down between 3,500 and 5,500 years ago, in a 'boggy fen/carr woodland environment, dominated by alder trees, together with reeds, rushes, sedge and ferns'.[61] Fragments of charcoal suggest the possibility of 'prehistoric occupation or exploitation of the landscape'.[62] The team included local artist Gail Dickerson and a sample of peat was set aside for her *Core Sample* project. A series of paintings appeared a year later and were exhibited locally – 'earth pigments' forming amorphous black smears on off-white paper, like oil slicks or a colony of amoebas.

When Roman engineers first laid their metalled roads across the land, this wild Britannia 'teeming with spirits and untamed humans', the Rockingham Anomaly would have posed a serious challenge.[63] It has long been known that the alignment of Stane Street – the Roman road from Chichester to the bridgehead at Southwark – deviates along the short stretch known as Newington Causeway. The name is a giveaway; here the road was raised above the waterlogged ground on an earth embankment (*agger*), with drainage ditches (*fossa*) on either side.* On my Streetfinder, the Causeway resembles the curved blade of a sickle and clearly tracks the western edge of the Anomaly before returning to its original alignment at Borough Tube station. It is here that Stane Street converged with another ancient highway, Watling Street – or as we know it, the Old Kent Road. Thus combined, the way proceeded at

---

* During roadworks in 1952, an elevated road of Roman origin was discovered underneath the present highway (Darlington, *Survey of London*).

last to London Bridge via a series of small gravel islands, presumably by means of another piled causeway.

Stane Street is not, however, the only Roman road believed to have been deflected by the presence of the Anomaly. The road from Portslade (Brighton) joins Stane Street at Kennington Park or Common, a site long associated with public executions and mass political gatherings (from the Chartists to Gay Pride). According to my own research, this convergence was made possible by a small adjustment of the route at Brixton – roughly where Villa Road meets Brixton Road. South of that point, the way aligns directly with London Bridge, but if unadjusted it too would have crossed the Anomaly.

A third and even more ancient route may also have been deflected by the disruptive geography of the Rockingham Anomaly. Before the founding of Londinium in AD 43, the most practical places to ford the river Thames were probably upstream and it is logical to suggest that the principal road through the region would have terminated there: at Stangate or the horse ferry to Westminster. Antiquarians have long searched for the route of this 'lost' section of Watling Street through south London, to Lambeth from the 'deep-ford' of the Ravensbourne at Deptford.

Following in the footsteps of William Stukeley (1722) and T. A. Codrington (1915), the esoteric fieldwalker John Chaple claims to have found this ancient track passing through the Rockingham Estate. 'I drew a pencil line on a map,' he wrote, 'and followed this as best I could to see if any traces were still remaining . . . To my astonishment I found this strong and unusual subsidence pattern on a council estate just to the north of Elephant and Castle.'[64] Chaple's theory seems fanciful to me; the boggy ground of the Anomaly would surely have provided a sufficient deterrent to prospective road-builders. In his *Bibliotheca Topographica Britannica* (1780–90), John Nichols proposed that the lost Watling Street passed further south, through St George's Fields, where, he noted, a number of Roman artefacts had been found.[65] In 1955 Ida Darlington suggested that it followed the course of 'the private road marked on seventeenth- and eighteenth-century maps across Walworth Manor and St George's Fields'.[66] Could this have been the route taken by the Roman general Plautius in AD 43?[67] Or even by Julius Caesar and his legions during their earlier, failed invasion of Britain in 54 BC? Classical sources tell of heavily armoured war elephants fording the Thames, causing local Catuvellauni fighters to flee in terror.

It's Friday prayers at the Baitul Aziz Islamic Cultural Centre. Worshippers are coming in ones and twos, walking silently towards the mosque or in discreet conversation. Soon the trickle is a stream flowing from every direction – down Harper Road from the Elephant or from the Borough through Trinity Church Square, from Long Lane and Great Dover Street, the Leather Market and the Bricklayers Arms. Young men in business suits and designer stubble; others in branded workwear or uniforms; elderly Bangladeshis with walking sticks and winter coats; Muslims of all classes and nationalities – Somali, South Asian, Arab and British. I have completed a circuit of the estate and now cross back through it, descending Bath Terrace. In the air around me – the buzz of anticipation, of shared time, of thanks to be given and prayers to be made.

There, at the heart of the Anomaly, where the road falls away and then levels out, two men with full beards greet each other like long-lost brothers and one puts out his arms, saying, 'Bring it in.' And as they embrace, I notice, written on the roof of a bicycle hangar that is fixed to the ground, there, on the side of the road, three words and a heart.

LOVE
ONE
ANOTHER
♥

First Contact

'I sey byyonde that myry mere
A crystal clyffe ful relusaunt;
Mony ryal ray con fro hit rere.'

PEARL, LATE FOURTEENTH CENTURY[68]

I SQUEEZE BETWEEN THE VEHICLES that are parked nose-to-tail in the yard outside the mosque. The last worshippers are hurrying inside. Two men in sharp suits – professional drivers – are sheltering beneath the open boot of a black people carrier, watching an Arabic sitcom on an iPhone. A bench made of bricks and crudely decorated tiles stands in the middle of the turning circle like a ruined throne, like Aslan's stone table. I skirt the edge of an abandoned adventure playground, its walls covered in graffiti tags, the tarmac floor carpeted with moss. The tarmac gives way to a gravel track, damp with fallen leaves, and I step through an invisible border into the green, hidden world of Dickens Fields.

In 1979 a team of trainee archaeologists uncovered human remains from wasteland by the boundary wall of the park. Here, on the northern margin of the Rockingham Anomaly, lay the body of a young woman. She was lying on her back in a shallow grave cut into the brickearth, 'head to the south-west, and arms by her side', and surrounded by grave goods.[69] A large wine jar imported from Europe lay by her head; a small rectangular mirror and a decorated bronze torc or neck-ring by her right foot; and by her left, two Samian ware dishes stamped with the maker's name in Latin. *Vitalis*: life-giving.[70]

Thirty years later, in 2009, the artist Roger Hiorns flooded an empty council flat on Harper Road with 90,000 litres of boiling-hot liquid copper sulphate. The chemicals had been imported from Italy in two shipping containers and were left to cool inside the condemned property on the Rockingham Estate. When, weeks later, the liquid was pumped out, what remained took everyone's breath away: the walls, floors and ceilings were entirely coated in glistening blue crystals. This former bedsit had become a spectacular, otherworldly space, like a dazzling ice cave or an abandoned structure from J. G. Ballard's *The Crystal World*.

They were soon within the body of the forest, and had entered an enchanted world. The crystal trees around them were hung with glass-like trellises of moss. The air was markedly cooler, as if everything was sheathed in ice, but a ceaseless play of light poured through the canopy overhead.[71]

Hiorns named his artwork *Seizure*. The title describes the kind of physical reaction one might expect to have in the space but also alludes to the unrelenting process of urban regeneration to which the area is subject. 'The sharpness and the oddness of it enlivens your senses, puts them in a different state,' he said. 'It's somehow like being a spaceman.'[72]

Harper Road Woman was buried on the periphery of an extensive Roman cemetery that stretched either side of the roads radiating south from London Bridge. Her skeleton now lies in a glass vitrine in the Museum of London. In 2017 a stone sarcophagus dating to the third or fourth century AD and containing the remains of a middle-aged woman was dredged from another dig on Harper Road, leading Southwark Council's heritage curator to describe the area as a 'complex ritual landscape'.[73] Many burials from this vicinity have been identified with immigrants from the Mediterranean and even with individuals of 'African or Asian ancestry'.[74] Harper Road Woman is the earliest of the bodies uncovered; she died between AD 50 and AD 70, when London was a small garrison town on the western edge of a vast empire stretching as far as the Persian Gulf. She may have lived through the destruction of Londinium by the Iceni queen Boudicca in AD 60/61 and even witnessed the first years of its reconstruction as a planned city.

But Harper Road Woman's own ethnic and cultural identities remain an enigma. A dark-haired, brown-eyed woman with northern European ancestry, she was buried lying down in a wooden coffin at a time when the more common practices were cremation (for Romans) or crouched burial (for Britons). The pottery and mirror found in her grave are in the continental fashion, the former probably made in the workshops of central France. Her magnificent torc, on the other hand, is decorated with designs associated with indigenous Celtic tradition: a 'ring-and-dot pattern . . . feather motifs and transverse hatched bands'.[75] Comparison with the armlets worn by Roman soldiers and the suggestion that the feather motifs represent peacock feathers – the Roman symbol of immortality – only add to the mystery. The torc, it has been suggested, is 'a "pidgin" artefact . . . representing a single creative response to a particular situation at the very beginning of Roman contact'.[76] Harper Road Woman's torc and mirror were found broken, her plates punched through with holes, in acts of apparent ritual sabotage whose meaning is unclear but which may have had a magical purpose: 'to transfer the metaphysical essence of the object to the realms of the shades'.[77]

Experiencing *Seizure* for the first time, said James Lingwood of Artangel, was like 'entering Tutankhamun's tomb'.[78] The wrecked mirror, the worshippers removing their shoes outside the prayer hall on Harper Road and the bedsit sparkling with crystals, azure-blue, share this in common: the transformational energy of ritual. 'There is a selection, a nomination of an object,' explained Hiorns, 'and that object then becomes crystallized. And then it becomes part of that language of an object, moved into the other realm – this realm of crystallization'.[79] Throughout my journeys across the city I have encountered again and again this sense of place as sacred, made holy through ritual. London was once known as the city of churches, but in today's increasingly secular society, perhaps it is this ancient impulse – to imbue our environment with magical potential – to which we will return.

In 2017 scientists at the Museum of London announced the results of DNA tests conducted on a group of Roman skeletons unearthed in the city. They had made an unexpected discovery. The early Roman burial from Harper Road, for decades known as Harper Road Woman, possessed male (XY) chromosomes.[80] The individual, they suggested, 'likely had a sex development disorder'.[81] This disorder might not have been identified or acknowledged during life; the morphology of the skull and pelvis, along with gendered grave goods, indicate someone presenting as female. 'The individual,' they continued, 'was identified as a woman by her community, a decision that we continue here and at the Museum.'[82]

It is possible that Harper Road Woman was affected by complete androgen insensitivity syndrome (CAIS), a condition in which a person develops female genitalia but with no uterus and undescended testes in place of ovaries. We can never know for certain the cause, nor how she lived with its physical, psychological or social effects. But today, at a time of growing recognition for transgender, non-binary and intersex people, her story offers a powerful testimony of gender diversity at the very beginning of London's own history. It is fitting that she was buried with a mirror, it being the ideal device by which to fashion her *own* identity.

In Dickens Fields, the grassy landscape undulates, as if disturbed by something underground; the rubble, perhaps, of terraced houses destroyed by a German V-1 rocket, a flying bomb. I cross the park, following a footpath that traces the line of a long-forgotten street. Deep craters brim with ivy, nettles, couch grass, hubcaps.

Flesh on earth.

Bone to air.

Dark river. The crystallized forest.[83]

First contact.

I have arranged to meet a local youth worker, Oli Rahman, after lunch. I want to get beyond the myth of the Anomaly, to find out what the Rockingham means to those who have actually lived there. I find Oli sheltering from the icy wind outside the Coronet, one hand gripping a leather-bound notebook, the other shoved into the pocket of his quilted jacket. He greets me warmly and we head back into the estate, already deep in conversation as we descend Meadow Row. Oli is the founder of Active Communities Network, a charity that uses sport to inspire young people and give them pathways into education, training and employment. ACN currently works in six areas across the UK and worldwide, but its methodology is grounded in the streets and yards of south-east London that Oli calls home.

When they moved to the Rockingham in the 1980s, Oli's was one of the first Asian families on the estate. He remembers when groups like the National Front stoked anti-immigrant sentiment among white residents. 'It's different nowadays, although racism is there in the background and it still comes out in times of stress,' he observes. The Rockingham is now home to one of London's largest Bangladeshi communities. Growing up, Oli's dad ran a garments factory in Whitechapel and his mother was a seamstress. He remembers walking across Tower Bridge carrying tiffin boxes for his dad's lunch – 'a bloodline connecting me back to the roots'.

We enter the large courtyard between Ellington and Longridge Houses. Oli points to a third-floor window. 'That was our flat,' he says. His eyes sparkle with a youthful energy that belies his salt-and-pepper beard. He gestures to the ground. 'We would play marbles right here. They were always getting lost in that drain,' he says, peering hopefully into a manhole. 'Look at this . . . this, what do you call it?'

'Bollard?' I prompt.

'Yeah! I remember leaping over that as a kid!' Oli shapes as if to move, but his hand remains firmly on his notebook.

In the middle of the courtyard is a low brick building containing an electrical substation, like a miniature version of the Faraday Memorial.

'We used to shin up that drainpipe too,' he says.

The Rockingham was no urban paradise. Oli remembers fights with gangs from the neighbouring Heygate Estate, and he now lives with his wife and two daughters in Lee Green, away from the 'hustle and bustle' of inner-city life. But his enthusiasm is more than mere nostalgia. 'I loved growing up on the Rockingham. It's a hidden gem. The bus routes don't come through here, even now, so people overlook the area. But we didn't feel deprived – we ran out looking for success.'

We walk to the corner of Harper Road, where some low planters once provided a handy 'cotch' for Oli and his friends. He seems suddenly quiet, lost in his memories. 'These estates shape people, shape communities, shape memories,' he says. I see now how the Rockingham is burnt into Oli's psyche, and into the DNA of his charity. I tell him about growing up in Herne Hill, how I once travelled the length of the alleyway behind our house dressed as one of the Three Musketeers. He smiles and nods along. 'You've got to let children explore,' he tells me, 'take risks, make mistakes and learn from them.'

Emboldened, I take out the Streetfinder. 'I want to show you something,' I say. The map almost falls apart in my hands and Oli has to help me hold it down on one of the planters. My index finger traces the outline of the Anomaly . . .

. . . and now Oli is striding down Rockingham Street, turning my map in his hands. 'Look how we're descending,' he says, breathlessly. 'We used to fly down here on our bikes.'

I am thinking about retreating glaciers, migrating rivers, ice cores melting, the peat at the centre of the hollow shining like a lake of black gold . . .

'This is it,' he says, and stops. 'The ditch.'

And sure enough, just before the dog-leg of Rockingham Street, the roadway drops into a distinct channel following the gap between Aird and Arrol Houses.

We stand there for a minute that seems like longer.

'Look at the wall,' says Oli. 'It's higher at that end, lower here.'

It's then I recognize the stretcher fences, remnants from the Second World War, arranged end to end above the wall like a chain of paper dolls, like cartoon ghosts.

When we part, Oli thanks me for sharing what I know about the Anomaly. 'I'll never forget it,' he says.

The towers of the new Elephant rise above the Rockingham, bossing the skyline.

Gallows

'to find a poison flow'
ALLEN FISHER[84]

I HAVE FINALLY ESCAPED the vortex of the Anomaly and emerge on the wide avenue of the Old Kent Road, just north of the Bricklayers Arms intersection. A white van roars past, blasting out Beyoncé's 'Single Ladies'. The *Old* Kent Road is, perversely, *new*-fangled; it wanders a little west from the original route. The prehistoric trackway known to the Roman colonizers as *Iter III* and to the Anglo-Saxons as Watling Street survives between housing blocks as the ruler-straight line of Tabard Street. The remains of a substantial temple complex dedicated to the Romano-Celtic god of war, Mars Camulos, were discovered at the northern end of this street, near Borough station, in 2002. An inscribed tablet unearthed from the site contains the earliest surviving written reference to London.

I'm back on the course of the Neckinger. The river once flowed beneath the road here using one of its aliases, the Lock Stream. A medieval stone bridge was discovered concealed beneath the highway during sewer works in the nineteenth century, a 'curious ancient structure' which, according to the news report of the time, must have witnessed 'passing armies', 'triumphant entries into the capital' and 'merry pilgrimages to St Thomas of Canterbury'.[85] That holy city seems a long way off today, although many of the roads and houses have since been renamed after characters from Chaucer's *Canterbury Tales*.

A crow is pecking at the mouth of a dustbin outside Pallant House, a yellow-brick council block raised in the footprint of the Lock hospital for lepers. A jogger stops at the pedestrian crossing, hands on hips, sucking in air. Tom Bolton reports that in August 1927, 'a Mrs Williams was standing in her back garden [in Rephidim Street] when the earth opened up and she disappeared into a pit full of black slimy water, from which she was pulled by her family, who could just see her hair above the surface'.[86] Rocque's map shows the Neckinger forming a long pool between the hospital and the Bull Inn, before surfacing within a network of drainage streams on the east side of the Kent Road. From here the river entered its industrial lower reaches where, under the tidal influence of the Thames, its flow was first harnessed by the Cluniac brothers of Bermondsey Abbey.

I follow Prioress Street past the redbrick towers of Hartley's Jam Factory – now recast as luxury apartment blocks – then cut through the surrounding low-rise estate to Long Lane. A portly bloke in a natty waistcoat – part Dickensian villain, part hipster dad – is sipping a pint of IPA outside Simon the Tanner. I stop to consult my map. Here, the Neckinger negotiated the neck of a gravel island or peninsula before following a wide channel of alluvium north into the Thames. The island is Bermondsey itself – *Beormund's ey* – and one branch of the river appears to have skirted its northern edge along Abbey Street (formerly Neckinger Road), where it once powered mills and supplied water for the area's innumerable leather tanneries. But the geography is unclear, provisional; in this shifting, riverside landscape it is almost impossible to distinguish the natural from the artificial. Rocque's map is full of man-made channels that snake like wild streams, and wild streams canalized and straightened by man. One archaeological study avoids naming the river at all but proposes that it flowed south-east in an ancient valley to join another stream, the Earl's Sluice, its journey north towards the Thames impeded by a 'land bridge . . . connecting Bermondsey Eyot to the mainland'.[87]

Two fire engines come wailing down Tower Bridge Road and the city seems to vanish, just for a moment. An old woman puts down her shopping bags. A young couple in matching flannel overshirts stop dead in their tracks. A toddler drops a small white rabbit on the ground. And now I'm walking down Purbrook Street, walking without thinking, following a row of trees between a small housing estate on the exact line of a drainage ditch marked by Rocque. It's already raining when I turn right into Tanner Street, which he called Five Foot Lane, whose course meanders like the stream it ghosts; then underneath the arches of the railway from London Bridge, where plumes of noxious steam discharge from unseen vents; to the crossroads at Druid Street, where microbreweries sit alongside mechanics' workshops and scrap-metal yards; and I can smell the river now, its salt mouth, the tang of vinegar, exhaust fumes, bin juice and cigarettes. I hear the rumble of a pneumatic drill and the scream of an angle grinder cutting stone – and there it is, at last: the dead river's mouth.

A family of mallards is dabbling in the thick yellow silt of St Saviour's Dock. I stand on a concrete parapet and look over the edge. It's low tide and the Thames has drawn back its grey-green mantle, retreating more than 300 metres to the main channel, where it laps against mudflats. Surface water pours from a drain set into the embankment beneath me and forms a silver rivulet working its way through the black sediment at the head of the dock. Traffic cones appear, half-submerged, like ancient stelae. Driftwood, road signs, a plastic fork. Someone is watching from a window in one of the tall, converted warehouses that line the waterway – an architect, perhaps, in black-rimmed spectacles.

The mouth of the Neckinger was first dug out by hand to form a dock nine hundred years ago by the monks of Bermondsey, when the stream was still navigable as far as the Abbey, but its character today is distinctively Victorian. A toxic atmosphere seems to rise from the slime of the dock bed, creeping up the tide-stained embankment walls like a fever. I follow Mill Street along the back of the warehouses towards the mouth of the dock. Two women in pencil skirts are sharing a single damp cigarette outside a recruitment agency. The warehouses are adorned with conspicuous signage: Shuters Wharf, St George's and Scott's Sufferance; Vogan's Mill and New Concordia; Butler's, Reed's and China Wharf. Fresh paint jobs for a vanished industry.

The final vestige of the Neckinger meets the Thames in a shallow gully wandering through the mudflats. The water is the colour and consistency of potter's slip; a slurry of claggy, oyster-grey fluid in which a set of faux-rattan garden chairs has found itself upturned and dumped. The intertidal zone is ambiguous territory, neither river nor solid ground – a suitable conclusion to a stream whose very existence is in doubt. I spot a shopping trolley, almost entirely submerged; a bottle of fizz and a circular blade; scaffolding poles and a child's grey sock. A modern footbridge spans the entrance of the dock and its steel struts remind me of the delicate latticework of a biplane. As I stand there, above the mud that is pockmarked, here and there, with little pools of standing water, I imagine, at that moment, being pulled underneath, as if in quicksand – first a foot, then up to the knee, then the other foot, and an arm, sinking ever deeper the harder I struggle, screaming voiceless cries, until my toes hit the bottom and I'm up to my neck like Winnie in Beckett's *Happy Days*. 'Oh no doubt you are dead, like the others, no doubt you have died, or gone away and left me, like the others, it doesn't matter, you are there.'[88]

'Form is a straitjacket,' said the poet Paul Muldoon, 'in the way that a straitjacket was a straitjacket for Houdini.'[89] I am starting to think of the lost river as a magic trick, an illusion, and of the Neckinger as the greatest escape artist, a mercurial thing. Before the Great Fire, the Neckinger had not drained into St Saviour's Dock at all but, instead, filled a large mill pond running parallel to the east.[90] Then, by the construction of various tidal ditches, the pond was later formalized into a kind of moat, enclosing an area of notorious slum housing known as Jacob's Island. When the social reformer Henry Mayhew visited in 1849, he dubbed it 'pest island':

> The running brook is changed into a tidal sewer, in whose putrid filth staves [planks] are laid to season; and where the ancient summer-houses stood, nothing but hovels, sties, and muck-heaps are now to be seen.[91]

It is here, on Jacob's Island, that my journey, and the history of the lost river, concludes. And so I double back along Mill Street, where a figure in an oversized parka is carrying a tray of cupcakes in a Tupperware box. The figure buzzes into a gated apartment complex where once stood the 'crazy wooden galleries', 'dirt-besmeared walls' and 'decaying foundations' described by Charles Dickens in *Oliver Twist*.[92] In an open-plan office, a bearded man is tapping at a laptop below a giant display of the company's brand values: Teamwork, Innovation, Authenticity. 'The air,' said Mayhew, 'has literally the smell of a graveyard, and a feeling of nausea and heaviness comes over any one unaccustomed to imbibe the musty atmosphere.'[93] Mayhew was not the only observer to identify Jacob's Island, and its polluted waterways, as a breeding ground for disease. The physician John Snow traced the source of the cholera epidemic of 1853–54 to a sailor living near by, in Marine Street.[94]

I am walking the line of Folly Ditch along Wolseley Street, between handsome apartment blocks and terraced houses. It is here that Dickens staged the grand finale of *Oliver Twist*. The murderer Bill Sikes, chased from his hideout to the rooftops of the island, forms a long rope into a noose by which he intends to rappel into the ditch and evade his pursuers; but then, suddenly startled by a vision of his dead lover's eyes, he loses his balance and falls to his death, killed by his own means of escape.

> The noose was on his neck. It ran up with his weight, tight as a bowstring, and swift as the arrow it speeds. He fell for five-and-thirty feet. There was a sudden jerk, a terrific convulsion of the limbs; and there he hung, with the open knife clenched in his stiffening hand.[95]

Surely the location and method of Sikes's demise were not coincidental; for it was here, on the north side of Folly Ditch, that the gallows once stood that gave the Neckinger its name. It is marked on a map of 1740 as 'Devol's Neckenger', an ancient place of execution which was later remembered by a public house, the Dead Tree.[96] Dickens returned to Jacob's

Island fifteen years after the publication of *Oliver Twist*. Folly Ditch had disappeared, filled in and covered over by the 'Bermondsey Improvement'.[97] The site of the Dead Tree had been inherited by another inn, the Ship Aground, whose name, he wrote, 'is wonderfully appropriate, for everything seems to have got aground there – never to be got off any more until the whole globe is stopped in its rolling and shivered'.[98]

The rain has stopped by the time I find the pub, tucked between Dockhead Fire Station and Farthing Alley. Four tiny England flags are quivering in the wind. A satellite dish and a CCTV camera are fixed to the wall below a row of wooden shutters and THE SHIP AGROUND in golden lettering. In the windows, a dim light is burning. Posters advertise live sport on TV – Champions League, FA Cup, Six Nations rugby. Happy days: I'll stop for a pint, another stormy blow-in, then walk the Thames Path home to Rotherhithe. I reach out and grip the door handle. Then something tells me to stop. I turn to face the street. Four long, black vehicles are moving slowly, silently past, on the line of Folly Ditch. A funeral cortège. The floral tribute reads, SISTER.

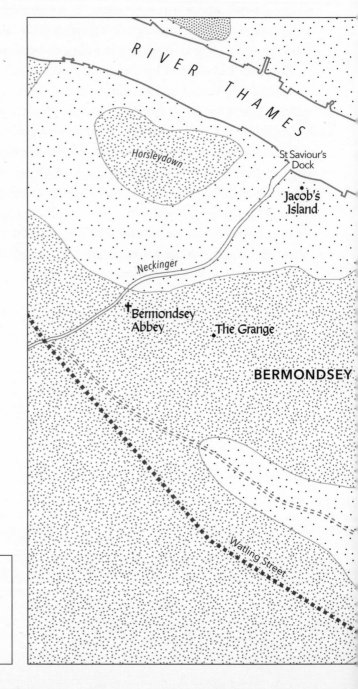

R I V E R   T H A M E S

Horsleydown

St Saviour's
Dock

Jacob's
Island

Neckinger

† Bermondsey
Abbey

• The Grange

BERMONDSEY

Watling Street

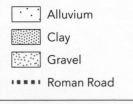

∴	Alluvium
░	Clay
∴	Gravel
▪▪▪▪▪	Roman Road

VII: BEATING THE BOUNDS

The Lost Island of Bermondsey

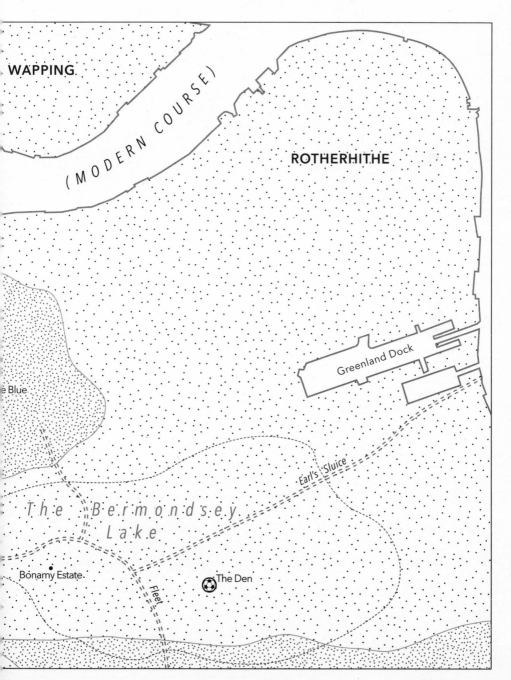

WAPPING

(MODERN COURSE)

ROTHERHITHE

Greenland Dock

e Blue

Earl's Sluice

The Bermondsey Lake

Bonamy Estate.

Fleet

The Den

Fragments

'CLAY,' SAYS JULIA, 'is the *quintessential* material.' She gestures to the glistening surface of the foreshore. 'And here, it's under your feet.' Julia Rowntree is an arts activist, a practising potter and is passionate about clay. 'It's where life began,' she enthuses. 'Clay is an incredibly absorbent material and scientists think that the first cellular life forms may have emerged from chemical reactions in the microscopic spaces inside it.'

We are standing below the stairs of Cherry Garden Pier, on a pebble beach only recently vacated by the mud-grey water of the Thames. I have returned to Bermondsey, just a short walk along the river from the mouth of the Neckinger, to find out more about the enigmatic substance that lies beneath the city. Julia is wearing Gore-Tex walking boots and a Louis Feraud silk scarf. 'Clay,' she continues, 'is universal, abundant and common to all cultures.' I spot the silver towers of Canary Wharf shimmering in the distance, beyond the bend in the river.

It's low tide. Across the city, mudlarks are descending to the foreshore to hunt for buried treasures in the alluvial gloop: fragments of discarded crockery, clay pipes, rare coins and trinkets from our maritime past. The river does not discriminate. Once, at the entrance to Surrey Basin, I stumbled across a wax figurine of Lord Shiva washed up on a pile of broken masonry. Another time, at Bellamy's Wharf, I discovered a novelty horse costume splayed out on the sand, its long, clownish horse-face fixed in a ghoulish smile. A Thames Clipper powers downstream, its twin diesel engines trailing a turbulent wake of frothy whitewater.

Cherry Garden was once at the heart of a bustling port city and marks the border between the Upper and Lower Pools of London (the Pool is the stretch of Thames between Limehouse and London Bridge). Its bucolic name is not without foundation; in 1664 Pepys reported carrying cherries home from the orchards here.[1] By the end of the eighteenth century, the wharves and warehouses of London were receiving more exotic cargo – tea and spices from India and China; sugar, coffee and rum from the plantations of the Caribbean – as well as domestic goods such as coal from the collieries of Durham, Northumberland and South Wales. In the heyday of the port, before the creation of inland docks on the Isle of Dogs, it was said that the river was so congested with ships that you could walk from one bank to the other without getting your feet wet. Today the foreshore of Bermondsey and Rotherhithe is littered with the remains of shipbreaking yards: skeletal timbers revealed at low tide; iron chains; bolts and scrap metal. I pick up a long, rusting nail from the beach and turn it in my fingers. It leaves a powdery red deposit on my skin.

As co-director of arts charity Clayground Collective, Julia has worked with hundreds of young people, including deaf children and those with limited communication, using clay as a vehicle for learning. 'As a society we are losing our hand skills,' she explains. 'Working with clay gives you a kind of embodied knowledge. It's the opportunity to have the earth in the room.' My mind skips back to the schoolboy hut-builders of Sydenham Hill Wood; and then to the plug of clay I extracted from the banks of the Ambrook, still drying out on my bookshelf at home. Clayground has commissioned public monuments, held exhibitions and organized workshops, foreshore walks and 'making' events across the country. They have even conducted research into clay deposits on Mars. Julia shows me a piece of a ceramic jug she has found on the beach. 'You can tell its age from the type and colour of the glaze,' she says. 'This one is Georgian.' She handles the small, brown fragment quickly, efficiently, using her free hand to sketch the rest of the vessel in the air.

We pick our way to the edge of the beach, where the view west towards Tower Bridge has been blocked by a huge, corrugated metal cofferdam (an enclosure built out into the river from which the water has been pumped). At Chambers Wharf, and other sites along the river, controversial works are underway for the Thames Tideway Scheme – the so-called 'super sewer' which upgrades Bazalgette's interceptor network with a new, 25-kilometre tunnel. If it works, the scheme will reduce the amount of wastewater discharged into the Thames each year from 62 million tonnes to 2.4 million tonnes. The scale and ambition of the super sewer is, as engineer Roma Agrawal puts it, 'mind-boggling'.[2] As well as the colossal main tunnel (7.2 metres in diameter), no fewer than twenty-one vertical shafts are being sunk into the edge of the river from Acton to Abbey Mills. At night the works emit a low, pulsating drone.

I notice, then, a strange rock balancing on a half-buried timber. A natural hole has formed in the surface – a perfect circle filled with water from the last high tide. 'It's a hagstone,' I say, and hold it in the palm of my hand.

I am beginning a new journey – here, at the northern edge of a lost landscape. Bermondsey. *Beormund's ey*. A refuge of dry ground in the shifting, flood-prone marshes of the south. A plan begins to form: a circular walk tracing the edge of the vanished island; where a great Abbey church once rose from terra firma; and where today, amid the ghosts of prehistoric routeways, of banished industry, an island people refuses to go quietly.

And now the seasons are turning. Daffodils loll heavy, veiled heads from the balconies of the riverside apartments of Bermondsey and Rother-hithe. The freshly cut lawns of the Dickens Estate release sweet perfume from the earth. We are grateful for crisp, cool days of sun, when the pale bricks of Globe Wharf glow like gold bullion and the river sparkles at dawn.

The first reports arrive like confetti on the wind, the sparks of a great conflagration five and a half thousand miles away. *Wuhan*. The name begins to stick in the throat. A city the size of London.

We take up vigorous hand-washing. Sunlight pools in the courtyard between our block and the next. A small boy waves and Martha waves back from behind the glass, beaming in a dinosaur jumper. My hands become dry and chapped; the folds of my fingers crack open like fault lines. Outbreaks of infection appear in Japan, South Korea, Italy and Iran. There are mass graves outside the holy Shia city of Qom. I dream of disaster. It's like it is in the movies, but slower, deeper.

I read that the surface of the virus is covered with club-like projections, spikes of glycoprotein that attach themselves to the host cell. *Corona*. From the Latin for 'crown'; from Ancient Greek *korōnè*, a garland or wreath; from Proto-Indo-European **(s)ker-*, to bend or to turn.

On Mother's Day, I take Martha to the woods in Rotherhithe to pick wildflowers: dandelions, cow parsley and marsh marigolds from the margins of an infilled dock. Sarah moves slowly across the flat, five months pregnant; she holds Zoom meetings cross-legged on the bed. I count up all the tinned food in the cupboards. The corner shop starts keeping toilet paper and hand wash under the counter like contraband. I panic-buy smoked salmon from Loch Fyne. I think again of Eliot: 'These fragments I have shored against my ruins', he wrote in *The Waste Land*.[3] One morning Martha asks, 'Daddy, are you sad?'

When the lockdown comes, at last, each step outside the flat feels like a furtive gesture, a provocation. The government permits one daily walk – for exercise. I take Martha to the foreshore at low tide to hunt for treasure and watch the black RIBs of the Met Police practising extreme manoeuvres in the river. With the parks closed, I find a spot by the road bridge on Beatson Walk where Martha can play while keeping her distance from joggers. She names my football 'Lisa' and carries it around like a newborn child. She performs the Downward Dog in the sunshine, then stretches her chubby hands to the sky, singing, 'Wind the bobbin up.'

Apart from these short excursions, we are marooned in the flat: Sarah, Martha and me. Days become weeks and the death toll rises. I disconnect from social media. We keep Martha's finds lined up on a table in the hallway: tesserae of fired clay, river-worn; bottle necks;

peculiar stones. I sign off messages to friends with, *From our little island to yours*, remembering that in ancient Rome apartment blocks were known as *insulae*.

London – a city of islands.

Keep safe, we write. *Keep well.*

One day I walk to Bermondsey to drop off supplies for a friend who is self-isolating in her flat. I find myself inadvertently tracing the northern edge of the island, beyond the protrusion along Cherry Garden Street. The wide avenue of Jamaica Road is eerily quiet, just delivery vans and motorbike couriers plying their trade along the dual carriageway. The chicken shop has closed its doors; so too the launderette and the ice-cream parlour with its American-style faux leather booths. Just past the Tube station, Jamaica Road veers north-west in a modern extension towards St Saviour's Dock. Its original alignment is preserved by a much smaller street that runs between a group of housing blocks and the railway viaduct. It is here, on the third floor of a yellow-brick apartment complex on the corner of Old Jamaica Road, that I find Abi's flat. I leave a bag of fruit on her doormat below a handwritten sign:

WE ARE SELF-ISOLATING.
DO NOT ENTER!

From inside I can hear the muffled voices of Abi Palmer and her partner, Golo. As I leave the building, I take out my phone and dial her number. Abi is a writer and artist who has lived in Bermondsey for four years. Her block is one of the smart new-builds that have sprung up in the past decade in this rapidly gentrifying part of south London. In fact, as Abi explains to me, the building is a former army barracks; once home to the 6th (Bermondsey) Battalion of the Queen's Royal Regiment. 'When I first moved in,' she reveals, somewhat cryptically, 'the house felt like a ship where everyone had come aboard at different times.' Abi lives with a range of physical disabilities and uses an electric mobility scooter to traverse the city; she part-owns the flat with the help of a disability waiver. 'We're surrounded by train lines and we have a balcony so we can watch the end of the world,' she says. Abi keeps a blue, inflatable tub in her bathroom to help ease her chronic pain; the tub is the subject of her strange, dreamlike memoir, *Sanatorium*.[4]

I tell Abi about the island in the marshes, Beormund's ey, and she says, 'Wow! That is *so* interesting.' Abi is a natural enthusiast whose speech is peppered with long, emphatic stresses. '*So* interesting,' she repeats. I hear a voice in the background. 'Golo would *love* that,' she adds.

According to my Streetfinder, I explain, Old Jamaica Road follows almost exactly the northern edge of the island, its dog-leg course mapping a shallow, bay-like recess in the gravel platform. 'It's almost like a coastal path,' I say. 'At high tide you'd have the river lapping at your front door.'

Abi laughs. 'We're always being told we're on the edge. The wrong catchment area. The wrong postcode. The doctor's surgery wanted to push us off the map.'

I ask Abi what it's like to travel around London as a disabled person.

'I feel marginalized by the city,' she explains. 'I'm constantly at war with urban planners and the natural world. I don't move through spaces intuitively, but have to negotiate steep kerb drops, tree roots and drainage ditches. Around here the roads are deep and it's hard to get on or off them. Bermondsey is still a working area, full of loading bays and utility roads for lorries. It's not designed for me.'

I have come so far on my journeys through London without ever considering just how privileged I am – as an able-bodied person and as a man – to explore the city almost without restriction. The landscape does not exert a neutral force on those who move through it, but projects our own unbalanced society back at us. What might an *inclusive* psychogeography look like; one that foregrounds the experiences of wheelchair users, say, or blind and partially sighted people; or creates space for night-walks where women need not fear harassment or assault? I think of the artist Noëmi Lakmaier, who crawled through the East End and into the City of London on her hands and knees in a 'slow and exhausting test of endurance' that lasted seven hours.[5] Lakmaier, a wheelchair user, was dressed in a smart business suit that became progressively soiled and ragged as she approached her destination, the Gherkin. The title of the work, *One Morning in May*, unconsciously echoes the opening lines of the fourteenth-century dream vision *Piers Plowman*, a poem that circles insistently around questions of social, economic and bodily inequality. 'Ac on a May mornyng on Maluerne hulles,' writes the dreamer, 'Me biful for to slepe, for werynesse of-walked.'[6]

I am crossing the unmarked boundary between the old parishes of Bermondsey and Rotherhithe; where, on my modified Streetfinder, the solid ground of the island gives way to the alluvial backwash of the river. The lead-covered spire of St Olav's – the Norwegian church – rises in the middle distance above the entrance to the Rotherhithe road tunnel: the southern portal.

I had an idea, I told Abi, of walking the entire circumference of the island, a performance intended to repeat the ancient custom of 'beating the bounds'. Like a country priest on Rogation Sunday, I would lead a procession of the faithful to the limits of my parish, I explained. We would carry boughs of birch or willow with which to beat whatever boundary stones we found, mapping the hidden island through streets and alleys, railway sidings and industrial parks. The way would be accessible, the group diverse. Like a family of wolves, we would move at the pace of our slowest member. Psalms and poems would be sung or read, beseeching God – or Southwark Council – for their divine protection of the land. Beormund's ey would live again, reanimated by the gestures we performed, the memories we made.

But now all my plans are in ruins. The city is locked down. Police are breaking up gatherings from Brixton to Aberdeen, dispersing revellers in breach of new rules on social distancing. A full circumambulation of the island would be impossible (and illegal). The Covid-19 pandemic is the single greatest challenge the world has faced in my lifetime. The risks are terrifying. I am making a will and have drawn up contingency plans for my business in case of death. On a good day we're at each other's throats; a slow burn of housework, shared childcare, cartoons on Netflix. On bad days, it feels like the end times. I remember, then, something Abi said about her experiences as a disabled traveller in the city, that you must 'innovate with the obstacles'. Back home, I take out my Streetfinder and a pen and begin to sketch out alternative routes. If I am to walk, I must walk quickly – and alone.

Lockdown

'SHIT, MAN!' CRIES A VOICE. 'Shit! *Shit!*'

The voice belongs to a leather-faced street drinker on the other side of the fence.

'Come on, man, leave the dog to be a dog,' says the voice, insistently.

The object of his displeasure is walking a small white terrier in the former churchyard of St Mary Magdalen. He – the dog walker – is wearing a hi-vis vest and a black surgical mask. The dog squats.

'Don't *force* him to shit if he doesn't *want* to!' shouts the drinker.

Pale sun strikes the boughs of a cherry tree, heavy with pink blossom. The drinker drifts away, muttering to the ground. I stifle a sneeze then reach to my face to carefully adjust the hiking scarf that is pulled up over my mouth and nose. The look I'm going for is Special Forces chic. But it's hay-fever season and my eyes are heavy and bloodshot behind a pair of reflective sunglasses.

A single-decker bus judders past towards Long Lane, devoid of passengers. Now maintained by the gardeners of Southwark Council, the churchyard is an oasis of parkland between fashionable Bermondsey Street and Tower Bridge Road. Today the streets are practically deserted, save for the dog walker, the street drinker and me. A row of tall gravestones leaning against a boundary wall marks, according to my Streetfinder map, the northern limit of the island. No other geological clues survive; the crenellated walls and weird, truncated tower of St Mary's – a medieval core in seventeenth-century white cladding – stand sentinel above a landscape whose edges have been flattened out.

Bermondsey is God's own country. Its meadows, fields and byways were once dominated by a Cluniac priory dedicated to St Saviour (Jesus) and known later simply as Bermondsey Abbey. A community of monks was first recorded at *Vermundesei* in a papal letter written in AD 715 to the great Mercian monastery at Medeshamstede (Peterborough) to which it was then subsidiary. St Mary's itself was established before 1290 as a small parish church serving the Abbey's secular workforce – the cooks, farmhands, labourers and stonemasons whose physical labour underpinned the spiritual toil of the clerics.

Just as at Westminster, the monastery at Bermondsey occupied a marginal position on an island surrounded by marshes. Both sites also flourished after being re-established several centuries after their original foundation: Westminster in the 960s or 970s by St Dunstan; Bermondsey in 1082 by a wealthy citizen of London called Alwinus Child. As well as the low-lying land in the immediate vicinity, which was quickly cultivated by the construction of dykes and drainage ditches, the Abbey was granted rate-paying properties in Dulwich, Balham, Croydon, Charlton, Rotherhithe and the City, as well as in more distant counties including Somerset and Leicestershire. By 1535 its annual income was valued at £548 – a substantial sum for the times, though a fraction of its more powerful neighbour. And while Westminster Abbey survived the purges of Henry VIII by rebranding as a Royal Peculiar, Bermondsey met the same fate of so many monastic institutions across the country: their powers dissolved, their assets seized and their lands redistributed to grasping courtiers and government stooges.

I cross Long Lane and enter Bermondsey Square. The site of the former Abbey close is occupied by a dark, timber-clad complex of flats and businesses surrounding a pedestrianized courtyard. The cladding looks clinker-built, giving the buildings the appearance of a Viking longhouse. The hotel, independent cinema and Turkish grill are shut. Just Sainsbury's Local remains open, its entrance watched by a diffident security guard. I stand in the middle of the empty square. There is nothing here. Then, out of nowhere, I hear the low, repeated note of a bell. A call to prayer. But what church is still open in these times? St Mary's, Rotherhithe or the Most Holy Trinity, Dockhead? Or perhaps St Anne's, the Hawksmoor church across the water in Limehouse? The wind changes direction and the bell is gone, swallowed up by another sound, from above: the rattle-drone of a Chinook airlifting medical supplies downriver to the NHS emergency field hospital at the Royal Docks.

On Good Friday a thousand people will die across Britain. At midnight the river will reverse its flow, our unborn child turning somersaults in the dark.

I follow Grange Walk into the interior of the island, where pink blossom explodes from a crab-apple tree and a father holds his young son tight to his chest. Two thousand years ago, a narrow neck of land connected Bermondsey to the 'mainland' of Southwark, a natural feature exploited by a trackway; the precursor to Long Lane.[7] Late Iron Age pottery found on the island is indicative, it is said, of 'small-scale pre-Roman activity, including settlement sites such as farmsteads'.[8] The island was also cultivated during the Roman period, with evidence of land reclamation and the cutting of ditches to prevent flooding on its margins. Waste dumps. Animal enclosures. Drovers' roads.[9]

Sunlight dapples the stuccoed walls of a row of old houses, with high gables and wooden shutters, which date to the late seventeenth century. Their pale-blue façades conceal the remains of a medieval stone gatehouse – the southern entrance to the Abbey complex. The houses lend the surroundings a picturesque air, as if they have been lifted wholesale from an English market town, and are quite at odds with Bermondsey's reputation as the home of belching factories and south London hard men. A few doors down, I find a set of wrought-iron gates guarding a cobbled yard behind Grange House, a handsome, two-storey property in London stock brick. Through the locked gates I make out a dark passageway covered, quite unexpectedly, in an elaborate fresco. Wild animals burst from the walls and ceiling – leopards, snakes and rearing horses – alongside scenes drawn from Classical myth. A set of keys hangs from a side door and jangles as a breeze passes through the yard.

I am following a path that once led to a large farm known as the Grange – a medieval descendant, perhaps, of the very earliest agricultural sites on the island. Rocque's map shows the farm compound still hanging on in 1746, but now enclosed by tanners' yards. In the nineteenth century, Bermondsey was known as 'the land of leather' – long before the doomed furniture chain. One factory, Garnar's, produced chamois for 'bookbinders, bootmakers and glovers' and survived at the Grange as late as 1981.[10] Another company, Christys', specialized in soft leather hats and still operates from its new manufacturing base in Witney, Oxfordshire. Today the noxious stench of the tanneries – the 'spicy miasma of lime and decay' as one author put it[11] – has been replaced by the distinctive aroma of fried chicken. Christys' is selling designer cotton face masks. A blue hatchback races past and, as it turns into St Saviour's Estate, a huge, hairy face appears at the passenger side window – the grinning visage of a teddy bear that I later realize belonged to a Tibetan mastiff.

'It feels like moving through a collage,' Abi had told me – and she was right. I am walking a landscape of fragments. Modern apartments in weathered timber and vintage tiling rise from the footprints of Victorian warehouses and face down the identikit blocks of a 1960s housing estate. Narrow alleys give way suddenly to vacant yards, wasteland, gaps in the street plan. I am following a tiny cobbled lane at the centre of the Grange, between half-completed flats and a derelict tannery garlanded with weeds, when a small man – wizened and bearded – appears from nowhere and almost stumbles into me, his mashed-up work boots catching on the crazy paving. When I turn to apologize, he has already vanished. A shaft of sunlight breaks through and I emerge on to Neckinger, the road that leads back north to the old mill pond. An eerie atmosphere has descended. Tufts of blossom hang, suspended, in the windless air. There is a low hum and the persistent bark of a dog from a third-floor balcony. I track the source of the hum to a vast redbrick substation, as tall as a cathedral, whose boarded-up doorways are covered in hazard signs that read: DANGER OF DEATH. In the distance, the Shard moves in and out of sight – a silver beacon catching the light.

Has it been three weeks or four? I am beginning to understand that isolation creates its own time: a languid movement of events unloosed from sequence that can suddenly collapse into moments of frightening clarity when everything seems to be at stake. Holy Week has begun. For Christians, we have stepped into a time outside of time; through ritual worship, our own lives synchronize with the events of Christ's final days. But this year, his entry to Jerusalem goes unmarked. Instead, I stand at the open window and applaud with our neighbours across Rotherhithe Street – a futile gesture of solidarity with those on the frontline. We do nothing. We change nothing. Sometimes the virus seems like a hoax, a waking dream from which we will soon be released.

I continue south, skirting the open ground at Bermondsey Spa, where joggers are doing government-approved loops of the park, each locked in to their own motivational playlist. A DHL delivery driver is tapping furiously at an entryphone at the gates of the Alaska Building, a converted sealskin factory which looms above the island like a beached, art-deco cruise ship. Seagulls wheel above the ice-white central tower as I pass, descending now towards the southern perimeter. At the bottom of Bacon Grove, two teenaged boys – one white, one black – stand back to back, comparing heights, joyously unselfconscious.

The road falls markedly then levels out and I find myself in a strange, suburban cul-de-sac. Rocque recorded a small ditch or stream flowing here from the direction of the Grange. Today one side of the street adjoins a low-rise estate of squat bungalows that would not look out of place in a seaside retirement village. On the other side stands a truncated terrace of smart, modern houses in the style of Taylor Wimpey or Barratt Homes, with off-street parking and folksy names. A middle-aged man looks up from polishing his Hyundai Ioniq outside *Marine Lodge*. I am still wearing my hiking scarf in the manner of a bandito; but this is no ordinary scene of suburban bliss that I am disturbing. The air is thick with brick dust and the tremendous sound of a mechanical digger hammering the ground, and high above the terraced houses two giant cranes are picking apart the condemned hulk of the Crosse & Blackwell pickle factory.

Here, on the southern edge of the former island, I encounter once more a dissonant geography; where ruined industrial megaliths compete with post-war infill. The effect is disorientating and my stride becomes suddenly cautious, unsteady. From somewhere I hear the buzz of a generator. I strain my neck and look up; a little white cloud of dust is rising from the open roof of the factory, like the contrail of an aeroplane, into the bluest of deep-blue skies.

Crosse & Blackwell produced canned goods here including soup, luncheon meat and baked beans, as well as bottled ketchup, fish pastes, salad cream, Worcestershire sauce and its signature relish, the famous Branston Pickle.[12] More recently, the site operated as a light industrial estate, with an art gallery and studios for creative businesses. Soon, luxury apartment blocks with heritage names will cluster in its shadows. The ruin is a Romantic fantasy; here, as everywhere in London, demand for housing outstrips the appeals of preservationists. But with less than a quarter of properties earmarked for social tenants, the development will surely only accelerate the marginalization of the established, working-class community in favour of wealthy professionals from elsewhere.

The old patterns repeat: decline and fall; rebirth and renewal. The island has always been porous, unfixed. Many Bermondsey families are descended, like my own, from immigrants from Ireland and Scotland; dockers and navvies dispatched from the Celtic fringe. 'London,' as Abi had said, 'is constantly recycling itself.'

It is five o'clock and Willow Walk is lit up like a film set. Low sun floods the pendulous boughs of a weeping willow, heavy with golden catkins; it pours through the gates of the Royal Mail depot and into the car park and loading bays, where a postal worker is taking his tea on an upturned pallet; it casts long shadows on the boundary wall of the former railway yard and makes of its barbed-wire crest a latticework of diamonds and other shining gems. The sunlight almost blinds the woman who is walking the steel-edged passage between the depot and a prefab warehouse, weighed down by grocery bags. I step aside and from behind a makeshift mask she nods a silent thank you. These tiny gestures of recognition sustain each day in lockdown. I hear a siren from the west and we both turn, instinctively, towards the dying light.

Willow Walk is an old road, marked as a nameless pathway through fields on Rocque's map. By the nineteenth century it was occupied by tannery yards, where 'oblong, rectangular pieces of "tan-turf"' could be purchased as a cheap source of fuel from 'skeleton frames about five or six feet in height'.[13] In 1810 a group of houses 'over the ditch' on the south side of the road is recorded under the curious name 'Jackson's Island' in Lockie's *Topography* but nowhere else; the ditch is untraceable and the site is now occupied by a commercial printing company.[14] In 1847 the London, Brighton and South Coast Railway established a goods yard on Willow Walk, adjacent to the ill-fated Bricklayers Arms terminus; it too has disappeared beneath the corrugated steel hangar of a parcel delivery depot. I pull out my Streetfinder to cross-reference my position with the geological record. If I am right, it appears that Willow Walk ran parallel with the interface between the gravel island and the surrounding swamp, an alignment that was later continued by Lynton Road along the line of a field boundary.*

The entire character of the landscape is changing; the dense, erratic composition of the island replaced by a low-rise terrain of trading estates, storage facilities and distribution centres. *This is it*, I think: the edge of the map. I cut south through the postal depot, where a large ventilation funnel emits a low metallic sound like a damp cough, and emerge on to Mandela Way. A white Ford Transit speeds past, followed by a flatbed lorry in British Racing Green. The street is bounded on both sides by anonymous sheds behind high, steel fences, such that, despite

---

* The late extension of this littoral route explains why the junction of Dunton Road with Willow Walk/Lynton Road is not a true crossroads but slightly offset.

its modernity, Mandela Way resembles a sunken lane – an ancient 'hollow way' through the flatlands of south Bermondsey. Here, at the head of an alluvial channel beyond the southern shores of Beormund's ey, a small army of delivery vans, public buses and waste-removal trucks is keeping London running. This hinterland is designed for vehicles, not pedestrians like me, sans lanyard, sans hi-vis, and to walk here feels like an eccentric pursuit, like trespass. On the empty pavement, a square of white paint has been sprayed, and inside it, in place of a tree, the single word *Tree*.

Mandela Way spits me out by a petrol station and a branch of Argos in whose vacant car park a small boy is kicking a partially deflated football. The traffic of the Old Kent Road, that genuinely ancient highway following the higher ground towards Deptford, is within earshot now; but instead I deflect due east at a roundabout and pursue a line of plane trees past low-rise housing developments.

Although there is nothing in the lie of the land to suggest it, Rolls Road tracks a little north of the underground stream known as the Earl's Sluice, which once flowed down from the hills beyond Camberwell, minutes from my childhood home, and is now contained in a sewer pipe. Its course north of the Old Kent Road has long divided the parishes of Bermondsey and Rotherhithe from those of Camberwell and Deptford, and an old stone marking the boundary between Surrey and Kent still stands near its mouth, on the Thames path by South Dock. Its meandering route is now represented by Rolls Road, Catlin Street and Rotherhithe New Road, but on Greenwood's map of 1828 the Sluice is shown running in ditches either side of a road marked 'Galley Wall'. There is still a Galleywall Road in Bermondsey, but somewhere else; at some point the name was relocated to a connecting track – the boundary path that Greenwood called Manor Lane. Writing in 1912, Walter Besant suggested that the name 'Galleywall' derives from a lost Roman quayside where galleys moored – an attractive proposition but one that draws more on his imaginative powers as a novelist than on historical scholarship.[15] The earliest surviving reference is found in a document of the mid-1500s – a list of lands owned by Bermondsey Abbey at the time of the Dissolution. It appears erroneously in the text as 'Salowe walle' and is amended in the margin to 'Galowe walle'[16] – a name glossed by one etymologist as the 'wall where a gallows stands'.[17]

If there *was* a gallows here, no trace of it survives. The junction of modern Galleywall Road with Rotherhithe New Road would have been a good location, as here three parishes converged. Today the spot is a craterous intersection overlooked by the railway bridge of South Bermondsey station and a haunted-looking branch of Greggs. Beyond this point, the Earl's Sluice appears to have continued in two, parallel channels, the northern of the pair following a dog-leg path marked 'Rogues Lane' on Horwood's map of 1799. In later maps, Rogues Lane is recorded as Rogers Lane. It survives today as a much-diminished side street, Corbett's Lane, named after an American-born shipwright, William Corbett, who was found guilty of the murder of his landlord and his wife in their house in Rotherhithe in 1764. After his execution at the Surrey Gallows on Kennington Common, Corbett's body was hung in chains from a gibbet 'on the road between Rotherhithe and Deptford' near the Jolly Gardeners, a Victorian boozer that has since been converted into short-term rental apartments.[18]

So, then, the condemned felon – cutpurse, fence or murderer – might have walked Rogues Lane to the Gallows Wall, an elevated bank-and-ditch causeway leading across the marsh from the Thames to a mysterious execution site. A simpler explanation presents itself. Perhaps the gallows in question was the one recorded on the Old Kent Road at St Thomas-a-Watering, where Chaucer's band of pilgrims stopped to water their horses in the Earl's Sluice and decide which of them would tell the first tale. The Sluice still runs beneath the Thomas A Becket, the former pub and boxing gym which is reputed to be haunted by the ghosts of three nuns and is currently operating as a Vietnamese restaurant. Meanwhile, the gallows has reincarnated on the wide pavement outside Tesco in the form of a luminous silver obelisk by kinetic sculptor Peter Logan. Some two centuries after Chaucer, it was here, in the shadow of Argos, DFS and Carpetright, that the Catholic recusants John Jones and John Rigby were hanged, drawn and quartered, with the latter suffering a particularly gruesome fate.

> He kissed the rope as it was put round his neck, and was offering his last prayers, when they were cut short by the impatience of the under-sheriff, and the cart driven away. The Martyr was immediately cut down, and the work of butchery begun while he was yet alive. His head and quarters were exposed in different places in the neighbourhood of Southwark.[19]

The tower blocks of Avondale Square come into view above Rolls Road; I feel as if I am moving through an avenue of giant standing stones. Since the roundabout by Argos, I have seen not a single soul. The way has been framed, on my left, by a high brick wall of considerable age. At the junction with St James's Road, the highway leading north climbs steeply and, as it does so, opens to a wide vista – back towards the island – and I realize, then, that I am standing at the apex of a bridge spanning what were once the railway tracks disgorging, like shoots of foliage from the Green Man's open gob, from the goods depot at Willow Walk; and that the high brick wall still illustrates the southern boundary of this vanished ground. I pull myself up and make out, in the wasteland underneath the bridge, the edge of an abandoned platform. Further down, a council work crew – four Polish lads in overalls and hi-vis vests – is making right a section that has partially collapsed and, as I pass, one of them looks up and smiles.

The strip development of light industrial estates and modern housing along Mandela Way and Rolls Road is bound, inextricably, to the history of the railway, just as the tracks themselves made use of empty meadowland between the island and the Sluice. The channel into which the Sluice drains predates even the island. Like its sister stream, the Neckinger, the Earl's Sluice probably exploited an ancient, abandoned route of the Thames dating to the late glacial period – a hollow both broad and deep that has come to be known as the Bermondsey Lake.

As the last of the sun strikes the pavement, I rejoin the Gallows Wall and proceed down Catlin Street in the direction of home. It's a forty-minute yomp back to Rotherhithe and I've already exceeded my daily allowance. The traffic has been light all day, but suddenly I sense that it has stopped altogether.

I, too, stop. And turn.

And listen.

A numbness travels down my body.

Silence.

Silence; then a tiny thing – a sound like the spinning of a hard disk, almost imperceptible. I realize now that, without quite knowing it, I have been walking off the island – Beormund's ey – into somewhere stranger still.

The sound grows louder and a single car approaches from the west – a vintage Citroën 2CV whose turquoise livery gleams with dappled light. It slows down as it passes and I catch a glimpse of the driver as she turns towards me wearing a floral facemask. It's as if she sees straight through me.

I look up, above the railings of a modern block, where a child has taped a painting of a rainbow to the inside of their bedroom window. I see then that I am standing directly beneath a timber scaffold – two crossed beams with a diagonal brace – the empty frame for an estate agents' sign that assumes, in that moment, the unmistakable form of a gallows.

Into the Lion's Den

MARTHA TURNED FOUR ON the day the UK death toll passed twenty-eight thousand. She ate smoked-salmon sandwiches and chocolate cake from a unicorn-themed table set as our extended families sang 'Happy Birthday' via Zoom – a gallery of grainy likenesses she barely acknowledged as true.

Once, in the days before the virus, I took Martha to the Horniman Museum in Forest Hill and let her run around the exhibits. She peered into glass cabinets at the shocked faces of taxidermied otters, grinning leopards and tigers, a fish with the hideous face of a monkey. 'Is it real or pretend?' she asked at every case, hardly stopping for breath once she had her answer. 'Real or pretend, Daddy? And this one – is it real or pretend?'

On the morning after Martha's birthday, I leave the flat and head south on the pretext of picking up a car seat for the new baby from my lock-up in south Bermondsey. I like to tell people I meet that I have a lock-up in south Bermondsey because it makes me sound like a character from *The Bill*. 'It's where I keep the bodies,' I say.

Some say the centre of Bermondsey is the Blue – the market and shopping precinct in the south-east of the island. But for many, the beating heart of Bermondsey is its famous football club, Millwall. It's here that I'm headed – into the lion's den – to explore again the industrial edgelands south of the island and discover the origins of Millwall supporters' fearsome reputation.

I walk in glorious May sunshine tempered with squalls of wind-whipped drizzle. I walk across the Rotherhithe peninsula, by the woods and playing fields, where chimes of tiny wrens burst from unchecked hedges. I walk across the empty road junction behind the shopping centre and through the car park of the big Tesco. A socially distanced queue has already formed outside the Express Fish Bar on Lower Road. I walk

317

to the crossroads where a cast-iron stink pipe rises from a traffic island, then follow the Earl's Sluice upstream to a deep railway cutting where the sewer has been miraculously lifted above the tracks in a fat, white tube. The air is thick with shreds of floating blossom and the vegetal stench of the fenceline fills my nostrils.

I am inspecting the wild grass where the tube emerges like a giant earthworm from the ground when, from out of nowhere, comes a jangly tune I recognize immediately as 'Greensleeves'. Ali Baba's Super Soft ice cream van pulls up by the railway cutting and the driver leans out of the window to greet a man in a grey tracksuit who is walking his daughter on a pink scooter. There is movement by the tracks: a family of foxes on the sun-drenched margins of the embankment. In the shadow of the elevated sewer, three scruffy cubs wrestle and chase each other through the undergrowth, while mother fox sits on her haunches on a little concrete podium, motionless and alert. *Are you real or pretend?* I think.

I follow the railway tracks down a street lined with recently pollarded trees. A youth smoking a joint bowls towards me; then a little girl in sparkly wellies. The verge is brimming with wildflowers – hollyhocks and gaudy dandelions – and a sprawling green shrub with large fuzzy leaves that I do not recognize. Before I know it, the way has opened up and I'm crossing a scrappy lawn enclosed on two sides by railways and overlooked by the smoking chimney of a waste disposal plant. A council bin is stuffed to burst with little plastic bags of dog poo. 'Ashley!' calls a woman hobbling across the grass with the help of a single crutch. 'Everything OK, yeah?' The tinny music of Ali Baba's van starts up again and as it drifts away towards the island the melody distorts into a creepy rendition of 'Yankee Doodle Dandy'.

'Oi! Keep your fucking voices down.'

A gang of men, forty-strong, is moving through the tunnel. The leader turns and raises his hand.

'Keep it quiet. Keep it quiet.'

A deep bass drone reverberates in the darkness.

And now they're rushing out, into the light, snarling like wolves, where another mob has assembled on the wasteland – a swaggering, ragtag army in Stone Island sweaters and blue jeans.

'You fucking wanker!' shouts the leader of the first group, Fred, played by south London-born Turkish Cypriot actor Tamer Hassan; and then his opposite number, Billy, played by British gangster film stalwart Frank Harper, pulls out a flare gun and the ruckus begins.

This organized brawl between two hooligan firms – the Chelsea Head-hunters and Millwall's notorious Bushwackers – forms the climax of the 2004 film *The Football Factory* and was shot on location in the fenced-off waste ground and industrial yards of SE16.[20]

I follow the path beneath a series of barrel-vaulted railway viaducts covered with graffiti; here the main line from London Bridge divides into its constituent branches, like an electrical cable released from its sheath. Between the tracks, the Shard directs its malevolent gaze, like the lidless eye of Sauron across Middle-earth.

Danny Dyer's lager-swilling anti-hero Tommy was brutalized in the murk of this tunnel; beaten, stamped on, his head caved in with a brick. Today a makeshift skate ramp has been built against one wall. A hipster couple cycles past on racing bikes. The bloke looks just like Björn Borg, right down to the stripy sweat band. I pass through the final viaduct and the pathway climbs to the rim of a concrete basin and I find myself, at last, looking out across the cantilevered roofs and colossal steel super-structure of The Den.

I had arranged to walk the perimeter of the stadium with an acquaintance, Chris Larkin – a lifelong Millwall supporter – but the lockdown has prevented our meeting face to face. When I call him, he is at home in the small Essex town of Manningtree and missing football. 'Jesus, I miss football,' he says, twice. 'It's like a structural deficit in my life.'

Chris grew up in Gravesend, out on the Estuary, with spells living in Peckham and Streatham in his twenties. He works at the *London Review of Books* and is a regular at the capital's poetry nights, where we met. But his first love is football. Millwall is a family affair; both his dad and granddad were fans. Like me, Chris was only ten years old when The New Den opened in 1993 – the first all-seater stadium in England to be built after the Taylor Report into the Hillsborough Disaster. Unlike the architectural mishmash of my own sporting alma mater, Selhurst Park, which is wedged between terraced streets and a branch of Sainsbury's, The Den occupies its island site between the railway lines with the hulking certainty of a championship boxer. Its metal exoskeleton – painted blue, the club's colour – gives the stands an industrial appearance, as if they might have grown organically out of the neighbouring waste disposal plant.

For Chris, the geography of The Den holds a powerful place in his imagination: 'On match days I walk from New Cross, or Queens Road, cutting through the housing estate where the old ground used to be, and soon I'm walking in a swathe of people, and we're scrambling up embankments, following desire lines towards the ground. I can do the route in my head.' Weekday matches are particularly special, when, he says, 'you can hear the trains going by in the floodlit dusk'.

Millwall has been in south Bermondsey since 1910, when the club moved from its original home on the Isle of Dogs. (The name 'Millwall' derives from the windmills built along the river wall on the western shore of that other peninsula.) The club makes much of its heritage in London's industrial heartlands. As Chris tells me, its location among the 'hidden facilitating industries' of the city underpins its identity as a 'no-nonsense club for the working man'. On the pitch, he continues, the fans still favour players who are 'rough around the edges and not shy of work – good honest pros who are fit for the area'. It's a far cry from what Chris calls the 'sanitized, anodyne' culture of the Premier League.

'I'm in enemy territory,' I say, half joking. But I get the sense it's not Millwall's south London rivals, Crystal Palace, to which he is referring, but the cash-rich megaclubs like Arsenal and Manchester City.

I follow the path above the Dockers Stand until I'm almost level with the railway tracks. Two boys speed past on roller skates. A bulldog sniffs at the verge then relieves itself. I ask Chris about Millwall's reputation for football violence; about the thuggish exploits of F-Troop and the Bushwackers. He demurs. 'We're no angels. But the problem has been exaggerated by the media. We're a pantomime villain that everyone loves to hate.'

'And what about *The Football Factory*?' I ask.

'It's a cliché, but there's some truth in it,' he says. For Chris, Millwall's famous chant, 'No one likes us, we don't care' (sung to the tune of Rod Stewart's 'Sailing'), is a declaration both of defiance and of a certain fatalism that is prevalent among supporters. '*Not* to be hated,' he says, quite without irony, 'would be a worse death than being relegated from the Football League.'

Perhaps something of the island mentality of Bermondsey lives on in this self-fashioning as embattled and derided; an enclave of working-class culture enduring, like a nodule of granite, as the new London of penthouses spreads in all directions. During the Blitz, Bermondsey was designated 'Target Area G' by the Luftwaffe; the north terrace of the old ground was even struck by a German bomb in April 1943. During the London Bridge attack of 2017, an unemployed man, Roy Larner, fought off knife-wielding terrorists with his bare fists while shouting, 'Fuck you, I'm Millwall!' He was stabbed eight times but survived, earning the nickname 'The Lion of London Bridge'.

At worst, however, this mentality gives rise to a tribal exceptional-ism that views outsiders with contempt. In the 1970s the terraces of Millwall were considered a fertile recruiting ground for far-right organi-zations such as the National Front. Larner was later caught on camera shouting racist abuse at students protesting at the Elephant and Castle against Trump and Brexit. Allegations of racism continue to dog the club to this day, although, as Chris is keen to point out, only a small minority of fans engage in the kind of bigoted chanting witnessed during their 2019 FA Cup win against Everton. The Millwall Community Trust, he adds, does 'a huge amount of work to support the local area' and runs football teams for children and people with disabilities.

As I descend into Bolina Road, I pass the Trust's headquarters – a corrugated blue shed behind the north stand. Millwall's emblem, the Lion Rampant, looks out from the club shop over a parade of vehicle repair shops and mechanics' yards. The pavement is lined with parked cars in various states of entropy: souped-up hatchbacks with their bonnets ripped off; pranged Hondas; the chassis of an ancient Saab licked clean for parts. A cocker spaniel spots me from a breaker's yard and crosses the forecourt to investigate. I hear the low pulse of an electric vehicle recharging. An engine revs wildly then cuts out. A small man emerges from behind a set of roller shutters and wipes his forehead with a rag. The spaniel follows me all the way down to the workers' caff and when I stop, to take a photo of the north and west stands silhouetted against the sky like a pair of giant anvils, he looks up with a quizzical gaze as if to say, 'Will you like me?'

If, as Chris proposed, a club's identity is 'formed by the landscape', then surely he, the spaniel, is Millwall's *genius loci* – the protective spirit of The Den. After all, he is like a lion, only smaller. Millwall's swagger is mostly smoke and mirrors; no one really wants to be hated, just to be heard. As the sociologist Garry Robson observed, 'The archetypal status of the Millwall fan is a vexed and complex one in which myth and reality have perhaps become so closely intertwined that even some of those most closely involved are unsure as to where the one might end and the other begin.'[21] I crouch down, proffer my open palm and, as the spaniel creeps towards me, I whisper, 'Are you real or pretend?'

For all the muscularity of its architecture, The Den lies on shaky ground. During construction, a thick layer of peat was encountered beneath the surface, requiring major adjustments to the design, taking into account seasonal movement within the soil.[22] The stadium now rests on concrete piles that were driven into the chalk bedrock underlying the site at an average depth of 19 metres. A venting system was installed underneath the ground-floor slabs for the purpose of removing any methane gas released from the ground (peat being formed of partially decomposed organic matter). As the spaniel turns and plods home to the breaker's yard, my nose suddenly fills with the putrid stink of fish. On the corner, a large man in a white apron is loading a box of fresh cod into a refrigerated van. It is fitting to find a fishmonger's here, at The Den, for I have walked into the invisible centre of a prehistoric lake.

In March 1992 archaeologists opened a trench in Bramcote Grove, 300 yards west of the present stadium, on ground cleared for new housing. What they discovered would transform our understanding of the prehistory of the London region. Beneath a covering of peat dating to the late Bronze Age emerged the preserved remains of an ancient wooden trackway. The trackway crossed a filled-in channel and was composed of two distinct phases: an earlier structure consisting of parallel lines of alder logs held in place by stakes; and a later iteration, dated to 1740–1530 BC, comprising a single line of oak logs with alder stakes on one side.[23] Only a small portion of trackway was revealed, but its alignment indicated that it was constructed 'as a means to traverse the marshy area between the gravels to the south and the edge of Bermondsey eyot'.[24] The logs overlaid thick clay silts and mud, suggestive of a late glacial water feature – the Bermondsey Lake – that had gradually silted up to form an expansive marsh fringed with birch and pine woodland. The lake itself appears to have formed in the abandoned channel of a river; a glacial stream was uncovered during the laying of a pipeline on Ilderton Road.[25] That the trackway was rebuilt at least once demonstrates that it was no temporary project, but a route sufficiently important to be maintained across successive generations. Two Neolithic flint axes had been already dredged from silt beneath the Bricklayers Arms in

1987, together with evidence of hearths and a platform of 'horizontal interlaced timbers' that may have represented a 'lakeside jetty'.[26]

Subsequent excavations at Marlborough Grove (1991) and the B&Q Depot on the Old Kent Road (1995) have revealed an extensive pattern of human activity on the margins of the lake. The burnt traces of hearths and scatters of worked flint (one containing over one and a half thousand pieces) are indicative of early Mesolithic hunting camps, strategically located on the high ground above the southern shore. Before it silted up, the freshwater lake would have been fringed by sedges, reeds and dwarf willows. Populations of deer, elk, aurochs and wild pig, as well as wild-fowl and fish, would have made it a rich and possibly stable focus for human groups and comparable to the landscape of the river Kennet in Wiltshire (which is home to numerous prehistoric monuments including Avebury Henge and Silbury Hill).[27] In this context, the Bramcote Grove trackway may have constituted an attempt to access the dwindling resources of the lake; to maintain traditional pathways in a changing world.[28] It may even have had some sacred significance, as has been suggested of the Bronze Age and Mesolithic jetties at Vauxhall, near the mouth of the Effra, where ritual deposits of weaponry have been found.

After its discovery in the spring of 1992, the trackway was temporarily 'reburied' beneath a polythene sheet and covered with damp peat to avoid air pockets. When, eight months later, archaeologists reopened the trench, they found the logs crawling with woodlice and covered in 'fungal bloom and growths'.[29] What had lain preserved in the anaerobic soil for over three and a half thousand years was now decaying before their eyes. A grainy photograph survives from the uncovering: four figures in hard hats holding a white shroud above the black earth, like priests embalming a corpse.

I collect the car seat from my lock-up on Record Street where it, too, has been entombed among audio equipment, mothballed props and boxes of unsold books, and then I head back north along Ilderton Road. The full extent of the Bermondsey Lake is unknown. It might have been as long as several kilometres from east to west.[30] I'm still well within its bounds when I reach a small enclave of two-room, brick bungalows hugging the embankment beneath the platforms of South Bermondsey station. Kids' bikes and plastic buggies stand forlorn on patches of unkempt lawn. A set of Portaloos is braced against the perimeter wall. It seems deserted, save an elderly man with improbably jet-black hair who is nailing wooden pallets together to form some sort of platform. In the window of an unhitched caravan a vinyl sticker declares JESUS IS LORD.

I have encountered the Travellers of Bermondsey before: young lads in branded sportswear and *Peaky Blinders* haircuts riding a pony and trap down Rotherhithe Street. In Irish, Travellers are called *an lucht siúil* – 'the walking people'. Traditionally, they have led a semi-nomadic lifestyle – like the Mesolithic hunter-gatherers of the lake – but today many communities have settled in local authority-run sites such as this one. It is not exactly a glamorous plot. According to the council's own records, the railway embankment was recently 'falling apart',[31] a retaining wall 'at risk of crumbling and sliding on to the site', and the access road was 'sinking' and waterlogged in winter.[32] New paving has since been laid through the site, but I can still make out signs of decay: a network of hairline fractures on the retaining wall.

There is something else here, stirring beneath the tarmac. The Peck – the river that gave Peckham its name – flows in a combined mains sewer down the centre of Ilderton Road, then joins the Earl's Sluice somewhere beneath the station. On Greenwood's map of 1828 the Peck appears as a pair of parallel streams tracking the parish boundary, a course that aligns exactly with the dense undergrowth behind the Travellers' enclave.

The confluence of two rivers is a powerful site – 'thickened water' as the poet Elizabeth-Jane Burnett puts it.[33] The people of the Iron Age considered them sacred and raised great funeral barrows on the high ground between them. It was, as Peter Ackroyd says, 'a place of votive offering . . . where the gods were meant to dance'.[34] Where, precisely, these two buried streams – the Earl's Sluice and the Peck – meet is a matter of debate. Could it be beneath my conjectured gallows site outside Greggs? Or, as Tom Bolton suggests, further east, where a series of drainage ditches once enclosed the little islet of St Helena's Tea Gardens?[35] The knotted tangle of railway lines, waste ground and industrial yards resists the kind of field-walking that might, to my mind, locate this mysterious union. Perhaps, instead, I might locate the site of the Bramcote Grove trackway, lost beneath modern housing. But not today. My time has run out.

Two men are talking in the shadowy interior of a scrap tyre yard. One sits cross-legged on an antique leather armchair like an emperor at court. I shift the car seat in my hands, my shoulders anticipating the weight of a child to come. The Bermondsey Lake has not yet given up all its secrets. My guide through the Rockingham at the Elephant and Castle, Oli Rahman, had told me of a council estate he knew that was, as he put it, 'literally sinking into the ground'. On the journey home, a fine rain begins to fall, releasing earthy scent; and when I look west, across the green expanse of Southwark Park, a rainbow has formed in the deep-blue sky above the island.

Sink Estate

I RETURN TO THE LAKE under the cover of night. A fierce wind is moving from the east – the kind you get before a storm – and the empty streets are strewn with blown debris. The night is fox time. They patrol the corners like street gangs, sniffing out the territory. This is my town, *my* town, they bark, then drift like phantoms into shadow.

I'm crossing the peninsula in the gathering dark when suddenly it seems as if I'm walking through the ruins of the Surrey Docks. Everything that once seemed fruitful and alive now seems to threaten from the margins. Old trees creak and groan; discarded takeaway boxes scuttle across my path like tumbleweed; a black plastic bag takes flight in the form of a bat.

I follow the old track of Trundleys Road, past the site of the former *Chymical Works*, then pass beneath the railway lines along Cold Blow Lane, where the road constricts through a series of tunnels, each one darker and more menacing than the last. A pathway once feared by visiting supporters to The Old Den, the tunnel walls are now daubed in tags for local gangs and drill groups: Deptford Ghetto Boys, Original Farm Boys, GAS Gang. A large dog fox tails me through the tunnel, then ghosts away in the direction of Monsoon Road. Perhaps he's heading for the Winchester, where Simon Pegg's band of thirty-something slackers shelter from the zombie apocalypse in the comedy horror film *Shaun of the Dead*: 'Go to the Winchester, have a nice cold pint, and wait for all this to blow over.'[36]

I cut back north across Ilderton Road, where joineries and timber yards sit alongside the corrugated metal sheds of Black Evangelical churches, then slip down a side road into a network of residential streets forming a rough triangle at the heart of the Bermondsey Lake. The wind has dropped and now the only sound is the distant hum of cars on Rotherhithe New Road. I have found myself in an inner-city suburbia of identikit terraced houses, their neat front yards defended by the stone figures of nymphs and dryads, water sprites and gurning gnomes. Some sport Union Jacks and bunting from the recent, muted VE Day celebrations. A front door opens and a middle-aged man in board shorts steps out and lights a cigarette. He is cradling a bottle of lager in his free hand. 'Evening,' I say, and as he nods I'm already doubling back to introduce myself.

'I'm looking for the site of an excavation,' I begin. 'From the early nineties. Can you help?'

He takes a swig then shakes his head. 'I've never heard anything like that. The houses on this side were all built in ninety-four,' he says. 'Back then there were scrap heaps everywhere.'

1994: the dates match up. I think I've found it: the site of the Bramcote Grove trackway.

When I tell him, the man seems nonplussed. Instead, he shrugs off his house slippers and approaches the pavement. 'That block on the corner used to be a box factory. Further down there was a chemical plant. Do you know the library at the Blue? Maybe you could find an old map of the area down there.'

The construction work leading to the discovery of the trackway must have been part of the regeneration of the area that culminated in the demolition of the surrounding Bonamy Estate by Barratt Homes in 1996. Built in the late 1960s with 'all the utopian optimism . . . for concrete high-density estates', within twenty years the Bonamy was falling apart at the seams; condemned by engineers, half-abandoned by its tenants.[37] The estate seemed destined for failure from the start, when it was revealed that the major shareholder in the building contractor, Kirk & Kirk, was none other than the Minister for Transport, Ernest Marples. Marples later fled to Monaco to escape prosecution for tax fraud, and is best remembered for his sexual fetish: to be whipped by prostitutes while wearing women's clothes.

'Thank you, keep well,' I say, and continue in the direction of the centre of the estate. A children's playground stands there, half-lit by streetlamps; the empty metal frame of the swing wrapped in hazard tape. I pass the Bramcote Arms, once a raucous Millwall pub, now washed out and boarded up like an old façade in a derelict backlot. I have read that the Earl's Sluice still flows beneath the estate towards its confluence with the Peck. At its lowest point the ground surface is nine metres below sea level. I walk from drain to drain along Delaford Road, flashing my little hand-held torch into the murky depths, hoping for the rushing sound of a sewer. But this is not the Fleet. A glossy SUV pulls out of a driveway and briefly catches me in its headlights, crouched in the middle of the road. If anyone asks, I'll say I've lost my wedding ring.

The Bonamy today is a tranquil, well-maintained mixed development of private and social housing; some of the properties here go for half a million or more. It's a far cry from the dim courtyards and forbidding walkways of the old estate, which was beset with 'damp, noise, faulty sewers and poor security' as well as frequent fires.[38] A black-and-white TV news report from 1983 shows the estate in all its eerie decrepitude.[39] The camera pans across an expanse of waste ground towards a dull-grey housing block, then cuts to an interior staircase where an elderly woman is reaching out her hand to show where the plasterboard has warped from damp and, behind the peeling wallpaper, split open like a fault line. Then we're outside again: a brick wall stained with rising groundwater; a broken, misaligned waste pipe.

Just as Metro Central Heights was diagnosed with 'sick building syndrome', the old Bonamy was said to suffer from 'concrete cancer'. Questions were raised in parliament. The local MP, Simon Hughes, blamed 'substantial defects' in the foundations.[40] The *Financial Times* filed a damning report of its own, criticizing the leaking roofs, corroded water mains, cracks and signs of movement in the concrete slabs, and generally poor standard of construction.

In the years before its demolition, the Bonamy became synonymous with urban decay. The estate provided the backdrop to the film *Nil by*

Mouth, a harrowing depiction of domestic violence and substance abuse which was the directorial debut of south-London-born actor Gary Oldman.[41] 'It was like an empty movie set,' Oldman said.[42] The estate was originally designed for two and a half thousand residents, but by the early 1990s a third or more had left. One reviewer likened the walkways to prison corridors, adding, 'It looks like a welcome stable for the four horsemen of the apocalypse.'[43] The ruined landscape of the Bonamy Estate was, in effect, the film's central character.

I managed to make contact with Mark Read, a former resident, by email. 'I lived on [the Bonamy] from the late 1960s to the early 1970s,' he wrote. 'The estate always looked dismal with the dark brickwork and lack of space between each block. I don't know what it was built on but there used to be a lot of unusual activity going on, as in ghosts. I know it sounds silly but the time I was there we did notice things going on.'

As in ghosts!

I pressed him further.

'It always had a spooky appearance and certain things going on. One night me and my family were settling down for the night when the letter-box started banging quite harshly. For several moments this continued, my dog was barking, and when my father managed to answer the door no one was there.'

A car backfires on the main road, towards the Gallows Wall. A scruffy young fox is rooting around in a scrap of grass, oblivious. I am starting to wonder if the demise of the Bonamy was down to bad workmanship alone, or whether more sinister forces were at play. There are no visible remains of the old estate, and the Bonamy Pharmacy on Rotherhithe New Road is the only external appearance of its name that I can find. As I reach the edge of the triangle of streets, here at the centre of the Bermondsey Lake, the wind picks up again. There is a sound like a scurrying rodent from a pile of household waste dumped by the bins.

In the late 1970s a teenaged music fan began to make trips down from Manchester to visit his pen pal at 91 Redlaw Way, in a 'maisonette of ramps and grey slabs' on the edge of the Bonamy estate.[44] His name was Steven Patrick Morrissey and, together with his pen pal, James Maker, he wandered the 'fog-bound' streets of south London like a Baudrillardian *flâneur*. He called the Bonamy 'the safest side of the tracks that are unsafe on both sides: a mishmash area'.

The two young friends, united by their love of the New York Dolls, would sit on the balcony of Maker's parents' flat drinking, talking and singing. One night, Morrissey claimed, they witnessed the astonishing sight of flying saucers 'hover[ing] low and slow over Bermondsey'.

> I stood on the balcony, and stared directly into one hovering ship, and it STOPPED in mid-air above me. Without a doubt, it was watching me![45]

I had set out to map a vanished island but found its opposite: a lake. I do not know if ghosts – or UFOs – are real or pretend. The fox in shadow. The knocking at the door. Two rivers meeting in the darkness underground. I do believe the past is carried with us, deep inside; something precious, unredeemable.

As I leave Bermondsey for the final time, a midnight haze descends and I glimpse, above the new estate, the towering chimney of the waste-disposal plant, where a red aircraft warning light is flashing off and on, off and on, against the cloudless night.

Alluvium	
London Clay	
Gravel and Silt	
Roman Road	
Medieval Road	
Outfall Sewer	

VIII: OLYMPIC CITY

Edgelands of the Lower Lea Valley

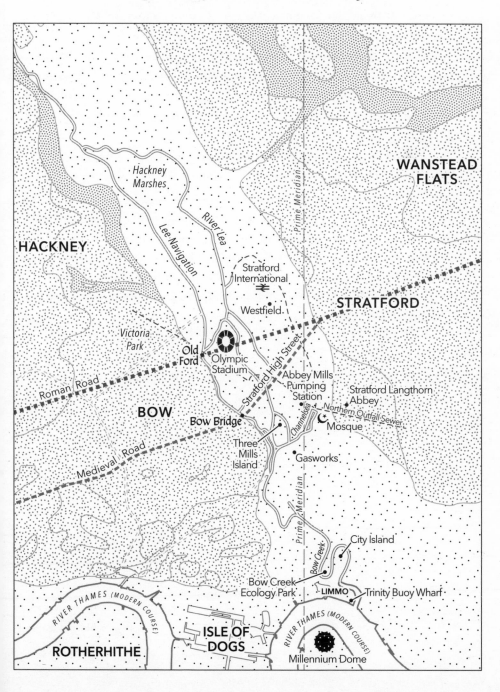

HACKNEY

Hackney
Marshes

Lee Navigation

River Lea

Prime Meridian

WANSTEAD
FLATS

Stratford
International

Westfield

STRATFORD

Victoria
Park

Old
Ford

Olympic
Stadium

Roman Road

Stratford High Street

Abbey Mills
Pumping
Station

Stratford Langthorn
Abbey

Northern Outfall Sewer

BOW

Bow Bridge

Mosque

Channelsea

Three
Mills
Island

Gasworks

Medieval Road

Prime Meridian

City Island

Bow Creek

Bow Creek
Ecology Park

LIMMO

Trinity Buoy Wharf

RIVER THAMES (MODERN COURSE)

ISLE OF
DOGS

RIVER THAMES (MODERN COURSE)

ROTHERHITHE

Millennium Dome

Marsh Yoga

*'... the right landscape in which
to lose ourselves. To start again.'*

Iain Sinclair[1]

WEEK EIGHT OF LOCKDOWN breaks us. Dog-tired and desperate, both of us trying to hold down full-time jobs, we admit defeat and Sarah takes Martha to stay with her parents, who are self-isolating too, in Edgware. 'It's only temporary,' she says. They'll be back in two weeks. It'll do everyone good.

At first the silence of the flat is thrilling, a miracle, and I rush around in an ecstatic whirl of productivity, but it soon becomes disconcerting, strange, and I grow lonely for the girls. I mither and mope, avoiding work by practising keepy-uppies in the bedroom. I stay up late and drink my way through the spirits cupboard. My stomach cramps, absent for months, return. Have I done the right thing? To put my work before the integrity of our family. What kind of man sends his wife and daughter away in a pandemic?

On 10 May Prime Minister Johnson, in a rare television appearance since his recovery from Covid-19, announces a partial relaxation of the lockdown. He bangs the table for emphasis, his trademark blonde tangles swept forward in an unconvincing attempt at a hairstyle. No one understands what he has said; the announcement manages to be both typically bullish and entirely contradictory. It's like Brexit all over again. But this time the impact is not theoretical, future projections composed on the fly. People are still dying in their hundreds every day.

Meanwhile, Martha is having a whale of a time, helping Nana in the garden and playing games with Nani. Sarah, when we speak on the phone, sounds rested too. 'The baby is moving more now,' she says. 'Her legs are pressing on my ribs.'

I tell Sarah that they've reopened the foreshore. 'I'll take Martha mudlarking again, when you're back.'

When I go down later that day, I find the surface of the beach covered in a layer of thick brown mud. It's like stepping through mucus and my trainers are covered in seconds. The river, on the other hand, is startlingly clear. Where sunlight hits the waves lapping the edge of a ruined dock, the sandy bottom is lit up like one of Damian Hirst's glass vitrines. Undisturbed by the constant turbulence of engines, the Thames is returning to its natural inclination; its payload of silt falls to the riverbed like the dregs of an unshaken aspirin. Grey seals – those strange hybrids of dog, fish and humanoid – arrive on the incoming tide, hunting for eels.

I walk beneath the slime-covered river wall and pocket a few trinkets: a pipe stem, a broken pot and a stone – another hagstone, a stone with a hole through its centre. A mother and her young son come down to explore, then a couple in their twenties (the girl excited, the boy indifferent). There are more people on the far shore, in Limehouse, where a strip of golden sand has been revealed below the western end of Narrow Street. A single pleasure craft sails downstream and when I wave its pilot – a bare-chested, piratical fellow – waves back. On closer inspection of my stone, I notice that its coating of gloopy mud harbours the tiny pink carcass of a water-shrimp, its legs curled into a translucent, gelatinous shell like a foetus.

That night I cannot sleep and when, eventually, I do, I dream of being hunted by the xenomorph from Ridley Scott's *Alien*. The future is unpredictable and frightening. 'I just can't imagine the baby actually being here,' Sarah tells me on the phone. 'It's like there's a blank screen in my mind where she should be.'

The next morning I turn the hagstone in my fingers as I work. It has eroded in such a way that it could almost be worn as a ring. My thoughts drift unexpectedly to a memory from fifteen years ago, when I first moved to east London from my childhood home: the survivors of the Aldgate bomb stumbling from the wreckage of the train, then picking their way through the darkness of the Circle Line.

The circle: a symbol reproduced seven years later by the five interlocking rings of the 2012 Olympics. And another memory: David

Beckham driving a speedboat down the Thames towards the mouth of
the river Lea, the Olympic torch aflame on the bow, passing beneath
Tower Bridge as fireworks explode into the night sky.

The Games have been dithering in the background of my journeys
across the city like a suppressed memory, the ghost in the machine.
There is a challenge I have been putting off for too long: a hike to the
Olympic stadium through the former industrial edgelands of the Lower
Lea Valley. It's too far east, I'd say. It's out of bounds. It's lockdown. And
besides, it's Iain Sinclair land – the subject of the London chronicler's
2011 polemic *Ghost Milk*. The closest I've managed to get, in all these
years, is the cavernous retail hangar of Westfield Stratford City.

And so a route begins to form in my mind. I will start in the marshes
of Hackney and work my way south, tracking the Lea through the Olympic Park all the way to its confluence with the Thames – to the easternmost
point of my journeys through the city. I pull out my old Streetfinder and
begin to scour the map for landmarks, waypoints. Gasworks. Railway
yards. A sewage pumping station. Britain's largest surviving tide mill.
The Lea is unlike any river I've followed before. Neither lost nor buried,
it flows entirely above ground through a landscape haunted by the ruins
of industry, and of empire; where ancient Roman pathways smoulder
beneath the half-built towers of the new London. There, at the edge of
the map where the Lea diverges in a tangle of smaller waterways, I make
out the elongated shape of an island – a deserted island in a dead-end
creek. I circle the island in red. Then mark it with an X.

X marks the spot.

Sarah and Martha come home the week the news turns to the adventures of the Prime Minister's chief political adviser. Dominic Cummings
is a demonic, smirking Gollum to Boris's bumbling Samwise Gamgee; a
contrarian and self-styled 'disrupter' who, it was revealed by a joint
investigation by the *Daily Mirror* and the *Guardian*, drove his family 260
miles from London to Durham (and then again on an infamous day trip

to Barnard Castle) in direct contravention of the lockdown rules he himself helped to draw up.

The death toll begins to fall and then, just as restrictions are lifted, it plateaus alarmingly. If the British took to lockdown like good boys and girls – dutifully queuing two metres apart and binge-watching Netflix – they now embrace their liberation with the wild-eyed fervour of a stag group in Ibiza. Across the Rotherhithe peninsula clouds of charcoal smoke drift from backyard barbecue parties. Packs of teenagers roam the streets on bikes and electric scooters. A second wave is coming, I'm sure of it. The weather doesn't help. It hasn't rained in weeks. Families picnic on scraps of parched parkland. Shirtless joggers do loops of the river path. In Minneapolis a Black man, George Floyd, is murdered by police, pressed to the ground by a knee to his neck for eight minutes and forty-six seconds. America is on fire. Protestors kneel and chant his dying words – 'I can't breathe' – as lines of riot cops advance.

In London, Peckham-born actor John Boyega addresses the crowd at Speaker's Corner through a loudhailer: 'Black lives have always mattered. We have always been important. We have always meant something. We have always succeeded regardless.'

There have been Black people in Britain since the Roman occupation. They are as much a part of the demographic weave of these islands as anyone. Boyega, the disenchanted stormtrooper from *Star Wars: The Force Awakens*, has thrown away the script and now reclaims the ancient folkmoot, the site of the vanished Ossulston.

'And now is the time,' he says. 'I ain't waiting.'

Siddhartha Bose strides towards me across Hackney Marshes in a natty black waistcoat and leather slip-on shoes. He's grinning and so am I – he's the first friend I've seen in three months. We touch elbows and head east, crossing the open ground together, towards the tree line. He has agreed to walk with me from the marshes, on the first leg of my journey down the Lea. 'So, what do you think about the protests?' Sid asks, earnestly. He always gets straight to the point. Hackney Marshes is common land, where anyone could once graze animals after harvest by exercising ancient Lammas rights. The expansive parkland was raised from its original level after the war using rubble from bombed-out buildings and now plays host to cricket matches and Sunday league football. Today, though, it is empty, save for a few locals launching googlies in the nets.

Sid spots a gap in the undergrowth – 'A portal!' – and we're through. He finds a path between unruly poplars, where dappled sunlight covers the ground, then stops. A bottle-green river is flowing in a tree-fringed channel about 50 feet from bank to bank. 'It's magic,' he says.

The Lea has come a long way to be here. Fed by rainwater falling in the Chiltern Hills, it descends from its source in the suburbs of Luton and passes through Hertfordshire to the county town of Hertford, where it turns south towards London, forming a series of reservoirs, filter beds and wetlands. During the Anglian glaciation (478,000–424,000 years ago) the meltwater from retreating ice sheets exploited its existing channel to cut a 'substantial valley', forming distinctive braided streams and, in some places, eroding the London Clay to expose the underlying rocks of the Lambeth Group.[2] Its name – Lea (or Lee) – is thought to derive from the Proto-Celtic root *lug meaning 'light' or 'bright' and the river may have been associated with Lugus, a god of the Celtic pantheon. 'Every time I come here, it's different,' Sid remarks. 'The light on the water is always changing.'

We stand there in silence for a while, listening to the wind through the trees, enjoying each other's company, watching the sunlight catching the current as it churns and eddies around submerged branches. River grass sways just below the surface like a carpet of human hair. A family of moorhens drifts by. 'It's very English,' Sid says, at last. 'Shadows. Light. Clouds moving. It's dreamlike, subtle. Like restorative yoga!'

Sid speaks in a mesmerizing Creole of poetry, hyperbole and self-deprecating jokes – like a Romantic bound in postmodernist clothing.

Several times today he will refer to 'the great summer of plague and unrest' as if he's quoting someone else, not his own invention. It's often difficult to work out if he's deadly serious or taking the piss.

'I've been trying to connect with nature,' Sid tells me, as we work our way along the riverbank. During lockdown he has been coming down to the Lea once a week to meditate and practise yoga. Two cocker spaniels have launched themselves from the opposite bank and are frolicking in the shallows beneath a weeping willow. A shirtless man has climbed into its branches and sits above the river like a water sprite, facing upstream, as another man lines up a shot from the bank with his DSLR camera. All along the path we find the grey, ashen remains of barbecues – 'the stubs of Druid fires' as Sid styles them. He stops and gestures towards a little pile of rubbish in a clearing: crushed cans and a discarded takeaway box. 'Fried chicken. That's *so* east London. The other day I came down here and some people from Hackney Wick were having a full-on rave in the middle of the river.'

Sid grew up in the Indian megacities of Kolkata and Mumbai, where, he says, 'nature is there to be tarnished, spoiled'. He has lived in Hackney longer than anywhere, plying his trade as a poet, playwright and academic – a freelance pen for hire. Ten years ago, we made his first theatre show together: an electrifying coming-of-age tale entitled *Kalagora* ('black man/white man'). I played producer – raising the cash, booking the theatres and running the lights – while Sid declaimed and sweated his way through a physically gruelling hour of performance in damp basements from Edinburgh to east Berlin. At the heart of the show was a glorious, degraded hymn to Mumbai, the 'animal city':

City bleeding city heaving city buying city fucking city jiving like big-balled mafia maderchods city crying city dying city slumming humming drumming becoming dinosaur city – scaffold skyscrapers, empire of ambition, built on lust and blood and spewing shit, oily diarrhoea. City of motion, like the sea – always same, always changing.

This is where your breed is born – half half, blackwhite, bastard of
bastards in the roaring city of bastards.[3]

We find a sheltered spot by the water, where two tree stumps are set a
metre or so apart amid dense vegetation. A forest of giant hogweed hus-
tles on the opposite bank and beyond it we can just make out the
perimeter fence of a railway. Eurostar International operates a maintenance yard here, at Temple Mills, where the Knights Templar once
owned a series of water mills straddling the Lea. *London: city of motion*,
I think. I show Sid a map I've drawn. 'It's called a braided river,' I say, and
use my finger to trace the network of canals and creeks surrounding the
Olympic stadium. I've been rereading *Ghost Milk*, in which Sinclair
dubbed the Lea 'a wig of snakes' – an image confirmed by the wormlike
lines of Rocque's map of 1746.[4] By then, I explain, many of the waterways of the 'Bow Back Rivers' were already several hundred years old,
dug out for mill streams or drainage channels during the Middle Ages.
I've marked the deserted island I want to visit, too. 'Nature is man-made,'
Sid adds, wistfully, as a canoeist glides silently upstream.

When Sid's family arrived in Mumbai, they settled first in the northern region of Andheri and then in Bandra, 'Queen of the Suburbs'. This
former Portuguese enclave, whose many churches give it a strong
Roman Catholic identity, is now home, Sid tells me, to Bollywood actors
and cricketing superstars. In 1989 the family moved again, this time to
Cuffe Parade, on the southern end of the peninsula. 'Mumbai is very
long and narrow,' Sid explains. 'When you travel through the city you
have the sense of moving between totally different places. The sea keeps
people sane.'

Bombay, as it was formerly called, was founded on an archipelago of
seven islands reaching out, like stepping stones, into the Arabian Sea.
The islands were given by the Portuguese to Charles II of England in
1661 as part of the dowry of his new bride, Catherine of Braganza. Bombay was soon under the authority of the East India Company, the ruthless

trading conglomerate that would grow to become *de facto* ruler of large parts of India until the Rebellion of 1857. Like the Knights Templar, 'the Company' is now considered to have been one of the world's first multi-national corporations. And like the Templars, they had investments on the Lea – downstream, at its confluence with the Thames.

Mumbai today is the result of a process of land reclamation that started in 1782 with the raising of a causeway (the Hornby Vellard) linking the seven islands and preventing the low-lying parts from flooding by the Worli Creek. In that same year, the East India Company faced armed insurrection in Bengal, led by the Pirzada of Sylhet; while in London engineers were completing the construction of the Lee Navigation, a canalized bypass of the river that would enable the more efficient transportation of goods to the Thames by way of the Hackney and Limehouse Cuts. Marine Drive and the slums of Colaba; Mumbai Central Station and the famous imperial arch, the Gateway of India – all are located on land reclaimed from the Arabian Sea. Mumbai is on the frontline of climate change. Nowhere is safe. 'During the monsoon,' Sid says, quoting his friend, the writer Jeet Thayil, 'the sea reclaims the city.'

Canalize. *Colonize*. Two words a single vowel adrift. They seem to me two reflexes of the same fundamental instinct.

In Bristol the divisive statue of Edward Colston, slave trader, has been toppled from its plinth and dumped into the harbour. Days later London follows suit. A statue of Robert Milligan, slave owner, is removed from West India Dock, the dock he lobbied to be built.

Colonize. *Canalize*.

Suddenly, Sid spots something in the water: a strange white object floating downriver. 'What is *that*?' he asks. 'It looks like a city in miniature.' We step on to the edge of the bank, where the soil is black and gives underfoot.

'I think it's a chunk of polystyrene,' I say, 'cut to fit around a laptop or something.' It wobbles midstream but stays upright. 'But you're right,' I add. 'It looks just like the Manhattan skyline.'

The current swirls and rolls in a square of golden sunlight, like sound waves collapsing back in on themselves, like black ink dispersing in a jar of water. Like *India* ink.

'We need to pay attention to all this,' Sid says, 'the language of nature – to what it's telling us.'

Neverland

'Grand Project development is accidental archaeology. A seance with ruins.'

Iain Sinclair[5]

THE EASTWAY HAS BLOCKED our path and we're forced to climb away from the Lea and navigate the treacherous intersection with the A13. The roof of the Olympic Velodrome appears ominously above a flyover carrying traffic east towards Leyton. It's a flying saucer, I think – a hyperbolic parabola clad in timber – or concept architecture from the latest instalment of *Alien*. Sinclair called the Games 'a theme park without a theme'.[6] But as we enter the Queen Elizabeth Olympic Park, Sid gifts me a zestier alternative, proclaiming, 'Welcome to the edgeland-neverland-post-capitalist-paradise!'

I have an idea I want to test out – that beneath the processional walkways and landscaped grounds of the park we might still trace the route of an ancient causeway across the marshes – an undiscovered section of the earliest Roman road from London to Colchester. It's getting late but Sid is game. We proceed south towards the centre of the park, following the river again as it passes beneath concrete road bridges echoing with deep vehicular rumbles. This is not the dystopian future imagined by J. G. Ballard. It's much worse; the footpaths are suddenly busy with enthusiastic joggers and fitness freaks performing step exercises on the embankments. The joggers are physical manifestations of digital cut-outs; they belong to the CGI renderings of the park that appeared in the press in the lead-up to the Games. The park is eight years old but it still feels half-built – a manicured non-space – scrubland patrolled by bored security guards in hi-vis jackets.

The valley of the Lea, wrote Sinclair, is 'damaged topography'.[7] Centuries of industrial exploitation have left the ground profoundly polluted by lead, arsenic, benzene, tars and oil – the 'ghost milk of dying industries'.[8] During levelling of the site for the Games, 800,000m^3 of excavated soil was cleaned using bioremediation or stabilization processes.[9] Dumps of radioactive paint from the former luminizing factories were reburied at depth

346

beneath impermeable membranes. Contaminated groundwater was pumped out of the aquifer, treated and discharged into sewers; wrecked cars and oil drums lifted from the bottom of the Bow Back Rivers. More ancient artefacts appeared too, from trenches sunk into the soft ground: a Roman coin; a Bronze Age axe; fragments of pottery, bone and flint from an Iron Age farmstead on the site of the future Aquatics Centre.

The Olympic stadium rises up before us on an island between the Lea and the City Mill River – a great white coliseum flecked with the claret-and-blue livery of its new tenants, West Ham United Football Club. In truth, it is not a beautiful or even, despite its size, an impressive arena. The architecture is functional – the tubular exoskeleton contains large-diameter trusses salvaged from North Sea pipeline projects – and I sense a faint nod to the postmodernism of the Pompidou Centre in Paris. The stadium attains neither the corporate polish of the Emirates nor the post-industrial menace of Millwall's New Den, but falls, flatly, somewhere in between. 'I've been inside only once,' Sid remarks. 'To see Guns N' Roses.'

West Ham's crest still bears the crossed hammers of the Thames Iron Works, where the club was founded, at the mouth of the Lea, in 1895. But their return to the river has been dogged by controversy: claims of backhanders and financial misconduct, crowd violence, pitch invasions and vociferous protests against the club directors. This was never designed to be a football ground; the raked seating is too low and set back from the pitch, leaving spectators detached from the action. It's like 'looking through the wrong end of a telescope', said one commentator.[10] Where the Boleyn Ground sat at the heart of a lively community on Green Street, fans arriving at the new stadium now find themselves stranded in a soulless wasteland.

We skirt the north-west corner of the island, stopping to admire Anish Kapoor's *Orbit*, a 376-feet-high steel helter-skelter denounced by Sinclair as a 'Meccano stack'.[11] The Indian steel magnate Lakshmi Mittal sponsored its construction so it must properly be called the ArcelorMittal

Orbit. Sid shrugs when I mention it: 'Big money meets big-name artist. It's Mittal, man.' More joggers are doing circuits of the stadium. Sid seems almost dumbstruck by the scale of the landscape. He's a man more suited to the shady banks of the Lea, or the graffiti-covered warehouses of Hackney Wick, than the monumentalism of the Olympic vision. 'It's so weird, it's just so weird,' he keeps saying. Then suddenly, out of nowhere, comes the sound of elevator music. We both stop in our tracks; piped jazz is drifting through the elevated concourse, above the artificial training pitch and across the dusty embankments of Marsh Lane. It seems to be coming from inside the empty stadium. Then the wind changes and it's an open window of the Bobby Moore Academy . . . and now the tree line marking the course of the in-filled Pudding Mill River. After a while, Sid says, 'I *know* this. It's *Jazz Samba*. By Stan Getz and Charlie Byrd.'

'It's so weird,' I say.

It's then that I notice the alignment of Thornton Street, a wide pedestrianized track leading to the east stand from the direction of Westfield and Stratford station. Could this be the lost causeway across the marshes we've been looking for?

It has long been suspected that the Roman military highway from London to Camulodunum (Colchester) crossed the Lea in the vicinity of Old Ford – a theory assisted by the presence, to the west, of Roman Road with its famous street market. Today the principal route across the Lea is familiar to many as the A11 between Whitechapel and Stratford (the 'Roman road-ford').[12] A major arterial route through east London, the A11 was rebranded 'High Street 2012' in time for the Games and fitted with 'Olympic family lanes' for the swift conveyance of VIPs to the stadium. West of the Lea, this road is not Roman but dates to the Middle Ages. In the twelfth century, the 'old ford' was replaced by a new crossing at Bow Bridge – England's first stone-arched bridge – and the road from London was adjusted accordingly. Use your finger to trace the route from Aldgate High Street along Whitechapel Road to the junction with Fieldgate Street and you will see how the highway clearly feints to the south. A deflection of only a couple of degrees in Whitechapel results in a divergence of half a mile at the Lea.

Fieldgate: fifteen years ago, this dog-leg street was on my route to work, the entrance to a labyrinth of grimy backstreets where halal butchers hauled huge joints of meat from dripping freezer vans and surplus cooking oil congealed in open wheelie bins. The history comes out thick here: the famous foundry where the Liberty Bell, Big Ben and the 2020 Olympic Bell were cast; the Victorian Gothic doss house where a young Stalin stayed while attending the Fifth Congress of the Russian Social Democratic and Labour Party; and the tiny nineteenth-century synagogue of Sha'ar Ya'akov (the Gate of Jacob), now engulfed by the vast East London Mosque. Until the middle of the eighteenth century, the 'field gate' opened to a network of rural footpaths crossing open land to Stepney; it marked, I think, the real limit of the City.

The original Roman road to the north and east, to Old Ford, was lost beyond this point. It is conspicuous by its absence from early cartography. Perhaps, as elsewhere in England, the remains of the distinctive Roman *agger* (embankment) were preserved only by field boundaries or unmapped tracks. Tracing the projection from Fieldgate Street, I have noticed something. The path aligns with (or runs parallel to) a number of modern roads running in a north-easterly direction towards Old Ford: Durward Street, Cephas Street, Colebert Avenue, Arbery Road and Saxon Road. Rocque, in 1746, recorded a series of linear earthworks on the same alignment, between Whitechapel Road and Old Montague Street, on land now occupied by student digs and a hostel for homeless men. Roman pottery has been found a little to the west, too – in Green Dragon Yard.[13]

Could these ghost-lines represent the original Roman route from London to the crossing of the Lea at Old Ford? I want to know more so I keep on digging.

In the cold winter of 1969–70, Harvey Sheldon, then a young amateur archaeologist, uncovered the remains of a substantial 'three-track high-way' south of Roman Road, as well as evidence of butchery and industrial tile-making.[14] First constructed during the time of the Claudian conquest of Britain (AD 43–87) the road was aligned on Aldgate and measured an impressive 67 feet across. (For comparison, the M25 motorway is mostly around 100 feet wide including hard shoulders.) The excavation was wedged between an abandoned railway line and the gardens of terraced houses soon to be demolished, a 'bitty, disruptive site' which nonetheless attracted the interest and assistance of local people including two workers from a furniture factory and a plumber 'with a fine eye for spotting finds'.[15] A photograph from the dig depicts Sheldon, with trademark spectacles and sleeves rolled up, lighting a pipe. Another shows him measuring the edge of a trench while volunteers, including local children, comb the ground with trowels or ferry soil in wheelbarrows. Just months before, a Roman sarcophagus had been discovered in nearby Parnell Road, one of many burials that would be unearthed in the area.

A further stretch of metalled road, with associated roadside settle-ment, was revealed by archaeologist Johanna Vuolteenaho in 2005. As well as Roman masonry, coins, animal bones and a *pila* (a tile from a hypocaust), four 'residual struck flints of possible Bronze Age date' were discovered, tantalizingly, within the brickearth, along with 'postholes and shallow pits'.[16] 'There may have been a cattle market at Old Ford,' she wrote, 'and the London–Colchester Road may have been used to trans-port food from Essex and East Anglia to *Londinium*.' Intriguingly, Greenwood's map of 1828 marks Roman Road as 'The Drift Way'.* Shel-don acknowledged the possible existence of a second road approaching Old Ford from due west, a theory endorsed by Smith (1910), Margery (1955) and others based on excavations in Old Street in 1867.[17] This

---

* 'Drift-way' is a variant of drove-way or drovers' road. These ancient routes were used to 'drive' cattle to market.

route passes north of the Roman city and may, therefore, have been part of an earlier, *pre*-Roman trackway continuing through Holborn and Marble Arch towards the tribal centres at Brentford and Staines.

If the course of the Roman roads west of the Lea is becoming gradually clearer, their presence in the swampland of the Olympic site itself remains entirely speculative. 'Surprisingly little' dating to the Roman period was found during extensive archaeological investigations: coins, ditches and remains of a wall, but nothing to indicate as much as a causeway, let alone a three-track, metalled highway.[18]

Sid and I look out across the broad valley of the Lea. The sun has not yet fallen below the horizon. The skyscrapers clustering on the Isle of Dogs shine like a mirage. 'It feels like being on a high mesa,' I say.

Sid spots his old haunts, across the canal, the Lee Navigation: 'There's Hackney Wick, the White Building, Fish Island.'

We climb down from our elevated position by the stadium and cross an empty car park. I keep looking back, to take a sighting of the landscape – Thornton Street, the ArcelorMittal *Orbit*, the stadium itself – but it keeps on rearranging.

Earlier, by a section of the Lea clogged with reeds, we had been talking about Observer Effect. 'How can we study something,' Sid asked, 'when we are a part of it?'

'Come on,' I say. 'Up here.'

And now we're scrambling up a steep embankment, where the thin grass has been scuffed to dirt: a desire line to the sky.

We step into the light of the Greenway – a ruler-straight trackway raised above the marshes. 'Wow!' Sid gasps as he reaches the summit.

'Smell that?' I ask.

Sid takes a breath, then wrinkles his nose.

'Down there's the Northern Outfall Sewer,' I say, pointing to a grille on the floor. A cyclist speeds past and a sulphurous odour fills the air.

'It's not that bad actually,' Sid notes. 'Like a wine cellar.'

The Greenway is waste disposal recycled as active living – a sewer you can walk or run or cycle on. From Wick Lane, the Outfall captures the flow from three of Bazalgette's giant interceptors (with two further, low-level sewers raised into its channel at Abbey Mills Pumping Station). The turds that had floated past me in the murk of the Fleet sewer would have passed this way on their journey to Beckton Sewage Treatment Works.

The Greenway has had some notable admirers. Visiting London in 1931 for negotiations with the British government, Mahatma Gandhi elected to stay in a hostel in the poverty-stricken East End. Each morning he took a 'pre-dawn hike' along the Northern Outfall, which was then known, more accurately, as Sewerbank.[19] Was Gandhi – the living embodiment of Indian resistance to colonial rule, in trademark dhoti and shawl – unwittingly tracking an ancient path through the marshes? The similarity of the Greenway with the elevated Roman causeway – the *agger* and ditch – is certainly arresting, but the alignment from Old Ford is all wrong. I look back, beyond the stadium, to the skyline of Stratford and line it up by eye and hand. The lost road would, I guess, have slipped between the towers and construction cranes at the beginning of the Broadway.

'I see the line,' Sid says, following my gaze, although I sense that he is humouring me. 'But where does it go?'

The Roman road to Colchester, I explain, once connected to an older highway between that city and the Iceni capital at Venta Icenorum (Caistor St Edmund). The combined route was later known as the Pye Road, after the Pie or Magpie Inn in the Suffolk village of Stonham Parva.[20]

The Greenway spits us out on Wick Lane and we loop around, searching for a way back down to the river. Sid seems more relaxed, having crossed back to the right side of the Lea. Someone's daubed a hammer and sickle and HANG BORIS on the back wall of a branch of

Toolstation. Sid goes to investigate an abandoned furniture factory on Old Ford Road. I realize later that it's the site of the manor house variously recorded as 'Gissing-place', 'Petersfield', 'King John's Palace', 'Great Place' and 'old place'. Its medieval gatehouse was known as Ivy Gate and survived as a Romantic folly until 1896. It was the likely setting of the amorous liaison between Rose and Lacy in Thomas Dekker's 1599 play *The Shoemaker's Holiday*. Sid is peering through the boarded-up, graffiti-covered entrance when I find the way ahead . . . which is also where our journey together ends.

Iceland Road descends to the ancient crossing of the Lea between modern flats and a condemned industrial yard. We cannot reach the river – it's hidden behind tumbledown walls and a faded sign for DIAL 4 PARTS – but there, above the trees, I see the southern tip of the Olympic stadium, and the ArcelorMittal *Orbit* perfectly aligned behind it on the conjectured route of the lost Roman causeway. At the bottom of the street, a metal gate leads to a concrete passageway brimming with weeds; but it too is truncated, blocked by a high wooden barrier.

This fly-tipped cul-de-sac is as close as we'll get. Car parts. Knotweed. Spent canisters of nitrous oxide.

Sid notices that the tarmac surface is broken, here and there, revealing cobblestones beneath. 'The street is a palimpsest,' he says, and I believe him. Sinclair wrote of Old Ford as a 'numinous locale in London's deep-topography', and I believe him too.[21] It seems to be a place where the layers of history might unfold before our eyes.

A manhole whispers and we both crouch down and peer into the darkness, where a stream is running deep below. Some say it's the Hackney Brook, but that river has long been diverted from its original course.

Sid points towards a bright-orange sign set on the wall of a ruined workshop. 'Look here,' he says, 'I think it's Yiddish.' The sign says:

WARNING
HAZCHEM

'That's not Yiddish,' I say. 'It means "hazardous chemicals".'

'Oh,' he says, then grins.

A man in a white vest appears at an open door above the yard. I turn to Sid and say, 'I thought this place was derelict.'

But he's not looking.

A bird has landed on the gate – black and white with a long tail and distinctive flash of blue. It hops on to the roof of the workshop, pauses, then drops into the passageway beyond.

'A magpie,' he says.

A magpie.

A pye for Pye Road.

Pandemonium

'Be not afeard; the isle is full of noises'
SHAKESPEARE, *THE TEMPEST*[22]

A VILLAGE GREEN. A GAME of cricket. Beehives. Children dancing around a maypole. Hay fields after harvest. Hedgerows. A single voice – a boy, stood high above it all – singing Blake's 'Jerusalem' to the famous tune by Parry –

> And did those feet in ancient time,
> Walk upon Englands mountains green[23]

– and now a phalanx of men survey the landscape, fifty Brunels in top hats and tails – and now a mighty shout and drums resound, a thousand-strong, on bin lids and steel buckets, and the giant oak that stands at the crest of a green, terraced mound begins to rise – as if pulled by unseen forces – and from the tear beneath its roots issue plumes of smoke – and figures, first a handful then a hundred, surface from the opening – soot-stained workmen trampling the turf, the weeds and wildflowers. Great chimneys rise, erupting from the earth – engines, anvils, levers – and from the edges bands of men and women in thick, drab work clothes cross the fields, the common land, together. The body of a woman is held aloft then falls and then is raised again. Then out of nowhere, stillness – a single poppy trembling in the floodlights.

I watched the opening ceremony of the 2012 Summer Olympics from my cousin's ground-floor flat in Anerley, on the southern slopes of the Norwood Ridge. We mainlined lasagne, red wine and speciality cheese long into the night – Dave, Kerry, Sarah and me. Back then, expectations for the Games were low. Deep in the shadow of the Great Recession, they were an extravagance the country could not afford. In *Ghost Milk* Sinclair conjured a vision of a ruined landscape, a paranoid hyper-reality of security patrols, unexploded ordnance and compensation money gone astray.

There were reports of ground-to-air missile systems being installed on top of local tower blocks, of checkpoints by the Lea manned by personnel in military fatigues. The '2012 game-show virus', as Sinclair dubbed it, was infecting everything in sight.[24]

I wouldn't have watched the opening ceremony at all, had it not been for the appointment of Oscar-winning filmmaker Danny Boyle as artistic director. The luminous spirit behind *Shallow Grave*, *Trainspotting* and *Slumdog Millionaire*, Boyle had previous with London. At the start of his 2002 zombie feature, *28 Days Later*, a bike courier – Jim – awakes from a coma in St Thomas's Hospital and wanders across Westminster Bridge and through the deserted streets of a post-apocalyptic city. After narrowly escaping the hordes of living dead, Jim finds shelter with a family living on the top floor of the Balfron Tower, another experiment in Brutalism by Ernő Goldfinger, which looms above Poplar on the west side of the Lea.

Boyle – magician of the edgeland, the empty space – had taken on the biggest stage of all, with an estimated global audience of nine hundred million. What transpired, that night, inside that giant bowl, was a spectacle like nothing I had seen before – a collective hallucination of Britain that interwove the patriotic with the punk, the sentimental with the surreal. All of us was there: Elgar's 'Nimrod' and The Clash; *East-Enders* and the *Empire Windrush*; the Suffragettes; the Pearly Kings and Queens; and forty Sgt. Peppers. 'God Save The Queen' was sung by a signing choir of deaf and hearing children. Dancer Akram Khan twisted and span underneath a glowing, yellow sun in a company of fifty-two – one for each of the victims of the London bombings. Performers colonized the terraced hill – a scale model of Glastonbury Tor – for an outdoor rave. Rapper Dizzee Rascal, born and bred in Bow, performed his chart smash 'Bonkers' in a jacket embroidered with his postcode, E3.

Our neighbour in Rotherhithe, John Odell, was one of the ten thousand volunteers recruited for the show. A photograph in his hallway shows him backstage in the costume of a miner – waistcoat, woollen trousers, flat cap – his face smeared with coal dust. It was, he told me, the 'standout moment' of his life (excepting the birth of his son, Oscar). John's section was known as 'the Warriors'; they were tasked with removing the pieces of fake turf from the opening set and unloading them offstage. 'Each piece was numbered,' he explained to me, 'so during rehearsals you had to be careful to return it to the correct position. It was like a giant jigsaw.' John was one of the workers who emerged from within the tor. 'I was so anxious about falling over,' he said. The organized chaos of 'Pandemonium' was the result of one hundred and fifty hours of rehearsals in a car park in Dagenham and then in the stadium itself. 'It pissed it down almost every day,' John recalled, 'and when it got wet the turf was incredibly heavy.' John's subgroup, or 'dump', of twelve volunteers included a vicar, a PhD student, a graphic designer and one man who was homeless. 'The Games were part of turning his life around,' John told me. 'We were all doing our bit. It didn't matter what your background was.'

Where Beijing, four years before, had demonstrated the power of national unity through tightly choreographed massed displays, Boyle's programme celebrated individual achievement, diversity and British eccentricity. When plans for the ceremony were leaked ahead of time, the *Guardian* sniped predictably at the 'rural idyll' of his first act. 'What on earth has Danny Boyle been smoking?' they grumbled. 'Where's the miserable Britain that we know and love?'[25] The cynics could never have anticipated the genius of his second act – the rupturing of the 'Green and Pleasant Land' by the 'Pandemonium' of the Industrial Revolution in what Boyle himself has called 'the biggest scene change in theatre history'. This was truly theatre for the Anthropocene: a celebration of human ingenuity and community tempered by a profound sense of loss. It seemed to me, also, to present an inclusive vision of British culture and identity; a vision in which multiple versions of the same story were allowed not only to exist but to actively compete against each other. Histories were written over but not written out – recorded instead as complex layers, like geological strata – and all watched over by the Glastonbury Tor, the sacred isle at the heart of Boyle's *Isles of Wonder*.

That night, Sarah and I took the last train back to London Bridge. The opening ceremony was only the beginning, a theatrical prelude to the main event. Bolt's sprint double; Phelps in the pool; the heroics of Jessica Ennis, Greg Rutherford and the irrepressible long-distance runner Mo Farah – these were all to come. We sat alone in an empty carriage, flushed with wine and optimism, and as we looked out east across the flatlands of Bermondsey and the Isle of Dogs, we glimpsed, for just a moment, a wall of flames erupting from the Olympic stadium and another from the Lea.

Overflow

*'the unseen was everything,
the unknown the only real fact of life'*
KENNETH GRAHAME[26]

I RETURN TO THE PARK a week later in blazing sunshine and retrace my steps up the canalized river. The east bank is bustling with lush foliage, reed beds and sluggish streams where shoals of huge, freshwater barbel patrol the shallows. I have arranged to meet a man for whom the Lea is a new frontline in the war against environmental degradation. A giant blue dragonfly hovers just in front of me, tracking my route in; and from the sun-kissed margins of an overpass comes the distinctive buzz of crickets.

I find Theo Thomas standing on a concrete parapet at the head of a small creek hidden in wetlands north of the stadium, in the shadow of the Westfield shopping centre.

'Come and take a look,' he says.

Beneath the parapet, a massive steel grille – 15 feet across – conceals the mouth of a storm drain known as a combined sewer overflow or CSO. A slick of oily sewage is floating on the surface of the water, either side of the bars. I climb down the concrete steps to the side of the sewer for a closer look: sanitary towels, an unravelled condom, human faeces in doughy clots. It glistens in the sunlight.

Theo is the founder of the independent charity, the London Waterkeeper – 'Defending rivers. Challenging polluters.' A lithe and nimble man with a shock of wavy brown hair, he seems custom-built for hacking through the undergrowth of the city's industrial edgelands. His Twitter profile shows him standing in a reed-fringed backwater, the dark river almost up to his waist. Theo has been observing this site, and others on the Lea and the Bow Back Rivers, since shortly after the Games, but he has only been able to gather accurate data on levels of oxygen in the water since 2019, when the outflow was fitted with an Electronic Duration Monitor. 'This overflow has already discharged twenty times this year,' he explains. 'Last year it was ninety-one. The sewage is a river killer.'

361

In May 2019, hundreds of dead fish were found floating in the Lea, victims of an unidentified pollution event. In February and March 2018 toxic oil spills were cleaned up by local volunteers. 'Whatever this is,' said Gill Walker from the Swan Sanctuary in Shepperton, 'it's certainly got a lot of diesel in it. It gets on to their skin and it's corrosive.'[27]

Three teenaged boys cycle past, doing wheelies along the footpath. Then a couple with a pushchair. 'People come here for solace, and for leisure,' Theo says, 'and they're walking just yards from stagnant, human waste. It's—' He pauses. 'Iniquitous.'

The sewage mostly comes from Leyton, he explains, as well as the new-builds on the eastern edge of the park. 'The infrastructure is over capacity due to the intensity of development. The Olympics had a budget of nine billion pounds. They could have spent some of it on this. If Bazalgette were here today he would be embarrassed. I mean, it's just a lot of concrete and a massive hole. "You're doing the same thing I did," he would say, "but less beautifully."'

I ask Theo what changes could be made to prevent further pollution into the river. More could be done to delay rainwater upstream, he tells me, before it overwhelms the sewer system. But the public also needs access to accurate data from the water companies, because, he adds, 'right now, we're in the dark. Is this area about connecting with nature or is it merely an extension of sewage infrastructure? A green glove over a sewery hand?'

There's a soft scraping noise coming from the mouth of the drain. Right on cue, a large brown rat emerges from the reeds and is now hopping up the steps towards us: a corpulent beast, sewer-fed, with piercing black eyes and a glossy russet coat. 'The River,' I almost hear him say, 'it's my world, and I don't want any other.'[28]

I turn to Theo – 'Was that stage-managed?' – but when I look back, Ratty has already slunk away.

*

Theo agrees to walk with me back through the Olympic Park and then along the Lea to Three Mills, where I will complete the middle section of my journey from marsh to mouth. 'The London Waterkeeper sounds like a historic title,' I say, as we approach the stadium, 'you know, like an alderman or a beadle.' The charity is comparatively young, Theo explains, created in 2014, but his work is inspired by an environmental movement founded in New York State in the 1960s. There, in 1983, the first full-time 'riverkeeper' was appointed to protect the Hudson River from industrial contamination and empower local people to hold polluters to account. Today the Waterkeeper Alliance unites over three hundred and fifty members from six continents in a common goal: to ensure 'drinkable, fishable, swimmable water everywhere'.[29] Through this global network, Theo is connected to water-, river-, bay- and coast-keepers from Lagos Lagoon to the Great Lakes, from glacial streams in the Himalayas to the bayous of the Mississippi Delta.

I remember something Sid had said on the riverbank: 'Water connects us.' Like Eliot before them, I think, Sid and Theo understand the flow of Lea to Thames, of Thames to ocean, and thence to mingle with the outwash of the mighty Rhine, the 'sunken' Ganges.[30]

The Lea is all rivers.

As we walk within a deep gully beneath the stadium, the sunlight reflecting on the water projects a shimmering wave-pattern on the side of a footbridge. 'During the Olympics,' Theo says, 'they would have commissioned an artist to make that for thousands of pounds. The river does it for free.' The disjuncture between the green and pleasant land and malevolent yet awe-inspiring industry played out in Danny Boyle's opening ceremony is now repeated in the park itself – the collision of concrete pipe and reed bed; a wetland paradise fed by combined sewers.

Before the building of the Lee Tunnel, Theo tells me, a staggering 40 per cent of Thames sewage derived from the Lea. The tunnel, London's deepest at 80 metres, opened in 2016 and reduced flood events, in one year, from thirty-five to three. 'This is a place to cherish,' he says, 'but there's a lot of melancholy here.' We reach the confluence of the river with the Lee Navigation at Old Ford, where Channel 4's morning show *The Big Breakfast* once broadcast from a spur of land between the water, then cross beneath the Greenway, where the Northern Outfall Sewer spans the Lea in huge exposed pipes. Dense bushes erupt from the crumbling embankment below Iceland Wharf, where I had been with Sid, where the river narrows just enough to suggest a fording point.

The atmosphere grows thick with damp, pre-storm heat. Sinclair wrote of the redevelopment of the Lower Lea Valley as 'anti-river, anti-flow'.[31] Theo talks of places, and people, lost, paid off and swept away by the all-powerful hand of the Olympic Delivery Authority – a furniture factory, film studios, the local fish industry – and also of lost opportunities. The new lock system on the Prescott Channel, he explains, was designed to allow barges to transport construction materials by water, rather than road, but it was finished too late to be useful for the Games. Instead, it has reduced the tidal range of the river, devastating intertidal habitats – reed beds and brackish backwaters where skittish fish and wading birds take refuge. 'The river's had the breath squeezed out of it,' he adds, solemnly.

We are roaming the brownfield land north of the High Street, Stratford, when the heavens open. It's as if someone's switched the lights off and turned the shower on full volume. Within seconds, the streets are running as storm drains. The sewers, choked with junk, fill up and boil over, like flooded sinkholes. Labourers in hard hats run for cover. Theo pulls on a bright-yellow cagoule. 'It's like the monsoon!' he shouts above the roar. The downpour comes at just the right time to illustrate a point. As a result of man-made climate change, we can expect more extreme weather in the future. In England, May 2020 was the driest on record. When sudden, heavy rain falls on sun-baked soil, stripped bare of vegetation, in a city of hard, impermeable surfaces, the sewers simply cannot cope.

The weather may be biblical, but Theo is cautious to avoid the apocalyptic tendencies of the environmental movement. 'It can be tiring,' he says, 'and people switch off.' Theo's activism is painstaking, unglamorous and incremental: the unseen labour of data collection and freedom of information requests. He doesn't pretend to have all the answers. 'It's about empowering citizens to hold the regulators to account,' he says. 'The more transparent a society is the happier it is, the less fetid.'

'Fetid?' I say.

'No, *fettered*. But fetid works too.'

The rain stops as quickly as it began and we are across the High Street in warm sunlight, following the Three Mills Wall River, a canalized waterway that is clogged up, here and there, with bright green pennywort. The west bank is fringed by new developments with names that echo the area's industrial heritage: Sugar House Island, Cooperage Yard, Botanical Mews. There were print works here too, producing Day-Glo paint, varnish, ink and dye. The channel ends at a modern weir complex which, together with the sluice and lock on the Prescott Channel, regulates the water level upstream. A dozen barges are moored end to end above the weir.

Knot Bothered.

Heart's Ease.

Nevermind.

And now, as if by sleight of hand, the channel has assumed the costume of a tidal stream. Though still contained by unforgiving sheet-metal revetments, the water has withdrawn a metre or more, exposing untamed reed beds and banks of thick green mud. Pea green. Sea green. Day-Glo. We come to a low wall within sight of the clock tower at Three Mills and I peer over. Two old footballs are nestled in the reeds; a pair of scissors impaled blades-up in the bog. Something else is thriving in the reed beds too: a tall, thrusting weed with clusters of purple, helmet-shaped flowers.

Himalayan or Indian balsam is an invasive species now so widespread in Britain that it's considered naturalized. 'It's pushing out the reeds,' Theo says. 'When they're ready the pods fling open and catapult hundreds of seeds up to seven metres away. It's colonizing the river-banks.' Himalayan balsam was first brought to Britain in 1839 by John Forbes Royle, superintendent of the East India Company's botanical garden at Saharanpur and a veteran of the Bengal Army. In that same year, the warship *Nemesis* set sail from Birkenhead Iron Works. Commissioned by the Secret Committee of the East India Company, the 'devil ship' was bound for China where she would see action in the First Opium War. *Nemesis* later operated out of Calcutta and Bombay, assigned with protecting Company property from pirates and popular insurrection. She was fitted with a Congreve rocket launcher, a weapon produced on the banks of the Lea at Three Mills on a model developed by Tipu Sultan, the Tiger of Mysore.

Statues may be coming down, but the ghosts of Britain's colonial past remain, haunting the former docks, the city's grand façades, the chopped and squishy landscape of the Lea. The Games – that great celebration of international accord – was just a moment in time, I know that now; Danny Boyle's rough magic is already wearing off. And now the liberal myths are working loose – Brexit, Boris, Britain First, the *Windrush* scandal. 'I felt optimistic and proud to be British,' my neighbour John had told me. 'I thought we were outward-looking, progressive, inclusive.'

Meanwhile, the work of the London Waterkeeper continues: hard graft, negotiation, pressure. For Theo, the real battle is against what he calls 'obfuscation'. 'Truth is being portrayed as contingent, arbitrary,' he says. 'It suits the people who seek to do us ill. We know the true state of our rivers. Now we need to hold the authorities to account.'

But Theo is an optimist. 'The roots of Himalayan balsam are shallow. They're easy to dig out. Some can be removed. It's all about finding a balance so the reeds can thrive too,' he says. Just then, a wading bird emerges from the riverbank; a balancing act on long, stalk-like legs. 'We have to be sentinels,' Theo adds, 'to keep democracy alive every day.'

Limmo

*'To move in earth's time is to
necessarily think outside the human'*
ELIZABETH-JANE BURNETT[32]

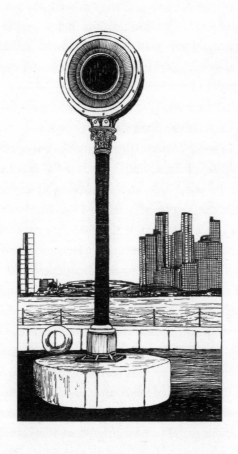

I ARRIVE IN LIMMO TO the music of screeching tyres: a silver hatchback flooring it out of the western roundabout of the Lower Lea Crossing.

Burnt rubber.

Mudflats.

Tidal swill.

I had crossed the river to get here, to walk the final stretch of the Lea, on an empty train from Rotherhithe, before trekking through the former maritime 'hamlets' of Wapping, Shadwell, Ratcliffe, Limehouse and Poplar – now one continuous development from the Tower of London to the Lea.

The river is where it ends.

'To start again. With a wiped slate.'[33]

Leamouth: Limmo: *Limbo*. The purgatorial energies of the place are overwhelming. Ruined dock walls stand in the shadows of half-built towers, open to the wind; sales and marketing suites for future homes; concrete flyovers sunk into alluvial swamp; the brine-stink of Bow Creek, as the Lea is called down here, where the channel loops back on itself in a series of hairpin bends. The Lea once formed the border between Wessex and the Danelaw and it still feels like frontier land – London's Wild East. On the near side, the Saxon kingdom of Alfred (urbane, Christian); on the far bank, the great heathen army of the Vikings under Guthrum. The earliest canalization of the Lea may date to this time, when in AD 895 Alfred ordered the draining of its lower reaches to prevent the Viking fleet reaching the Thames from their base in Hertford. In the middle of the roundabout a giant figure surveys the traffic heading across the Lea – the three legs and disembodied face of Allen Jones's *Aerobic* (1993) – a rusting, sheet-metal Matisse whose feet are barbed like arrowheads, like something dredged from the water.

I find a bench by Bow Creek and carefully disinfect my hands with antibacterial gel before wolfing down a shop-bought sandwich. A couple in matching Lycra stop for a photo, their beaming selfie framed by an island of green wilderness on the opposite bank, where dense vegetation spills over the steel revetments at the water's edge. Storm clouds are gathering to the north as I cross to the island by a modern footbridge. The bridge spans the creek just below the nine-lane flyover of the A13 and also runs parallel with an abandoned single-track railway built in 1848 to carry goods between Canning Town and the East India Dock. The railway bridge is now covered with graffiti and rendered inaccessible by forests of weeds and nettles at either end. Nevertheless I notice that a nylon hiking tent has been pitched on the empty trackway directly above the freezing tidal water. A fourth crossing – an ornamental pipe bridge carrying gas into London from the Beckton works – is remembered by a solitary brick pier on the east bank. The tent shakes violently in the wind gusting downstream.

The island across the water, I discover, is not wilderness at all but a carefully managed ecology park squeezed, ingeniously, on to a teardrop peninsula inside a loop of the creek. A branch of the Docklands Light Railway splits the narrow bar in two such that the park appears, in places, to be merely an extension of the railway verge. The geography is hair-raising. As I move along the island, deserted trains rush past on an elevated viaduct to the southern shore, where they appear to launch, unmanned, back across the creek, soaring like rollercoaster cars above the Lower Lea Crossing. The DLR track extends a dead-end railway siding marked on old maps and aerial photographs – the only visible feature of an otherwise muddy, contaminated wasteland. During the construction of the park in 1996, traces of mercury were detected in the ground, leading to the addition of an extra 40cm of topsoil.[34] Where the Olympic Park struggles to contend with the vast scale of the Lea Valley, the Bow Creek Ecology Park has the benefit of intimacy; it takes around ten minutes to complete a circuit on footpaths brimming with red clover and ox-eye daisy. Locals appear alone or in pairs: a jogger by a reed-filled mere; two women sharing a spliff in a shady bower beneath the railway embankment. Small white butterflies explode from bushes as giant bumblebees stumble, nectar-drunk, amid the wildflowers. I disappear into the undergrowth for a piss and for a moment, in the darkness between trees, I could be almost anywhere but here.

An information board tells me how the park's wetlands are fed by groundwater from a borehole sunk into the mud to a depth of twelve metres. A pump is used to regulate the levels in two ponds connected by a weir. Every September an area of meadow is deliberately inundated 'to mimic the natural flooding of a river floodplain'. Here, as Sid observed, the natural is artificial – a simulacrum of the real thing. But the human is also part of nature; we are hustling at the edge of the frame, observers of a world to which we, too, are subject.

I follow the path out of the park and along Bow Creek. In this cork-screw geography, the east bank is now west, and across the mudflats another peninsula emerges. In shape it is an inverse facsimile of the first, a little larger perhaps; but in place of the dense foliage of the ecology park it is crammed with towering modern apartment blocks. The sheet metal revetments have been capped with brand-new concrete blocks and stainless-steel railings on which two men in matching polo shirts are leaning.

In truth there is nothing 'flat' about the mudflats of Bow Creek. They swell and heave with the submerged ruins of innumerable wharves and slipways, timber piles and river stairs – here folding and unfolding like a satellite image of mountains, here fractured by deep gashes filled with rubble, nails, car tyres, rusting exhausts, chicken wire, road signs, aluminium cans, traffic cones, shopping trolleys, waste pipes and, a little upstream, a large steel litter bin. Everything that could have fallen into the creek has done; and everything that has done is covered in the same claggy, grey liquor. It is hard to resolve this hazardous, post-industrial topography with the upmarket development on the opposite bank. Unlike the upper reaches of the Lea, Bow Creek remains defiantly tidal. It is a dynamic environment that cannot easily be tidied away.

I cross a footbridge spanning the creek and City Island appears, as it is designed to, like a miniature version of Lower Manhattan. The name is a marketer's invention – a place that is dense with history now reduced to its simplest forms. Island. City. City. Island.

I have been here once before, for an exhibition inspired, I was told by the enthusiastic curator, by my last book of poems.[35] (The exhibition's title, *on my island none of this would be true*, was borrowed from my poem 'Security'.) Two years ago, the peninsula was still heavily cloaked in hoardings and as I made my way from Canning Town in the rain I remember being funnelled down dark corridors between construction sites manned by sullen work crews. The gallery was a mysterious, dimly lit space buzzing with interesting art-school types dressed in black and the beer was free. The exhibition programme promised to explore 'the interpretations and contradictions that islands summon in our mind, ranging from remote lands where reptiles exist in a permanent Palaeolithic state, to places where identities and cultures meet to do commerce and forge empires'. The stand-out piece was by Israeli sculptor Naama Arad, a sort of butcher's curtain made of a giant shredded Xerox copy of the Arch of Constantine in Rome.[36] I spent the whole night resisting the temptation to walk right through it.

For all the crassness of its branding, City Island is a miracle of imagination (and engineering). A decade ago the peninsula was uninhabited wasteland – a forgotten limb in a remote part of east London. Its last tenant, Pura Foods, left in 2006; their distinctive metal cylinders, used to refine vegetable oil for use in margarine, were dismantled or destroyed. Today the peninsula is home to a burgeoning community of young professionals looking for a foothold near Canary Wharf. They call themselves, cutely, 'the islanders' and benefit from amenities including a clubhouse, gym and an 'authentic-Italian grocer's shop' (hyphen theirs).[37]

A Daimler limousine is parked outside the angular new home of English National Ballet. A passing dignitary or benevolent patron, I wonder? Around the back, five or six young dancers are lunching on a triangle of grass, as keen as meerkats. The site's developer, Ballymore, is a canny outfit run by Irishman Sean Mulryan. In a world where media barons and hedge-fund sensations dress and behave in the manner of Brooklyn hipsters, this former bricklayer knows how to exploit the soft power of culture and the arts for commercial gain. On City Island, the communal amenities are wrapped together in a membership of an 'exclusive arts club' (a club, I note, without any demonstrable 'art'). The website foregrounds profiles of the island's creative residents: an animator, ceramics artist, photographer and filmmaker. But there are signs on every corner to remind the casual walker that this is private land. The island has the atmosphere of a resort town out of season. I pass through the central plaza, where an adult woman is learning to ride on a child-sized skateboard, and locate the gallery I had visited before. A collection of furniture – all Scandi-chic – has been stacked outside: the contents of a flat awaiting its new owner.

Rocque recorded this peninsula as 'Good Luck Hope' on his map of 1746. Back then it belonged to the Manor of Stepney and was occupied by meadows, a fishery, a farm and a large house known as Handle/Han-bury/Handlebury Hall.[38] 'Hope' derives from the Old English word *hop*, interpreted by Gelling as a 'piece of enclosed land, e.g. in the midst of fens or marshes or of wasteland generally'.[39] She also noted a possible connection to the Old Norse term *hóp*: 'a small land-locked bay or inlet, salt at flood tide and fresh at ebb'.[40] It is tempting to imagine that here, at the boundary between Wessex and the Danelaw, both meanings might once have held true – that the Hope might have been a place shared across two rival languages. As for 'Good Luck', its origins remain obscure, although the bend of the river around the peninsula was known as Good Luck Reach. Perhaps it was simply the message delivered to departing sailors as they approached the mouth of the Lea.

In 1810 Good Luck Hope was purchased by Sir Robert Wigram, a prominent merchant of the East India Company. Like the botanist John Forbes Royle, Wigram trained as a surgeon before joining the Company;

in 1762 he was apprenticed to Dr Joseph Allen, Master of the College of God's Gift – the precursor to my old school in Dulwich. But while Royle dedicated his life to the study of the natural history of India – publishing on Hindu medicine, fibrous plants and the flora of 'Cashmere' – Wigram used his time overseas to develop a profitable line in the trafficking of opiates, with sidelines in privateering and whale hunting. Royle's name lives on in the name of a genus of flowering plant (*Roylea*) and a small Himalayan mammal (the Royle's pika). Wigram fathered twenty-three children and was remembered in his obituary as 'one of the greatest importers of drugs in England'.[41]

I leave the LEGO skyscrapers of City Island behind and continue to track the meandering river south. Two anglers, a father and son, are reclining on camp chairs underneath the DLR flyover.

'What do you fish in here?' I ask.

'Anything,' replies the son, a gangly teenager in grey joggers. 'Bass. Eels. But nothing today. And we've been here all morning.'

I think of the outflow pipe upstream, in the Olympic Park, spilling raw sewage into the river. It's a wonder anything survives at all. On the far bank a series of half-built towers diminishes into the distance like a set of matryoshka dolls. A turf-covered mound rises above the water's edge, where giant hogweed has once again ingrained like something from *Invasion of the Body Snatchers*.

'Good luck,' I say to the boy. 'Good luck and Godspeed.'

In summer 2012, with the Olympic Games in full swing two miles upstream, a pair of colossal tunnel-boring machines (TBMs) were delivered to a construction site here, on the east bank of Bow Creek. Dubbed Elizabeth and Victoria, the TBMs were fitted with state-of-the-art laser guidance technology and fearsome rotating cutterheads, but they operated on the same fundamental principles as the tunnelling shield pioneered by the Brunels on the Thames Tunnel (1825–41). In October 2012, the machines were lowered 40 metres into the ground, ready to begin their mission: to excavate two 8.3-kilometre-long tunnels from the Limmo Peninsula to Farringdon, as part of the Cross-rail project. Today the grassy mound conceals a ventilation shaft, with an access point for maintenance crews cut into its eastern flank. Like a clone of Danny Boyle's model of Glastonbury Tor, the mound is designed to be opened up, to disgorge hi-vis-wearing workmen from its steel-and-concrete core.

Extensive geohazards had already been identified on the Limmo Peninsula long before the cutterheads began to spin. Preliminary studies of the ground revealed that here the clay through which the TBMs would be cutting was 'heavily fissured with numerous discontinuities'.[42] These fissures, or faults, some more than a metre long, resulted in a reduction in the shear strength of the clay, making it more susceptible to structural failure. Hydrogeology tests also recorded unusually high groundwater pressures in the underlying permeable deposits – a situation that would require the 'dewatering' of those formations by means of sinking additional well shafts. Results from further testing indicated 'connectivity' between these strata and the chalk aquifer beneath; the fissures have created vertical pathways in the rock through which groundwater can flow in ways that are both unusual and impossible for engineers to predict.[43]

I have encountered drift, or scour, hollows before on my journeys across the city. Hunting the Fleet south of King's Cross, I located a glitch in the clay, 250 metres in length, filled with gravel and 'black deposit' in the vicinity of two ancient springs: Black Mary's Hole and Bagnigge Wells. And in the backstreets north of the Elephant and Castle, I stumbled across the Rockingham Anomaly, a subterranean feature so profound it seems to have infected the surrounding estate with a mysterious energy. Limmo completes the set – a holey trinity of sites where the bedrock of the city has been ruptured by unseen forces from deep within the earth.

No fewer than three drift hollows have been identified near the mouth of the Lea. It is suspected that these hollows, together with 'several tectonic features' in the wider area, are responsible for the unstable ground conditions encountered during the Crossrail works.[44] A new theory has emerged in recent years, a theory that would explain the presence of these subterranean anomalies. The extensive faulting and subsidence revealed by analysis of boreholes drilled during the construction of both the Crossrail and Lee tunnels may be the result of a much larger geological phenomenon known as 'inversion', in which the entire London Basin is very slowly being 'uplifted' (raised) by the ongoing convergence of the African and European plates.[45] Far from being inert 'relics' of the last Ice Age, then, the hollows may be evidence of 'deeper driving processes' taking place over millions of years: the tectonic collisions which raised the Alps and formed the Mediterranean Sea.

One of the three hollows at Limmo, a gravel-filled depression in the chalk bedrock, appears to be located a matter of yards from the ventilation shaft; its epicentre is lost beneath the undergrowth of the Lower Lea Crossing. Another underlies the East India Company's former shipyard at Blackwall (later operated by Wigram). The third and final hollow is cast adrift below the main channel of the Thames, where its waters mingle with the contaminated outflow of the Lea. This is where I'm heading, to complete my journey from marsh to mouth.

I cross the neck of land between Bow Creek and the East India Dock Basin, where migrating tern and black redstart nest on rafts floating in the brackish water and where the margins of the salt marsh have been colonized by yellow buttonweed. A row of abandoned sheds comes into view. The corrugated metal walls are stamped *THAMES IRON WORKS* in blocky white capitals. More signs appear, relics from the industrial past:

MATHERS

WHALE OIL

EXTRACTION

DITCHBURN AND MARE

SHIP

BUILDERS

☙GOODLUCK HOPE

Goodluck Hope. But the hand is pointing in the wrong direction. I've just come from there. It should be pointing north. I hear the familiar rumble of polyurethane on tarmac. The skateboard novice must have followed me from City Island and is now rolling down the potholed street towards me, her arms outstretched for balance.

The stencil signs are too good to be true: heritage reproductions by Ballymore. The way to the mouth is flanked by deserted building sites where the concrete shells of high-rise towers rest on exposed steel piles. I stop outside Ballymore's sales suite and take a photograph through the frosted glass. Inside, a scale model of the Limmo Peninsula glows with concealed lights. Goodluck Hope is no mistake. The southernmost arm of the peninsula was traditionally known as Orchard Place, after the main road running through it, but today it has been rebranded with the name of its northern neighbour. The name is emblazoned on logos everywhere, the double *o* of 'Goodluck' bound together like links on an iron chain.

This heritage hijacking is characteristic of new developments in London's former industrial zones. In 2017 Ballymore opened an 'experience centre' in a derelict boat shed on the peninsula.[46] The shed was dressed as if for an immersive theatre performance. Potential buyers entered a covered courtyard where a large wood-burning chimney had been installed – to evoke the forges of the former iron works – then passed through a 'grove' of real palm trees beneath exposed steel girders. At the business end was a mock-up of an apartment, dubbed the 'exhibition space', and finally a 'boardwalk' overlooking the Thames where champagne was served by eager young men in business shirts.

Orchard Place was once a tight-knit, working-class community served by a few shops, a school and several pubs. Known locally as 'Bog Island', the peninsula was prone to flooding and infested with rats. There were claims of inbreeding. In the 1890s the local priest, Father Lawless, described the islanders as 'hardly human . . . incarnate mushrooms'. [47] By the 1930s the area had been declared one of London's worst slums. The old houses were demolished and residents shipped out to Poplar and beyond – three hundred of them in 1936 alone.

The modern repopulating of the Limmo at City Island and Good-luck Hope is heralded by the degraded, euphemistic language of the advertising agency. 'It is not just about selling an apartment,' preached Ballymore's head of brand design, Matt Gavioli, 'it's about selling an exciting shared experience of what life might be like living on a develop-ment by promoting the overall sense of place.'[48] For Roger Black, creative director, east London is a 'land of opportunity'.[49] But not for all. A one-bedroom flat in Goodluck Hope will set you back a cool half a million, while the top-floor 'lofts' start at £1.1 million. Many units have already been sold off-plan to foreign buyers as investments or second homes. Ballymore even operates a sales office in Hong Kong. Beyond the PR hype and gestures towards 'place-making', there is a real risk of the Limmo becoming another 'zombie neighbourhood' – a heritage theme park overlooked by 'ghost towers'.[50] By then Ballymore, and their atten-dant cast of bespectacled architects and branding flunkies, will already have moved on to somewhere new.

It is with genuine relief and excitement, then, that I arrive at Trinity Buoy Wharf. Like a pilgrim reaching Finisterre, I can go no further. This is the edge of the world, where Lea meets Thames.

I step through the gates and into a large courtyard where a boy is practising wheelies under the watchful eye of his father.

'Don't fall off,' the father says.

'I'll try not to, Dad,' replies the boy, sarcastically.

First established in 1803 as a storage and maintenance depot for river buoys and lightships, the wharf now survives as a thriving centre for the creative arts. Its workshops, warehouses and refurbished shipping containers provide studio and office space for artists and arts organizations. English National Opera has a set store here, and Thames Clippers operates a pier on the riverfront. One container houses a café which I am surprised to see open today. I stand outside the door, fiddling with my face mask. 'Don't worry, you can come in,' says a young woman, carrying a tray of pastries.

The wharf is full of quirky discoveries. A black cab is parked on top of the café with an apple tree appearing to grow out of its roof. Opposite, two female nudes are perched on iron girders projecting from a large, redbrick building. Both are works by blacksmith-turned-artist Andrew Baldwin, whose kinetic sculptures are encountered elsewhere in the wharf. Around the corner I find Fatboy's, a classic 1940s steel-clad diner that started life in New Jersey. At the centre of the complex is an experimental lighthouse built in 1864–6 to test maritime lighting equipment and train lighthouse keepers. Michael Faraday, the Newington boy, carried out research into optics within another, earlier lighthouse on the site, which was demolished in the 1920s.

I take my espresso along the seawall of Trinity Buoy Wharf to where the river empties into the Thames. Bow Creek, Lea or Lee, it doesn't matter now – the currents blend without so much as a ripple on the surface. Can it be slack tide already? I take a deep breath: the air is fresh but with a briny tang. Banks of storm clouds threaten from the south but will not break. Two kayakers are paddling downstream from Shadwell Basin. The colossal white marquee of the Millennium Dome squats on the far shore, its western side brushing an invisible line: the prime meridian. From above, the Dome resembles a giant clock face. Twelve yellow support towers represent the months of the year and its diameter measures 365 metres: a metre for each day. I listen to the swell; the creaking of ropes; the echo, I think, of a struck bell. I record the names of the boats moored on the floating pier: *Bandit*, *Storm Clipper* and *Twin*

Star – the ancient little catamaran that ordinarily would be ferrying passengers between Canary Wharf Pier and Rotherhithe.

The Thames seems to stretch out in all directions from this point, more like a great grey lagoon than a river. I am scanning the seawall for a mark, a sign of something lost. The Ordnance Datum – the standard reference from which all measurements of vertical height derive – was once taken from Mean Sea Level at Trinity Buoy Wharf.* I have spent so long exploring this vertical city that I am anxious to locate where this spot is marked. But today the tide is too high. I find, instead, the source of the echo: a large bronze bell rigged to the outside of the seawall. This is one of seven *Time and Tide Bells* installed by artist Marcus Vergette across Britain. The bells are activated by the rising and falling of the tide, and their innovative shape enables one strike to sound a series of notes – a melody of waves.

A toddler is attempting to climb the base of a tall periscope-like sculpture which is set back a few yards from the wall. I don't blame her; it looks just like a 'voice trumpet' from Teletubbyland. Designed by artist Laura Williams, this is *Alunatime*, the world's first tidal-powered moon clock. The face lights up with rings of LEDs to indicate the lunar phase, the position of the moon in the sky, and the ebb and flow of the tide. A larger version of the clock – 'larger than Stonehenge' – was planned for the North Greenwich Peninsula but the project has been on ice for years.[51]

Meanwhile, the experimental lighthouse no longer serves its original purpose but instead contains the musical installation *Longplayer*. Conceived by Jem Finer and launched at midnight on 1 January 2000, this arresting project is programmed to play variations of the same piece of music without repetition for one thousand years, at which point it will repeat in its entirety for another millennium. A bank of computers inside the lighthouse controls an instrument composed of 234 Tibetan

---

* The Ordnance Datum was subsequently taken from the Victoria Dock in Liverpool and, since 1921, from Mean Sea Level at Newlyn Harbour, Cornwall.

singing bowls and gongs, set out in a pattern of concentric rings. *Long-player* has already been playing without pause for twenty years when I visit the wharf, although today I cannot go inside to experience it first-hand. The lighthouse is closed during lockdown.

I collapse into one of the deck chairs that are laid out by the seawall and bring up a YouTube recording on my phone instead. The music comes in waves. Ominous aircraft drones and wavering, ethereal tones form, reform and dissipate. Bells ring and buzz; round notes harmonize then oscillate – sound on the edge of silence. Prayer. Breath. The music of deep time.

'Stretching way back to my childhood, I wanted to understand time,' explains Finer, formerly of Celtic punk band The Pogues. 'Being shown the stars through a telescope and told that what I was seeing was thousands of years in the past, to me it was a mystery.'[52]

Longplayer reaches forward to the future but also backwards, through the human story, to something elemental, *pre*-human. A thousand years ago in the story of these islands, the inheritors of Alfred's Wessex were now ruled by the Viking Cnut, who styled himself *ealles Engla landes cyning* ('king of all England').[53] Cnut, who cut a channel through the flat-lands of the Thames; who raised a wooden palace on the isle of thorns; who could not turn back the tide. Rewind another thousand years from then: on the western edge of the Roman empire an archipelago is slowly coming into focus – a land of wild woods and jagged coastlines, rich in tin and timber, a place of 'mystic terror' governed by a shadowy elite of philosopher-priests. Now zoom in: a broad river valley appears, fringed with fertile wetlands; two low gravel hills;[54] and a stream of freshwater rippling amid bright pebbles.[55]

The Dome, the Ordnance Datum, *Longplayer*, *Alunatime* and the *Time and Tide Bell* have transformed this tiny peninsula at the mouth of the Lea into something akin to a ritual landscape; a space designed to heighten our encounter with time, to celebrate its power in the form of the moon and the tide.

Where humankind once raised great barrows and pyramids to honour the dead and make certain their passage to the afterlife, contemporary monuments such as those at Trinity Buoy Wharf render into physical form the inner psyche of a new age of anxiety. They are, in essence, attempts to comprehend the afterlife of humanity itself.

'The Anthropocene,' wrote Robert Macfarlane, 'requires us to undertake a retrospective reading of the current moment . . . a "palaeontology of the present" in which we ourselves have become sediments, strata and ghosts.'[56]

I face downstream, to where the Thames sweeps out east towards Woolwich. The Thames Barrier is just out of sight – a chain of giant steel flood gates protecting London from the destructive force of a storm surge. The barrier is halfway through its designed lifespan and sea levels are rising. With modifications it might last till 2070.

Three local lads around my age have settled into chairs a little further down and are talking excitedly in a seamless mix of English and Bengali. One of them is planning to do Hajj next year. Another has just had his second child. 'Have you seen the new flats? On the Creek?' he asks. 'They're nice you know.'

'Nah, man,' says the third. 'I couldn't live there. I'm old school. I want a house in Poplar near my ma.'

To settle in London, wrote Ackroyd, is 'to be part of the present moment moving into futurity.'[57] I look out to the river, to the point where, deep beneath the water, the southernmost drift hollow was discovered. It feels like the perfect spot to end my journey down the Lea.

A fault in the bedrock.

All that time compressed into the earth.

A thousand years, I think – it's nothing.

Meridian

'"Why are you scared, Little Bear?" asked Big Bear.
"I don't like the dark," said Little Bear.
"What dark?" said Big Bear.
"The dark all around us," said Little Bear.'

MARTIN WADDELL[58]

How could I have forgotten? In all my rush to reach the mouth, I had overlooked the one place I had set out to discover. The Lea is the most complex, resistant landscape I have encountered. I must go back, one final time, to trace a secret stream to the wild, deserted island at the heart of it. I make a call, confirm arrangements. My walking partner will drive the short journey from his home in Harringay, where the Hampstead Ridge gives way to the Lea Valley in a series of perilous escarpments.

I find my father admiring the impressive architecture at Three Mills. He is wearing a Hawaiian shirt and a disposable dust mask, like the man who's come to do your skirting boards. It is the hottest day of the year so far; my forearms glisten with perspiration as I take a swig of water. Today is the first time I've seen my dad in fifteen weeks. A survivor of throat cancer with ongoing medical issues, Dad has been shielding from Covid-19, with his wife Hannah, since before the lockdown. For a gregarious man with a love of music and the arts, the isolation has been hard to bear. 'I've felt very lonely,' he confesses, and hands me a book he has bought for Martha: *Can't You Sleep, Little Bear?*

The Lea has been an industrial zone since the Middle Ages. In 1085–6, the Domesday Book recorded at least eight mills on the river. The remaining structures here at Three Mills date to the late eighteenth and early nineteenth centuries and include the House Mill, the largest tidal mill in the world. 'Look how steeply pitched the roof is, Tom. It's double-height. Dormer windows to provide light for workers and access doors for hoisting up sacks of grain to the upper floors.' Dad proves a valuable guide; since his retirement from teaching, he has been taking courses in architectural history. '*This* is most unusual,' he continues, probing across the cobbled yard. 'Pointed arch windows in the Gothic style. And a hexagonal clock tower. No, sorry. *Octagonal.*'

Three Mills is one of London's hidden treasures – an enclave of the old city encircled by artificial waterways and mill streams. The water-wheels no longer turn, but you can still make out the runnels where the ebb tide flowed, powering millstones that once ground grain for flour and, later, gunpowder and gin. As well as the mill buildings themselves, the island contains TV and film studios and a public park known as Three Mills Green which, today, is full of picnicking families. At low tide wading birds explore the shallows, migrants from the south. I tell Dad my plan and he agrees: we will head downstream, then find the path that cuts off-piste through wasteland to an elusive tributary of the Lea, the Channelsea River. I'm excited. I've been anxious to make this journey for weeks.

Dad and I follow a slender spit of land to Bow Locks, passing a barricaded footbridge and a narrowboat selling pot plants, flowers and herbs from its roof, then veer east, away from the river. Seven giant gas holders rise up before us: the cast-iron skeletons of the abandoned Bromley-by-Bow gas-works. It's here, in the early 1800s, that William Congreve established a weapons factory for the production of his experimental rockets. An iron plate on the base of one of the gas holders reads '1827' but the rest of the text is indecipherable, worn away by rain and rust. In 2013 plans were drawn up to convert the gasworks into a Victorian-inspired zoological garden for a competition of speculative architecture.[59] The zoo would be self-sufficient, powered by biogas produced on-site from animal waste. The gas cylinders would become enclosures for animals, with the sur-rounding land flooded for ponds and fisheries. Its creators, David Wakefield and Robert Nimmo, dubbed their vision 'A Lost World'.

We are descending the empty road past dense foliage when we come to the edge of a vast industrial estate – a labyrinth of waste plants, warehouses, vehicle depots and scrap-metal yards stretching all the way to Canning Town station. Amazon and Sainsbury's operate giant distribution centres here, on the rutted east bank of the Lea. Two morose women in overalls are smoking outside Greencore, the sandwich manufacturer.

'Are you sure you know where you're going?' Dad asks.

My Streetfinder is no use here, so I pull up Google Maps and zoom in. A footpath is marked heading north-east through a tongue of thick woodland, but when we find the entrance it has been blocked off by a steel palisade topped with anti-climb spikes. Beyond the fence the tarmac path disappears into the trees like a hollow way. 'I don't think they want you to go through,' Dad says, already turning back.

The land beyond the trees, a seven-acre wedge of scrub between the railway and the Channelsea River, was acquired by the Islamic missionary group Tablighi Jamaat in 1996. The group currently operates a small mosque from a squat prefab surrounded by barbed-wire fences and electricity pylons. Plans for a 'mega-mosque' capable of holding seventy thousand worshippers have come to nothing, despite several iterations of the design. The initial vision, from 2005, resembled a 'giant walnut whip, eccentrically spiralling out of control' and met with vociferous opposition from locals and right-wing activists.[60] Although avowedly non-political, Tablighi Jamaat promotes a conservative interpretation of Islam, stressing adherence to religious practices as they were at the time of the Prophet Muhammad. Their name means 'Society of Preachers' and members are encouraged to strive for spiritual perfection – to become *al-Insān al-Kāmil*, 'the complete person'. The group was founded in north-western India in 1926 as an offshoot of the Islamic revivalist movement known as Deobandi, which developed in response to British rule in India, eight years after the Rebellion of 1857.

Congreve, Wigram and the East India Company; Gandhi, Tipu Sultan and Tablighi Jamaat – for all its utopian fantasies, this landscape is a haunted place, riddled with the ghosts of empire. I'm pondering all this as we retrace our steps back to Three Mills Island and across the green, where a shirtless man is doing keepy-uppies in the baking sun.

'Look how much he's sweating,' Dad remarks. My father is rarely

385

without an opinion. When we're out walking, he delivers a regular commentary on the people we pass: their appearance; their behaviour; and, most of all today, their proximity to him. It's his way, I think, of mediating his experience of a world that seems to be spinning out of control – and it's a habit I have inherited.

We cross the Prescott Channel just above the new locks. A young boy on a bike races past on the narrow towpath. 'Sorry, mate,' he says, as Dad steps into the verge. Here, two rows of chain-link fencing separate the path from the concrete wasteland surrounding a massive steel industrial building. Station F is the latest addition to the sprawling Victorian pumping station of Abbey Mills. It shimmers in the heat like a silver-grey aircraft hangar or an upturned prison hulk. The gas holders reappear in the distance, so we know we're on the right track.

In 1994 the historian Dan Cruickshank tracked down the remains of the lost Euston Arch to this obscure waterway, where they had been dumped in 1962 'to fill a chasm in the bed of the channel'.[61] Built in 1838 as the monumental entrance to Euston Station, the Doric-style sandstone archway was the largest of its kind in the world. Cruickshank had spent fifteen years searching for it – a steampunk Indiana Jones in the tweed jacket of a country gent. Video footage shows a crane raising the very first piece from the channel: a massive, fluted slab of one of the columns. 'My God, it's brilliant, absolutely brilliant,' exclaimed Cruickshank. Then: 'Bloody hell.'[62]

The fence continues past a grassy promontory, which I reveal to Dad was the site of the first two series of Channel 4's *Big Brother* (2000–2001). He is less impressed by this and strides ahead. The *Big Brother* house was designed as a walled compound, whose perimeter was lit up by floodlights and patrolled by security guards with German shepherds. The complex was surrounded by water on three sides and by Station F on the fourth, and was connected to the TV studios on Three Mills Island by a footbridge. Twenty-four cameras kept contestants under constant surveillance for sixty-four spellbinding days of viewing.

Back then, reality TV felt exciting and new – not the mind-numbing parade of attention-seekers and minor celebrities it has become today. 6.9 million people tuned in to watch the eviction of former City broker 'Nasty' Nick Bateman, who was found to have been manipulating housemates' votes, playing them off against each other like stocks in a volatile market. The winner of series one, Scouse bricklayer Craig Phillips, was that rare thing in television: warm-hearted, genuine, a deserving winner. He donated his £70,000 prize fund to a friend to pay for her heart and lung transplants. As he left the house, fireworks were launched into the night sky above the gasworks in unintended tribute to Congreve's rocket factory.

At the end of the channel, two bewildered teenagers are stumbling arm-in-arm from the dark portal in the trees into which Dad has disappeared. I follow and as I cross the threshold the air feels suddenly thick, as if the world is closing in. I smell weed and then another, deeper vegetal perfume – the rotten scent of a riverbank. Dad is hurrying ahead. 'Wait up,' I call, but he doesn't hear me.

He swerves off the footpath out of sight, then calls back: 'I'm going for a slash.'

For a moment I'm alone, and through a break in the trees I see that the path is elevated above an impenetrable forest of reeds and Himalayan balsam leading down to the boggy margins of a tidal stream. At last, the Channelsea River emerges from the map, with a shopping trolley half-sunk into its western shore. It's low tide and the water is shallow enough to ford, I think, in a pair of sturdy boots. What else is down there, underneath the gloop? Perhaps an empty magnum of champagne from the finale of *Big Brother 2*?

In the last century, the Ordnance Survey marked this path as 'Long Wall', a raised embankment presumably constructed to defend the surrounding pastureland of Mill Meads. Its name brings to mind the ancient flood barriers raised in the marshes of Lambeth, Bermondsey and the Isle of Dogs. Today Long Wall is a recognized wildlife corridor, buzzing with songbirds, moorhen, feral pigeons, snipe and gulls.[63] The

German hairy snail has dug into the mudflats. Kingfishers and a kestrel have been observed hunting near by. Dad reappears from behind a bush and we continue down the path together. 'This is beautiful,' he says. 'We could be in the middle of the countryside.' At night common pipistrelle bats can be heard foraging along the tree line.

Suddenly Dad stops and points across the river. Sheet piling. Wasteland. A District Line train hurtling towards West Ham.

'Look,' he says.

And, yes, I see it too: the tangled southern tip of an island.

X marks the spot.

Islands have fascinated me since childhood. I used to dream of crossing the stagnant lake in my local park in Herne Hill to explore a scraggy islet that always seemed to have had some new piece of street furniture dumped on its banks. Channelsea Island is a different beast altogether. Shrouded in colossal weeping willows and choked with rampant brambles, it appears more like a primeval forest or something out of *The Adventures of Huckleberry Finn*.[64] Giant hogweed has colonized the margins and draws my eye towards a series of ruined structures half-obscured by undergrowth. The island is owned by Tablighi Jamaat but remains both uninhabited and off-limits; an old iron footbridge from the mainland is stopped with a bung of impenetrable foliage. Sprawling chemical works existed on the east bank of the Channelsea from the nineteenth century, producing sulphuric acid and other toxic materials. The footbridge was built in the first half of the twentieth century to connect the works with associated industrial buildings on the island itself, which included a circular storage tank for chemicals.

Remarkably, I later discover that someone has recently managed to get to the island: an intrepid kayaker named Ian Tokelove. Only a week before our visit, Tokelove and his companion paddled up the Channelsea at high tide and penetrated the dense vegetation to the interior. A series

of photographs appears to illustrate the aftermath of a nuclear apocalypse: abandoned, windowless rooms clogged with fallen branches and
rusting industrial artefacts; menacing pipes covered in cobwebs and
creepers. It is a vision from the Anthropocene: a future projection of a
post-human world where giant hogweed proliferates like carnivorous
plants from *The Day of the Triffids*. This is 'poisoned land'.[65] In some
places, the soil was unnaturally red and friable. In one building, Tokelove
found a 'crucible, wired up to melt metals or other substances'; in another,
a row of cylinder chains attached to the wall like prison shackles.[66]

Tablighi Jamaat's mega-mosque was described in the press as 'an
alien symbol', but in truth the claims of the spiritual on this isolated area
stretch back almost nine hundred years.[67] The Channelsea Island was
constructed in the eleventh century to accommodate a series of tidal
mills owned by the Abbey of St Mary's, Stratford Langthorne. The Abbey
was founded in 1135 and was one of England's largest and wealthiest
Cistercian foundations, with extensive properties in Essex and lucrative
rights to milling on the river Lea.

On 3 April 1300 the Abbey received a visit from Edward I, the Hammer of the Scots.[68] He was carrying a relic acquired from the Welsh
kings of Gwynedd: a fragment of the True Cross known as *Croes Naid*
('the Cross of Neath'). During his stay at Stratford Langthorne, the King
is said to have made 'offerings' to the *Croes* together with a thorn from
the Crown of Thorns. The *Croes* was last recorded at the Tower of London
in 1552 but has long since vanished.

At the time of the Dissolution, the Abbey attracted a net annual
income of £511 – a figure comparable to that of St Saviour's, Bermondsey. Its grounds once dominated the eastern side of the Channelsea; the
stream on the near side of the island is still known as Abbey Creek.
Stratford Langthorne did not escape the turbulence of 1381, but was
ransacked by protestors marching towards London from Essex. Goods
were pillaged and ancient charters burned to ash. What little remains of
the original buildings now lies beneath the railing sidings of Stratford

Market Depot, where Jubilee Line trains recharge after a long day of ferrying shoppers to Westfield and back.

A heavy atmosphere hangs over the island, as if something – or someone – has not been laid to rest. A few decades after the foundation of the Abbey in the mid-twelfth century, reports began to emerge of paranormal visions within the monastic community. Some claimed to have experienced 'demonic temptations', others to have observed first-hand the intercession of saints, the Blessed Virgin and even Christ Himself as salvation from 'purgation' in Hell. The stories were collected by Peter of Cornwall, the prior of Holy Trinity, Aldgate, and published in his *Liber revelationum*. I imagine him in the role of Brother Cadfael or Umberto Eco's monkish detective, William of Baskerville, travelling up the old Roman road from the city to this marsh-bound outpost.[69] One day during Mass, he recorded, Abbot Arnold witnessed 'an angel descend from heaven, in a bright light and with the odour of celestial grace, into the Stratford choir and sprinkle the monks with incense from a golden thurible which made them sing more sweetly'.[70]

I have been performing Google deep dives on my laptop and have come up trumps. I'm not the only writer to have been drawn to this strange and magical place. The island features in the first book of *The Twelfth Odyssey*, a series of self-published fantasy novels by Derrick Herbert. In this bizarre mash-up of Norse mythology, Arthurian legend, speculative fiction and space opera, Herbert proposes Channelsea Island as the meeting point of two energy lines: the 'blue wall of energy' of the Greenwich prime meridian and a 'shimmering curtain of green energy . . . they had followed from Kings Cross'.[71] Here, at this cosmic crossroads, the wizard Merlin and his Muggle comrades attack the malevolent 'Revenants' or 'Black Sorcerers', rushing across the footbridge armed incongruously with assault rifles, TASERs, C-4 and a flamethrower. Herbert channels Peter of Cornwall's medieval visions in his portrait of the island as a *thin place*, where the air is thick with sprites, nymphs and faeries.

*

Heavenly visions, faeries and energy lines – deep in lockdown fever it almost could be true. As the path divides and then emerges into light, I remember my earlier descent into the Mithraeum, the temple by the Walbrook, and the violent encounter of the marble tauroctony: a vision of the cosmos where the powers of good and evil are 'locked in eternal, equal, conflict'.[72]

Dad is rushing on. He's eager to get back to Three Mills before his parking ticket runs out. Besides, he doesn't like to hang around. We reach the Greenway, where the Northern Outfall Sewer spans the Channelsea on its slow descent to Beckton. The island has petered out along a line of precarious reed beds and collapsed timbers, and the mudflats are peppered with junked car tyres. A large white office block rises above the mud on the far bank; its tenants include a caterer of 'soul food' and a company that manufactures industrial air compressors. After the dissolution of the Abbey of Stratford Langthorne, the land along the riverbank here was leased to the Dean of Salisbury, Peter Vannes. A native of the Tuscan city of Lucca, Vannes was part of an unsuccessful diplomatic mission to the Pope in 1528 during which the English argued for Henry VIII's marriage to Catherine of Aragon to be declared void. Vannes acquired a dwelling house, outbuildings, gardens, orchards, a hay barn and stable on the banks of the Channelsea, together with a property known as 'le Gestenhall'. Remarkably, this dormitory or guesthouse was still in use as late as the 1840s, three hundred years later.[73] Its final occupants were Lascars, Indian sailors who worked on British ships.

The river itself is culverted not far beyond this point. It burrows deep beneath the shopping centre in a flow-less pipe, before eventually connecting with the network of waterways within the Olympic Park, including the Combined Sewer Overflow I visited with Theo, the London Waterkeeper.

Two girls are performing an elaborate dance routine by the railings. One girl leans back, grinding her hips, while the other, taller girl shrugs and gestures to the camera. Tinny R&B emits from a phone propped up on a bollard. As we pass, the shorter girl looks up, caught unawares, and bursts out laughing: 'We're not on TikTok, I *swear*! We're rehearsing!'

I look across at Dad. His mask is down. He's beaming. 'Carry on, you're doing great!' he says, and marches on. This little adventure has been good for him, I think. Bazalgette's monumental pumping station appears through a steel fence and Dad stops to take a look. 'The Cathedral of Sewage' is an architectural amalgam – a Byzantine basilica with flourishes of Italian Gothic, Romanesque and Moorish design in alternating yellow and red brickwork. When the station opened, in 1868, a local official complained of its exorbitant cost, remarking that this 'elegant structure in a swamp . . . might be taken for a mosque or Chinese temple'.[74] It is a fitting end to my time in the Lower Lea Valley. For the Lea is not an edge, but a conduit connecting the past with the future, the local with the global.

I look down across the creek. A large grey heron is standing stock-still on a tyre. I had wanted to stay longer here, to find a way of getting closer to the island, to unearth, perhaps, some proof of its occult power. I will have to settle, instead, for this: a landscape witnessed as a blur, at speed, following somebody I love.

The heron scans the water and is gone.

All the world is on the Greenway: young and old, rich and poor, cyclists, walkers and rampaging, sun-drunk toddlers. We power-walk towards Three Mills on the same path Gandhi took in 1931 on his pre-dawn hikes along the Sewerbank. We're moving so fast that we fail to notice the line incised into the pavement where the Greenway crosses Abbey Lane. It's only later that I realize what we'd missed.

Derrick Herbert was right about one thing.

It was the prime meridian.

Coda:

A ROSE BY ANY OTHER NAME[1]

'There are many ghosts and they travel with me'
AL JOSHUA[2]

1

IN OCTOBER 2019 I returned to the Aldgate hole – to the gap in the city where all these journeys began. Aldgate: where Richard of Cornwall compiled his 'Book of Revelations'; where, two centuries later, Chaucer conjured dream-visions of melting palaces and parliaments of squabbling birds; and where now the ruins of a playhouse, the Boar's Head, had finally been unearthed.

Archaeologist Heather Knight appeared at the gate and ushered me through the barriers. It was the last days of the excavation; mechanical diggers were poised to backfill the trenches she and her team from MOLA had cut into the brickearth. Gone were the grassed-over spoil heaps, the bramble jungle, the fly-tips. The ground crunched underfoot: wet gravel. And from the deep cut on the eastern edge I could make out the stumps of stone foundations, sticking up from the mud like rotten teeth.

Heather led me into the site office, a large Portakabin where two more archaeologists were wolfing down lunch from the burger van on Goulston Street. She showed me a selection of finds: discarded oyster shells, glassware and fragments of beer mugs, a pair of crossed spoons and a bent window latch, half a dozen clay pipes and a fossilized horn core. 'Aldgate was the epicentre for horn-working in London,' she explained. 'There were forty members of the Worshipful Company of Horners working on Middlesex Street alone in around 1641.' The chalk and brick foundations that Heather and her team had carefully brought into the light would once have supported timber structures, 'traces of the inn's lodging spaces that were later converted into seating for the audience'.[3] They had found finials from the tops of Tudor money boxes. These small, disposable ceramic pots were commonly used in

Elizabethan playhouses to collect ticket earnings; they have given us the modern phrase 'box office'. When they were full, the boxes would have been broken open and thrown away. An eighteenth-century kiln for the firing of pipes had also emerged, remarkably preserved, from the ground.

I had been following Heather's investigations into early modern London since her discovery of the Theatre in Shoreditch – an event that made national headlines in 2008. In contrast, the Boar's Head, a converted inn lost beneath the rubble of a V-2 bombsite and truncated by the abandoned Tube tunnel to the south, risks being ignored as 'an also-ran' – a footnote in history. But Heather is a fierce champion of the more obscure playhouse. 'We should be fighting its corner,' she said. 'The Boar's Head doesn't have that Shakespeare factor, but it was integral to the drama scene in the early seventeenth century, staging city comedies with characters the audience would recognize, everyday London life, topical stuff, gossip.'

For this briefest of moments, the playhouse was open again to the sky; to the noise and traffic fumes of the roundabout; to the sideways glances of pedestrians heading east to Whitechapel. The discovery of the Boar's Head precedes the delayed but inevitable redevelopment of the hole. Its remains will be left *in situ*, Heather explained, and spanned by the foundations of the new building – a twenty-four-storey accommodation block for students. The developer has promised to preserve the archaeology in the tower's footprint, while a new 'community performance space' will celebrate the site's theatrical history. As Heather walked me around the perimeter, I felt a strange sense of loss – not for the theatre, as it had now been found, but for the no man's land *before* the excavation, a place between places.

'As archaeologists we're comfortable with change,' Heather said. 'We know that nothing lasts for ever.'

The anomalous energies of the hole have begun to dissipate.

The portal is closing but I'm not yet ready to leave.

2

The Boar's Head; Newington Butts; the Theatre and the Curtain in Shoreditch – I have started to think of London's lost playhouses as sites of power connecting my journeys across the map, as vital to my understanding of the city as its hidden rivers, its ancient churches, islands and holy wells. If the spirit of London is its people, then what are these playhouses but ruined temples, ablaze with what Chris McCabe calls 'midnight fire': the latent energies of poets and players, groundlings and gallants?[4]

From the ghosts of Banquo and Old Hamlet to the spiritualist seances of the Victorian age, the theatre has always been the natural place in which to summon the supernatural. So let me conjure you a ghost.

A grainy video is recovered from an amateur filmmaker's attic and posted on the internet.[5] The year is 1989. Bankside, Southwark. The sky is a blank white screen – it saturates the world in light – and as we see through a chain-link fence, the camera trembles slightly. There are people by the hoardings. There are people on the bridge. There are people on the wooden platform raised on scaffold poles above the ground and there are people in the ground itself. There are people in the street, caught in silent tableaux in flat caps and knitted jumpers; in denim, perms and summer suits. They clap politely when local MP Simon Hughes hands the microphone to veteran Hollywood actor Sam Wanamaker. 'This whole area,' he says, 'is, I think, one of the most important areas in the world, if not *the* most important area of Western civilization.'

The video cuts to night, a vigil, Hughes again, and then the camera pans across the crowd and there she is: my mother, resplendent, out of time, with a fresh-cut rose in the lapel of her luminous white blazer.

The discovery of the foundations of the Rose in Southwark on 31 January 1989 was a pivotal moment not only for the history of early modern drama in London but for the future preservation of Britain's cultural heritage. Faced with imminent destruction under the footing of a ten-storey office block, and without legal protection, the partial remains were in a perilous condition. On 2 March a temporary extension was granted to the Museum of London team, who worked around the clock to uncover as much of the playhouse as they could. Finds trays filled up with the ephemera of Elizabethan London:

> orange pips, Tudor shoes, a human skull, a bear skull, the sternum of a turtle, sixteenth-century inn tokens, clay pipes, a spur, a sword scabbard and hilt, money boxes, quantities of animal bones, pins, shoes and old clothing.[6]

Six days later the stage of the theatre emerged from the waterlogged ground.

Constructed in 1587 for the impresario Philip Henslowe, the Rose was a purpose-built, polygonal amphitheatre with an external diameter of 72 feet. Established earlier than its larger neighbours, the Swan (1595) and the Globe (1599), its stage was home to the leading dramatist of the time, Christopher Marlowe, and also presented early works by Shakespeare. In 1592 the Rose was expanded (its diameter increasing to 79 feet) and fitted with machinery to represent 'the heavens' consisting of a 'hoisting device which enabled a throne or other vehicle to be lowered from the roof above the stage'.[7] Along with Henslowe, whose surviving account book or 'diary' supplies much of our knowledge of the early modern theatre industry, the prime mover in the history of the Rose was Edward 'Ned' Alleyn, celebrated as the greatest actor of his generation.

When the story broke, it was once again actors who stole the show. National treasure Dame Peggy Ashcroft led a makeshift cast of stars from stage and screen including Ian McKellen, Judi Dench, Ralph Fiennes, Vanessa Redgrave and James Fox. Laurence Olivier sent messages of support from his deathbed. Director Peter Hall persuaded Dustin Hoffman to drop by. And 007 himself attended press conferences in the shape of Timothy Dalton. On 9 May 1989 Simon Hughes addressed the House of Commons, winning an unlikely supporter in Prime Minister Margaret Thatcher. By 14 May – the final day of the excavation – the Rose found itself in the middle of a media frenzy. Christine Eccles reported that 'thousands rallied around the chalk-white skeletal geometry unearthed in the dark Southwark mud.'[8] As darkness fell, a hardcore of protestors prepared for a long, hot night.

My mother is on camera for almost thirteen seconds. It is the only time I have. She holds a cigarette in her right hand; her left lodged in a pocket. Her face is locked in fierce concentration and then she turns, two seconds in, as if a voice from behind the crowd has called her name. At nine seconds, she stoops in genuflection, collects her handbag from the ground and then she's gone, conveyed off-stage in motion blur. In May 1989 she was thirty-seven – the age I am now.

> *Through all the drama – whether damn'd or not –*
> *Love gilds the scene, and women guide the plot.*[9]

These lines, by Richard Sheridan, were cut, on my mother's instruction, into the Scottish granite of her headstone. There always was something more exciting behind the curtain, in the half-light of the wings after the show had ended. The pun on 'plot' was hers as well, I'm sure of it. As Shakespeare wrote, 'This green plot shall be our stage, this hawthorn-brake our tiring-house.'[10]

I do not know if my mother stayed all night. Somehow I doubt it; she was not the camping type. Some of her sixth-form students certainly did. 'The night was fortunately warm,' recalled Sarah Gregory, 'and our spirits were kept high by donations of chocolate, bagels and other provisions.'[11] Earlier that day Gregory and other students from Alleyn's School (including a seventeen-year-old Jude Law) had performed extracts from

Dr Faustus for the assembled crowd, 'with Eileen Chivers fearlessly playing the part of Lechery'.[12]

At midnight the site was formally handed back to the developer, Imry Merchant. Padlocks were changed. But then, at 4.30 a.m., protestors reoccupied the Rose. By dawn the octogenarian Peggy Ashcroft had resumed her position on a camp stool inside the perimeter fence. Shortly after 6 a.m. a fleet of lorries arrived with a cargo of sand to backfill the remains but found their path blocked – 'A line of people, arms linked, moved in front of them.'[13] Remarkably, after a brief stand-off and then further negotiation with the developer by phone, the lorries turned around and left at around 7 a.m.

That day a campaign group was hastily assembled, its committee 'elected from the street'.[14] Hughes was the obvious choice for chair. My mother, the schoolteacher, was among those selected to represent the interests of the local community. Over the next four weeks the future of the Rose hung in the balance, subject to furious negotiations between the campaign committee, Imry Merchant, the Museum of London, English Heritage and the Secretary of State for the Environment. Meanwhile the archaeology itself lay abandoned and exposed to the elements in the middle of a heatwave. Eccles compared the playhouse to a 'patient in coma . . . intravenously fed on a permanent drip'. '[Visitors'] concern,' she continued, 'was expressed by gifts of roses or cards embellished with the aphoristic sayings of the Bard.'[15]

A second all-night rally was held on 11 June but by then the writing was on the wall. The developer had already agreed to redesign their tower at an additional cost of £10 million. Six steel columns, each a metre thick, would span the remains of the playhouse to create an 'office on stilts'. Lacking both financial backing and political will, the campaign's alternative proposals came to nothing. On 15 June the Secretary of State declined to schedule the Rose as an ancient monument and the remains were reburied, 'swathed in an impermeable shroud'.[16]

*

When she was dying, my mother made me a promise: to come back as a ghost and haunt me. I wanted that so much that for years I swore I had felt her presence standing by my bed at night or glimpsed in a haze of waste heat outside a classroom window; a haze so like the cloud of smoke curling from the lit end of a Marlboro Red it was as if she was waiting just out of sight below the sill. She kept her stash of cigarettes in a cabinet in the dining room, always the same brand, stacked in bricks of two hundred procured on the ferry crossing along with cut-price bottles of Gordon's gin. By the time the cancer had spread to her lungs and bones it was already too late.

Mum died three years before the remains of the Rose were reopened to the public, with an accompanying exhibition space, in the basement of Imry Merchant's tower. Today the foundations of the playhouse lie beneath multiple strata of protective backfill. First comes a layer of Buckland sand, in which a leaky hose pipe is positioned for the purposes of maintaining the correct moisture level. The sand is covered with an impermeable plastic membrane, followed by 'weak mix' concrete – designed for flexibility. The whole footprint is then covered by several feet of water.

'The pond isn't essential,' Jane Sidell tells me; it is designed to prevent evaporation from the concrete. Jane is Historic England's Inspector of Ancient Monuments and has been visiting the Rose once a month for the past twenty-one years to monitor the remains. 'You'll find me sloshing around in my waders quite happily,' she chuckles down the phone. Along with most of the country's cultural infrastructure during the Covid-19 pandemic, the Rose has shut its doors. Its busy programme of talks and fringe theatre shows has been put on ice and Jane is restricted to emergency visits only.

Back in the late sixteenth century, outbreaks of bubonic plague were a constant menace to London's flourishing theatre scene. Playhouses were considered sites of potential infection as well as crucibles of social unrest. The Rose itself was closed down numerous times between 1592 and 1596. The excavations of 1989 revealed an intimate venue whose yard would have been packed with 'groundlings' as tightly as a rush-hour Tube. 'Plague signifies urban catastrophe,' wrote Sally Barnden, 'a vertical slice across the horizontal trajectory of normal existence.'[17] Cures proliferated like fake news. Henslowe recommended a 'good dryncke for the pestelence' consisting of lily root boiled in white wine.[18] Ned Alleyn advised his wife to pray daily, wash the doorstep and spread 'reue [rue] and herbe of grace' on the window sills.[19] Alleyn retired from acting in 1597. He was just thirty-one years old. 'Legends persisted,' wrote Eccles, 'that his nerve had never been quite the same since he counted an extra devil, or two, on stage during *Dr Faustus*.'[20] In another performance of Marlowe's supernatural thriller, the structure of the theatre itself is said to have 'cracked and frighted the audience.'[21] Henslowe's diary contains inventories of props and costumes including a 'Hell mought' (Hell mouth) and a 'robe for to goo invisibell.'[22]

Deep in lockdown, I spend an evening clearing out the wooden chest in which I keep my mother's things: old photographs, school reports and love letters; a bundle of newspaper clippings from the 'Save the Rose' campaign; the microcassette from her answering machine. The discovery of each new relic triggers a cascade of memories. Inside an oval, leather-covered pot, I find two partially melted sticks of wax which she sometimes used, eccentrically, to seal important letters, together with a brass stamp debossed with the image of a rose. Another box contains sherds of ancient pottery – 'souvenirs' from a ruined amphitheatre on the Greek island of Euboea which my mother insisted we visit despite warning signs and barbed-wire fencing. And now a rose again: this time garnishing the resin mould of a reproduction cameo brooch.

I pull out a crumbling scrapbook from the bottom of the chest and drop it on the dining-room table. Something brown and terrible shoots out and scuttles across the table into a pile of unpaid bills. I open the cover and out shoot two more: centipedes the length of my index finger. I trap one in a tin as the others disappear into the nearest skirting board. The centipede is an ancient species; its oldest recorded fossils date to the Late Silurian Period, making them roughly contemporary with the deepest rocks ever to have been found beneath London.[23] These ones must have been feeding on the glue from the binding, slowly ingesting my mother's archive in the darkness of the chest.

That night I dream that I am back in the basement of Alleyn's School, Dulwich. It's after hours and dimly lit corridors stretch out in all directions. The hum and creak of pipes. A door scrapes opens and I enter a dark passage overflowing with props and period costumes from my mother's plays: ruffs and corsets; imitation daggers and wooden canes and huge leather boots from *Captain Stirrick*; ballgowns, britches and a papier-mâché dragon; rails and rails of great coats stinking of mothballs. The air is thick with particles of dust and with each furtive step clouds of chalk-white make-up powder blossom in the half-light. A bare bulb flickers at the end of the passage where two eyes glint in the shadows – the snarling face of a red fox staring out from a forest of fur coats and scarves – and now I put out my hand, and now I'm reaching through the fur in the darkness of the wardrobe, and now I'm stepping forward into light . . . into the bright, cold light of the hospital, into the room she died in.

'How do you know what is real and what is pretend?' Martha asks again one day.

To be a child of three or four is to live in an enchanted world in which metaphor has the power of a spell. I comment on a set of crude wooden figures Martha is playing with and she corrects me.

'They're not *like* fairies, Daddy. They *are* fairies.'

And then she waves an invisible wand: 'Fairy . . . *Wishenpoof!*'

A phrase from the Latin Mass floats to the surface.

Simili modo   In a similar way

And another.

Mysterium fidei   The mystery of faith

CODA

London is enchanted ground, no longer merely the 'unreal city' of Eliot's *Waste Land* but glorious hyperreality: a hundred million possible Londons, present and past, imagined, unintended, forgotten and reborn. Time is all around us, passing through our bodies, imperceptible as radioactive particles, ethereal Wi-Fi signals.

I had set out, armed with a tattered map, to discover what lies beneath the streets. But I have found myself descending deeper into the layers of my own life than I had expected – from the trauma of losing a parent to the uncanny joy of becoming one myself.

I pull out the map one final time. London is unforgiving. The map is a brittle relic, mangled, torn to pieces. And yet, I think, I've hardly even scratched the surface.

The chalice and the basin. The invisible river. A hole in the city.

'To survive,' wrote Umberto Eco, 'you must tell stories.'[24]

These are mine.

'I'd like to see the Rose properly re-excavated before I die,' Jane Sidell told me, wryly. 'You don't forget how special it is . . . when the wind is howling down Park Street.' The weak-mix concrete protecting the remains is very slowly decaying, releasing alkali materials into the water above. The Rose Theatre Trust has launched a fundraising campaign to uncover the complete footprint of the playhouse, install a new conservation system and build a visitor and arts centre.[25] 'It's freezing cold in winter,' Jane said, 'and I'm often there on my own. But sometimes it is lovely and peaceful.'

Wearing thick rubber waders and a hard hat, Jane collects data from pipes sunk into the layers covering the archaeology before carefully analysing their chemistry. Two of these pipes penetrate the natural gravel beneath the playhouse and record varying levels of water saturation depending on time and season. The remains of the Rose lie within the tidal influence of the Thames – permeable ground which, Jane explained, 'the tide recharges twice a day.' It's a miraculous image – the brackish ooze of the river slowly leaching south towards the buried playhouse; the water following unseen pathways; flow and fault-line; the whole, invisible world beneath the city.

Evelyn Mary is born at St Thomas's Hospital on 21 July 2020. From the same room on the seventh floor I watch the same sun dip behind the Palace of Westminster, only this time Big Ben is silent and the famous clock tower is sheathed in scaffolding. Sarah's contractions come every six minutes, then every five. I keep the times on a sliver of paper:

14:12
14:17
14:22

Just before 4 p.m., the same midwife, Lauren, leads us down the corridor to the birthing pool – a large, ceramic bathtub standing in the middle of a darkened room. The water is glowing with purple light from LEDs concealed within the tub. I lean in and Sarah grips my hand and we count breaths together. 'In, two, three, four, five, six . . . and out, two, three, four, five, six, seven, eight.'

And then, at 4.13 p.m., I watch my daughter swim towards me through the light, her tiny arms and legs cycling in slow motion, and for that moment, as she is held by water, time appears to fold and stretch as fabric all around us in the room and if the cord around her neck was removed before or in that fraction of a second I will never know nor need to.

There is a story, recorded by the Venerable Bede, from the court of Edwin, the pagan ruler of Northumbria in the seventh century. A counsellor, eager for the king to convert to the new religion, compares the passage of a life to the flight of a sparrow through a warm hall.

The sparrow, flying in at one door and immediately out at another, whilst he is within, is safe from the wintry tempest; but after a short space of fair weather, he immediately vanishes out of your sight, passing from winter into winter again. So this life of man appears for a little while, but of what is to follow or what went before we know nothing at all.[26]

Human time is shallow time, this smallest moment our gift, over in 'an eagan bryhtm', the twinkling of an eye.[27] Birth, death: these are the windows to another place, 'þære tide þe us uncuð is' – that time which is unknown to us.

After a few days the little blackened nub of Evelyn's umbilical cord, sealed with a medical clamp where I made the cut, drops off. It is the last trace of her connection to the womb. I scoop it up and pop it in a plastic tub in the fridge – a relic to join the pond juice I gathered from the Vale of Health, the fluid and the lump of clay from the Ambrook.

We are born from water. Our bodies are made of it.

'She's a Cancer,' Sarah says, reading from her phone with Evelyn clamped to her left breast. 'Cancer is a water sign, symbolized by the crab. Ruled by the always-changing moon, the Cancer baby has mood swings as often as the tides change.'

Evelyn. Her name is a jolt from my mother's. *Eileen* – from the Irish for 'bringer of light'.

3

'Enter Ghost'
SHAKESPEARE, *HAMLET*[28]

An email arrives from the Rose. I have been permitted to make a short, socially distanced visit to the site. My heart is beating out of my chest. *This is where my journey will end.* Bankside. My personal ground zero.

I dig out an old photographic print from the chest. The Museum of London, 1990. A posed PR shot behind a table of artefacts dredged from the remains of the playhouse: myself, Simon Hughes MP, Peggy Ashcroft and the archaeologist Harvey Sheldon with his three young children. Sheldon, champion of the Roman road at Old Ford, went on to direct the excavation of the Rose. I am six or seven years old. I stare down the lens, doe-eyed, with Hughes's hand on my right shoulder. I am wearing a plaid shirt and a bomber-jacket-style sweater. Dame Peggy is caught mid-flow, pointing left, out of shot. She would die a year later, aged eighty-three.

'If the land, like the body, can hold a trauma . . . it can also, perhaps, hold a healing.'[29] In her 'geological memoir', the poet Elizabeth-Jane Burnett seeks solace in the soil of Devon, in her late father's fields. I walk to the Rose on the hottest day of the year, charged with this same hope – that things unsaid might now be spoken.

In the late 1980s, before the reconstruction of Shakespeare's Globe and the arrival of Tate Modern in a disused power station, Bankside was an edgeland of decaying industrial sites and empty warehouses. Even when I first started walking the city alone, in the early 2000s, the area still seemed dark, dirty and ignored. For years a derelict building on the west side of Rose Alley was daubed with an enigmatic message; a howl of futile indignation against the bright lights and big money of urban renewal.

CODA

I KNOW I HAVE LOST

Today the graffiti has gone and Imry Merchant's tower block is swathed in protective wrapping like a shoe box in a giant Jiffy bag. Its upper floors have been gutted, a trellis of bare concrete open to the sky. Workmen in hard hats appear on the street then vanish into a mysterious archway. I walk beneath the scaffolding into a cool, dark interior.

'In hot weather, this is the place to be,' says Celia Gilbert, the Rose's site manager, as she opens up. The modest anteroom in which I find myself is part gift shop, part box office and part theatre bar. On performance days, drinks are served in plastic cups from a trestle table. A scale model by architect Nick Helm illustrates the proposed redevelopment of the site, with a new performance space raised on a wooden deck above the re-exhumed remains of the playhouse. Trustee Maurice Hindle arrives wearing a red bandana like an outlaw from an old Western. I am holding a microphone and a set of headphones. 'I thought I would make an audio recording from the space,' I say. 'To focus my mind.'

Celia and Maurice are no fools; they know exactly what (or who) I'm here to listen for. I pass through a curtained doorway and the temperature drops again – it's like entering a void – and now I'm edging across a floorboarded platform towards a black railing and the darkness beyond. I spot the huge steel girders installed above the remains to support the weight of the tower. The ceiling is rigged here and there with thick metal chains; they hang motionless in the dark like meat hooks in an abandoned slaughterhouse. I look down over the railings and across the cavernous basement, where the 'pond', as Jane Sidell called it, ripples gently from some unknown draft. A single shaft of sunlight pierces the gloom; it shimmers on the surface.

I put on my headphones, hold the microphone over the railings and listen. Through thick static comes the steady drip, drip of water as if from a faulty tap, but this is soon submerged beneath the deep booms of

407

building work upstairs, like thunder heard at a distance. If I had hoped for the silence of contemplation, then I have come on the wrong day. A sound like something being dragged, metal on metal, fills my ears; my own breath; a buzz of electrical interference. And then a demonic banging starts, filling the room with noise.

Celia returns and flicks a switch and lines of gaudy red and yellow lights appear in the water, marking the positions of the foundations below – the interior and exterior walls of the playhouse, two iterations of the stage. I see now that the pond is not a regular shape, but instead resembles a natural pool, being contained by undulating banks of scuffed grey concrete. There's even a tiny island in the middle of the shallow water.

'It's a bit like a penguin enclosure,' I note. But really I'm thinking about all the geological anomalies I have encountered on my journeys across the city. I'm thinking of the drift hollows at Limmo and beneath the Rockingham Estate. The shape of the pond even bears an uncanny resemblance to one of the pools marked on Rocque's map near Black Mary's Hole. I'm thinking about the Bermondsey Lake.

What on earth am I doing here, kitted out like a quack investigator from *Most Haunted*? What am I hoping to witness? The crackle of an EVP? The devil Mephistopheles rising from the water like a skull-faced Baron Samedi? Or Dame Peggy on her folding chair, refusing to be moved? Lengths of metal piping are poking out of the ground all over the place like crude antennae. They remind me of the poles left impaled in the Thames foreshore by mudlarks to indicate where they have been digging.

Celia gestures to the far shore. 'The times when I've had to go down there to operate the intruder alarm, being on my own at night here, not for many minutes, just either coming in first or being the last to live—'

She stops.

'To *leave*, I mean. There is a feeling that there could be something here. It has an eerie quality.'

CODA

'I love the lights,' Maurice adds. 'They're suggestive of a skeleton.'

Although I don't say it, they remind *me* of the birthing pool at Tommy's. 'The contemporary Rose,' wrote Barnden, 'stages performances in the time between excavation and restoration: as repetition, as reminder, as attempts to make contact with the other time that lies unresolved under its floor.'[30]

The foundations of the playhouse are safely locked beneath concrete, plastic and sand – I know that – but through the presence of water the space is filled with a sense of immanence. Perhaps, I think to myself, if I could just perform one final ritual. An act of connection, of healing. For Mum. For the Rose. For all the lost and buried places. The water is just there. I could almost reach out and touch it. The deep city. The body incorruptible.

My mother left behind a little red notebook, dated 23 February 1996. I found it at the bottom of the chest, beneath a stack of formal letters from undertakers, stone masons, insurers, etc. – the paperwork of death. 'I am writing this as a journal to you to say all the things I want to say to you,' it begins. The journal runs to just eight short handwritten pages. I will never know why she did not write more, in the ten months she had left. 'This is for you to keep and read when I'm not here to speak to you myself . . .'

I'm alone again, the air thick with static. I close my eyes as if to pray, but no words come. I'm still that thirteen-year-old boy, lost in grief, trying to see ghosts.

Five months of lockdown has taken its toll. By August the chronic back condition that has dogged me for years has become unbearable. One morning I wake to nerve pain so intense it takes me five attempts to get out of bed. My left leg feels like it's about to burst and the only relief is to lie down flat on the floor. I make an emergency appointment with an osteopath and gather the strength to walk to the clinic.

I stumble as far as the bus stop and lie down on my stomach on the narrow plastic seat. 'You've done your back in,' observes a helpful woman waiting for the C10. I pull myself up and make it another hundred yards to the corner of Rotherhithe Street where I collapse again, groaning, on a scrap of lawn. A younger woman comes out of her flat to see if I need help. *Get up*, I say to myself. *Get up, you bastard.* I stagger across the peninsula with pain shooting down my hamstring and into my calf. By the time I cross the old dock entrance, I'm dragging my foot like a brick. It's taken thirty minutes to make a five-minute journey and I'm only halfway there.

I'm lurching down a dappled, gravel footpath through an avenue of woodland when I collapse again. My head is spinning and I'm gasping for air. I lie prone on the grass to let the pain subside, whispering *shit, shit, shit* to the soft, cool floor. A songbird calls from the trees overhead with the falsetto ringtone of a blue tit. I watch an ant negotiate a forest of dried leaves one inch from my face. I smell the sweet aroma of soil, the tannic scent of shredded fag ends.

Maybe, I think, I could just stay here till nightfall.

The sun passes into cloud.

And now the pain begins, slowly, to recede. I lay my hands flat on the earth and I breathe it in deep.

There is no door in the mountain-side. Only this.

This path. This earth. This broken, sacred ground.

Notes

Prologue: Mapping

1   *The Shawshank Redemption*, dir. Frank Darabont (Columbia Pictures, 1994).

I: Sinkhole

1   Ken Worpole and Joe Orton, *The New English Landscape* (Field Station, 2013).

2   The block has been well documented by Paul Talling at www.derelictlondon. com/offices.html.

3   The full planning applications can be viewed at planreg.towerhamlets.gov.uk (ref. PA/10/00336 & PA/11/01571).

4   Interview in *Spitalfields Life*, 23 September 2013, www.spitalfieldslife. com/2010/09/23/tubby-isaacs-jellied-eel-stall-aldgate.

5   *Guerrilla Exploring*, www.guerrillaexploring.com/gesite/public_html/index. php?option=com_content&view=article&id=390:ges250-aldgate-east-disused-station-london.

6   It is probable *A Sack Full of News* was based on the popular jest-book of the same name. See Terhi Rantanen, *When News Was New* (Wiley-Blackwell, 2009) and John Payne Collier, *The History of English Dramatic Poetry to the Time of Shakespeare: and Annals of the Stage to the Restoration* (London, 1831), vol. 3.

7   For a detailed account of the Boar's Head see Wickham, Berry, Ingram (eds), *English Professional Theatre, 1530–1660* (Cambridge University Press, 2000).

8   W. Ron Hess, *The Dark Side of Shakespeare* (iUniverse, 2002).

9   Wickham et al., *English Professional Theatre*.

10 Ibid., p. 468.

11 Herbert Berry & C. Walter Hodges, illus., *The Boar's Head Playhouse* (Folger Shakespeare Library Press, 1986). Berry's two conjectured plays are *A Pleasant Conceited Comedie Wherein is Shewed How a Man May Chuse a Good Wife from a Bad* (1602) and *The History of the Tryall of the Cheualry* (1605). Thomas Heywood was a member of the Worcester's Men and one of six men who stood bond for the company's purchase of Browne's lease in 1601.

12   William Shakespeare, *Hamlet* (1600–1). II.2 and IV.2.

13   Berry, *The Boar's Head*.

14   Geoffrey Chaucer, *Troilus and Criseyde* (Everyman, 1953).

15   Photographs of the panels can be viewed at the website of graphic design agency Thomas Matthews: www.thomasmatthews.com/project/aldgate-subways.

16   Andrew Hough and Hannah Furness, 'London 2012 Olympics: Heavy Rain Leaks into Velodrome and Soaks Marathon', *Telegraph*, 5 August 2012.

17   Caroline M. Barron, 'Chaucer the Poet and Chaucer the Pilgrim' in Rigby and Minnis (eds), *Historians on Chaucer: The 'General Prologue' to The Canterbury Tales* (Oxford University Press, 2014).

18   Geoffrey Chaucer, *Troilus and Criseyde*, Book II, 22–25, *The Riverside Chaucer* (Oxford University Press, 1987).

19   Ibid., Book V, 666 and 730.

II: Return to the Source

1   John Ruskin, 'Herne-Hill Almond Blossoms' in *Præterita: Outlines of Scenes and Thoughts Perhaps Worthy of Memory in My Past Life* (1885–89). The art critic and preeminent Victorian (1819–1900) grew up in a house on Herne Hill and called the area home for most of his life.

2   Eric Mottram, 'Herne's Descent', *The Book of Herne* (Arrowspire Press, 1981).

3   Allen Fisher, *Place* (Reality Street Editions, 2005).

4   Nicholas Barton, *The Lost Rivers of London* (Phoenix House/Leicester University Press, 1962).

5   Quoted in Jon Newman, *River Effra: South London's Secret Spine* (Signal Books, 2016).

6   Ruskin, 'Herne-Hill Almond Blossoms'.

7   Edward Thomas, 'First Known When Lost' in *Selected Poems* (Everyman's Poetry, 1997).

8   Michael Glover, 'Great Works: Lordship Lane Station, Dulwich (1871), Camille Pissarro', *Independent*, 23 July 2010.

9   Dante's *Inferno* (Canto I, line 2): '*mi ritrovai per una selva oscura*'.

10   Alice Oswald, 'Poem', *The Thing in the Gap-Stone Stile* (Oxford Poets, 1996).

11   Barry MacSweeney, 'In The Orchard Twining Daisies with Sheila', *Tears in the Fence*, 28 (Spring 2001).

12   Laura Reynolds, 'The Sad Story of the Hermit of Dulwich', Londonist.com, 13 October 2017.

13   *The Morning Post*, 5 January 1803.

14   @portalsoflondon, Twitter.com, 7 December 2017.

15 @PhilH86835657, Twitter.com, 28 March 2019.

16 There is no evidence to support the story, but it is repeated in Diana Evans's novel *Ordinary People* (Chatto & Windus, 2018), which is set in this part of south London.

17 Martin Knight has provided the most comprehensive analysis of the Ambrook valley on his website: www.martindknight.co.uk/MKsResearch.html.

18 In 2011–12, entomologist Richard 'Bugman' Jones discovered 197 species not formerly recorded in Dulwich and Sydenham Hill Woods, including rare beetles and wasps. 'Sydenham Hill Wood Update', *The Dulwich Society* website, 21 March 2012.

19 Newman, *River Effra*.

20 This story probably originates from a report in *The Times* in May 1818 which describes the discovery of bodies in 'the creek at Kennington', i.e. the mouth of the Effra. See Newman, *River Effra*.

21 J. B. Wilson, *The Story of Norwood* (1973), quoted in Newman, *River Effra*.

III: Liquidity

1 Eliot, *The Four Quartets* (1943).

2 This claim is made in *The Old Straight Track* (1925), which first established Watkins's revolutionary and much-contested theory of 'ley lines'.

3 The etching is by Charles Grignion after an illustration by Samuel Wale and is held by the Wellcome Library, London: wellcomeimages.org/indexplus/image/V0010613.html.

4 'Richard Serra – Talk with Charlie Stone (2001)', YouTube, 21 May 2011: http://www.youtube.com/watch?v=KEvklGKd6uE.

5 Nick Elsden, private correspondence, 2013.

6 Quoted in Sir William Monson, *Megalopsychy: Being a Particular and Exact Account of the Last XVII. Years of Q. Elizabeths Reign, Both Military and Civil* (1682).

7 Ojay, 'London Bridge Sewer', 28DL Urban Exploration: https://www.28dayslater.co.uk/threads/london-bridge-sewer-2014.95628.

8 Steve Duncan, 'London Underground: The Walbrooke Stream/London Bridge Sewer', Undercity: http://undercitywebsite.blogspot.com/2009/03/london-underground-walbrooke.html.

9 Eliot, *The Four Quartets*.

10 Gillian Darley, *John Soane: An Accidental Romantic* (Yale University Press, 1999).

11 Brian Dillon, *Ruin Lust* (Tate Publishing, 2014).

12 *Daily Mail*, 9 July 2009: www.dailymail.co.uk/news/article-1198268/City-party-king-Anjool-Malde-leaps-death-rooftop-restaurant-terrified-lost-job.html.

13 Independent, 12 October 2012: https://www.independent.co.uk/news/uk/home-news/witnesses-tell-horror-seeing-suspected-suicide-rooftop-coq-d-argent-restaurant-8208806.html

14 Julian Hill and Peter Rowsom, *Roman London and the Walbrook Stream Crossing: Excavations at 1 Poultry and Vicinity, City of London* (Museum of London Archaeology, 2011).

15 Kevin Lynch, *The Image of the City* (The MIT Press, 1960).

16 *Daily Mail*, 10 April 2013: http://www.dailymail.co.uk/news/article-2306443/The-Bloomberg-Place-Construction-Site-Archaeological-dig-London-heralded-capitals-important-excavation.html.

17 Penny Jones, 'The Momentum of the High Speed Bull', Datacenter Dynamics, 13 March 2013: archive.datacenterdynamics.com/focus/archive/2013/03/momentum-high-speed-bull.

18 *Liquid City* is the title of a 1999 book by Marc Atkins and Iain Sinclair. The phrase is repeated in Sinclair's 2013 limited edition book *Swimming to Heaven: The Lost Rivers of London*, where I first encountered it.

19 Robert Browning, 'The Pied Piper of Hamelin', *Dramatic Lyrics* (1842).

20 Robert Macfarlane, *Underland* (Hamish Hamilton, 2019).

21 Umberto Eco (trans. William Weaver), *Foucault's Pendulum* (Secker & Warburg, 1989).

IV: Descent

1 Joseph William Bazalgette, 'On the Main Drainage of London, and the Interception of the Sewage from the River Thames' (The Institution of Civil Engineers, 1865).

2 Alexander Pope, *The Dunciad* (1743).

3 Received by email on 16 January 2013.

4 Bazalgette, 'On the Main Drainage of London'.

5 Ibid.

6 The line is taken from a report in the *Daily Telegraph*, 10 October 1859. There is another, more recent urban myth concerning albino pigs that has been propagated by the writer Iain Sinclair.

7 Aaron Angell, 'The Fatberg: An Affluence of Effluence', *ArtReview* (Summer 2018).

8 William Shakespeare, *Richard III* (1633). III.4.

9 St Thomas Aquinas, *Quaestiones Disputatae de Malo* (1267).

10 Museum of London Archaeology Service/Crossrail, *Assessment of Archaeology Impacts: Technical Report*, 2/6 (2005). Investigations in Ely Place have also uncovered a Roman ditch and 'indeterminate Roman cut features'.

11 In *Roman London* (1926) Gordon Home presents the font as the most convincing evidence of any Christian church in Roman London.

12 *A Brief Guide to the Mediaeval Chapel of St. Etheldreda Ely Place*, undated.

13 Style of Samuel Scott, *c.* 1750, *The Thames and the Fleet Canal* (The Royal Collection).

14 Jonathan Swift, 'A Description of a City Shower', *Tatler* (October 1710).

15 Charles Dickens, letter to William de Cerjat, July 1858.

16 John Stow, *A Survey of London* (1598).

17 Father Kit Cunningham, *St Etheldreda's, Ely Place* (Scala Arts and Heritage Publishers, 2013).

18 Canon David Meara, *St Bride's Church* (Jarrold Publishing, 2014).

19 Simon Webb, *Unearthing London: The Ancient World Beneath the Metropolis* (The History Press, 2011).

20 William Hone, *The Every Day Book* (1826), vol. 1.

21 This claim is reported in various places without citation, including by prehistorian Paul Bennett: megalithix.wordpress.com/2018/01/20/st-brides-well/.

22 St Bride Foundation website: stbridefoundation.wordpress.com/2015/03/05/traces-of-the-swimming-pool.

23 Tom Bolton, *London's Lost Rivers: A Walker's Guide* (Strange Attractor Press, 2011).

24 From Baynes's advertisement in the *Post Bag*, quoted in Walter Thornbury, *Old and New London: Volume 2* (Cassell, Petter & Galpin, 1878).

25 Iain Sinclair, *Swimming to Heaven: The Lost Rivers of London* (The Swedenborg Society, 2013).

26 John Rogers, 'Black Mary's Hole', *the lost byway*, 28 March 2006: http://thelostbyway.com/2006/03/black-marys-hole.html.

27 George Clinch, *Marylebone and St. Pancras; their history, celebrities, buildings, and institutions* (London, 1890).

28 William Harrison Ainsworth, *Jack Sheppard* (Galignani and Company, 1840).

29 Neal Stephenson, *The System of the World* (William Morrow, 2004).

30 Bolton, *London's Lost Rivers*.

31 John Bevis, M.D., *An Experimental Enquiry Concerning the Contents, Qualities, Medicinal Virtues of the Two Mineral Waters of Bagnigge Wells, &c.*, (1767/1819). Quoted in *The Gentleman's Magazine* (F. Jefferies, 1813), vol. 83, part 2; vol. 114.

32 *London and its Environs Described* (R. & J. Dodsley, 1761).

33 *Notes & Queries*, series 7, vol. 1 (John C. Francis, 1886).

34   From the *Sloane Catalogue of the British Museum*.

35   Brother Fabian, *Contributions to a History of the Thames* (1886).

36   Francis W. Readers, 'Note on an Arab Water-Bottle' in *Transactions of the London and Middlesex Archaeological Society*, New Series, vol. IV (Bishopsgate Institute, 1922).

37   J. Burnby, 'John Conyers, London's First Archaeologist' in *Transactions of the London and Middlesex Archaeological Society*, 35 (1984).

38   *The Archaeology of Greater London* (Museum of London, 2000).

39   Ainsworth, *Jack Sheppard*.

40   Chesca Potter, 'The River of Wells': insearchofholywellsandhealingsprings.com/source-first-series-contents/the-river-of-wells.

41   Reviews from Tripadvisor.com.

42   Arnold Bennett, *Riceyman Steps* (Cassell and Company, 1923).

43   Jondoe [pseudonym], 'Lost Bagnigge': http://www.sub-urban.com/lost-bagnigge (2010).

44   J. Copywell [William Woty], 'Bagnigge-Wells', *The Shrubs of Parnassus. Consisting of a Variety of Poetical Essays, Moral and Comic* (J. Newbery, 1760).

45   A. W. J. G. Ord-Hume, *Barrel Organ: the Story of the Mechanical Organ and its Repair* (George Allen & Unwin, 1978). Quoted in 'Lost Bagnigge'.

46   Harold Bayley, *Archaic England: An Essay in Deciphering Prehistory from Megalithic Monuments, Earthworks, Customs, Coins, Place-names, and Faerie Superstitions* (Chapman & Hall, 1919).

47   Robert Macfarlane, *Underland* (Hamish Hamilton, 2019).

48   F. G. Berry, 'Late Quaternary Scour-hollows and Related Features in Central London', *Quarterly Journal of Engineering Geology and Hydrogeology* (The Geological Society, 1979), vol. 12.

49   M. G. Sumbler, *British Regional Geology: London and the Thames Valley* (HMSO for the British Geological Survey, 1996).

50   William Shakespeare, *Macbeth*, ed. Sylvan Barnet (Signet Classics, 1963). I.3.

51   Further information on the geology of Hampstead Heath can be found courtesy of UCL's Earth Sciences department: www.ucl.ac.uk/earth-sciences/impact/public-engagement/londons-geology/londons-geology-fieldwork/hampstead-heath/geology-hampstead.

52   Celoria, Scot and Spencer, 'Eighteenth-Century Fieldwork in London and Middlesex: Some Unpublished Drawings by William Stukeley' in *Transactions of the London and Middlesex Archaeological Society*, 22 (1968).

53   David Furlong, 'London's Leys': http://www.davidfurlong.co.uk/leyslond1.htm.

54   Rachael Getzels, 'Killer Crayfish Nip Nude Swimmers in Hampstead Heath Ponds', *Ham & High*, 21 September 2012; Arthur Martin, 'Poles Found

Guilty of Stealing Crayfish from Hampstead Pond ... Where They Have Been Attacking Swimmers', *Daily Mail*, 1 November 2012.

55 Richard Sharkey, *The Tales of the Walrus* (Xlibris, 2013).

56 John Thomas Smith, *Nollekens and his times* (H. Colburn, 1828).

57 Percy Bysshe Shelley, *Adonais: An Elegy on the Death of John Keats* (Charles Ollier, 1821).

V: Floodlands

1 Geoffrey Chaucer, 'Parliament of Foules' in *The Riverside Chaucer*, ed. F. N. Robinson (Oxford University Press, 1988).

2 Daniel Wright, 'Box of Delight', 10 February 2016: thebeautyoftransport.com/2016/02/10/box-of-delight-westminster-underground-station-london-uk.

3 The technical detail here is drawn from Robert Mair and David Harris, 'Innovative Engineering to Control Big Ben's Tilt', *ingenia*, 9 (August 2001).

4 These descriptions are from two nearly contemporary chroniclers and are quoted in David Sullivan, *The Westminster Corridor* (Historical Publications, 1994).

5 In 'Thorney Problem', *Geoscientist Online* (The Geological Society, September 2016), Desmond Donovan argues that the Westminster branches of the Tyburn have been misidentified and are in fact man-made drainage channels.

6 John Morris, *Londinium: London in the Roman Empire* (Weidenfeld & Nicolson, 1982).

7 Sidell, Wilkinson et al., *The Holocene Evolution of the London Thames* (Museum of London Archaeology Service, 2000).

8 Simon Webb, *Unearthing London: The Ancient World Beneath the Metropolis* (The History Press, 2011).

9 Sidell et al., *The Holocene Evolution*.

10 Ibid.

11 Webb, *Unearthing London*.

12 Peter Brook, *The Empty Space* (Atheneum, 1968).

13 Matthew Payne and Warwick Rodwell, 'Edward the Confessor's Shrine in Westminster Abbey: Its Date of Construction Reconsidered', *The Antiquaries Journal*, 97 (The Society of Antiquaries of London, 2017).

14 Matthew M. Reeve (assisted by Bradley J. Fuller), commentary on Plate 1.16 of *Vetusta Monumenta* (The Society of Antiquaries of London, 1724): scalar.missouri.edu/vm/vol1plate16-edward-the-confessor-shrine.

15 Sally Badham, 'Edward the Confessor's Chapel, Westminster Abbey: The Origins of the Royal Mausoleum and Its Cosmatesque Pavement', *The Antiquaries Journal*, 87 (The Society of Antiquaries of London, 2007).

16 Brook, *The Empty Space*.

17 Ibid.

18 John Hollingshead, *Underground London* (Groombridge and Sons, 1862).

19 *100 Years of GOGGS: 1917–2017* (HM Treasury, The History Network, 2017).

20 Ibid.

21 William Hone, *The Table Book* (1827).

22 Hollingshead, *Underground London*.

23 Jodi Picoult, *My Sister's Keeper* (Atria Books, 2004).

24 Gaia Vince, *Adventures in the Anthropocene* (Chatto & Windus, 2004).

25 Robert Macfarlane, *Underland* (Hamish Hamilton, 2019).

26 Tom Chivers, 'Petrus', *Dark Islands* (Test Centre, 2015).

27 Chivers, 'Ecosystem', *Dark Islands*.

28 Ruth Bloomfield, 'Waters Recede But Nightmare Continues for Flood Victims', *Evening Standard*, 31 March 2014.

29 Nathan Bailey, *The Antiquities of London and Westminster. Being an Account of Whatsoever is Ancient, Curious Or Remarkable, as to Palaces, Towers, Castles, Walls, Gates, Bridges, Monasteries* (H. Tracy, 1722).

30 Sidell et al., *The Holocene Evolution*.

31 Caroline Shenton, *The Day Parliament Burned Down* (Oxford University Press, 2012).

32 Ibid.

33 Matthew Smith, 'Did You See These Strange Lights Above Meltham Last Night?', *Huddersfield Daily Examiner*, 1 November 2019.

34 Quoted by Andrew Woodcock, '"You took your time": Boris Johnson Heckled on Visit to Flood-hit Yorkshire', *Independent*, 13 November 2019.

35 'Fishlake Flooding: Fears for Village as More Rain Due', *BBC News*, 11 November 2019.

36 G. M. Hopkins, 'The Windhover' (1877) in *Selected Poetry* (Oxford University Press, 1998).

37 Kathleen Jamie, 'A Lone Enraptured Male: Review of *The Wild Places* by Robert Macfarlane', *London Review of Books*, 6 March 2008.

38 David Sullivan, *The Westminster Corridor* (Historical Publications, 1994); *The Westminster Circle* (Historical Publications, 2006).

39 Sullivan, *The Westminster Corridor*.

40 His obituary, by Piers Plowright, appeared in the *Independent* on 22 August 2015.

41 Sullivan, *The Westminster Corridor*.

42 Sullivan, *The Westminster Circle*.

43 Tom Bolton, *London's Lost Rivers: A Walker's Guide* (Strange Attractor Press, 2011).
44 Sullivan, *The Westminster Circle.*
45 Ibid.
46 Westminster City Archives, 'London's Market Gardens: the Neat Houses', *The Cookbook of Unknown Ladies*, 25 October 2013: lostcookbook.word-press.com/2013/10/25/neat-houses.
47 Peter Whitfield, *London: A Life in Maps* (The British Library, 2006).
48 Councillor Andrew Smith, 'Update to Housing, Finance and Regeneration Policy and Scrutiny Committee', 18 March 2019: westminster.moderngov.co.uk/documents/s31753/5%20-%20CMfHS%20Update.pdf.
49 Henry Angelo, *Angelo's Pic Nic* (John Ebers, 1834). Quoted in Henry Benjamin Wheatley, *London Past and Present* (John Murray, 1891).
50 Sullivan, *The Westminster Corridor.*
51 Sullivan, *The Westminster Circle.*
52 Ibid.
53 Ibid.
54 Clement Walker, *Anarchia Anglicana* (1649).
55 As suggested by Patricia Wright, *The Strange History of Buckingham Palace* (The History Press, 2008).
56 Sullivan, *The Westminster Circle.*
57 Tom Gillespie, *Daily Express*, 18 January 2018.
58 James I, speech to the Star Chamber, 1616. Quoted in Charles Howard McIlwain, *The Political Works of James I* (Harvard University Press, 1918).
59 Sullivan, *The Westminster Corridor.*
60 Jessica Freeman, 'Middlesex in the Fifteenth Century: Community or Communities' in Michael Hicks (ed.), *Revolution and Consumption in Late Medieval England* (Boydell & Brewer, 2001).
61 F. H. W. Sheppard, 'The Acquisition of the Estate' in *Survey of London: Volume 39, the Grosvenor Estate in Mayfair, Part 1 (General History)* (London County Council, 1977, 1–5).
62 W. H. Black, 'Observations on the Recently Discovered Roman Sepulchre at Westminster Abbey' in *Transactions of the London and Middlesex Archaeological Society*, 4 (1875).
63 Iain Sinclair, *Lud Heat* (Albion Village Press, 1975).
64 Sullivan, *The Westminster Corridor.*
65 Ibid.
66 Jessica J. Lee, *Two Trees Make a Forest* (Virago Press, 2019).
67 Denise Riley, *Time Lived, Without Its Flow* (Picador, 2019; first published Capsule Editions, 2012).

68   Ibid.

69   The statue is a copy of *Homeless Jesus* by Timothy Schmalz, first installed at the University of Toronto in 2013.

70   R. S. Thomas, 'The Empty Church' (1978).

71   Sinclair, *Lud Heat*.

72   This is the first line of Louis MacNeice's 'The River in Spate', *Selected Poems* (Faber and Faber, 1988).

73   'The Guardian View on Parliament's Move: Be Bold, Leave London', *Guardian*, 1 February 2018.

VI: Dead River

1   John Gibbens, 'London Bride', *London Bride* (Contraband Books, 2018).

2   Nicholas Barton, *The Lost Rivers of London* (Phoenix House/Leicester University Press, 1962).

3   Tom Bolton, *London's Lost Rivers: A Walker's Guide* (Strange Attractor Press, 2011).

4   diamond geezer, 28 April 2010: diamondgeezer.blogspot.com/2010/04/neckinger-i.html.

5   Michael J. Allen, Rob Scaife, Nigel Cameron and Chris J. Stevens, 'Excavations at 211 Long Lane, Southwark, Part 1: Prehistoric Neckinger-side Environment in Southwark and Its Implication for Prehistoric Communities', *London Archaeologist*, 11 (Winter 2005).

6   Gibbens, *London Bride*.

7   Bolton, *London's Lost Rivers*.

8   The first three plants were identified with Lambeth Marsh by the botanist John Gerard in *The Herbal Or General History of Plants: The Complete 1633 Edition as Revised and Enlarged by Thomas Johnson* (1633; first published 1597); the latter as 'Blue Hairy Heart's-Ease' in Abraham Rees, *The Cyclopaedia; Or, Universal Dictionary of Arts, Sciences and Literature* (Longman, Hurst, 1819), vol. 37.

9   *The Illustrated London News*, 1 July 1848.

10 Fred G. Bell, *Engineering Geology and Construction* (CRC Press, 2004).

11 J. G. Ballard, *Concrete Island* (Jonathan Cape, 1974).

12 Lost Rivers Brewing Company: lostriversbrewery.com.

13 William Blake, *There is No Natural Religion* (1794).

14 Alexander Gilchrist, *Life of William Blake* (Macmillan, 1863).

15 'St George's Fields: Enclosure and Development' in *Survey of London: Volume 25, St George's Fields (The Parishes of St. George the Martyr Southwark and St. Mary Newington)*, ed. Ida Darlington (London, 1955).

16 John Burgoyne, *The Maid of the Oaks* (1774).

17 Robert Dighton, *Labour in Vain – Or, Fatty in Distress* (1783).

18 Gerard, *The Herbal*.

19 William Curtis, *Flora Londinensis, Or, Plates and Descriptions of Such Plants as Grow Wild in the Environs of London* (1777–98).

20 Terry Trainor, *Bedlam. St. Mary of Bethlehem* (2012).

21 William Blake, *Jerusalem: The Emanation of the Giant Albion* (1804–1820). It is unclear if these lines relate specifically to the Bethlem Royal Hospital in Southwark. In 'Lambeth and Bethlehem in Blake's Jerusalem' in *Modern Philology*, vol. 48, no. 3 (1951), David V. Erdman argues for an identification with the Dog and Duck and with the Asylum for the Indigent Blind housed in its building after 1810.

22 Recorded by Richard Horwood in his map of 1799.

23 W. H. Black, 'Observations on the Recently Discovered Roman Sepulchre at Westminster Abbey' in *Transactions of the London and Middlesex Archaeological Society*, 4 (1875).

24 Edward Geoffrey O'Donoghue, *The Story of Bethlehem Hospital from Its Foundation in 1247* (Button & Company, 1915).

25 Robert Seymour's updated edition of John Stow, *A Survey of the Cities of London and Westminster* (1753). See also: John Entick, *A New and Accurate History and Survey of London, Westminster, Southwark, and Places Adjacent* (1766).

26 O'Donoghue, *Bethlehem Hospital*.

27 Confusingly, two other stones by the same name are recorded in Southwark by a court document of 1720: one 'near the wall' of the King's Bench Prison; the other in Long Lane. Richard Gude, *The Practice of the Crown Side of the Court of King's Bench, and the Practice of the Sessions* (Pheney, Sweet et al., 1828).

28 O'Donoghue, *Bethlehem Hospital*.

29 *Geraldine Mary Harmsworth Park Masterplan* (Foster + Partners, 2017).

30 William Shakespeare, *Twelfth Night*, ed. Herschel Baker (Signet Classics, 1965). III.3.

31 Anna-Kaisa Tadayon and Robert Benson, 'St Mary's, Elephant and Castle, London: Geotechnical and Geoenvironmental Interpretative Report' (Card Geotechnics Limited, May 2012).

32 William Maitland, *The History and Survey of London* (1756).

33 John O'Connell, interview with Aphex Twin, *The Face* (October 2001).

34 Laurie Johnson, 'High and Dry at Newington Butts: The Genesis of the Permanent Playhouse' in *Before Shakespeare*, 2 August 2017: beforeshakespeare.

com/2017/08/02/high-and-dry-at-newington-butts-the-genesis-of-the-permanent-playhouse.

35 Bill Halden, *Melody Maker*, 8 March 1958.

36 Justin Berkmann, 'How We Made: Ministry of Sound', *Guardian*, 13 November 2018.

37 Ibid.

38 Bolton, *London's Lost Rivers*. Beyond here the Neckinger appears to have formed a part of the old boundary between the parishes of St George and Newington.

39 From Goldfinger's translations of his collaborator Auguste Perret.

40 Michael John, 'Tearing the City at the Seams # 18 – The Amazingly Dreary Elephant & Castle': doveswillrust.blogspot.com.

41 Michael Hacker, Rob Scaife and Peter Collins, 'The Rockingham Street Anomaly, Southwark: A Geoarchaeological Evaluation' (London Geodiversity Partnership, Preliminary report, April 2019).

42 Christopher Menary, *The Former Duke of Wellington Public House: An Archaeological Evaluation Report* (Museum of London Archaeology Service, 2006).

43 Ibid.

44 Ida Darlington, *Survey of London* (London County Council, 1955), vol. 25.

45 *Joseph Lancaster Nursery Site, London Borough of Southwark, SE1 4EX: An Historic Environment Desk-Based Assessment* (Pre-Construct Archaeology Ltd, June 2017).

46 Charles Booth, *Life and Labour of the People in London* (Macmillan, 1902–1903).

47 Graham Dawson, 'It's Walworth but Where Is It?' in *Surrey Archaeology Society Bulletin*, 343 (November 2000).

48 Ibid.

49 John Gibbens, sleeve notes to *Rockingham Street* by The Children (Touched Phono, 2002).

50 *Breaking Barriers: Community Cohesion, Sport and Organizational Development* (Active Communities Network, 2017).

51 F. G. Berry, 'Late Quaternary Scour-hollows and Related Features in Central London', *Quarterly Journal of Engineering Geology and Hydrogeology* (1979) vol. 12.

52 Hacker et al., 'The Rockingham Street Anomaly'.

53 Ibid.

54 J. N. Hutchinson, 'Possible Late Quaternary Pingo Remnants in Central London', *Nature* (284, 1980).

55   Patrick D. Nunn, 'The Development of the River Thames in Central London during the Flandrian', *Transactions of the Institute of British Geographers*, New Series (1983), vol. 8, no. 2.

56   Ibid.

57   Ibid. Borehole data from Tarn Street supports Nunn's theory: 'The presence of [Holocene] gravels at the base of the sequence suggests this part of the Rockingham anomaly was mostly likely formed by a flowing channel, rather than as a "periglacial sink hole" within the earlier terrace gravels.' Craig Halsey, *Report on Geoarchaeological Monitoring of Boreholes at Tarn Street TAZ 06* (Museum of London Archaeology Service, 2007).

58   Geoarchaeologist Mary Ruddy believes the Rockingham Anomaly to be 'probably a small pingo that is peat filled due to compaction/subsidence. So, although it may have formed and largely infilled during the last cold stage (the Devensian) the Holocene sediments (probably Neolithic and Bronze Age peats) formed on top have slumped/caved in on the subsiding, softer sediments in the hollow'. Private correspondence, 2012.

59   Hacker et al., 'The Rockingham Street Anomaly'.

60   Diana Clements, 'Exhibition Report: Core Sample Temporary Exposure', *Magazine of the Geologists' Association* (2019), vol. 18, no. 1.

61   Hacker et al., 'The Rockingham Street Anomaly'.

62   Ibid.

63   Bernardine Evaristo, 'AD50' (2001). Poem displayed above Harper Road Woman at the Museum of London.

64   John Chaple, 'London's Missing Roman Road', *Britain's Hidden History*: www.johnchaple.co.uk/watling.html.

65   John Nichols, *Bibliotheca Topographica Britannica* (1780–90).

66   Darlington, *Survey of London*.

67   Morris proposed that Plautius constructed an 'engineered and metalled road' from 'Westminster to the Medway bridgehead on an alignment of 103½° (13½°)'. John Morris, *Londinium: London in the Roman Empire* (Weidenfeld & Nicolson, 1982).

68   J. M. Dent (ed.), *Sir Gawain and the Green Knight, Pearl, Cleanness, Patience* (Everyman, 1976).

69   Martin Dean and Michael Hammerson, 'Three Inhumation Burials from Southwark', *London Archaeologist* (1980), vol. 4, no. 1.

70   Redfern, Marshall, Eaton and Poinar, '"Written in Bone": New Discoveries about the Lives and Burials of Four Roman Londoners', *Britannia*, 48 (2017).

71   J. G. Ballard, *The Crystal World* (Jonathan Cape, 1966).

72   Charlotte Higgins, 'Seizure, Glistening Cave of Copper-sulphate Crystals, Moves to Yorkshire', *Guardian*, 13 June 2013.

73   Judy Aitken, 'They Came, They Saw, They Conquered', *The Elephant Magazine*, 12 (Winter 2018).

74   Redfern, Gröcke, Millard, Ridgeway, Johnson and Hefner, 'Going South of the River: A Multidisciplinary Analysis of Ancestry, Mobility and Diet in a Population from Roman Southwark, London', *Journal of Archaeological Science*, 74 (2016).

75   Redfern et al., ' "Written in Bone" '.

76   Jonathan Cotton, 'Harper Road, Southwark: An Early Roman Burial Revisited' in Clark, Cotton, Hall, Sherris and Swain (eds), *Londinium and Beyond: Essays on Roman London and Its Hinterland for Harvey Sheldon* (Council for British Archaeology, 2008).

77   Ibid.

78   Higgins, 'Seizure'.

79   *Studio Visit: Roger Hiorns*, video interview with Stephanie Gervais for Christie's website: www.christies.com/features/Goldsmiths_Roger_Hiorns-5605-3.aspx.

80   Redfern et al., ' "Written in Bone" '.

81   Ibid.

82   Ibid.

83   Ballard, *The Crystal World*.

84   Allen Fisher, *PLACE* (Reality Street Editions, 2005).

85   'Ancient Stone Bridge Discovered in Kent Street', *The Illustrated London News*, 29 January 1848. The Lock Bridge is sometimes confused with the bridge near St Thomas-a-Watering, where the Old Kent Road was crossed by a stream from the south (the Earl's Sluice).

86   Bolton, *London's Lost Rivers*.

87   Robert Cowie and Jane Corcoran, 'The Prehistoric, Roman and Later Landscape Between Watling Street and Bermondsey Eyot: Investigations at Rephidim Street and Hartley's Jam Factory, Bermondsey', *Surrey Archaeological Collections*, 94 (2008).

88   Samuel Beckett, *Happy Days* (Grove Press, 1961).

89   Paul Muldoon in Dennis O'Driscoll (ed.), *The Bloodaxe Book of Poetry Quotations* (Bloodaxe Books, 2006).

90   Richard Newcourt and William Faithorne, *An Exact Delineation of the Cities of London and Westminster and the Suburbs Thereof* (1658).

91   Henry Mayhew, 'A Visit to the Cholera Districts of Bermondsey' in *The Morning Chronicle*, 24 September 1849.

92   Charles Dickens, *Oliver Twist* (1837–38).

93 Mayhew, 'A Visit'.

94 Amanda J. Thomas, *Cholera: The Victorian Plague* (Pen and Sword, 2015).

95 Dickens, *Oliver Twist*.

96 William Rendle and Philip Norman, *The Inns of Old Southwark and Their Associations* (Longmans Green, 1888).

97 Charles Dickens, Letter to Angela Burdett Coutts, 7 January 1853, in Jenny Hartley (ed.), *The Selected Letters of Charles Dickens* (Oxford University Press, 2012).

98 Ibid.

VII: Beating the Bounds

1 Samuel Pepys, Monday, 13 June 1664, *The Diary of Samuel Pepys* (https://www.pepysdiary.com/diary/1664/06/13/).

2 Roma Agrawal, *Built* (Bloomsbury, 2018).

3 T. S. Eliot, *The Waste Land* (Boni & Liveright, 1922).

4 Abi Palmer, *Sanatorium* (Penned in the Margins, 2020).

5 Noëmi Lakmaier, *One Morning in May*: www.noemilakmaier.co.uk/html/omim.html.

6 William Langland, *Piers Plowman: A New Annotated Edition of the C-text*, ed. Derek Pearsall (Liverpool University Press, 2008).

7 A pre-Roman timber and brushwood trackway was discovered beneath Long Lane in the 1990s. Howe, Jackson, Maloney and Saich, 'Archaeology in Surrey 1997–9', *Surrey Archaeological Collections*, 87 (2000).

8 Cowan, Seeley, Wardle, Westman and Wheeler, *Roman Southwark Settlement and Economy* (Museum of London Archaeology, 2009).

9 Ibid.

10 Debra Gosling, *Bermondsey & Rotherhithe Through Time* (Amberley Publishing, 2012).

11 Simon Ings, *Dead Water* (Atlantic Books, 2011).

12 Gosling, *Bermondsey & Rotherhithe*.

13 Edward Walford, 'Bermondsey: The Abbey' in *Old and New London: Volume 6* (1878).

14 John Lockie, *Lockie's Topography of London* (1810).

15 Walter Besant, *London, South of the Thames* (A & C Black, 1912).

16 *List of the Lands of Dissolved Religious Houses* (Kraus Reprint Corporation, 1964), vol. 4: Surrey–Isle of Man.

17 A. D. Mills, *A Dictionary of London Place-Names* (Oxford University Press, 2001).

18 Andrew Knapp and William Baldwin, *The Newgate Calendar* (J. Robins & Co., 1825), vol. 2.

NOTES

19   Richard Stanton, *A Menology of England and Wales, Or, Brief Memorials of the Ancient British and English Saints Arranged According to the Calendar, Together with the Martyrs of the 16th and 17th Centuries* (Burns & Oates, 1892).

20   *The Football Factory*, dir. Nick Love (Momentum Pictures, 2004).

21   Garry Robson, *'No One Likes Us, We Don't Care': The Myth and Reality of Millwall Fandom* (Berg Publishers, 2000).

22   Bill Reid (Director, Thorburn) in 'Building Study: Millwall Sets Safety as Its Goal', *The Architects' Journal* (September 1993).

23   Christopher Thomas and D. J. Rackham, 'Bramcote Green, Bermondsey: a Bronze Age Trackway and Palaeo-environmental Sequence', *Proceedings of the Prehistoric Society*, 62 (1996).

24   Jane Sidell, Jonathan Cotton, Louise Rayner and Lucy Wheeler, *The Prehistory and Topography of Southwark and Lambeth* (MoLAS, 2002).

25   Manca Petric, 'Archaeological Desk Based Assessment: Land at 62 Hatcham Road and 134–140 Ilderton Road' (February 2018).

26   Ibid.

27   Ibid.

28   Ibid.

29   Evelyn Johnsen, 'A Question of Reburial', MA thesis (NTNU Trondheim, 2009).

30   Sidell et al., *The Prehistory and Topography of Southwark and Lambeth*.

31   Southwark Council, Minutes of London Gypsy and Traveller Forum, 13 October 2016.

32   Southwark Council, Minutes of Bermondsey and Rotherhithe Community Council, 29 April 2013.

33   Elizabeth-Jane Burnett, *The Grassling* (Allen Lane, 2019).

34   Peter Ackroyd, *Thames: Sacred River* (Random House, 2008).

35   Tom Bolton, *London's Lost Rivers: A Walker's Guide* (Strange Attractor Press, 2011).

36   *Shaun of the Dead*, dir. Edgar Wright (Universal Pictures, 2004).

37   'Jam Tomorrow! Some history and notes on the regeneration and gentrification of North Southwark & Bermondsey: Part One: 1900–1987', *Southwark Notes*: southwarknotes.wordpress.com/archive-resources/southwark-1900-1987.

38   *Construction News*, 8 December 1994.

39   *Thames News*, 14 August 1983.

40   HC Debate (11 June 1986), vol. 99, col. 456.

41   *Nil by Mouth*, dir. Gary Oldman (20th Century Fox, 1997).

42 Gary Oldman, interviewed in Stephen Lowenstein (ed.), *My First Movie* (Faber and Faber, 2000).

43 Weyman Bennett, 'Real lives', *Socialist Review* (October 1997).

44 Morrissey, *Autobiography* (Penguin, 2013).

45 Morrissey, Letter to Lindsay Hutton, quoted in Tony Fletcher, *A Light That Never Goes Out: The Enduring Saga of the Smiths* (Random House, 2013).

VIII: Olympic City

1 Iain Sinclair, *Ghost Milk: Calling Time on the Grand Project* (Hamish Hamilton, 2012).

2 Diana Clements, 'The Geology of London', *GEO ExPro* (2012), vol. 9, no. 3.

3 Siddhartha Bose, *Kalagora* (2010), dir. Russell Bender. Unpublished script.

4 Sinclair, *Ghost Milk*.

5 Ibid.

6 Ibid.

7 Ibid.

8 Ibid.

9 The present information is drawn from 'The Olympic Park – Soil Cleaning', a video produced by NBS TV/RIBA (2011).

10 Andrew Anthony, ' "It's soulless here": Why West Ham Fans Are in Revolt', *Observer*, 29 April 2018.

11 Sinclair, *Ghost Milk*.

12 Margaret Gelling, *Place-Names in the Landscape* (Phoenix Press, 1984).

13 Heather Knight, 'Green Dragon Yard, Old Montague Street, London EC1, London Borough of Tower Hamlets. An Archaeological Evaluation' (MOLA, 1999).

14 Harvey Sheldon, 'Excavations at Lefevre Road, Old Road', *Transactions of the London and Middlesex Archaeological Society* (1970), vol. 23, no. 1.

15 Harvey Sheldon, interview with Becky Wallower, 'Roman Road in a Railway Cutting', *London Archaeologist* (Summer 2007).

16 Johanna Vuolteenaho with Ian Betts, Alan Pipe and Beth Richardson, 'New Evidence for the London–Colchester Roman Road and Adjacent Settlement at Bow/Old Ford', *London Archaeologist* (Spring 2010).

17 Reginald A. Smith, 'A New View of Roman London', *Journal of the Royal Society of the Arts* (1910), vol. 59, no. 3030. Ivan Margery, *Roman Roads in Britain* (Phoenix House, 1955).

18 Vassil Girginov, *Handbook of the London 2012 Olympic and Paralympic Games: Volume One: Making the Games* (Routledge, 2013).

19 James D. Hunt, *Gandhi in London* (Promilla, 1978).

20   James Edward Albone, 'Roman Roads in the Changing Landscape of Eastern England *c.* AD 410–1850', unpublished PhD thesis (University of East
Anglia, 2016).

21   Iain Sinclair, *Swimming to Heaven: The Lost Rivers of London* (The Swedenborg Society, 2013).

22   William Shakespeare, *The Tempest*, ed. M. M. Mahood (Penguin, 1968). III.2.

23   William Blake, preface to *Milton: A Poem in Two Books* (1804–11).

24   Sinclair, *Ghost Milk*.

25   Patrick Kingsley, 'The Dystopian Olympic Opening Ceremony that Britain
Deserves', *Guardian*, 13 June 2012.

26   Kenneth Grahame, *The Wind in the Willows* (Methuen, 1908).

27   Ramzy Alwakeel, 'River Lea Oil Spill: Boats Stopped Between Tottenham
and Hackney Wick to Contain Pollution Outbreak One Week On', *Hackney
Gazette*, 20 February 2018.

28   Grahame, *The Wind in the Willows*.

29   Waterkeeper Alliance: https://waterkeeper.org/who-we-are.

30   T. S. Eliot, *The Waste Land* (Boni & Liveright, 1922).

31   Sinclair, *Swimming to Heaven*.

32   Elizabeth-Jane Burnett, *The Grassling* (Allen Lane, 2019).

33   Sinclair, *Ghost Milk*.

34   Gloria Sellers, Tony Hutchings and Andy Moffat, 'Learning from Experience: Creating Sustainable Urban Greenspaces from Brownfield Sites', *WIT
Transactions on Ecology and the Environment*, 94 (2006).

35   Tom Chivers, *Dark Islands* (Test Centre, 2015).

36   Naama Arad, *EL AL* (2012). Midrasha Gallery of Art, Tel Aviv.

37   Ballymore Group, *London City Island*: www.londoncityisland.com.

38   'Leamouth Road and Orchard Place: Historical development' in Hermione
Hobhouse (ed.), *Survey of London: Volumes 43 and 44, Poplar, Blackwall and
Isle of Dogs* (London County Council, 1994).

39   Gelling, *Place-Names in the Landscape*.

40   Ibid.

41   *The Annual Register, Or, A View of the History, Politics, and Literature of the
Year 1830* (1831).

42   Emilio Linde-Arias, David Harris and Richard Ghail, 'Engineering Geology
and Tunnelling in the Limmo Peninsula, East London', *Quarterly Journal of
Engineering Geology and Hydrogeology* (2018), vol. 51, no. 1.

43   Ibid.

44   Linde-Arias et al., 'Engineering Geology and Tunnelling in the Limmo
Peninsula'.

45   R. C. Ghail, P. J. Mason and J. A. Skipper, 'The Geological Context and Evidence for Incipient Inversion of the London Basin', *Proceedings of the XVI European Conference on Soil Mechanics and Geotechnical Engineering* (2015). See also: Jennifer Scoular, Richard Ghail et al., 'Retrospective InSAR Analysis of East London During the Construction of the Lee Tunnel', *Remote Sensing* (2015).

46   Ballymore Group, 'Goodluck Hope: London's Lost Village', YouTube, 29 June 2017: www.youtube.com/watch?v=JcgYdCA5jRc.

47   'Leamouth Road and Orchard Place: Historical Development'.

48   Ballymore Group, 'Storytelling and Emotional Excitement is a Key Part of the Marketing Process': www.ballymoregroup.com/feature/storytelling-and-emotional-excitement-is-a-key-part-of-the-marketing-proces.

49   Ballymore Group, 'East London – the Land of Vast Opportunities': www.ballymoregroup.com/feature/londons-pioneering-spirit-moves-east.

50   David Hencke, 'Zombie Neighbourhoods: London's Disappearing Voters', *Byline Times*, 5 December 2019.

51   Aluna: www.alunatime.org.

52   Great Big Story, 'A Symphony to Last a Thousand Years', YouTube, 18 June 2017.

53   Sarah Foot, 'The Making of Angelcynn: English Identity before the Norman Conquest', *Transactions of the Royal Historical Society* (1996), vol. 6.

54   John Morris, *Londinium: London in the Roman Empire* (Weidenfeld & Nicolson, 1982).

55   In the twelfth century William Fitzstephen wrote: '*Sunt etiam circa Londoniam ab aquilone sub urbani fontes praecipui, aqua dulci, salubri, perspicua, et per claros rivo trepidante lapillus*' ('There are also round about London in the Suburbs most excellent wells, whose waters are sweet, wholesome and clear, and whose streams ripple amid bright pebbles'). William Fitzstephen, *Descriptio nobilissimi civitatis Londoniae*, ed. James C. Robertson, *Materials for the History of Thomas Becket, Archbishop of Canterbury*, 7 vols. (*Rerum Britannicarum medii aevi scriptores*, 67, 1877).

56   Robert Macfarlane, *Underland* (Hamish Hamilton, 2019).

57   Peter Ackroyd, *London: The Biography* (Chatto & Windus, 2000).

58   Martin Waddell and Barbara Firth, *Can't You Sleep, Little Bear?* (Walker Books, 2013).

59   Abi Grogan, 'Architects Vie to Regenerate London's Forgotten Spaces', *Engineering & Technology*, 9 October 2013.

60   Oliver Wainwright, 'The "Mega-mosque" and the "Mega-church": The Battle Over London's Sacred Sites', *Guardian*, 29 October 2015.

61 Jaya Narain, 'Historic Railway Arch Destroyed by 60s Planners to Be Rebuilt After Remains Were Found Dumped in River', *Mail Online*, 24 September 2009.

62 EustonArch, 'Euston Arch: Dan Cruickshank Finds Piece in the River Lea', YouTube, 13 April 2008.

63 Thames Tideway/Tunnel Thames Water Utilities Limited, Application for Development Consent (Ref. WWO10001), 'Environmental Statement, Volume 25: Abbey Mills Pumping Station Appendices' (January 2013).

64 Mark Twain, *The Adventures of Huckleberry Finn* (Chatto & Windus, 1885).

65 Brian Dillon, *Ruin Lust* (Tate Publishing, 2014).

66 Ian Tokelove, 'Channelsea Island, a Former Chemical Works Reclaimed by Nature', *Remote London*, 10 June 2020.

67 Wainwright, 'The "Mega-mosque" and the "Mega-church"'.

68 Madeleine Gray, 'The Cross of Destiny', 21 March 2015: https://www.heritagetortoise.co.uk/tag/croes-naid/.

69 Umberto Eco (trans. William Weaver), *The Name of the Rose* (Harcourt, 1980).

70 Joanna Marie Royle, 'Transitional Holiness in the Twelfth Century: The Social and Spiritual Identity of Domina Christina of Markyate', PhD thesis submitted to the University of Glasgow (June 2008).

71 Derrick Herbert, *The Twelfth Odyssey: Book 1: Coda* (2016).

72 John Morris, *Londinium: London in the Roman Empire* (Weidenfeld & Nicolson, 1982).

73 Thames Tideway, 'Environmental Statement'.

74 'Cost of Abbey Mills Pumping Station', *The Builder*, 26 September 1868.

Coda: A Rose by Any Other Name

1 William Shakespeare, *Romeo and Juliet*, ed. Joseph Bryant (Signet Classics, 1964). II.2.

2 Al Joshua, 'Terra Firma' (recorded by Orphans & Vandals), *I Am Alive and You Are Dead* (Ambiguous Records, 2009).

3 Carly Hilts, 'Elizabethan Fringe Theatre', *Current Archaeology*, 359 (January 2020).

4 Chris McCabe, 'The Revenger's Tragedy', *Speculatrix* (Penned in the Margins, 2014).

5 Richard Miller, 'Save the Rose – (Short Version) a Documentary about the Rose Playhouse – Bankside, London', YouTube, 16 May 2014.

6 Christine Eccles, *The Rose Theatre* (Nick Hern Books, 1990).

7 Ibid.

8 Ibid.

9 Richard Brinsley Sheridan, *The Rivals* (1775), ed. Elizabeth Duthie (A & C Black, 1990). Epilogue.

10 William Shakespeare, *A Midsummer Night's Dream*, ed. J. H. Walter (Heinemann, 1964). III.1.

11 Writing in the Alleyn's School magazine and quoted in Eccles, *The Rose Theatre*.

12 Eccles, *The Rose Theatre*.

13 Ibid.

14 Ibid.

15 Ibid.

16 Ibid.

17 Sally Barnden, 'Site-Specificity, Archaeology, and the Empty Space at the Contemporary Rose Playhouse' in *Shakespeare Bulletin* (2017), vol. 35, no. 2.

18 Philip Henslowe, *Henslowe's Diary*, ed. R. T. Rickert (Cambridge University Press, 2002).

19 Quoted in Nigel Wheale, *Writing and Society: Literacy, Print and Politics in Britain 1590–1660* (Routledge, 2005).

20 Eccles, *The Rose Theatre*. The apocryphal story seems to derive from an account of a visit to Dulwich College by the antiquarian John Aubrey in 1673.

21 Thomas Middleton, *The Black Book* (1604).

22 Rickert (ed.), *Henslowe's Diary*.

23 M. G. Sumbler, *British Regional Geology: London and the Thames Valley* (HMSO for the British Geological Survey, 1996).

24 Umberto Eco (trans. William Weaver), *The Island of the Day Before* (Secker & Warburg, 1995).

25 The Rose Playhouse: www.roseplayhouse.org.uk/discover/future-plans.

26 A. M. Sellar (trans.), *Bede's Ecclesiastical History of England* (George Bell & Sons, 1907).

27 Sharon M. Rowley, *The Old English Version of Bede's Historia Ecclesiastica* (D. S. Brewer, 2011).

28 William Shakespeare, *Hamlet*, ed. Edward Hubler (Signet Classics, 1964). I.1.

29 Elizabeth-Jane Burnett, *The Grassling* (Allen Lane, 2019).

30 Barnden, 'Site-Specificity'.

Thanks

To David Buckland at Cape Farewell, who commissioned *Adrift*, from which the idea of this book first emerged. To his colleagues Mary Paterson and Patrick Holden for facilitating the project. To Kira Milmo at Bishopsgate Institute and Bea Colley and Erica Jarnes at Southbank Centre for supporting my walking performances along the 'lost' rivers Walbrook and Neckinger.

To all those with whom I walked, talked and corresponded during the writing of *London Clay*: Tom Bolton, Siddhartha Bose, Father Tom Deidun, Rachel Dowse, Nick Elsden, Colin Fenn, Celia Gilbert, Maurice Hindle, Hannah Hood, Sophie Jackson, Leafcutter John, Heather Knight, Chris Larkin, Nick Murray, John Odell, Abi Palmer, Natasha Powers, Oli Rahman, Mark Read, Julia Rowntree, Mary Ruddy, Harvey Sheldon, Jane Sidell, Rob Smith and Theo Thomas.

To Sharon Ament and Natasha Carlish for encouraging me to keep going when I had lost all hope.

To Chris Gribble and Peggy Hughes at the National Centre for Writing in Norwich for supporting my work.

To Chris McCabe, poet and friend.

To Sophie Scard at United Agents, for giving me a second chance and for having the right words at the right moments.

To Susanna Wadeson at Transworld, for taking a risk and changing my life. For falling into the same river twice.

To Sharika Teelwah for her incisive editorial eye, her care and friendly encouragement.

To Bella Bosworth for the rigour of her copy-edit. To Kate Samano, Josh Benn and Becky Wright for vigorously checking and re-checking the typescript. To Irene Martinez and John Walson for designing such a striking cover. To Clare Varney at Lovell Johns for her detailed cartography; Rohan Daniel Eason for his remarkable illustrations; and Phil Lord for supervising it all. To Tabitha Pelly, Ruth Richardson and their teams for getting the word out.

To Larry Finlay, Katrina Whone and everyone else at Transworld/ Doubleday for welcoming me and supporting this book.

To my colleagues and authors, for letting me skive off work to write this.

To my family, every one of you, for checking in, for helping out, for keeping me sane. And, especially, to Angela Dustagheer (Nani) for providing a seemingly endless supply of free childcare.

To Matt Glithero, for fixing my back.

To my father, Chris Chivers, for believing in me.

To my wife, Sarah Dustagheer, for everything else and more than I could ask.

To my girls, Martha and Evelyn. Look: Daddy's written a book.

Index

Abbey Creek 389
Abbey Lane 392
Abbey Mills 298, 386
Abbey Mills Pumping Station 352, 392
Abbey Street 287
Abbots Manor Estate 216, 217
Acton 298
Agas map 92, 153
Aldersgate 94
Aldgate 8–42, 88, 94, 110, 125, 253, 263, 337, 349, 350, 394
Alfred the Great 368, 380
All Hallows-on-the-Wall 87, 103
Alleyn, Edward 'Ned' 25, 26, 49, 397, 401
Alleyn's School 25–6, 48, 398, 402
Altab Ali Park 25, 38
Amandinus, Valerius 188–9
Ambrook 43, 53, 62–4, 66–70, 72, 73, 140, 170, 297, 405
Anglo-Saxons 57, 95, 143, 148–9, 166, 189, 190, 194, 211, 212, 226, 271, 286, 368
Anthropocene epoch 203, 204, 358, 381, 389
Antonius Pius, Emperor 204
Aphex Twin 263
Appold Street 95
Aquinas, Thomas 144
Arbery Road 349
Arnold Circus 84, 86
Arsenal FC 321
Arthur, King 117

Auckland Hill 76
Avery Farm Row 218
Avondale Square 314
Aylesford Street 214

Bacon Grove 309
Bagnigge House 155, 158
Bagnigge Wells 148, 158–9, 160, 250, 251, 374
Bagshot Formation 164
Balfron Tower 357
Bank of England 105, 106, 108, 109, 110
Bankside 89, 271, 396, 405, 406
Barbican 85, 100
Barge House Stairs 236
Barry, Charles 186
Bath Terrace 270, 277
Battersea Power Station 218
Bayeux Tapestry 190
Bazalgette, Joseph 52, 102, 120, 133, 147, 180, 206, 298, 352, 362, 392
Beatson Walk 299
Beckton 137, 147, 352, 369, 391
Bede 404–5
Belgravia 210, 211, 219, 220, 221
Bellamy's Wharf 296
Bentham, Jeremy 84, 213
Bermondsey 4, 106, 125, 265, 287, 293, 296–8, 300–15, 317, 320, 321, 323, 332, 359, 387
Bermondsey Abbey 287, 288, 298, 305–6, 307, 313, 389

Bermondsey Improvement 291
Bermondsey Lake 315, 323–5, 326,
    328, 331, 408
Bermondsey Square 306
Bermondsey Street 305
Besant, Walter 312
Bethlehem Hospital 100, 252, 253,
    254, 258
Bethnal Green 13
Beulah Hill 52
Big Ben 181, 184, 185, 199,
    349, 404
Big Brother 386–7
Bishop of Ely's Palace 142
Bishopsgate 13, 25, 90,
    94, 100
Black Ditch of Limehouse 51
Black Lives Matter 339, 343
Black Madonna 156, 159
Black Mary's Hole/Well 155–7, 159,
    160, 162, 273, 374, 408
Blackfriars 147, 240
Blackfriars Bridge 157
Blackwall 375
Blake, William 60, 212, 246, 247–8,
    252, 356
Blitz, the 19, 200, 205, 321
Blomfield Street 100
Boar's Head playhouse 22–6, 41, 42,
    89, 394, 395, 396
Bolina Road 322
Bonamy Estate 329–32
Booth, Charles 271
Borough station 275, 286
Boudicca 101, 166, 167, 280
Boudicca's Mound 166
Boundary Estate 84, 85
Bow Back Rivers 342, 347,
    361, 367

Bow Bridge 348
Bow Creek 368–71, 373, 375,
    378, 381
Bow Creek Ecology Park 369–70
Bow Locks 384
Boyn Hill Gravel 47
Bramcote Grove 323, 324, 326, 329
Brent, River 52, 164
Brentford 226, 351
breweries 119
Brexit 184–5, 186, 206, 213, 239, 241,
    268, 322, 336, 366
Brick Lane 37
bricks, yellow stock 5, 13, 63
Bride Lane 149
Bridewell 89, 148, 149
Bridget, St 148, 150
British Geological Survey 4, 159
Brixton 46, 47, 52, 56, 258, 276
Brixton Prison 47
Brixton Road 53, 276
Brixton Water Lane 52
Broad Street 94
Broadgate Circle 96
Broadgate Exchange 95
Broadgate Tower 90, 91, 94, 109
Broadwall/Broad Wall 237
Broadway 352
Brockwell Park 47, 49, 53
Bromley-by-Bow gasworks 384
Bronze Age 16, 97, 166, 189, 323, 324,
    347, 350
Brook, Peter 192, 195, 196
Brook Drive 254, 258, 259, 261
Browne, Robert 24, 25, 26
Brunel, Isambard Kingdom 28,
    356, 373
Brunel, Marc 373
Brutus 117

Buckingham Palace 202, 220, 221,
    222, 225
Buckingham Palace Road 222
Bucklersbury 112, 115, 116
Bulinga Street 212
Bulunga Fen 212, 272
Burbage, James 89
Burbage Road 47
Burgh House (Hampstead) 210–11
Byron, George Gordon,
    Lord 64, 174

Cabinet War Rooms 200
Caesar, Julius 277
Calthorpe Street 159, 160
Camberwell 17, 46, 312
Camberwell Old Cemetery 272
Camden 157
Camlet Street 84
Canary Wharf 2, 165, 183,
    296, 371
Canary Wharf Pier 379
Canning Town 369, 371, 384
Cannon Street 101, 114, 117,
    118, 254
Cape Farewell 86
Carlisle Lane 246
Catherine of Aragon 142, 391
Catherine of Braganza 342
Catlin Street 312, 315
Catuvellauni 277
Cephas Street 349
Chalybeate Well 174
Chambers Wharf 297
Channelsea Island 388–90, 391
Channelsea River 384, 385, 387, 388,
    389, 391
Charing Cross 46
Charles II, King 342

Charlotte Road 88
Charterhouse 147
Charterhouse Street 146
Chaucer, Geoffrey 27, 31–5, 182, 286,
    313, 314, 394
Cheapside 110
Chelsea FC 319
Cherry Garden Pier 296
Cherry Garden Street 300
Chick Lane 153
Christina Street 91
Church of the Immaculate
    Conception (Farm Street)
    229–30
Churchill, Winston 200
City Island 371–3, 376, 377
City of London 29, 31, 90, 255
City Mill River 347
City Road 86
Clapham 17, 186, 258
Clapton 5
Clarkes well 147
Claygate Member 56, 164, 170
Claylands Lane 53
Cleaver Square 53
Clerkenwell 34, 147, 150, 153,
    154, 155
Clerkenwell Catacombs 153
Clerkenwell Road 153
Clerk's Well 152, 153
climate crisis 203
Cloak Lane 117–18
Cnut 190, 259–60, 380
Cold Blow Lane 328
Coldbath Fields 154
Coldbath Square 154
Colebert Avenue 349
College Green 191
College Hill 118

Combined Sewer Overflow 361, 391
Commercial Street 19
Copthall Street 103, 104
Corbett's Lane 313
Cornhill 13, 106, 117
Coronet Theatre 265, 266, 282
Council of British Druid Orders 166
County Street 266
Courtauld Institute of Art 58
Cousin Lane 119, 122
Covid-19 pandemic 298–9, 302–3, 308–9, 317, 336, 338–9, 383, 400–1, 409
Cox's Walk 58, 59, 69
Crescent Wood 68
Crescent Wood Road 64
Crescent Wood Tunnel 65, 66
Cricklewood 3, 167
Cringle Dock 180
Cripplegate 94
Cromwell, Thomas 103
Crosser Street 248
Crossness 52
Crossrail 97, 100–1, 374, 375
Croxted Road 53, 59, 72
Crystal Palace 57, 58, 65, 66, 164
Crystal Palace FC 57, 214, 320, 321
Crystal Palace Park 79
Crystal Palace and South London Junction Railway 58, 65
Crystal Palace transmitter 165
Curtain playhouse 89, 396
Curtain Road 87, 88, 89, 90, 91, 100

Dalston 87
Danelaw 368, 372

de Mandeville, Geoffrey 211
Dean's Yard 193
Dee, John 117
Dekker, Thomas 353
Delaford Road 330
Den, The 319–23, 328, 347
Deptford 56, 276, 312, 313, 328
Deptford Creek 274
Devil's Highway 227
Dewy Pond 66–7, 69
Dickens, Charles 146–7, 290–1
Dickens Fields 277, 282
District Railway 17, 183
Docklands Light Railway 369, 373
Domesday Book 211, 383
Doulton family 75
Dowgate Hill 117
drift hollows 160, 161, 308, 374
Druid Street 288
Druids 166, 189, 190
Dulwich 46, 52, 59, 62, 69, 72
Dulwich & Sydenham Hill Golf Club 69–70
Dulwich College 25, 59, 62, 68, 373
Dulwich Hospital 46
Dulwich Road 47, 51
Dulwich Wood 54, 60, 64
Dunstan, Archbishop of Canterbury 188, 306
Durward Street 349
Dylan Ap Thuin 166

Eagle Wharf 214
Ealdgate 29–35
Ealing 164
Earl's Sluice 287, 313, 314–15, 318, 325–6, 330
Earth-mothers 172

East India Company 342–3, 366, 372, 375, 385
East India Dock 369, 375
East London Mosque 37, 349
Eastern Cluster 90, 126
Eastway 346
Ebury 210, 218
Ebury Bridge 210, 217
Ebury Square 210, 218–19
Ebury Street 210, 220, 221, 222–3, 225
Eddowes, Catherine 18
Edgar, King 188
Edgware Road 227
Edward the Confessor 190–1, 194, 195–6, 204, 211
Edward I, King 389
Edward III, King 186
Edwin, King of Northumbria 404
Effra, River 4, 49, 50–3, 61, 69, 72, 73, 76, 77, 79, 125, 324
Effra Parade 52
Effra Road 52
Eldon Street 98
Electric Avenue 53
Elephant and Castle 157, 253, 256, 258–66, 268, 269, 270, 276, 277, 284, 321, 326, 374
Eliot, T. S. 84, 104, 123, 299, 363, 403
Elizabeth I, Queen 196
Eltham 204
Ely Place 73, 140, 142–3
English Defence League 37, 38–9
English National Ballet 371–2
Eocene Epoch 5
Etheldreda, St 143
Euston Arch 386
Euston station 157, 386

Eye/Eye Cross 220–3, 225, 231

Falconbrook 51
Falmouth Road 270, 272
Faraday, Michael 378
Faraday Memorial 263, 264, 268
Farringdon 146, 374
Farringdon Road 143, 145, 152, 153, 154
Farthing Alley 291
Fatberg, Whitechapel 139–40
Fawkes, Guy 204–5
Field of Eye 211, 220
Fieldgate Street 349
Finsbury Avenue Square 96
Finsbury Circus 101, 102, 255
Fish Island 351
Fitzjohn's Avenue 201
Five Fields 220
Fleet, River 89, 134–75, 201, 237, 250, 253, 274, 352, 374
Fleet Street 147
floods 205–6, 208
Folly Ditch 290, 291
Forest Hill 54, 317
Fortunata (slave) 112
Frankfurt Road 46
Friars' Mount 85

Galleywall Road 312–13
Gallows Wall 313, 315, 331
Gandhi, Mahatma 352, 385, 392
Gatesborough Street 91
Gentleman Johnny 251
Geoffrey of Monmouth 189
George IV, King 149
Geraldine Mary Harmsworth Park 250

INDEX

Gherkin, the 2, 30, 90, 165
Gipsy Hill 52, 64
Globe Theatre 89, 397, 406
Globe Wharf 298
Good Luck Hope 372
Goodluck Hope 376, 377
Goulston Street 12, 13, 15, 18, 394
Government Offices Great George Street (GOGGS) 198–201, 202
Grange Lane 59
Grange Walk 307
Gray's Inn Road 159
Great Bagshot River 164
Great Dover Street 277
Great Eastern Street 87, 90
Great Exhibition (1851) 57
Great Fire (1666) 12, 205, 289
Great Horse Pond 89
Great North Wood 54–5, 75
Great Peter Street 209
Great Stink 146
Great Storm (1987) 60
Great Swan Alley 104
Green Dragon Yard 349
Green Park 202
Green Street 347
Greenway 351–2, 364, 391, 392
Greenwich 2, 167, 379, 390
Grenfell Tower 216
Grosvenor Canal 217
Grosvenor Place 225
ground-penetrating radar (GPR) 195
Guthrum 368
Guy's Hospital 174

Hackney 90, 92, 341
Hackney Brook 353

Hackney Cut 343
Hackney Gravel 154, 159
Hackney Marshes 339–40
Hackney Wick 87, 341, 348, 351
Half Moon Lane 49, 51
Half Moon pub (Herne Hill) 49, 51
Hammersmith 186, 205
Hampstead 4, 153, 201, 214
Hampstead Brook 146, 170, 171–2, 175
Hampstead Heath 2, 162, 164–75
Hampstead Ponds 168–72
Hampstead Ridge 164, 383
Hampstead Water Company 173
Harold Godwinson 190
Harper Road 270, 273, 277, 279, 281, 284
Harper Road Woman 279, 280–2
Harringay 383
Hatchett's Bottom 173
Hatton Garden 146
Henry III, King 194
Henry VII, King 196
Henry VIII, King 142, 148, 222, 306, 391
Henslowe, Philip 397, 401
Herbal Hill 143
Hercules Road 247, 248
Herne Hill 45–9, 51, 52, 56, 59, 240, 254, 258, 284, 388
Hewett Street 89
Hexham Road 79
Heywood, Thomas 25
High Street (Stratford) 364, 365
Highgate 164
Highgate Brook 146, 167–8, 170
Hither Green 3
Hockley-in-the-Hole 153, 154

440

Holborn 146, 351
Holborn Circus 143
Holbourne Bridge 153
Hollingshead, John 197, 202
Holy Trinity (Aldgate) 390
Holywell Mount 87, 91
Holywell Priory 89
Horniman Museum 317
Horseferry Road 209
House of Commons 191, 206, 398
House of Lords 187, 205
House Mill 383
House of Occupations 255
Houses of Parliament 6, 181, 209
Hoxton 86
Hyde Park 57, 211, 227
Hyde Park Corner 210, 225

Iceland Street 353
Iceland Wharf 364
Iceni 166, 280, 352
Ilderton Road 323, 324, 325, 328
Imperial War Museum 250
Iron Age 325, 347
Isle of Dogs 297, 320, 351,
    359, 387
Islington 157
Islington Local History Centre 152

Jack the Ripper 18–19
Jacob's Island 289–91
Jamaica Road 300
James I, King 154, 222, 226
Jewel Tower 186–7, 198
Jewish community 17, 18–19
John of Gaunt 34, 142

Keats, John 174, 175
Kennington 52

Kennington Common 276, 313
Kennington Oval 250
Kennington Park 276
Kennington Road 251, 253
Kentish Town 146
Kenwood House 170
King's Cross Road 155, 157
Kings Cross station 37, 157, 162
King's Scholars' Pond Sewer 188,
    202, 213
Kingsland Road 90
Knights Hospitaller 147, 153
Knights Templar 147, 342, 343

La Neyte 211, 216, 217, 219
Lambeth 46, 206, 236, 237, 240, 246,
    247–8, 250, 252, 258, 274, 276
Lambeth Group 47, 159, 273, 340
Lambeth Marsh 184, 237–8,
    246, 387
Lambeth Road 250, 251, 253, 254
Langley Silt 13
Lavender Hill 5
Lea, River/Valley 4, 30, 33, 164, 226,
    333, 338, 340–4, 346–52, 357,
    359, 361–6, 368, 370, 374–5, 377,
    378, 380, 383–5, 389, 392
Leake Street 243–5, 255, 270
Leamouth 368
Lee Navigation 343, 351, 364
Lee Tunnel 363, 375
Lewisham 204
Leyton 362
Lillington Gardens 214
Lily Place 143
Limehouse 274, 296, 337
Limehouse Cut 343
Limmo Peninsula 367,
    368–81, 408

Lincoln Inn Fields 109
Lines of Communication 91
Liverpool Street station 19, 37, 40, 91, 95, 96, 97, 98, 100, 112
Lock hospital 236, 266, 286, 287
Lock Stream 236, 273, 286
Loders well 147
London Basin 375
London bombings (2005) 40–1, 337, 357
London Bridge 4, 237, 276, 280, 288, 296, 319, 321
London Bridge Sewer 102
London Clay 4–5
London Eye 239
London Stone 117, 254
London Wall 100, 102
London Waterkeeper 361, 363, 366, 391
Long Lane 277, 287, 305, 306, 307
Long Wall 387
Longmoore Gardens 215
Lord Mayor's stone 253–4
Lordship Lane station 58
Lothbury 106, 108
Lower Lea Crossing 369, 375
Lower Marsh 238, 243, 244, 245, 246
Lower Pool of London 296
Lower Road 317
Ludgate 94, 106
Ludgate Hill 114, 117
Luke Street 91
Lynton Road 311

Mandela Way 311–12, 314
Mansell Street 28, 30
Mansion House 114

maps 3–4
Marble Arch 227, 228, 351
Marine Street 290
Marlborough Grove 324
Marlowe, Christopher 397, 399, 401
Marsh Lane 348
Marshalsea Prison 24
Mary, Queen of Scots 196
Marylebone 201
Marylebone Lane 201
Mathews the Hairyman 61–2, 68
Mayfair 202, 211, 228
Mayhew, Henry 289, 290
Meadow Row 273, 282
Mellitus, Bishop of London 188
Mesolithic period 324, 325
Metro Central Heights 268–9, 330
Metropolitan Drinking Fountain Association 119
Middle Walbrook 103
Middlesex Street 28, 394
Middleton, Thomas 72, 259
Mile End Green 33
Mile End Road 90
Mill Mead 387
Mill Street 288, 290
Millbank 206, 208
Millbank Prison 212, 213
Millennium Dome 378, 380
Millwall FC 317, 319–23, 328, 330, 347
Ministry of Sound 265
Mithraeum 116, 126–8, 391
Moorfields 103, 252
Moorgate 94, 102
mORGANICo 272
Most Holy Trinity (Dockhead) 306
Mount Pleasant 154, 173

Museum of London 139–40, 280, 281–2, 406
Museum of London Archaeology (MOLA) 105, 115, 116–17, 394, 397

Narrow Street 337
Narrow Wall 237
Neckinger, River 233, 236–7, 246, 250, 253, 255, 256, 258, 259–60, 265, 266, 269, 271, 273, 274, 286–90, 308, 315
New Cross 87, 186, 320
New Inn Broadway 89
New Kent Road 265, 266, 271
Newgate 94
Newington 157, 253, 259
Newington Butts 259, 263, 265, 396
Newington Causeway 265, 266, 268, 269, 275
Nile Place 266
North Greenwich Peninsula 379
North Kensington 216
Northern Outfall Sewer 351–2, 364, 391
Norwood 4, 5, 53, 64, 165
Norwood Hermit 61–2, 68
Norwood High Street 76
Norwood Ridge 56, 57, 64, 66, 68, 72, 164, 356
Norwood Road 49, 59, 73
Notting Hill 17

Old Blue Last 85, 87, 90
Old Castle Street 37
Old Ford 348, 349, 350, 352, 353, 364
Old Ford Road 353, 406

Old Jamaica Road 300, 301
Old Kent Road 275, 286, 287, 312, 313, 324
Old Montague Street 349
Old Nichol 84
Old Street 28, 86, 350
Olympic Games 30–1, 39, 337–8, 346, 348, 356–9, 361, 362, 363, 364, 366, 373
Olympic Park 31, 338, 346, 361–3, 369, 373, 391
Olympic Stadium 347–8, 351, 352, 353, 359, 361
Olympic Velodrome 346
One Poultry 111, 115
One Tree Hill 58
Orchard Place 376, 377
Ordnance Datum 379, 380
Ordnance Survey maps 22, 387
Ossulston 211, 225–8, 231, 253, 339
Oswulf's stone 226
Oval cricket ground 53, 250
Oxford Street 201, 211, 227

Paddington 137
Palace of the Bishop of Ely 142, 143
Palace of Westminster 180, 181, 184, 186–7, 190, 205–6, 231, 404
Paleys upon Pilers 31, 41
Panyer Alley 227
Paris Garden 250
Park Lane 225, 226
Park Street 227, 403
Parliament Hill 164, 165, 166, 167, 170
Parliament Square 199

Parliament Street 198
Parnell Road 350
Paxton Tunnel 66
Peartree Court 143
Peasants' Revolt 33, 38, 142
Peck, River 325–6
Peckermans Wood 64
Peckham 72, 258, 320,
    325, 339
Penge Peak 57
Pentonville 155, 161
Pepys, Samuel 216, 296
Peter of Cornwall 390
Peter Street 89
Petticoat Lane 12, 37, 38, 210
Petticoat Lane Market 28
Piers Plowman (Langland) 302
Pimlico 187, 188, 202, 211,
    212, 213
pingos 273, 274
plastiglomerates 203
Plautius 277
Plough Yard 88
Plumtree Court 143
Poplar 357, 377, 381
Portcullis House 184
Post Office Railway 160, 161
Prescott Channel 364, 365, 386
prime meridian 390, 392
Princes Street 108, 109
Principal Place 91
Prioress Street 287
Project Habakkuk 153
Pudding Mill River 348
Purbrook Street 287
Pye Road 352, 354

Quaggy, River 51, 204
Queen Victoria Street 112

Queen's Diamond Jubilee Galleries
    189
Queens Road (Peckham) 72, 320

Radwell 147
Ralph, Earl 211
Ravensbourne, River 204, 276
Ray Street 152
Record Street 324
Redlaw Way 331
Regent's Canal 162
Regent's Park 201
relict channels 274
Richard II, King 34
Richard of Barking, Abbot of
    Westminster 216
Richard of Cornwall 394
riots (2011) 37–8
Rivington Street 87
Rockingham Anomaly 269, 273–7,
    279, 282, 284, 286, 374
Rockingham Estate 269–73, 276, 279,
    282–4, 326, 408
Rockingham Street 269, 270, 273,
    274–5, 284
Rocque, John 52, 87, 91, 155, 161, 212,
    227, 238, 250, 253, 254, 259, 271,
    286, 287, 307, 309, 311, 342, 349,
    372, 408
Rogues/Rogers Lane 313
Rolls Road 312, 314
Romani travellers 64, 85
Romans
    artefacts 97, 104, 106, 117, 126, 137,
        227, 270, 276, 347, 349, 350, 351
    buildings 16, 105, 112, 145, 148,
        270
    cemeteries/burials 100, 101, 188–9,
        280–2, 350

city of Londinium 12, 90, 94, 125, 276

conquest 156, 166, 188, 339

farming 307

gates and walls 29, 40, 103, 148, 237, 246

gods/goddesses 114, 116, 150, 189, 286

harbours 146, 312

roads 33, 98, 112, 211, 259, 275–7, 286, 338, 346, 348, 349–51, 352, 353, 406

Roman empire 116, 380

slavery 112

temples and shrines 108, 116, 126–8, 145, 147, 148, 286, 391

Rose Alley 406

Rose playhouse (Bankside) 396–9, 400, 401, 403–4, 405–9

Rotherhithe 4, 105, 125, 205, 212, 274, 291, 297, 298, 299, 302, 312, 313, 315, 317, 339, 379

Rotherhithe New Road 312, 313, 328, 331

Rotherhithe Street 185, 309, 325, 409

Royal London Hospital 40

Royal Observatory (Greenwich) 2

Ruskin, John 45, 52

Saffron Hill 143

St Anne's (Limehouse) 306

St Bartholomew's Hospital 85, 147

St Benet Sherehog 111

St Botolph's (Aldgate) 28, 30

St Bride's (Fleet Street) 147, 148–9

St Chad's Well 148

St Clement Danes 85

St Dunstan-in-the-West 85

St Etheldreda's (Ely Place) 73, 140, 142–6, 147, 148, 150

St George's Cathedral (Southwark) 254

St George's Fields 250, 251, 252, 254, 258, 276, 277

St George's Spa 251

St James the Less (Pimlico) 214

St James's Road 314

St John's (Clerkenwell) 153

St Leonard's (Shoreditch) 86

St Martin-in-the Fields 85

St Mary-at-Hill 73, 78

St Mary, Benedictine Nunnery of 147

St Mary le Strand 85

St Mary Magdalen (Bermondsey) 305, 306

St Mary Matfelon (Whitechapel) 25, 33

St Mary's (Newington) 259

St Mary's (Rotherhithe) 306

St Mary's (Whitechapel Road) station 19

St Mary's Abbey (Stratford Langthorne) 389, 390, 391

St Mary's Priory 153, 156

St Michael Paternoster Royal (College Hill) 118

St Mildred's (Bread Street) 110

St Olav's (Hart Street) 302

St Oswulf Street 212

St Pancras 155, 240

St Pancras Hospital 162

St Pancras Old Church 147, 161, 162

St Paul's Cathedral 2, 110, 114, 117, 165

St Peter's monastery (Thorney Island) 188

St Philip's (Clerkenwell) 157

St Saviour's Dock 288, 289, 300
St Stephen Walbrook 114–15
St Thomas-a-Watering 313
St Thomas's Hospital 180, 199, 237,
    246, 357, 404
Saxon Road 349
scour-hollows 160, 161, 273,
    274, 374
Selhurst 56
Selhurst Park 320
Severus Alexander 97
sewers 133–40, 147, 297–8, 351–2,
    361–4, 391
Sha'ar Ya'akov synagogue 349
Shadwell Basin 378
Shakespeare, William 23, 89, 143, 163,
    256, 355, 395, 397, 398, 405, 406
Shard, the 2, 165, 308, 319
Shell Centre 239
Shepherd's Bush 204
Shepherd's Well 201, 214
Shoreditch 84, 85, 86–92, 118, 126, 396
silkworms 222, 225
Sinclair, Iain 154, 227, 230, 335, 338,
    342, 345, 346, 347, 353,
    356–7, 364
Skinners well 147
Smithfield 146, 253
Smithfield Market 153
Snow Hill station 153
South Bermondsey station 325
South Dock 312
South End Road 175
South Hill Park 171
South Kensington 183
South Street 227
Southbank Centre 239
Southwark 46, 49, 106, 237, 253, 254,
    258, 271, 275, 307, 396, 398

Southwark Park 326
Southwark Playhouse 265
spas 52, 89, 90, 148, 155,
    251, 309
Speakers' Corner 228, 339
Spitalfields 100
springs 53, 67, 76, 86, 89, 114, 120,
    158, 172, 201, 374
  healing 147, 154, 250–1
  see also spas; wells
Square Mile 6, 110
Staines 351
Stalin, Joseph 349
Stane Street 259, 275–6
Stangate 237, 246, 276
Stave Hill 125
Stepney 4, 349
Stewfen 271–2
Stockwell 258
Stradella Road 51
Strand 250
Strand Ley 85
Stratford 31, 33, 348, 352, 364
Stratford Langthorne 389–90, 391
Streatham 320
Streetfinder, Collins 3, 5
Studio Weave 31
Sudbury, Simon, Archbishop of
    Canterbury 34
Surrey Basin 296
Surrey Docks 125, 328
Swan playhouse (Southwark) 397
Swedenborg, Emanuel 154
Swiss Cottage 201
Sydenham 52
Sydenham Hill 55–65, 297

Tabard Street 286
Tachbrook 188, 202, 213

Tachbrook Street 214, 215
Tanner Street 287–8
Taplow Gravel 47
Tarn Street 270
Tate Britain 212
Tate Modern 406
Tavistock Square 40
tectonic plates 375
Temple Mills 342
Thames Barrier 381
Thames House 209
Thames Path 291, 312
Thames, River 105, 114, 379
    alluvial floodplain 4, 84,
        206, 250
    bridges 106
    confluence with the Lea 338, 343,
        375, 377, 378, 380
    confluence with the Neckinger 236,
        288–9
    confluence with the Tyburn
        210, 214
    confluence with the
        Westbourne 210
    crossings 188, 209,
        237, 276
    during Covid-19 pandemic 337
    embankments 4, 189, 206
    and the Fleet 146, 147
    floods 205–6, 381
    gravel terraces 47, 98, 201, 266,
        269, 301
    islands 6, 187–91, 210–23, 231, 287,
        298, 301, 306–15
    northward migration 274
    sewage 363
    tide 122, 189, 403–4
    tributaries 51–3, 69
    and the Walbrook 104, 123

Thames Tideway Scheme 297–8
Thames Tunnel 28, 373
Thames Water 135, 136
Theatre (Shoreditch) 89, 395
Thorney Island 187–91, 196, 202, 204,
    206, 209, 210, 231, 380
Thorney Street 209
Thornton Street 348, 351
Three Mills 363, 365, 366, 383–4,
    391, 392
Three Mills Green 384
Three Mills Island 385, 386
Three Mills Wall River 365
Tideway 134
Tivoli Corner 108, 109
Tode well 147
Tokenhouse Yard 105, 115
Tothill Fields 212, 215
Tottenham 164
Tower Bridge 2, 37, 114, 236, 283,
    297, 338
Tower Bridge Road 287, 305
Tower Hamlets 13, 29, 37, 90
Tower of London 34, 167,
    205, 389
Toynbee Street 37
Trafalgar Square 3
Treasury 198, 199
Trinity Buoy Wharf 377–80, 381
Trinity Church Square 277
Trocadero 265, 268
Trundleys Road 328
Tulse Hill 46
tunnel boring machines
    (TBMs) 373–4
Turnmill Brook 146
Tyburn, River 164, 188, 198, 199–203,
    210, 211, 212, 213, 214, 215, 220,
    222, 223, 237, 274

Tyburn milestone 228
Tyburn Tree 227
Tyler, Wat 33

Upper Marsh 238, 246
Upper Pool of London 296
Upper Thames Street
    118, 120

Vale of Health 173–5
Vannes, Peter, Dean of
    Salisbury 391
Vauxhall 106, 261
Vauxhall Bridge 53
Vauxhall Bridge Road 213
Venta Icenorum 352
Victoria 187
Victoria, Queen 222
Victoria station 58, 217, 240
Victory Arch 238
Vikings 190, 368, 380
Villa Road 276
Vine Street Bridge 143

Walbrook 81, 86–128, 237, 252, 255,
    274, 391
Walbrook Wharf 122
Walworth Manor 277
Walworth Road 258
Wandle, River 52, 274
Wandsworth 274
Wapping 4
Warner Street 154
Warwick Way 215
Waterkeeper Alliance 363
Waterloo International station 239–40
Waterloo station 4, 184, 236, 238,
    239, 241
Watkins's Ley 87, 90

Watling Street 106, 227, 275,
    276–7, 286
Well Walk 174
Wellington Arch 225
wells 52, 89, 120, 147–8, 152, 155, 172,
    174, 201
    holy 147, 148, 149, 150, 156
    see also spas; springs
Wentworth Street 37
West Ham United FC 347
West Norwood 51, 74, 75
West Norwood Cemetery 53, 72–8,
    162, 167, 212
Westbourne, River 4, 164, 188, 201,
    210, 211, 220
Westfield shopping centre 338, 348,
    361, 390
Westhorne Avenue (Eltham) 204
Westminster 106, 167, 181, 184,
    186–96, 198, 204–6, 210–11, 217,
    218, 222, 253, 274, 276
Westminster Abbey 187, 189, 190–1,
    193–6, 199, 204, 211, 218,
    222, 306
Westminster Bridge 199, 357
Westminster Bridge Road 246
Westminster Bridge station 183–4,
    189, 194
Westminster Delta 177, 186, 206,
    210, 231
Westminster School 193
Westow Park 76
Whalebone Court 104
Whitechapel 17, 18, 30, 40, 253, 283,
    348, 395
Whitechapel High Street 15, 17, 37,
    38, 40
Whitechapel Road 19, 28, 90,
    139, 349

INDEX

Whitefriars 147
Whittington, Richard 'Dick' 118
Wick Lane 352
William the Conqueror 147
Willow Walk 310–11, 314
Winterbrook Road 49
Wolseley Street 290
Woodliffe, Oliver 23, 24, 25

Woolwich 205
Worship Street 91
Worshipful Company of
    Horners 394
Wren, Sir Christopher 2, 109,
    110, 114, 115, 147

York Road 239, 241

Tom Chivers is a writer, publisher and arts producer. He was born in 1983 in south London. He has released two pamphlets and two collections of poetry, the latest being *Dark Islands* (Test Centre, 2015). His poems have been anthologized in *Dear World & Everything In It* and *London: A History in Verse*. He was shortlisted for the Michael Marks and Edwin Morgan Poetry Awards and received an Eric Gregory Award in 2011.

Tom has made perambulatory, site-specific and audio work for organizations including LIFT, Cape Farewell, Humber Mouth and Southbank Centre. He was writer in residence at Bishopsgate Institute and associate artist of the National Centre of Writing. In 2009 he presented a documentary for BBC Radio 4 about the poet Barry MacSweeney. In 2011 an animated film of his poem 'The Event' was broadcast by Channel 4's *Random Acts*. He lives in Rotherhithe with his wife and daughters.